small wars

Small Wars

Low-Intensity Threats and the American Response Since Vietnam

Michael D. Gambone

Legacies of War
G. Kurt Piehler, Series Editor

The University of Tennessee Press
Knoxville

The Legacies of War series presents a variety of works—from scholarly monographs to memoirs—that examine the impact of war on society, both in the United States and globally. The wide scope of the series might include war's effects on civilian populations, its lingering consequences for veterans, and the role of individual nations and the international community in confronting genocide and other injustices born of war.

First Edition.

The paper in this book meets the requirements of American National Standards Institute / National Information Standards Organization specification Z39.48–1992 (Permanence of Paper). It contains 30 percent post-consumer waste and is certified by the Forest Stewardship Council.

Library of Congress Cataloging-in-Publication Data

Gambone, Michael D., 1963–
Small wars: low-intensity threats and the American response since Vietnam / Michael D. Gambone. — First ed.
p. cm. — (Legacies of war)
Includes bibliographical references and index.
ISBN-13: 978-1-57233-914-9 (hbk.)
ISBN-10: 1-57233-914-4 (hbk.)
1. Low-intensity conflicts (Military science)—History.
2. Intervention (International law)—Government policy—United States.
3. United States—Military policy—History—21st century.
4. United States—Military policy—History—20th century.
5. Military history, Modern—20th century
6. Military history, Modern—21st century
I. Title.

U240.G33 2013
355.02'15—dc23 2012028719

To

MAJOR JOHN McGARRY
U.S. ARMY SPECIAL FORCES

Contents

Illustrations

Foreword

Over a generation has passed since the United States forces completely withdrew from Vietnam in 1975. Although President Gerald R. Ford urged Americans to put the conflict behind them as the war drew to a close, Americans have ever since debated the legacy of this conflict. The terrorist attacks of September 11, 2001, against the World Trade Center in New York City and the Pentagon in northern Virginia sparked a renewed interest in studying the legacies of the small wars fought by American forces. In this study, Michael Gambone makes an important contribution to understanding the legacy of the Cold War, especially Vietnam in shaping what President George W. Bush labeled the "Global War on Terror." Although Bush and those who supported the war in Iraq in 2003 used rhetoric that evoked the good war's struggle against Nazi Germany, the parallels with Vietnam and earlier small wars are much more significant.

Gambone is not the first scholar to observe the strong propensity of political and military leaders to want to refight the Second World War. After the fall of Vietnam, successive presidents and their policymakers stressed the need to focus renewed attention to facing the conventional and nuclear threat posed by the Soviet Union, especially in Europe. While not disputing the need to bolster's West Europe's defense in this period, Gambone stresses that this Cold War stance offered a less ambiguous model for structuring American strategic doctrine and forces. But as Gambone shows exhaustively, small wars remained an uncomfortable reality that evoked significant public debate and controversy, especially the decision by President Ronald Reagan to intervene in the civil war in El Salvador and topple the Sandinista regime in Nicaragua.

Asymmetric warfare is not unique to the struggle against Al Qaeda and other terrorist groups based in Afghanistan and elsewhere. Before the 9/11 attacks, American armed forces were already involved in seeking to combat drug traffickers in a number of Latin countries, most notably in Columbia beginning in the 1990s. With a few exceptions, military historians have largely ignored this long-standing military involvement in Colombia along with the wider war on drugs. Given the recent escalating violence by drug lords against the Mexican Government, the utility of using military force in the drug wars may have greater relevance to American policymakers.

Equally valuable in this study is Gambone's discussion of the growing use of military contractors. Although political scientists, policy analysts, and economists have considered the question of privatization of military functions, Gambone is one of the first historians to examine the question and place this trend into a wider context. As Gambone's analysis makes clear, this pattern is not simply a "one-time" response to strains placed on American forces during the wars in Afghanistan and Iraq.

In writing this book, Gambone is part of a tradition that studies military history in order to help guide policymakers and military leaders. As series editor, I wanted to add this work to the Legacies of War in order to contribute to the debates regarding the best strategy and tactics to prevail in small war at such institutions as the Army War College, National Defense University, and RAND. But it is my hope that it finds a readership among scholars and average citizens who seek not only to better understand the legacy of the Vietnam War, but also the continuing need of the United States to wage a series of low-intensity wars to protect American national interests.

G. Kurt Piehler
Florida State University

Acknowledgments

This book enjoyed the support of more people than I can accurately count. I would like to thank many of those who helped with the research, writing, and revisions that made it a better product at each stage.

Without access to primary source documents, this project would have been impossible. My thanks to Geir Gunderson at the Gerald R. Ford Library and David Stanhope at the Jimmy Carter Library and Museum. The staffs serving the Army Heritage and Education Center, the Ronald Reagan Library, the George H. W. Bush Presidential Library, and the National Archives and Records Administration were equally generous with their time and guidance.

Kudos to the Rohrbach Library staff, particularly Joanne Bucks and Dawn Boody, who kept up the deluge of interlibrary loan material as my work proceeded over the years.

I would also like to express my appreciation to Dr. Nancy Gentile Ford and Dr. Kurt Piehler for their understanding of military history and the important perspective it lent my writing.

For my wife, Rachel, who has spent more than twenty years working as my primary editor and adviser, I can once again express my ongoing amazement that I had the right amount of luck to find her.

Lastly, I would like to thank my son, Michael, now a young man and a scholar in his own right. He is not a historian, instead focusing his interests on math and science. However, in his pursuits, I am always reminded of a wider world outside my desk.

Abbreviations

AFQT	Armed Forces Qualification Test
AFRICOM	Africa Command
AUC	Autodefensas Unidas de Colombia
AWOL	absent without leave
CAP	Combined Action Platoon
CAP	Combined Action Program
CENTCOM	Central Command
CIA	Central Intelligence Agency
CIDG	Civilian Irregular Defense Group
CMTC	Combat Mission Training Center
CORDS	Civilian Operations and Revolutionary Development Support
CPA	Coalition Provisional Authority
CSCE	Conference on Security and Cooperation in Europe
DEA	Drug Enforcement Administration
DOD	Department of Defense
EU	European Union
FARC	Fuerzas Armadas Revolucionarias de Colombia
FBI	Federal Bureau of Investigation
FMLN	Frente Farabundo Martí para la Liberación Nacional
FSLN	Frente Sandinista de Liberación Nacional
GAO	General Accounting Office

GRM	graduated response matrix
GWOT	Global War on Terror
IED	improvised explosive device
IFOR	Implementation Force
ISI	Inter-Services Intelligence
JCS	Joint Chiefs of Staff
JTF	Joint Task Force
JRTC	Joint Readiness Training Center
MACV	Military Assistance Command, Vietnam
MAP	Military Assistance Program
MAS	Muerte a Secuestradores
METL	mission essential task list
MILF	Moro Islamic Liberation Front
MIST	Military Information Support Team
MPRI	Military Professional Resources Inc.
MSP	Mutual Security Program
MTT	Mobile Training Team
NATO	North Atlantic Treaty Organization
NCO	noncommissioned officer
NGO	nongovernmental organization
NSC	National Security Council
NSDD	National Security Decision Directive
NSDM	National Security Decision Memorandum
NTC	National Training Center
NVA	North Vietnamese Army
NWO	new world order
OOTW	operations other than war
OSS	Office of Strategic Services
PLO	Palestine Liberation Organization
PMC	private military corporation
RDF	rapid deployment force
RDO	rapid decisive operations
RMA	Revolution in Military Affairs
SALT	Strategic Arms Limitation Treaty
SCC	Special Coordinating Committee
SEAL	Sea, Air, and Land (team)
SEATO	Southeast Asia Treaty Organization

SOCCENT	special operations Command Central
SOCOM	Special Operations Command
SOF	Special Operations Forces
SOUTHCOM	Southern Command
START	Strategic Arms Reduction Treaty
TRADOC	Training and Doctrine Command
UNITAF	Unified Task Force
UNOSOM I	United Nations Operation Somalia
UNOSOM II	United Nations Operation Somalia
USAID	U.S. Agency for International Development
VC	Viet Cong
WHORM	White House Office of Records Management
WMD	weapons of mass destruction

Introduction

If the legacy of misplaced analogies which the past has bequeathed to the Vietnam debates is even half equaled by the misplaced analogies which Vietnam bequeaths to the future, error will compound error in a positively horrifying manner.

—Samuel Huntington in James J. Wirtz, "The 'Unlessons' of Vietnam"

The Nature of Contemporary American War

Contemporary American conflict is defined by the ongoing war on terror. Attempts to disrupt terrorist organizations such as Al Qaeda and to discover the whereabouts of Osama bin Laden have absorbed years of effort, hundreds of billions of dollars, and thousands of American lives. The latter objective was only finally realized in May 2011. As George W. Bush promised almost ten years before bin Laden's death, the United States committed "every means of diplomacy, every tool of intelligence, every instrument of law enforcement, every financial influence, and every necessary weapon of war—to the destruction and defeat of the global terror network."[1] This effort has substantially expanded both civilian and military capabilities. The war on terror comprises a vast and intricate network of operations dedicated to peeling away the cultural, political, financial, and military layers that encompass America's new enemy. We now fight in a war that lacks boundaries, geographical or otherwise. This point was driven home with the creation of the Department of Homeland Security in 2002, the largest single reorganization of the U.S. federal government in its history.[2]

The war on terror has also transformed the U.S. military. The invasion of Afghanistan introduced the world to the concept of "rapid decisive operations" in 2001 and again during Operation Iraqi Freedom in 2003. What resulted initially was widespread celebration over the fact that the U.S. armed forces had successfully bridged the gap between the Cold War and the new century. Whether employing special forces and CIA paramilitary operatives, backed with the "brilliant" weaponry available to the world's last remaining superpower, or a more conventional force against Saddam Hussein, it appeared that the nature of modern war had changed in the United States' favor.[3]

This hope proved short-lived, however. In practice, the initial "global war on terror" proved to be immeasurably complex, ugly, and, most important, indecisive. The successful invasions of Afghanistan and Iraq produced neither peace nor stability, even in the short term. Chaos reigned in many parts of these "liberated" countries, a product of crime and simple desperation as much as overt terrorism. In the face of rampant, bitter fighting between ethnic and religious factions, the U.S. military had few answers. When confronted with a low-intensity war against insurgents, U.S. forces fought successfully, as was the case in Fallujah in 2005, but with little attention to collateral damage. In the meantime, improvised explosive devices and an increasingly well-organized insurgency set the tempo of operations.

"Small wars" currently reside at center stage in U.S. military thinking. They dominate the most active parts of our debates over strategy, readiness, and future leadership. It was no coincidence that Martin E. Dempsey and David H. Petraeus both benefited from their ability to prosecute our current small wars when they took charge of the JCS and the CIA. Authors such as Rupert Smith argue that the current emphasis on insurgency, terrorism, and other irregular forms of conflict is long overdue. Smith believes that the First Gulf War against Iraq and the Yom Kippur War of 1973 were simply the echoes of an obsolete past, notable for their singular rarity in recent history. From this perspective, conventional fighting, waged by massed, industrial armies, is nearly extinct as a viable means of warfare, replaced by the broad and diverse array of conflicts that we see today.[4]

However, recognizing change is only a first step toward under standing its basic nature. Although this book addresses the causes of the United States' many conflicts since Vietnam, it is our proposed solutions that occupy most of the story. How did U.S. policy makers respond to the multiplying challenges to U.S. security after 1973? What factors influenced their decisions? What was the end result? Hopefully, the chapters that follow will lend themselves to these and other questions.

Vietnam Analogies

History is a useful and problematic device to understand the present. When the respective conflicts in Iraq and Afghanistan bogged down, analogies to the Vietnam War began almost immediately. Some appeared accurate, at least on their face. The prospect of a quagmire in which U.S. forces were indecisively engaged with insurgents became a real possibility as Iraqi stability unraveled and militants in Afghanistan proved stubbornly resilient against a long-term occupation. Moreover, the lack of clarity on the battlefield produced a string of civilian casualties that alienated Iraqis and Afghanis, as well as the American public. By June 2006 a majority of Americans (57 percent) asked by the Opinion Research Corporation believed that American troops had committed atrocities in Iraq.[5] On a broader scale, the stalemate that emerged in Afghanistan and Iraq also severely eroded support for the war at home. A March 2008 poll by the *Washington Post* and ABC news reported that 63 percent of respondents believed that the war in Iraq was not worth fighting.[6] The situation was indeed similar to the one presented in Leslie Gelb's landmark 1979 study *The Irony of Vietnam: The System Worked,* in which the author described public opinion as the "essential domino" in the war.[7]

But just how far do Vietnam analogies with the current global war on terror apply? Judged simply through the lens of pubic opinion, comparisons break down almost immediately. In the present day, the military as an institution is nowhere near as vilified as it was in the sixties and seventies. Contemporary opinions about the military are notable for separating individuals in uniform from the war itself. Consequently, even as Iraq teetered on the brink of sectarian civil war, a September 2006 Gallup poll recorded a 72 percent favorable rating for U.S. military personnel, double that which supported military operations in the country.[8]

A more inclusive, in-depth comparison of the Vietnam War and current conflicts produces an even greater array of discrepancies. How does the contemporary U.S. order of battle stand up against its historical predecessor in terms of training, doctrine, personnel, and equipment? What about the enemy it faces? Are there distinctions that separate Al Qaeda and other terrorists from the North Vietnamese Army and the Viet Cong? Other factors, from terrain to basic ideology, also beg examination. Understanding these differences becomes important to revealing the true nature of the current war and the validity of applying the lessons of history.[9]

Yet, it is clear that Vietnam continues to have a profound legacy for American policy and the U.S. military. One analyst observed in 2004 that the fundamental source of the so-called Vietnam syndrome was not military defeat, but a crisis of faith in liberal, distinctly Western institutions such as free elections and open markets. When the United States failed to "save" South Vietnam, its Wilsonian civilizing mission "to make the world safe for democracy" suffered what many considered a mortal blow.[10] Reconstructing the commitment to liberal institutions became an ongoing enterprise in the decades between 1973 and 2001. This effort was readily visible throughout the Reagan years, during George H. W. Bush's declaration of a "new world order" in 1991 and subsequent U.S. efforts to shape policies after the collapse of Soviet communism. When George W. Bush declared the September 11 attacks to be an assault on "our freedom of religion, our freedom of speech, our freedom to vote and assemble and disagree with each other," he picked up a thread almost thirty years in the making to frame the new war against terrorism.[11]

Similarly, Vietnam has been profoundly important to the American military. For decades military leaders and academics have struggled with its value to history and the U.S. defense establishment. A substantially large school of thought chooses to treat Vietnam as an aberration produced by a lack of commitment to strategic interests or operational standards. Initiated by Colonel Harry Summer's landmark book *On Strategy* (1982), this theory endorses the idea that the war in Southeast Asia was a black mark to be erased by a more rational application of policy and appropriate resources.[12]

Conversely, over nearly forty years much effort has been dedicated to gleaning positive lessons of Vietnam. Instead of dismissing the war as failure of misapplied conventional power, many authors have instead focused on the many counterinsurgency and pacification programs applied to South Vietnam, particularly after 1968, when Creighton Abrams and William Colby took charge of the U.S. war effort.[13] From this perspective the Army's Civilian Irregular Defense Groups (CIDG) or the Marine Corps Combined Action Program (CAP) serve as examples of successes in Vietnam, ones that both validate past military policies and offer potentially useful models for America's present conflicts.[14]

Whether deflecting or embracing the value of Vietnam, either approach risks overapplying potential historical lessons. A clearer analysis requires a handful of basic features that lend balance and depth to the narrative. One such feature is a fundamental definition of small wars. While simple on its face, "small wars" cover a potentially vast historical and conceptual area. Refining the basic idea as to what these conflicts comprise will be crucial to this study. The second feature must include both the military and nonmilitary factors that pertain to small wars. This distinction has been the subject of significant debate among military historians.[15] Yet, understanding the proper proportional value of military, political, social, and economic factors to small wars is essential to establishing a more complete history.

The Nature and History of Small Wars

Small wars are nothing new to history. For millennia, combatants on one side or more have applied unconventional or irregular methods to prevail. In Europe the practice has been described as *Volk im Waffen* (people in arms) or *petite guerre.* In Spain, the term "guerrilla" can be traced as far back as 1611.[16] However, for much of this period, irregular units—the Chausser, Tirailleur, or Jäger—were essentially light forces serving as adjuncts to the conventional militaries that dominated the battlefield.

Small wars have also been the province of those resisting great power. These individuals have been variously described as partisans, bandits, guerrillas, insurgents, or terrorists. They have persisted over the centuries because their manner of fighting is sometimes effective at deflect ing enemies with greater military power. The prolonged, indecisive, and frustrating nature of irregular warfare was also very effective at sapping an opponent's will to fight. Thus, by definition, small wars include actions that are overtly political as well as military. Over the centuries, empires and democratic republics have proven equally susceptible to this type of struggle.

From the time of their founding, the American colonies embraced the concept of small wars. To borrow Russell Weigley's famous term, the "American way of war" bore little resemblance to European convention as the first settlements along the Atlantic seaboard adapted their security needs to local conditions.[17] Later, as it matured as a nation during the industrial revolution, the United States slowly steered its military affairs to accepted exemplars such as the British navy and the German general staff.[18] However, even as it actively sought out modernity, the American military did not totally forget the lessons of its past. Techniques employed on the American frontier of the nineteenth century would later reappear in the Philippines and Latin America.[19]

This work primarily will concern itself with responses to small wars. The methods adopted by great powers to prevail in these conflicts have been as diverse as the conflicts themselves, especially in the modern era. Responses to irregular opponents cover a broad spectrum of options, from punitive expeditions designed to destroy local resistance to continually evolving efforts at what we now define as nation building.[20] Some are utilized in combination, depending on the era or a particular conflict. American forces fighting in the Philippines at the turn of the twentieth century adopted both punitive and pacification measures against insurgents. The same techniques appeared during a succession of American interventions in Latin America and the Caribbean prior to World War II. The U.S. Marine Corps eventually published the *Small Wars Manual* in 1940 to reflect the bitter lessons of its campaigns against enemies in Nicaragua, Haiti, and the Dominican Republic.[21] The practice of creating a dedicated counterinsurgency doctrine reached a peak during the Cold War, when the United States confronted revolutionary upheaval on a global scale. In places as disparate as Guatemala and South Vietnam, a generation of special forces soldiers, intelligence agencies, and civilian aid workers attempted to counter the threat of small wars while addressing their socioeconomic and political foundations. Results were, at best, problematic. In Latin America, billions in American assistance resulted in stability, but at the cost of U.S. sponsored dictatorships.[22] In South Vietnam, initial optimism regarding progress in the countryside was overwhelmed by a communist movement that proved far more resilient than American assistance.

Two concurrent and complimentary trends emerge when studying the history of small wars. The first is the sense that the conflicts themselves, difficult to define in even basic terms like "irregular" or "unconventional," are dynamic in nature. For example, a popular revolution might originate from local causes and later adopt external ideology and material support, such as in the case of twentieth-century Nicaraguan *sandinismo*.[23] In more recent times, the growth of vast urban sprawls has changed the very environment in which insurgent networks operate. Similarly, modern communication technology has made their message impossible to contain, while readily available precursors for weapons of mass destruction make the modern militant a formidable foe.[24]

Great power responses to small wars possess similar dynamics that are equally hard to categorize. For much of recorded history, policies that addressed irregular threats have been almost entirely military in nature. Even where regular forces incorporated unconventional features, such as the use of native auxiliaries, the practice normally appears as an adjunct to conventional military operations.

The military's dominance over fighting small wars began to change in the twentieth century. Policy makers in many nations realized that civilian functions had a distinct value in undercutting popular support for irregular forces. Programs variously described as "pacification," "civic action," or "support and stability operations" proved useful in fighting unconventional enemies.[25] A country that could build roads and sink wells or provide rudimentary medical care had an opportunity to win what Vietnam-era Americans described as "hearts and minds." As a consequence, however, the concurrent use of civilian and military institutions effectively blurred the lines between two distinct policy spheres and organizational cultures.[26] Today, as many official documents like *Field Manual 3-24: Counterinsurgency* (2006) indicate, the methodologies applied to modern conflict are a complex mélange of civilian and military effort.[27] The inclusion of nongovernmental organizations (NGOs) into this mix has complicated the creation and execution of policy even further. Understanding the particular roles played by these actors and, perhaps more important, which had greater influence over policy decisions, is a difficult process at best.

Bridging the Gap between Vietnam and the Present

As John Lewis Gaddis once noted in *Strategies of Containment* (1982), historians can be grouped into two camps: "lumpers" and "splitters."[28] This study clearly falls within the former category. Its methodology will follow a descending order of U.S. strategic, doctrinal, operational, and tactical approaches to small wars after 1973. The intent is to provide context and a sense as to how these various layers of policy and decision making interacted and affected the military history of American small wars.

In this vein, it is important to address a narrative that is the sum of many parts. I include matters of politics and economy in addition to individual leadership tendencies and the intellectual debate on matters of national security. In addition, many nonmilitary factors pertain to this study. Simply put, American military policy exists within the public domain, and it reflects, justly or not, the political, economic, and emotional priorities of the public and the national leadership alike. Consequently, resulting military strategy, doctrine, and action are a product of compromise as much as, or perhaps more so, than military necessity.

Using both distinctly military and nonmilitary approaches to the topic of small wars, this book addresses a number of questions that apply to the post–Vietnam era. Perhaps the most obvious is what exactly happened in the years separating Vietnam from America's current wars? It is almost certainly true that Vietnam nearly ruined the American military. The Vietnam syndrome reflected a public crisis of faith in war as a legitimate means of foreign policy.[29] It was also a crisis of faith within the military institution. How were these and other problems addressed in the decades separating the fall of Saigon from September 11?

This story takes the reader through the armed forces' nadir in the seventies, when the American military struggled with the substantive and psychological legacies of Vietnam, the early years of the all-volunteer force, and a public forum averse to funding needed reforms. The narrative also includes the Reagan "revolution" as it applied to a renaissance in American military affairs in the eighties, an event punctuated by the rapid, unanticipated victory during Operation Desert Storm in 1991. The new world order (NWO) that followed in the wake of Desert Storm offered anything but clarity for American policy makers, particularly with respect to matters of national security. Far from heralding a period of peace, free-market growth, and democratic expansion, the nineties proved to be a case study in the longevity of intractable ethnic, religious, and racial strife. September 11 brought the threats inherent in this new international reality home, to the shock and dismay of the country. Since 2001 the United States has actively pursued a series of wars against terrorism and insurgency that have resulted in the largest number of military deployments since Vietnam.

A history of American military affairs after Vietnam involves more than a simple chronology of comparative events. It must also address the policy decisions and doctrinal changes defining each respective era. An important lineage of presidents, from Nixon to Obama, and their respective national security teams, each have left an important stamp on American military policy in the last four decades. Similarly, the Pentagon has continually developed and reconsidered doctrine in an effort to address prevalent threats to American security. Consequently, terms like "active defense," "AirLand Battle," and "rapid decisive operations" serve as important milestones on the military timeline. For the most part, the Cold War governed U.S. military priority and shaped policy and doctrine over most of the period under examination. Without question, the desire to counteract a presumed Soviet threat directly affected planning, training, weapons development, and unit organization. As such, it is important not to underestimate the institutional and cultural inertia created by the Cold War or its impact on military decision making even today.

Although the Cold War was important in shaping the context of American military history between Vietnam and the present, it did not dominate its every feature. While the U.S. armed forces maintained their strategic nuclear deterrent and mobilized for a Warsaw Pact invasion at the Fulda Gap, they also prepared for and conducted numerous low-intensity conflicts after 1973. Consequently, as Carter Doctrine came into being to assert American strategic interests in the Persian

Gulf, U.S. special forces prepared for the Iranian hostage rescue mission. When the Reagan administration deployed Pershing II missiles to Western Europe, the CIA fostered an insurgency against the Soviet Union in Afghanistan. When the United States joined Operation Provide Hope to deliver food aid to Somalia in 1992, U.S. special forces were instrumental in assuaging fears within local tribes that humanitarian assistance was not a prelude to new colonialism. A careful examination of U.S. military history makes it clear that, although Al Qaeda and the Taliban have introduced mainstream America to the concept of asymmetrical war in all its various forms, this type of conflict has been an active part of U.S. policy for many years.

It appears then that the military history of the United States between Vietnam and the current war on terror is a diverse and complex narrative that cannot easily be reduced to a comparison of two points on a timeline. To understand the period from 1973 to the present day, it is necessary to take a comprehensive approach, one that includes key leaders, a descending array of policy decisions from the strategic to the operational level, and the methods developed to implement them. In this manner, a more complete picture of modern American military history may emerge.

Additionally, a study of the time period should consider many intangible factors directly related to policy and doctrine. As mentioned above, institutional culture is an important part of the narrative. Within the American military, the current generation of leaders embodies both the burdens of Vietnam and the recovery that followed in the eighties. In a sense, their decisions reflect an aversion to the risks of potential quagmires, but also an abiding sense of confidence in American military capabilities. How did these factors affect the military's willingness to learn and adapt? Was this willingness equally shared across the ranks and within the civilian leadership, or, as has been the case with past reformers like Emory Upton, Billy Mitchell, or Hyman Rickover, did inertia prove to be a formidable enemy?

Lastly, this history must assess the effectiveness of the small wars the United States has actually fought over the past forty years. Combat is the first and best test of security policy and military doctrine. From the multitude of low-intensity wars that the United States has fought since Vietnam, it is possible to derive a better understanding of not only American military effectiveness, but also the country's ability to adapt to the unexpected consequences normally produced by war. The final, practical application of these small wars may be the best means to understand how much or, conversely, how little progress the United States has made in prosecuting conflict abroad.

1

The Cold War and Limited Conflict

The fundamental lesson to draw from the misadventures of the counterinsurgency era is the one already emphasized by many—the lesson of the limits of American power. It is also of importance that we should understand in what way our power, great as it is, can be challenged by a few thousand ragged jungle fighters armed with a dedicated leadership, a tested theory, and great patience.

—Douglas Blaufarb, *The Counterinsurgency Era: U.S. Doctrine and Performance, 1950 to the Present*

After 1945 limited war became a dangerous and permanent reality in the world. With the concurrent introduction of atomic weapons into military arsenals and the rapid demobilization of most Western armies, small-scale conflicts proliferated, particularly outside of Europe in the so-called Third World. "Brushfire wars," as they were defined in the fifties, spread to nearly every portion of the Southern Hemisphere. Prompted by newly won freedom from European colonialism, unresolved political conflict, poverty, or ethnic animosity, few regions of the non-Western world escaped bloodshed. Joining these local conflicts were larger regional wars in the Middle East, between India and Pakistan, in Southeast Asia, and Korea. A number of these, as was the case with Israel, produced periodic clashes that stretched over decades. In the former French colony of Indochina, warfare of varying degrees of intensity remained constant for decades.[1] Scholars have claimed with good reason that the second half of the twentieth century was more deadly than the first.[2]

Despite these challenges, most nations kept their conventional force structures, doctrines, and weaponry largely intact and unchanged after World War II. In part, this was because conventional armies retained their value as forces in place, necessary to hold, protect, and administer territory. Immediately after World War II, the Allied militaries were essential to the stability and reconstruction of the defeated Axis powers. Later they became critical to maintaining the collective security treaties that started with NATO in 1949 and continued for the remainder of the century. Throughout the Cold War, American and Soviet conventional forces essentially became agents of the status quo. For most of the U.S. military, this meant projecting force to key positions surrounding the USSR and limiting communist expansion while controlling the prospect of escalation to a thermonuclear exchange between the superpowers.[3] Although the American military trained incessantly and regularly updated its weapons, tactics, and leadership, the bulk of U.S. military forces assumed a dormant role during the Cold War, awaiting a call to battle that never came.

For the American national security establishment throughout the Cold War, the central problem was discerning a productive use for military power. The obstacles to this were formidable. Once Japan surrendered, the country essentially abandoned military readiness for its traditional focus on domestic priorities.[4] Demobilization and the needs of the impending baby boom took center stage in the public debate and appropriations hearings. Satisfied that it had sacrificed enough to defeat global fascism, the American people clamored for housing, jobs, and amenities unseen since the Great Depression.[5] Consequently, the once formidable American military plummeted in size from approximately 12 million arms at the peak of World War II to just 1.7 million in 1947.[6]

Despite an increasingly isolationist focus, American global responsibilities multiplied after World War II. Less than two years after the war, Great Britain announced its withdrawal from the eastern Mediterranean, forcing a fait accompli on Harry Truman, who committed the United States to Greek and Turkish independence from communism and, by extension, the world.[7] After 1947 American commitments proliferated from the Truman Doctrine and NATO to SEATO, CENTO, and innumerable bilateral defense agreements in the fifties.[8]

But how best to bridge the gap between responsibilities and resources? One response was to fall back on technology, a traditional American method of meeting military need. During the Cold War this decision took the form of atomic and nuclear weapons married to strategic airpower.[9] For many planners, the nuclear option represented a manageable compromise that offered a sustainable response to American security responsibilities. Even before Eisenhower's adoption of the New Look, atomic weapons and airpower dominated discussions regarding the future of American military power. In the approaching age of "push button" war, some speculated that the days of the infantry were over.

The Korean War proved these pundits wrong. Brutal, bloody contests continued, resulting in hundreds of thousands, if not millions, of military and civilian casualties. While massive conventional armies patrolled territory along the communist bloc, and strategic nuclear forces stood at the ready, conflict continued to spread. Small wars clearly emerged within the gap between strategic forces held in readiness and unstable parts of the world vulnerable to conflict. If technological solutions to the problem were insufficient—this fact itself a dawning, debated reality in the fifties—it was equally clear that the human element had to be reintroduced back into the military equation.[10] The question remained: how best to close this gap?

The OSS Legacy

Postwar advocates of small, unconventional forces borrowed extensively from the World War II experience. Although there was no single definition of special operations, the war created a broad spectrum of doctrine and expertise pertinent to new and innovative forms of military operations. Both the Axis and Allied forces, for example, adopted mass airborne operations during the war. From the invasion of North Africa onward, American airborne formations emphasized mobility over firepower in order to strike and seize key objectives far behind enemy lines until relieved by heavier forces. Ranger units employed by the U.S. military emphasized similar elements, albeit on a much reduced scale, and focused particularly on commando-style raids against key tactical targets. Still smaller special operations units performed even more specialized tasks. Navy demolition teams that preceded marine and army landing forces were emblematic of the elite special forces of the period. Yet the common thread that linked all of these units together was their overall dependency upon conventional forces. As was proven time and again, in the invasions of North Africa, Sicily, and Normandy, airborne units fought well but were largely at the mercy of the enemy until relieved by armored spearheads. Ranger and commando units were best suited to raiding specific targets that had little, if any, impact on the tactical or strategic course of the war.[11]

During World War II true unconventional warfare waged by American forces was the province of the Office of Strategic Services (OSS). Throughout the war, this agency handled clandestine sabotage, intelligence gathering, and supported the escape and evasion of downed fliers. OSS teams also advised and supported local guerrilla units in areas as diverse as France, China, and Japanese-occupied territories throughout the Pacific and Asia.[12]

Doctrinally, the OSS approach to unconventional warfare repeatedly clashed with conventional military thinking, which refused to recognize it as an integrated part of the military. Both the Pentagon and most senior American commanders in the field dismissed OSS functions as entirely separate and distinct from military operations, pigeonholing clandestine operations as the province of spies rather than soldiers. The same stigma was attached to OSS operators who, deservedly or not, gained the reputation as cowboys operating too far outside military discipline to gain either institutional recognition (and promotions) or doctrinal traction. Once the war was over and special units disbanded, with the exception of some airborne units, the prejudice against military special forces remained intact, in some forms, for decades.

The American military failed to reconcile OSS operations with conventional military doctrine in the postwar. This was a genuine tragedy, particularly in light of the fact that, as conventional forces fell victim to budget cuts and public apathy after 1945, proliferating low-intensity conflicts repeatedly demonstrated the value of small units of well-trained specialists. Instead, the American military establishment tended to conflate the old World War II–era ranger or commando mission with special operations units based on the OSS model. This preference was not an accident. If a peacetime OSS unit was to be formed, American military leadership remained highly skeptical about the risks associated with maintaining guerrilla or resistance movements behind the Iron Curtain. These would, by definition, draw the U.S. military into the clandestine world of civilian subterfuge, a highly risky place where few senior officers wanted to tread in a political climate dominated by Joseph McCarthy. The OSS, along with the Army Rangers and most Navy underwater demolition teams, disbanded in 1945. Few military leaders objected when responsibility for clandestine missions passed to the embryonic Central Intelligence Agency two years later.[13]

Military special operations forces did not reappear until June 1952, when the U.S. Army officially activated the 10th Special Forces Group. The OSS model dominated the brainchild of Aaron Bank and other officers with clandestine experience in World War II and 10th Group's structure, training regimen, and equipment. Veteran OSS cadres conducted much of the unit's initial training at Fort Bragg, North Carolina, and emphasized creating and maintaining contacts with local resistance forces. European immigrants, actively recruited by the Army for their language skills and anticommunist commitment, formed a core group within the special forces community in the fifties and early sixties. Once the unit completed training, it deployed to its primary area of operations in Europe.[14]

Although the 10th Special Forces Group represented a victory over institutional inertia, it suffered from a number of profound deficiencies. The most obvious was geographical. Aaron Bank's creation was intended to lead partisan movements and raids behind the Iron Curtain in the event that the Cold War became hot. As a result, its training, equipment, and, most important, linguistic and cultural skills focused on Central and Eastern Europe. Although the special forces soldier of the period was without question highly trained and motivated, his skills were significantly limited in many of the areas of the Third World, where they were most needed. Special forces units that deployed with increasing frequency to Latin America and Southeast Asia found their effectiveness blunted until they could adapt to new circumstances, a task that took years to develop in some cases.

Containment and Military Assistance

While the postwar U.S. military struggled to adopt specific units to the task of small-scale military operations, the mission fell by default to service members assigned to America's growing military assistance programs. Again, World War II established a working precedent with the implementation of Lend-Lease aid, which provided assistance to not only the major allies like England and the Soviet Union, but also nations liberated from German occupation. In late 1944, for example, Lend-Lease aid was used to equip eight new French divisions.[15]

In the two years following World War II, American policy makers embraced military assistance as a cost-effective mechanism that would rescue obsolescent, surplus equipment from mothballs and provide American allies with an adequate means to be responsible for their own security. More important, allied ground forces, maintained overseas at key positions, would displace the risks of combat to foreign sons and satisfy an American public leery of spending blood for fuzzy Cold War objectives.

The Inter-American Treaty of Reciprocal Assistance of 1947, or the Rio Pact, established the baseline for collective security and U.S. military assistance in the postwar.[16] From the late forties onward, the Defense Department established a network of military missions throughout Latin America that was responsible for training host nation armed forces, the distribution of military aid, and the inclusion of these countries in U.S. strategic planning.[17] Latin American cohorts received training directly from American advisers and attended military schools located in the Panama Canal Zone, as well as within the United States.

The first American advisory effort designated to directly counteract communism was in Greece and Turkey. As noted above, the eastern Mediterranean witnessed the open collapse of British dominion after 1947 and the subsequent American commitment, as Truman articulated it, to "support the free peoples who are resisting attempted subjugation by armed minorities or by outside pressure."[18] To this end, the Truman Doctrine allocated $400 million for military and economic aid.[19]

The bulk of American military assistance went to the 100,000-man Greek national army (GNA) in order to improve its ability to defeat communist insurgents led by the Communist Party of Greece (KKE). Communist victory was a real possibility. By August 1947 guerrilla numbers had increased to over 22,500 troops, almost doubling their numbers at the time Truman first announced the new U.S. doctrine. In contrast, the GNA was a demoralized, ineffective organization that was overly committed to conventional tactics. Prior to 1947, it had failed miserably to defeat the insurgency.[20]

The American military advisers who arrived in 1947 did not attempt a massive increase of the Greek conventional forces, fearing that the host country would require permanent U.S. aid to maintain its forces. Instead, they focused upon qualitative improvements in individual and unit training, troop morale, and logistics. With these basic goals in mind, the U.S. mission reconciled communist containment with a cost-effective approach to collective security.[21]

American assistance also demanded basic institutional reforms from the Greek military and its government, conditions that proved difficult to meet in practice. A CIA report from January 1949 described Greece as "a running sore, calling for constant doctoring but unable to respond to treatment."[22] However, the national army was able to register important victories against insurgents by the end of the year and was largely able to break the back of the guerrillas aligned with the KKE. Eventually, with American assistance, the Greek military made considerable improvements, particularly in the use of tactical airpower, and was able to destroy major guerrilla formations. At the start of the fifties, after three years of fighting, desertions began to seriously erode insurgent forces remaining in the country.

At the start of the fifties, American policy makers appeared ready to expand beyond the Truman Doctrine. In October 1949, Harry Truman signed the Mutual Defense Assistance Act, which provided more than $1.3 billion in military assistance to NATO, Greece, Turkey, Iran, South Korea, and the "general area" of China.[23] American military aid addressed three specific objectives: to reconstitute defense industries in Western Europe; to direct weapons to rebuild host nation militaries; and to provide technical assistance and military training.[24] The act permanently anchored the United States to European rearmament through NATO and created a new pipeline of military assistance to the failing French military effort in Indochina.[25] As the fifties progressed, it would eventually evolve into even more ambitious projects, such as the Military Assistance Program (MAP) and the Mutual Security Program (MSP).

Korea

Korea was not a war known for its military innovations. For three brutal years, the conflict in northeast Asia was fought with the surplus materiel and equipment left over from World War II. The same standards held true with respect to small unit operations. Korea represented a very limited return to past form left over from 1945. The U.S. Army allowed the brief re-creation of Ranger companies used as scouts, raiders, and assault troops. However, because of high casualties, the units were disbanded by August 1951.[26]

During the war, there were also tentative efforts to form Korean "partisan" units to conduct the war north of the front lines once the latter had stabilized after 1951. The basic premise for the units was derived directly from the U.S. experience during World War II. Volunteers for these partisan units were drawn from the ranks of northern refugees. The American Far East Command eventually trained and equipped approximately 22,000 guerrillas to conduct raids and intelligence missions behind communist lines.[27]

The Korean partisans proved to be a limited success at best. Once the front lines firmed up, communist forces routinely swallowed up units infiltrated into North Korea. Efforts to create a guerrilla movement and interdict military traffic failed miserably in the last two years of the war. Of 272 personnel parachuted behind northern lines between 1952 and 1953, none returned.[28]

Small Wars and the Nuclear Military

During the Eisenhower years, MAP seemed the ideal vehicle for American national security policy. It provided the means—weapons, training, and equipment—for collective security cooperation and promoted the idea that American allies would assume responsibility for their own defense. MAP's cost effectiveness clearly attracted the president, who openly worried throughout his term in office whether "national bankruptcy or national destruction would get us first."[29]

Collective security left responsibility for strategic deterrence to the United States. Secretary of State John Foster Dulles explained the basic intent of the "New Look" in 1953: "The basic decision was to depend primarily upon a great capacity to retaliate, instantly, by means and at places of our choosing. Now the Department of Defense and the Joint Chiefs of Staff can shape our military establishment to fit what is our policy, instead of having to try to be ready to meet our enemy's many choices. That permits a selection of military means instead of a multiplication of means. As a result, it is now possible to get, and share, more basic security at less cost."[30] The fifties subsequently became the decade of Air Force ascendancy, wherein successive generations of B-36, B-47, and B-52 long-range strategic bombers carried the nuclear firepower necessary to keep communism at bay. In contrast, the Army saw its post-Korea ranks diminish from 1.5 million personnel in 1953 to 998,000 just four years later.[31]

For strategists, military assistance was attractive because it offered a clear division of labor. Complementing the nuclear forces in the American arsenal, collective security assistance provided a second layer of defense for the United States, a "second fence," as Senator Claude Pepper called it, which would produce strategic defense in depth.[32] The idea of using indigenous forces in place also seemed to make more sense since they already possessed the local area knowledge essential to combating insurgent threats to security.

The initial focus of MAP and other U.S. assistance programs was Europe. Approximately $1.2 billion of the $1.3 billion first allocated for the MAP went to NATO countries as well as Greece and Turkey.[33] However, after 1954 the U.S. Mutual Security Program, which consolidated military and technical assistance, expanded both the amount of aid to $5 billion and its application to American allies abroad.[34] Within three years, the United States had collective security agreements that included forty-two countries. By 1957, 6,000 American military advisers were stationed abroad and responsible for the logistical support and training of foreign military forces comprising 4.7 million personnel, the equivalent of 200 American divisions.[35]

As the fifties came to a close, American defense assistance also began to shift from building local forces that mirrored the U.S. military to programs more closely related to counterinsurgency. In 1957 the Office of Assistant Secretary of Defense for International Security

Affairs received additional funding for projects that included civil engineering, health care, and education. In addition, training courses offered by the American military included "civic action" instruction for advisers dispatched to hotspots around the world. In 1960 one of the U.S. military's first civic action teams was dispatched to Guatemala.[36]

The leadership of American ground forces was less than sanguine about these developments. In his memoirs, Army Chief of Staff General Maxwell Taylor decried the New Look as the "Great Fallacy" and little more than old airpower "dogma" with "Madison Avenue trappings." He would characterize the fifties as the Army's "Babylonian Captivity."[37]

Many of these criticisms were valid. Well into the second Eisenhower administration, it was readily apparent that the New Look lacked flexibility. Nuclear deterrence meant little in the world's proliferating brushfire wars.[38] As early as 1954, when the president balked at interven tion to save the French garrison at Dien Bien Phu, it was clear that U.S. military capabilities could not address the sliding scale of military and strategic demands placed upon them.[39]

Conventional forces were also lacking. In a desperate effort to maintain their relevance in the nuclear age, American ground forces contorted existing doctrine to make themselves relevant to policy makers. The Army and Marine Corps that finished the decade remained armor-plated and road-bound, with tactical nuclear weapons and missile systems grafted onto reorganized regiments in a poorly conceived effort to survive the New Look.[40]

The expanding military assistance program that accompanied the New Look had its own significant failings. National intelligence estimates regularly recognized that a general war with the Soviets was unlikely in the medium term and that Moscow would continue an aggressive campaign of subversion and support for local insurgencies against American allies on a global scale.[41] Yet, while American assistance trained hundreds of thousands of allied troops, most of these were deployed in smaller versions of the U.S. Army and wholly unsuited for counterinsurgency war. The resurrection of communist forces in South Vietnam at the conclusion of the fifties and the absolute failure of the local military were but one illustration of a larger problem. Even where American military personnel were prepared to address local insurgency, they faced formidable obstacles of indigenous incompetence, nepotism, and corruption.[42]

Fifteen years after World War II, it was clear that American military policy had failed to adequately address the challenge of small wars. Strategic priorities remained centered on nuclear deterrence rather than local insurgency. Although billions were invested in military assistance projects on a global level, the end product was, at best, problematic. The dramatic and unexpected success of the Cuban revolution against the Batista regime in 1959 punctuated the point. The conventional wisdom, which had already begun to shift a few years earlier, now focused on more effective means to win low-intensity conflicts. When the incoming Kennedy administration assumed its new mandate, the new team was bound and determined to successfully fill apparent gaps in U.S. national security policy.

The New Frontier and the Alliance for Progress

At the start of the sixties, much of the world suffered from chronic upheaval. By 1960 all of French West Africa and French Equatorial Africa were free. Seventeen new African nations emerged between 1960 and 1961 as Europe withdrew from the continent.[43] Few of these new countries enjoyed even basic stability. In Southeast Asia, war spread in the years following French withdrawal. The Diem government in Saigon found itself increasingly under siege by the resurgent Viet Cong. In Laos, communist-backed insurgents threatened the very existence of the country. Throughout Latin America, instability increasingly became the rule rather than the exception as ten military governments were toppled between 1956 and 1960.[44]

As was the case with the previous administration, Kennedy believed that the problem was not only instability but also outside exploitation of it. As a senator, he had made his stance clear in 1959: "So in practice, our nuclear retaliatory power is not enough. It cannot deter Communist aggression which is too limited to justify atomic war. It cannot protect uncommitted nations against Communist takeover using local or guerrilla forces. It cannot be used in so-called brush-fire wars. . . . In short, it cannot prevent the Communists from nibbling away at the fringe of the free world's territory or strength."[45] Walt W. Rostow, who joined the administration as deputy special assistant for National Security Affairs, would remark to candidate Kennedy in 1960 that the Soviets "were going to give us hell in the underdeveloped areas."[46]

Kennedy was determined to prevail over these challenges. Communist supported insurgencies were red meat for the self-described "ultrarealists" in the administration who saw the benefits at home and abroad of fighting small wars throughout the world. In *The Best and the Brightest,* David Halberstam noted the sincerity of both Kennedys, McGeorge Bundy, and other principle leaders: "that this attitude also made one less vulnerable to attacks from the right about softness on Communism did not hurt: it dealt at once with totalitarians abroad and wild men at home. Force was justified by what the Communists did; the times justified the acts which decent men did not seek, but which historic responsibilities made necessary."[47]

The prospect of fighting small wars abroad had an additional, special resonance within the administration. Roger Hilsman, who worked in the State Department's Bureau of Intelligence and Research, had led guerrilla forces behind Japanese lines in Burma. Secretary of Labor Arthur Goldberg had been an OSS operative in Europe. Throughout the Kennedy administration were men who had fought as junior officers in World War II, "tempered by war, disciplined by a hard and bitter peace," the very same generation he so prominently featured in his inaugural.[48]

Consequently, Kennedy embarked upon an effort to counter Soviet aggression across a wide military spectrum. In terms of substance, it meant the largest defense increases since the Korean War. Regular ground forces jumped from 875,000 to over 1 million troops during his first year in office. Smaller conflicts also received their due. In February 1961, National Security Action Memorandum (NSAM) 2 designated $100 million toward "paramilitary and sub-limited or unconventional wars."[49]

In terms of actual policy, counterinsurgency emerged as the most important component of American small war planning and operations. NSAM 131 (June 1961) mandated a series of multiagency training programs to study the history of popular rebellions and to develop means to prevent them. The Army responded by creating Free World Liaison and Assistance Groups comprised of administrative, logistical, and combat personnel who would provide both security training and "civic action" programs to countries threatened by communist-backed insurgencies.[50]

Latin America became an important test bed for this new approach. As was the case with much of the Third World, the prerequisites for instability permeated the Western Hemisphere. A 1961 National Intelligence Estimate concluded: "It appears to us very likely that during the next decade or two the Communist element among the revolutionary forces will grow in size, although its growth in influence would not necessarily be proportionate to its growth in size. The important question is not whether communism grows, but whether the non-Communist revolutionary forces can grow more rapidly, can control the revolutionary movement, and can achieve an acceptable level of momentum and progress in social, economic, and political change."[51] As far as Washington was concerned, the question was not whether a new revolution would threaten the hemisphere but when.

There was also a consensus that the primary source of future trouble for Latin America was Castro's Cuba. An American intelligence report from January 1961 noted definitively that Cuba was "a symbol of spontaneous popular revolution and a base for subversive operations."[52] Ernesto "Che" Guevara would later write that the revolution had "showed plainly the capacity of the people to free themselves by means of guerrilla warfare from the government that oppresses them."[53] Castro repeatedly echoed Guevara in his lengthy speeches before mass rallies: "Cuba will never become cowardly, Cuba will not step back, the Revolution will not be detained. . . . The Revolution will march ahead victoriously! . . . We shall continue to make our fatherland an example that will make the Andes mountain range into the Sierra Maestre of all America."[54] Thus, whether Cuba represented a precedent for aspiring Latin American insurgents or a Soviet entry into the Western Hemisphere, or both, the potential threat to U.S. interests appeared obvious at the time.

Unfortunately, Kennedy's first public entry into Latin American anticommunism was the Bay of Pigs fiasco in April 1961. The CIA paramilitary operation to train and support Cuban exiles in their effort to "liberate" Cuba from the Castro regime represented the apex of the agency's influence in Washington and its subsequent fall from grace.[55] More important, the CIA's failure did little to check American resolve to combat insurgency or the Cuban threat. McGeorge Bundy called the Bay of Pigs "a brick through the window" that had exposed a poorly conceived plan, but not its basic objectives.[56] In practice this meant that future operations would increasingly fall to the military rather than a civilian intelligence agency.

Only a few weeks into his administration, Kennedy was already considering American military assistance that placed "more emphasis on the development of counter-guerrilla forces." After the Bay of Pigs, the State Department recommended the possible creation of a "Caribbean Security Force" and later agreed that the United States should consider "organizations whose missions are in the counter-subversion, guerrilla and counter-guerrilla area."[57] To pursue these policies, the administration formed the Special Group (Counterinsurgency) in January 1962 as an appendage of the National Security Council (NSC). It included such diverse agencies as the U.S. Agency for International Development and the Justice Department and was chaired by Maxwell Taylor, a World War II paratrooper and later ambassador to South Vietnam. Officially, the Special Group has a dual purpose:

> a. To insure proper recognition throughout the U.S. Government that subversive insurgency ("wars of liberation") is a major form of politico-military conflict *equal* in importance to conventional warfare.
>
> b. To insure that such recognition is reflected in the organization, training, equipment, and doctrine of the U.S. Armed Forces and other U.S. agencies abroad and in the political, economic, intelligence, military aid and information programs conducted abroad by State, Defense, AID, USIA, and CIA.[58]

In practice, this meant that American counterinsurgency efforts would shift from the covert world of the intelligence community to open policy practiced by the Defense Department. From 1961 onward, this translated into a major commitment of resources and leadership. When Kennedy came into office, the total cost of Latin American military assistance was $49 million. For fiscal year 1962, the Defense Department recommended an increase to $112 million for grant aid, civic action projects, and credit sales. Military assistance levels remained high for much of the remaining decade.[59]

The change in policy also prompted direct U.S. involvement in planning and counterinsurgency operations within host countries. American officials also began organizing joint military exercises to foster cooperation between regional militaries. Over time, American advisers became intimately involved with not only military training but also police and civic action projects as well. To this end, the Agency for International Development created the Office of Public Safety in 1962 to coordinate security planning between local governments and U.S. officials.[60]

A number of military actors were responsible for Latin American training in the sixties. Many of the more traditional U.S. military attaché offices and military advisory groups familiar since World War II remained in place to conduct conventional training. However, new counterinsurgency doctrine was the primary province of American special forces units deployed throughout the region.

At the time, public acclaim made special forces soldiers into something akin to pop culture heroes of the era. A *Newsweek* story captured the image in a style reminiscent of an Ian Fleming novel: "From now on, President Kennedy told the Joint Chiefs of Staff, the Special Forces would no longer languish in the shade of the atomic missile, and they would, in fact, take on a series of new duties. The hard-muscled wielders of knife and garrote would teach their back-alley arts to fighters for freedom in the jungles of Southeast Asia, the savannas of Central Africa, wherever revolt and terror encroach."[61] Real life tended to be more mundane, but no less important, as the special forces effort grew in size and scope throughout the sixties. Teams initially drawn from the 7th Special Forces Group based at Fort Bragg, North Carolina, were dispatched to supplement the work performed by military advisory groups already stationed in Latin America as early as 1961. After April 1963, additional soldiers were deployed from the 8th Special Forces Group stationed at Fort Gulick in the Panama Canal Zone.

Between 1962 and 1967, 600 special forces mobile training teams eventually served in nineteen Latin American countries. In 1965 alone, U.S. personnel trained 41,000 Latin America soldiers.[62]

What these men managed to accomplish has been subject to intense debate ever since. During the sixties, the military regime in Guatemala became one of the largest recipients of U.S. military assistance. American aid enabled Guatemala to bolster its police, military, and paramilitary militia to combat a leftist insurgency active in the country. American assistance allowed the Guatemalan military to launch Operation Zacapa in October 1966, which combined airmobile units for search-and-destroy operation against rebel strongholds with a system of *comisionados*—temporary civilian militia—and a series of civic action projects.

Widespread human rights abuses followed in the wake of these operations. Right-wing death squads, such as the Mano Blanca, became commonplace and caused thousands of civilian casualties. Acting in concert with regular military units and the *comisionados,* these groups summarily executed rebel sympathizers and opponents of the government led by Julio César Méndez Montenegro. Between November 1966 and March 1967 an estimated 8,000 civilians died during internal security operations.[63]

The U.S. military's willingness to set aside viable counterinsurgency practices for what could be construed as state-supported terrorism later drew considerable criticism. Michael McClintock's 1992 book *Instruments of Statecraft* examined in particular the use of fear as a deliberate part of counterinsurgency doctrine. Contemporary publications such as *Field Manual 33-1: Psychological Operations* (1965) specifically endorsed terror as a standard military practice: "In many situations, the tactical commander may select the type of ordinance to be employed solely based on the psychological effect it will have on the guerrilla force. Historically, the employment of napalm has produced psychological effects on guerrilla forces."[64]

Events in Guatemala signaled a disturbing trend throughout Latin America in the sixties. As the decade progressed, national governments increasingly shifted toward military rule. Between 1961 and 1969 there were a total of sixteen military interventions in Latin America. A series of coups in Brazil (1964), Argentina (1966), and Peru (1968) prompted the State Department to comment at the end of the decade that: "The military's control of government in the three countries, which include half the area's population, and their determination to retain power for an indefinite term have been widely regarded as placing in question the future of constitutional representative government in Latin America."[65] The same was no doubt true of the military regimes that controlled the Dominican Republic, El Salvador, Ecuador, Paraguay, and Nicaragua. However, as the massacre of protestors in Mexico City during the 1968 Olympics proved, ostensibly more liberal Latin American governments were not immune from acts of overt oppression.

Another unforeseen consequence of U.S. military policy was a regional arms race. At the heart of counterinsurgency doctrine in Latin America was the assumption that the United States could cultivate local military action under controlled circumstances. Policy makers believed that hundreds of millions of dollars in military spending would purchase leverage to dictate the terms of local military practices. In this scenario, Latin American militaries were to be relatively compliant appendages of U.S. security policy.[66]

Events proved these assumptions to be badly mistaken. Many Latin American countries, particularly those in South America, simply chose to spend money far in advance of U.S. assistance. Between 1965 and 1968, Peru (12.3 percent), Brazil (11.9 percent), and Venezuela (6.3 percent) all substantially increased their defense budgets. Large amounts of money went not to low-intensity counterinsurgency operations, but to submarines, supersonic jet fighters, and surface ships, weapons that Peruvian finance minister Pedro Beltran dismissed as "expensive toys, already obsolete."[67] Responding to this criticism, Latin American militaries turned U.S. rhetoric back on itself and cited the ongoing contingencies of the Cold War. Chile justified naval modernization due to the need to protect "our lines of communication" along its 3,000-mile coastline.[68]

Consequently, Latin American arms imports increased significantly during the sixties. When the United States balked at providing modern weapons systems, local militaries turned to Western European sources that offered better prices. Chile opted for British Hawker Hunter jets when American officials refused a request for the advanced F-5 fighter. Peru sought out French Mirage-5 fighters when Washington appeared reluctant to supply more modern aircraft for its air force.[69] European arms agents commonly used what the State Department described as "aggressive and imaginative salesmanship" to promote their wares. Latin American countries interested in military purchases found better prices as well as low-interest, long-term loans and favorable credit rates. Between 1965 and 1970, arms sales from five countries (England, France, Canada, Italy, West Germany, and the Netherlands) jumped significantly from $57.4 million to $418.3 million.[70]

In the end, the counterinsurgency campaign initiated by Kennedy largely succeeded in stamping out leftist rebellions but produced unforeseen consequences that would undermine long-term stability in Latin America. Military regimes that were the beneficiaries of U.S. military assistance and foreign purchase became highly adept at handling guerrilla wars. Che Guevara's death in Bolivia in 1967 highlighted the failure of Cuban-sponsored popular revolutions.

Successful counterinsurgency exacted a high cost, however. Measured in human terms, U.S. military objectives in Latin America were won at the expense of thousands of lives as well as the rule of law. Fear was an effective tool to win order, but, as history has proven, state coercion produced diminishing returns over time. In the next decade, many of the dictatorships that prevailed over insurgents would find themselves hard pressed by renewed rebellion.

In basic economic terms, the militarization of Latin America also created significant long-term problems. The regional arms race that surged forward through the sixties was as expensive as it was unnecessary. Yet most major Latin American nations continued purchases that were both irrelevant to small-scale warfare and economically unsustainable. The energy crises of the seventies and the decline in basic commodity prices repeatedly drove this latter point home.[71]

Intervention in Vietnam

While U.S. military policy unfolded in Latin America, it is clear that the Vietnam War exerted a much more profound influence on how America planned for and fought small-scale conflicts. As many studies of the conflict have noted, U.S. involvement in Southeast Asia began in World War II, when OSS teams actively supported the Viet Minh and other insurgent groups against the Japanese. After 1945, with postwar

European solidarity in mind, American policy shifted to support the French reoccupation of Indochina. By the Korean War, Washington underwrote a significant portion of the French war effort in Southeast Asia as well as its NATO membership. When the Military Assistance Program was created, $75 million was allocated for the "general area" of China.[72] By 1954 U.S. assistance for the French war effort amounted to more than $1 billion, a total of 78 percent of the money spent for the war in Indochina.[73]

American involvement escalated after the French phase of the war ended in 1954. Due largely to U.S. diplomatic efforts, South Vietnam was officially recognized by the Southeast Asia Treaty Organization (SEATO). A year later, Ngo Dinh Diem became a U.S. proxy and benefited from significant political and economic support that allowed his regime to survive early challenges and consolidate its power.[74]

The most important component of the U.S. effort in South Vietnam was its military assistance program. Even as the last French contingents departed the country, the American military advisory group essentially embarked upon the creation of a large conventional force that could protect the country from a conventional invasion on par with what had threatened Korea in 1950. Their specific goal, which reflected most American military aid programs in the fifties, was to construct eight regular divisions and three tactical air wings to replace departing French forces.[75] Five years and many hundreds of millions of dollars later, the advisory group had largely succeeded in its mission. In 1960 the South Vietnamese Army consisted of 150,000 soldiers organized in a manner that more resembled NATO forces on duty in West Germany than Southeast Asia. Vietnamese units were trained to maneuver in synch with their field artillery units, at this point comprised of 105mm howitzers and 4.2-inch mortars. The entire enterprise, once deployed, was road-bound and logistics heavy.[76]

Predictably, the same military, when faced with a dedicated communist insurgency after 1957, collapsed under the weight of improper training and doctrine, politicization of the officer corps, and blatant incompetence. In the first four months of 1960, the South Vietnamese army lost over 1,000 weapons of all types, while recovering only 150 from guerrillas. According to the South Vietnamese Ministry of Defense, national forces were losing enough weapons each month to equip an entire Viet Cong battalion.[77]

As the South Vietnamese war effort faltered, the United States increasingly inserted itself into the conflict to prevent collapse. Communist gains against the Diem regime conjured up images of a failure on par with the loss of China in 1949, a prospect that was politically and strategically untenable in Washington. Consequently, during the early sixties, a combination of events and the deliberate actions of the new Kennedy administration introduced U.S. forces into the entire spectrum of Vietnamese conflict.

Before the mass deployment of conventional U.S. forces in 1965, American military activity in South Vietnam was a relatively small-scale affair. American helicopter units provided direct combat support to the South Vietnamese military under operation FARMGATE.[78] Covert programs against North Vietnam, such as OPLAN 34A conducted by the CIA, also defined a great deal of increased intervention without public exposure.[79] These initial projects, managed by civilian intelligence operatives, established a strong precedent that continued throughout the war. The Phoenix Program, a much larger effort to attack the Viet Cong "infrastructure" through a combination of counterintelligence and selective assassination continued long after the American military build-up in South Vietnam.[80]

In the meantime, the United States supported a series of projects designed to separate South Vietnamese civilians from the Viet Cong and win popular support. Initial efforts, such as the abortive "Agrovilles" and the "Strategic Hamlet" program, were primarily conducted by the Saigon government but received significant American assistance for what the U.S. country team initially believed were proactive steps against insurgents.[81]

After the collapse of the Diem government in November 1963, the United States took charge of the counterinsurgency war. Strategic hamlets were rebranded under the New Life Hamlet Program. In the early stages of American intervention, a variety of U.S. agencies embraced the responsibility for reforming counterinsurgency in South Vietnam. The CIA created "counter-terror teams" (later renamed Provisional Reconnaissance Units) that attempted to replicate the tactics and structure of the Viet Cong. The U.S. Agency for International Development took a more conventional approach when it took responsibility for training the national police under the Public Safety Program.[82] A small component of the American military advisers also participated in the counterinsurgency effort. Army special forces took charge of Civilian Irregular Defense Groups from the CIA in 1963 and, with their counterparts in the South Vietnamese special forces, trained and armed more than 50,000 local troops drawn from tribes in the Central Highlands and along the Laotian and Cambodian borders.[83]

Among the American conventional forces stationed in South Vietnam, the Marine Corps were clearly the most intent on fostering a small unit approach to the war. Early in their tenure, the Marines created Combined Action Platoons (CAPs), where small groups of Americans served combat tours stationed with local South Vietnamese units. While some individual efforts proved highly successful and created an important degree of camaraderie between Americans and South Vietnamese, overall the CAP program was only partially effective. It was hamstrung by the fact that it received little support from higher command. Only a tiny portion of the total Marine Corps effort in South Vietnam was dedicated to the combined platoons, reaching a total of only 144 units.[84]

Taken as a whole, the initial U.S. counterinsurgency effort in South Vietnam proved to be a patchwork of sometimes redundant or contradictory programs that were poorly coordinated with each other and the growing mass of conventional units in the country. Ultimately, U.S. policymakers saw the problem not in terms of method or doctrine, but as a matter of better bureaucratic organization. This was essentially the motive behind the decision to group all counterinsurgency efforts under a single office, the Civilian Operations and Revolutionary Development Support (CORDS) in May 1967.[85] CORDS was a bold move that placed a civilian, Robert Komer, at the head of the U.S. counterinsurgency effort. Komer was able to introduce a significant degree of rational planning to American operations and enjoyed substantially greater cooperation with both Military Assistance Command, Vietnam (MACV) and corps-level commanders. By the end of the sixties, there was some evidence that CORDS was succeeding against the Viet Cong. Estimated Viet Cong and North Vietnamese Army strength had declined, along with large-scale, battalion-sized attacks. In 1970 U.S. Hamlet Evaluation System estimated that 75 percent of the South Vietnamese population was "secure."[86]

Yet, in the end, CORDS did fail. Despite the optimistic projections assembled by MACV, stability in the countryside was a tentative prospect at best. Clearly, the ineptitude of the Thieu regime was responsible for this failure, as was the Nixon administration's concessions to North Vietnam at the Paris peace talks.

However, a number of military factors also account for the abortive counterinsurgency effort in South Vietnam. One clear indicator was the American preference for the "big war" against the Viet Cong and North Vietnamese Army forces. Although U.S. commanders tinkered with their methodology during the sixties, a large-scale war of attrition based on overwhelming firepower essentially defined the American war effort. More important, as Jeffrey C. Clarke and other scholars have noted, when "Vietnamization" began in 1969, the American military institution passed this standard directly to the South Vietnamese, ensuring that their efforts would be heavily dependent on conventional forces and an unsustainable consumption of military materiel.[87]

The vast, expensive, and vulnerable logistical infrastructure built by the United States during the Vietnam War also significantly influenced American operations.[88] In order to sustain the war of attrition in the field, far more manpower was expended on support functions than combat units. For a modern military unit in the sixties, this meant that a ratio of at least three support troops to every combat soldier was an unbreakable standard.[89] It was an open secret throughout the conflict that most troops stationed in South Vietnam were there in a logistical capacity. Sustained combat with VC and NVA units was a rare experience for most American personnel.

Yet, even where regular American units operated in the field, commanders believed that they possessed the flexibility to win a counterinsurgency war.[90] Both the Pentagon and MACV embraced doctrine governing dismounted patrolling and small unit operations as adequate to defeat insurgents on their own terms. The Marine Corps CAP program was emblematic of contemporary confidence in existing conventional force structure and training.

In the end, the bias toward conventional operations proved disastrous to the American war effort in South Vietnam. The progressively increasing scale of search-and-destroy operations, coupled with massive U.S. Air Force bombing, generated hundreds of thousands of refugees who fled the countryside and CORDS counterinsurgency programs.[91] The imperfect vessel that was South Vietnam broke under the pressure of social suffering and a growing popular backlash against military escalation. Even where CORDS was marginally successful, it was undercut by corruption and incompetence from the local level all the way to the South Vietnamese national leadership in Saigon.

For the entirety of the Vietnam War, American leaders allowed the counterinsurgency effort to be dominated by a military frame of reference. Where political reforms were necessary to create legitimacy and popular support, the U.S. focused on security first, allowing Cold War priorities to take precedence over democracy or the rule of law.[92] Where social and economic programs might have produced stability, the United States played lip service to winning "hearts and minds" as it waged a war of attrition against communists in the countryside. While on the NSC staff in the first year of the Kennedy administration, Robert Komer had presented the core elements of a viable counterinsurgency policy:

> What we are really driving at is that internal security measures, counter-guerrilla operations, and a broad range of civic actions essentially deal with manifestations of a central problem encountered in many of the underdeveloped countries. This problem involves the critical area where internal political, economic, and social tensions interact with external manipulation and/or local initiatives for irregular forms of armed violence or civic disturbance. The resulting disorder can take different forms, varying considerably from one country to the next. But in all cases it has deep roots in civil turmoil which is *not originally* of a military nature.[93]

Unfortunately, the complexities, and the commitments, that Komer proposed were largely ignored both in Latin America and, later, South Vietnam. In both cases, the "big war"—whether delineated by anticommunist containment or an emphasis on conventional warfare—took precedence, with all their inherent faults.

Conclusions

American leaders were clearly cognizant of the fact that small wars had a particular relevance to the Cold War. Truman's warning in 1947 about subversion by "such methods as coercion, or by such subterfuges as political infiltration," had the same traction a decade later when the Eisenhower administration assembled plans to fight brushfire wars in the Third World.[94] When John Kennedy became president, it was clear that he not only wanted to accept America's commitment to low-intensity war, but also win them once and for all. Given the understanding of the threat and the obvious desire to prevail, why then did this effort end so badly?

The prospective costs of victory obviously gave American leaders a reason to pause. In terms of military funding, successive administrations reverted to historical American form after World War II and gutted defense spending. The forties and fifties, with the obvious exception of the Korean War, were notable for an ongoing search for military economy, a "bigger bang for the buck," as contemporary policy makers defined the solution. More important, there was little likelihood that the American public was willing to commit the manpower necessary for successful low-intensity warfare. The postwar period was characterized by declining public tolerance for risking American lives. Truman's disastrous decline in popularity during Korea and later mass protests against the draft in the sixties indicated the new and expanding boundaries of this sentiment.

Institutional inertia within the American military was also a powerful obstacle. Faced with budgetary retrenchment after 1945, the uniformed services clung to the doctrines, weaponry, and organizational structures burnished by victory over the Axis. In the fifties, when the New Look held sway, the service branches scrambled to shoehorn nuclear weapons into their existing tactics and training. Hindsight has provided some perspective on how absurd some of these efforts were, particularly some of the schemes to incorporate tactical nuclear weaponry into a future battlefield. At the time, however, they represented a desperate search for relevancy at the height of the Cold War. More important, it was this New Look military that deployed to Vietnam, encumbered by supersonic aircraft, heavy formations, and a leadership prepared to fight Soviet armor pouring through the Fulda Gap in West

Germany. The special operations troops that Kennedy and the popular press lavished with so much attention were but a tiny percentage of the American military. They remained so as U.S. forces escalated their effort in South Vietnam and the "big war" began in 1965.

While the Vietnam War was clearly influenced by the factors above, the totality of America's withdrawal from South Vietnam and its collapse two years later created their own legacies. Later studies of the war would take note of the massive cost of the war, not in only in the isolated context of Cold War defense budgets, but also in terms of the holistic damage it inflicted upon the U.S. economy long after the conflict was over.[95] On the other side of the spectrum were the intangible costs of Vietnam. Henry Kissinger and a generation of academics would devote considerable thought to the war's impact on American prestige abroad as well as the permanency of "Vietnam Syndrome" at home.[96] How the U.S. military and its civilian leadership might respond to such a disastrous turn of events was an open question.

2

The Seventies Nadir and Recovery

> *We were in transition from the draft to the all-volunteer force. As we dragged ourselves home from Vietnam, the nation turned its back on the military. Many of our troops, in Army shorthand, were "Cat Four," Category IV, soldiers possessing meager skills in reading, writing, and math. They were life's dropouts, one step above Category V, those who were considered unfit for Army service. Today [1995], about 4 percent of the Army is Cat Four, while in those days the figure was closer to 50 percent.*
>
> —Colin Powell, *My American Journey*

The seventies were a decade defined by a profound sense of aftermath. They began with continued, vicious divisions within American society, rising crime rates, and declining economic fortunes. Political developments only contributed to the bitter atmosphere. Although Nixon's landslide electoral victory in 1972 put to rest questions about a presidential mandate that had dogged the previous contest, the Watergate scandal quickly ripped away public faith in the government. Overall, the seventies were, in the words of one recent historian, "grim, tasteless years that are best put out of mind."[1]

The American military found itself in much the same situation as the rest of the country. The start of the seventies saw the war in Vietnam finally winding down. Troop withdrawals, promised by the Nixon administration and highly popular with the public, proceeded apace. By the end of 1971, 175,000 American troops remained in South Vietnam, of which only 75,000 were combat forces.[2] However, the outflow of American forces was not simply a means toward an end. The single-minded nature of U.S. pullout essentially defined the conventional wisdom of the moment. Contemporary American leaders saw the Vietnam War more as the end of an era than the beginning of a new age. The president drew this important distinction in a 1970 press conference that would eventually become known as "Nixon Doctrine": "We are not involved in the world because we have commitments; we have commitments because we are involved. Our interests must shape our commitments, rather than the other way around."[3] Within the military itself, the Pentagon also wanted desperately to leave behind the drug use, breakdown in discipline, and declining morale that had become endemic problems within the service. An escape from Southeast Asia offered at least the potential for a new start that could arrest these trends and save the military as an institution.[4]

What would bedevil both civilian and military policy makers was the final treatment of the war. Was it an aberration, forced upon the military by poor decisions generated from successive presidential administrations? Or had the American prosecution of the war in Vietnam revealed larger, systemic failures within the military establishment as a whole? Neither of these paths presented particularly easy choices for the White House or the Pentagon under ideal circumstances. What they faced instead was a turbulent economic, political, and social context that made meaningful reform as problematic as it was necessary.

American Military Policy at the End of the Nixon Era

If there was one trend that was clear at the beginning of the seventies, it was that war was an option of rapidly declining importance to the United States. During his first term, Richard Nixon built a national security strategy predicated on selective military withdrawal abroad and a greater emphasis on diplomacy. The massive deployment of American airpower against North Vietnam during the Easter Offensive in 1972 and, again during the so-called Christmas bombing campaign at the end of the year, were literally a last gasp, an exception to a trend that saw the United States becoming increasingly reluctant to flex its military muscle.[5] As the war wound down, superpower summitry became the new rule. America's final year in South Vietnam was overshadowed by well-publicized meetings in Peking and Moscow that reconstructed the Cold War template and garnered Nixon political accolades that served him well during his reelection bid. In 1973 the Paris Peace Treaty removed whatever emphasis the administration had on military action in Southeast Asia and punctuated a new period of withdrawal from direct global military intervention.

The unforeseen consequences of the Watergate scandal punctuated self-imposed restrictions on the use of American power. In August 1974, fully 65 percent of respondents to a Gallup poll believed that there was enough evidence to bring Nixon to a trial before the Senate. Upon departing the White House in disgrace that same month, Nixon enjoyed a 24 percent approval rating.[6] When Barry Goldwater told Republican leaders in the midst of the debate over impeachment that "we can be lied to only so many times," the tough-minded Arizona Senator actually lagged behind the public consensus on the president.[7] Although the Nixon's resignation clearly marked the endpoint of a tragic personal decline, it was the collapse of presidential legitimacy that made Watergate important to the modern era, particularly as it applied to national security policy. Watergate was the finale of what Arthur Schlesinger Jr. called the "imperial presidency," a status enjoyed by chief executives throughout the Cold War that had granted them significant latitude with respect to foreign policy decisions.[8] Overt intervention in Korea and Vietnam had signified public trust and congressional acceptance of national security contingencies over standing constitutional procedures and normal peacetime expectations (e.g., the draft). Even where covert actions were less publicized, Nixon's predecessors enjoyed significant discretion, a fact that every president after 1945 increasingly accepted as a mandate for action.[9]

Unfortunately, when Gerald R. Ford assumed the presidency in the furor that followed Watergate, he enjoyed none of this tolerance or any of its derivative benefits. During his abbreviated term, Ford failed to win legislative support for either direct military action or, more important, substantive military aid for American allies. In a 1975 debate over additional aid to South Vietnam, New York Senator Jacob Javits bluntly informed the president that "I will give you large sums for evacuation, but not one nickel for military aid."[10] The 94th Congress was clearly a resurgent branch prepared to fill in the political vacuum created by Nixon's departure. Lawmakers embraced oversight as an overriding priority, whether this applied to weapons sales, intelligence work, or the definition of U.S. fishing rights. The Congress also openly challenged prospective new overseas involvement. After the collapse of South Vietnam, legislators proved extremely reluctant to indulge in further overseas entanglements. This led to a ban on military grant assistance to Chile after the coup against Salvador Allende Gossens in 1973. Later, when members of Congress sympathetic to Ford's foreign policy challenges in Africa made a move to preempt a ban on aid to Angola, it was decisively defeated in the House 323–99 and 72–26 in the Senate.[11]

By mid-decade it was also clear that public priorities had shifted from guns to butter. According to an October 1975 Gallup poll, respondents considered the most important problems confronting the United States to be "the high cost of living" (57 percent) and unemployment (21 percent). In contrast, "international problems" gathered 4 percent of the poll responses.[12] High energy costs and the declining viability of American manufacturing framed much of the public discourse on foreign affairs. Combined with congressional recalcitrance and the weakened state of his own office, Ford faced a steep climb over a limited time span as he addressed pressing national security demands.

The Ford Administration and National Security

When he assumed office in 1974, most Americans expected Gerald Ford to be a caretaker who would occupy the White House without making much of an impact on domestic or foreign policy.[13] Although historians have since noted Ford's admirable personal convictions and character, his service as president, particularly regarding military affairs, was limited by a significant lack of experience. As a member of Michigan's congressional delegation, Ford served on the House Defense Appropriations Subcommittee after 1953 and the Foreign Operations Administration Subcommittee from 1956 to 1964. During this period, he had the opportunity to offer questions to foreign policy principals in the State and Defense Departments regarding spending but did not participate in the formation of grand strategy.[14]

In terms of active foreign policy, Ford followed the diplomatic emphasis established earlier by Nixon. Within a year of assuming office, the hallmark of his administration would be the Helsinki Conference, where discussion focused on human rights within the Soviet bloc. Ford hoped that a mutual understanding regarding this one issue would eventually create momentum behind the SALT II nuclear arms treaty with Moscow.[15] Under his guidance, it appeared that détente would enjoy a life beyond Watergate.

Ford's one dramatic brush with military decision making occurred during the 1975 Mayaguez incident. The U.S. response to Cambodia's seizure of a 480-foot container ship and its crew was the one distinct military action ordered by his administration.[16] From the start, the president adopted an aggressive position, siding with Secretary of State Kissinger in his support of military strikes against Cambodia. Ford consequently ordered Marine and Navy units into the region to rescue the captive crew and bomb targets in Cambodia. In doing so, he provoked an open break with Defense Secretary James R. Schlesinger, who remained skeptical that U.S. forces could successfully rescue the hostages.

American special operations forces were ready and available for the Mayaguez operation. A Navy SEAL team stationed in the Philippines was alerted for the mission, but not deployed to provide reconnaissance of the hostage site before the Marine assault began.[17] Lacking good intelligence prior to the mission, American forces suffered nearly a hundred casualties (forty-one killed and fifty wounded) in the assault, only to find the Mayaguez empty and the prisoners already released by Cambodian authorities.[18]

Beyond the tactical deficiencies of the Mayaguez rescue mission, the operation proved to be a primer on many failures that would repeatedly appear in the post-1975 American military. In one respect, the operation proved to be a case study on the problem of military micromanagement. Ford reflected in his memoirs about being miffed at poor intelligence and "high-level bumbling" in the defense establishment when the time came to accurately execute his orders, particularly those applying to air strikes against Cambodia.[19] The rescue mission also illustrated a significant split within the Ford's national security team. Schlesinger and senior military commanders were extremely averse to conducting yet another operation in Southeast Asia so soon after the withdrawal from South Vietnam. Unlike the civilian leadership, led by Ford and Kissinger, they had no desire to commit U.S. forces to a mission with even a limited objective. This civil-military friction clearly retarded the rescue mission's operational success. Military command on the ground accepted the letter of civilian orders rather than their spirit. They focused on reducing potential risk rather than aggressively pursuing the mission. This reticence explains the absence of adequate reconnaissance assets on site. More broadly, it also highlighted the boundaries of a civil-military schism over the use of force abroad.

The public reaction to the Mayaguez mission was also illustrative of the post-Vietnam era. Press coverage of the operation was mixed at best. The *New York Times* called it a "domestic and foreign triumph."[20] However, a column by Anthony Lewis in the same paper referred to the American action as "Barbarous Piracy."[21] The response in Congress proved to be an altogether different story. Federal lawmakers saw the Mayaguez operation as a litmus test for the War Powers Act. Senator Mike Mansfield (D-MT) criticized the failure to consult with Congress as required by the law. After the mission was completed, Senator Thomas Eagleton (D-MO) introduced three separate amendments to the War Powers Act to plug loopholes in the law and requested a Government Accountability Office investigation of the Cambodian strikes.[22]

Overall, the Mayaguez operation was a minor departure from the Ford administration's overall approach to military affairs, which could be best described as one of conceptual and budgetary retrenchment. American defense priorities at the time were clearly expressed in National Security Decision Memorandum 348, "U.S. Defense and Military Posture," published in January 1977. According to the document, the three primary areas of American military interest were, in rank order: a sustainable strategic nuclear balance with the Soviet Union; "an adequate American contribution to the defense of the NATO area"; and a global capability to "meet those challenges outside the NATO/Warsaw Pact area."[23] Official policy recognized that U.S. military forces might be needed "for a wide variety of possible conflicts." However, the final short paragraph of a four-page document focused more on acquiring base rights and a transportation infrastructure abroad than meeting low-level military threats on par with those recently abandoned in South Vietnam.[24]

Secretary of Defense James Schlesinger hammered home this new set of priorities throughout his tenure at the Pentagon. In a 1974 speech before the National Security Industrial Association, he described the post-Vietnam period as an "age of transition."[25] What the United States needed, according to this school of thought, was to restore its focus to the primary security threat to American interests, namely the Soviet Union. JCS Chairman, General George S. Brown echoed this refrain two years later when he warned the Senate Armed Services Committee that "there is mounting evidence that the Soviet Union is pressing forward vigorously with massive programs for near-term deployments involving every facet of offensive strategic power."[26] Both the joint chiefs and the defense secretary believed that the best way to ameliorate this problem was to shift military appropriations and doctrine. When Schlesinger testified before Congress on February 1975, he made note of the fact that the Soviets "now devote more resources than the United States in most significant categories of defense. In overall Research and Development, they outstrip us by 20%; in General Purpose Forces by 20%; in Procurement by 25%; and in Strategic Nuclear Offensive Forces by 60%."[27]

Simple facts, readily accessible to most Americans at the time, drove these points home. By the mid-seventies, the Soviet conventional force structure was formidable, with eighty-eight Warsaw Pact divisions deployed or near NATO and another forty divisions stationed in the Far East.[28] Moreover, as the SALT I negotiations had made abundantly clear, Soviet nuclear forces had already moved past the point of parity with the United States. These challenges required American policy makers to devote considerable attention to nuclear and conventional military readiness. They would also be very costly. After factoring in inflation, Schlesinger predicted the need to increase U.S. defense spending from $104.7 billion in 1976 to $148 billion by 1980.[29]

But the defense secretary was politically savvy enough to understand the obstacles he faced in asserting these new priorities. In regular public speeches, Schlesinger rejected the post-Vietnam critique of America's global role and its military as a form of "national dyspepsia" that threatened national strategic interests. Although he acknowledged skepticism regarding bloated budgets and "voracious bureaucrats" in the Pentagon, he also warned that complacency was leading U.S. military power down a dangerous path that revisited America's isolationist past. In a January 1975 speech before the Economic Club of New York, he stated that the United States Navy would drop below 500 ships for the first time since 1939, and that the number of service members under arms was "no higher than that reached in the pell-mell demobilization after World War II."[30] In order to meet basic defense needs, the American military was in desperate need of renovation and restructuring. Weapons and equipment worn out by overuse or made obsolescent by improvements in technology required replacement and refitting. More important was the next generation of tactical and strategic weapons systems necessary to counteract Soviet dominance in sheer numbers of troops, tanks, and missiles.

However, despite these appeals, the Defense Department was unable to stave off what Schlesinger described as "deep, savage, and arbitrary cuts" in defense appropriations for fiscal year 1976.[31] The previous year, appropriations for defense had been cut from the initial Defense Department recommendation of $97.9 billion to $90.5 billion, a 7.5 percent reduction.[32] In 1976 lawmakers appeared somewhat more willing to recognize the threat posed by the Soviets in principle. Schlesinger's replacement Donald Rumsfeld claimed before congressional leaders in March 1976:

> No one chart or statistic can provide the complete picture—but a sweeping look at resources, procurement and R&D efforts, equipment construction rates, force level changes, and shifts in relative capability can make clear what has taken place. A collection of such graphics is presented here, with appropriate explanations and caveats.
>
> The facts drive one to a clear conclusion that the U.S. must act now to arrest these adverse trends, by providing real increases for national security, unless the U.S. is willing to alter our policy of maintaining "rough equivalence." It is my conviction that the

> American people are not willing to accept a policy of inferiority.[33]

Unfortunately, his encouragement proved to be of limited value. A 1976 budget resolution set a $112 billion dollar limit on defense spending, only $1.3 billion below the president's initial request but inadequate to keep pace with inflation.

Efforts to revamp American doctrine during the Ford years also suffered from significant limitations. In basic terms, U.S. policy makers wanted to restore the Eurocentric approach to national security policy that had dominated much of the Cold War.[34] During his time at the Pentagon, Schlesinger made the defense of Western Europe his first priority. The so-called Schlesinger Doctrine, expressed in the 1974 National Security Decision Memorandum 242 (NSDM 242), restructured U.S. nuclear deterrence and returned to the European theater as the centerpiece of U.S. strategy. NSDM 242 essentially posited a nuclear "trickle down" effect, wherein a viable U.S. strategic capability would legitimize the nuclear umbrella over NATO that would, in turn, backstop conventional forces in place to defend the region against the Warsaw Pact. In theory, Schlesinger Doctrine would check the most important Soviet threat to America's primary global political, economic, and military interests.[35]

In a less tangible but nonetheless important sense, Schlesinger saw in a return to Europe an opportunity to reconstruct a sense of purpose. Across the Iron Curtain stood a known enemy in an order of battle that made sense to troops in the field as well as the command structure in Washington. The predictability of the Soviet threat and the responses necessary to meet it offered the defense establishment a purchase point and the traction that had been absent for so many years during the Vietnam War. In sum, the European theater of operations offered what Schlesinger would refer to in his farewell remarks as secretary of defense as "a revitalized sense of history."[36]

Unfortunately, Schlesinger's new doctrine was compromised from the start, ironically by United States' policy. One outcome of the budgetary battle fought over defense on Capitol Hill was the impact of spending reductions on American alliances abroad. Throughout the entirety of the Vietnam War, from 1964 to 1973, the United States had provided NATO with $9.1 billion in military assistance.[37] With the conclusion of the conflict and subsequent reductions in defense spending, Washington wanted its Western European allies to shoulder a greater proportion of the regional defense burden. NSDM 293 (1975) directed efforts to encourage these countries "to increase their defense expenditures, to undertake force improvement programs to upgrade their military hardware, and, most importantly, to make more effective use of existing defense resources by reducing the overlap and duplication that exists in many areas of NATO activity." In principle, improvements in these areas would strengthen NATO, ease the ongoing burden on American defense spending, and address the problems that military assistance created for the U.S. balance of payments.[38]

Predictably, Schlesinger Doctrine almost immediately faced resistance abroad. One immediately apparent challenge was the fact that America's NATO allies had their own "revitalized sense of history." Rather than approach the Cold War in the seventies as an opportunity to rebuild military deterrence, European leaders wanted to find methods to ameliorate tensions. Led by West Germany's chancellor Willy Brandt, "Ostpolitik" offered an attractive alternative to a new round of nuclear and conventional military confrontations along the Iron Curtain.[39] Consequently, when the Soviets supported initiatives such as the Conference on Security and Cooperation in Europe (CSCE) that addressed items such as prior notification of major military exercises and troop movements, both NATO and neutral states were readily willing to participate.[40] The CSCE effectively rendered Schlesinger's new doctrine moot by offering collective security based on increased cooperation between East and West.

Cooperation was also cheaper than American proposals. Globally, the 1973 oil crisis provoked what Thomas J. McCormick describes as the "quiet depression" that affected advanced nations and the Third World alike.[41] In the seventies, the common denominators of inflation, trade imbalances, and increasingly restive constituencies appeared throughout the world and were differentiated only by their severity. Faced with skyrocketing energy costs and their own declining industrial bases, few European countries wanted to shoulder a greater burden for NATO defense. Thus, in simple economic terms, Schlesinger's centerpiece for American strategy was untenable before it was proposed.

Outside of Western Europe, attempts to pursue American national security policy fared badly during the Ford years. Interestingly, the debate did not involve sending military forces to new conflicts overseas per se. American withdrawal from South Vietnam and the War Powers Act had rendered that discussion moot for the moment.[42] Instead, the debate centered on foreign military assistance. In his capacity as Ford's Secretary of State, Henry Kissinger complained that restrictions on aid to the beleaguered Saigon government had created an unfortunate snowball effect in Congress.[43] Throughout the mid- and late seventies, lawmakers were diligent in cutting appropriations for foreign military assistance and setting specific limits on presidential discretion in using it. A September 1974 NSC memorandum warned that "Senate amendments do not consider the unpredictable future, and restrict flexibility in solving the human ills of the world, and will particularly hamper attempts for peace in the Middle East, Cyprus, and Southeast Asia."[44] Kissinger, for example, personally opposed a congressional plan to phase out MAP grants in favor of loans for foreign military purchases. In a memo to president Ford, he pointed out that "grant assistance is an important diplomatic tool for the achievement of our own interests. The U.S. needs it as a quid pro quo for political support, use of bases and facilities and, to a limited degree, to strengthen allies with shared national security interests. In many cases the use of MAP provides the only leverage with nations faced with real or potential threats to their security."[45]

Despite Kissinger's objections, Congress largely had its way. While security assistance to Israel increased under Ford, aid to Third World countries allied with the United States was generally cut—in some cases, significantly. Indonesia, Thailand, and Zaire all saw reductions. Military support for Ethiopia fell by 25 percent during fiscal year 1976.[46]

Although the debate over foreign military assistance clearly illustrated the shift in bureaucratic power from the "imperial" executive branch to the legislature, it is more important as an illustration of American military priorities in the late seventies. As NATO and Warsaw Pact forces maintained their respective vigils along a heavily defended but peaceful border separating Eastern and Western Europe, warfare raged in the underdeveloped world. Once Vietnam was reunified, violence spread into Cambodia and north along the border with China. Leftist guerrillas in Latin American, repeatedly quashed by security forces in the sixties, gained a new lease on life during the seventies. As America celebrated its bicentennial, insurgent movements returned to El Salvador and began coalescing into a revolution against the Somoza regime in Nicaragua.[47] Africa in particular witnessed a significant increase in fighting all throughout the seventies, much of it supported by foreign sponsors. According to U.S. intelligence estimates, between 1977 and 1979, the Soviet Union provided Ethiopia with $2.1 billion in military assistance—tanks, artillery, MIG aircraft, and air defense—in addition to 1,300 military advisers and between 15,000 and 17,000 Cuban combat troops. During roughly the same time period, 1975 to 1979, Angola received between $400 and $450 million in Soviet military aid, as well as Cuban military personnel, whose numbers peaked at 25,000–30,000 in 1977.[48]

During Gerald Ford's abbreviated term, American military power suffered at all levels. At the very top of the national command structure, the country's first unelected president struggled with the basic question of his own legitimacy before the Congress and the public. Where Ford did attempt to define himself within the context of the Cold War, it was in the diplomatic rather than the military arena. Fresh from the American retreat from Vietnam, he had no desire to revisit military affairs in any serious manner. His secretary of defense, James Schlesinger, also openly attempted to jettison the war in Southeast Asia by rebuilding American military strategy with familiar tools and objectives: nuclear deterrence in support of conventional forces organized under the doctrine of collective security in Europe. Schlesinger Doctrine was a return to the past, almost to the point where it skipped over a decade and revisited American defense policy in the Eisenhower era.

It proved impossible to return to the halcyon days of the Cold War, however. The United States lacked the political clout to impose its will upon its European allies. Farther abroad, where conflict threatened in Asia, Africa, and Latin America, the Ford administration also lacked the political capital necessary to win funding for military aid. Unable to rediscover the past and unable to face present challenges, the prospects for reconstructing either the American military as an institution or the national security policy seemed bleak indeed.

Military Affairs in the Carter Administration

The 1976 presidential election did little to dispel a sense of American military decline. The contest held amidst bicentennial celebrations reflected one of the electoral cycles in the United States that periodically rejects the status quo. In this case, the public chose a relatively obscure southern governor whose primary mandate was to distance the country from the scandal and partisanship of the immediate past and address the troubles affecting Americans at the moment. When Jimmy Carter arrived in Washington, these priorities were overwhelmingly domestic in nature. According to a January 1977 Cambridge Survey, the first four areas of public concern were jobs/unemployment (78 percent), tax reform (52 percent), stimulation of business and the economy (50 percent), and welfare system reform (44 percent). The desire to reshape foreign policy garnered 14 percent of the responses, below reducing the defense budget (18 percent).[49]

In the area of foreign policy priorities, the new administration promised a departure from standard Cold War practices. Carter's secretary of state, Cyrus Vance, noted in his memoirs that before considering relations with the Soviet Union, economic strategy, or human rights, his objective was that "our foreign policy should be understood and supported by the American people and the Congress."[50] Carter echoed this promise of greater public accountability and took it a step further by making human rights the issue essential to reestablishing American credibility at home and abroad. Alluding to the founder of the colonial Massachusetts Bay Colony, John Winthrop, he wanted the United States to become "a beacon of light for human rights throughout the world."[51] By refocusing American action away from confrontation, Carter saw his policy as the "wave of the future throughout the world."[52] And it appeared that he was intent on reaching that goal. In meetings with congressional leaders in March 1977 regarding U.S. foreign assistance, the White House emphasized America's "credibility as a nation concerned with world poverty" and "our constructive leadership of the North-South dialogue."[53] Even Carter's normally hawkish national security adviser, Zbigniew Brzezinski, tended toward the themes of normalizing global relations through non-military means such as closer political and economic relations, referring to this approach as "constructive global engagement."[54]

Despite its new emphasis on revising both the ends and means governing American foreign relations, Carter and his national security team took great pains to make sure it was understood that defense remained a critical component of American policy. However, it became clear over time that the administration rarely approached military affairs with the same interest in innovation as it had toward diplomacy. Consequently, the familiar Cold War template, inherited from Ford, persisted under Carter. When administration officials spoke of sound military practices, they referred to the strategic nuclear balance or collective security structures such as NATO. When the Third World was introduced into the discussion, in countries such as Angola or Somalia, it was framed within the context of Soviet interests.[55]

At the end of the Carter administration, Brzezinski claimed that the president was responsible for the third major revision of strategic military doctrine during the Cold War. He considered the first to be John Foster Dulles's adoption of "massive retaliation" in the fifties as the guiding light of American thinking. In the following decade, "mutually assured destruction" held sway as Soviet and U.S. nuclear arsenals approached relative parity. Interestingly, Brzezinski skipped over Richard Nixon before proceeding to the final evolution of American doctrine in the late seventies, which he described as "essential equivalence" in both conventional and nuclear forces. Essential equivalence recognized the United States was unlikely to enjoy the type of military balance that had allowed Dulles to threaten the Soviets with blunt force. Brzezinski's approach was more pragmatic in nature, proposing to essentially preserve the military status quo while tinkering with military affairs on the margins. In practice, this meant maintenance of the conventional force balance in Europe through upgrades in weaponry (to include tactical nuclear weapons) and training. At home, the national security adviser advocated improvements to civil defense, the military telecommunications infrastructure, and mobilization planning. The one innovation that Brzezinski offered was the creation of a rapid deployment force (RDF) that would be ready to intervene in global hot spots during times of crisis. However, given its relatively small size and slow development, the RDF had little impact on American military policy under Carter.[56]

A fundamental question the Carter administration faced was how best to achieve his own limited military goals. Funding was a clear problem. In his memoirs, Carter specifically took note of the 35 percent decline in real dollars spent on defense from 1969 to 1977.[57] He was astute enough to understand that the appropriations necessary to redress the many military gaps between the United States and the Soviet Union would not be forthcoming in his stewardship. In a notable departure from the previous administration, Carter did not revert back to Schlesinger's alarmist rhetoric regarding the consequences of military decline. Instead, rather than simply spending its way back to parity, the administration focused upon increased military efficiency.

Efficiency had an important appeal to the former naval officer. It was axiomatic that Carter sought a better performing military institution. The seventies were rife with stories of poor recruiting standards and discipline—among many other problems—that begged for official attention. But Carter's interest went deeper than simple military utility. When he reflected later on the topic of military efficiency, the president was adamant about the negative impact the various defense lobbies had on the military's basic functions.[58] In some respects, his administration was reminiscent of the Robert McNamara era, which attacked the redundancy of equipment, doctrine, and missions within the defense establishment. Critical to Carter's approach to governance was his insistence that American defense policy, like policy in general, emphasize effectiveness over the parochial agendas of entrenched special interests.

This particular worldview also affected Carter's approach to nuclear arms. Improvements in strategic weapons promised increased lethality and a credible deterrent to the Soviet Union. However, running parallel to more efficient weapons system was another major objective: the justification for nuclear arms reductions. It was clear throughout his term that Carter wanted to go beyond simple renewal of the Strategic Arms Limitation Treaty and move toward permanent cuts in both the U.S. and Soviet arsenals. In a very important sense, the president's core beliefs, freely expressed in Carter's advocacy of human rights, remained intact. Abandoning the pragmatism of previous administrations in favor of higher principles of international behavior, Carter expressed his own moral abhorrence of the nuclear bomb and promised a new direction for American nuclear strategy in the late seventies.[59]

While, admittedly, Carter's practical desire for efficiency as well as his intent to reduce nuclear armaments were far ahead of their time, in 1977 they placed the president on a collision course with the Pentagon. Early in his presidency, the Joint Chiefs of Staff were relatively confident that Carter would leave untouched a number of modernization programs started under Nixon and Ford. All the major military branches expected to keep pet projects each deemed critical to American defense. The Air Force had the B-1 bomber, the Navy at the time was promoting construction of a 90,000-ton Nimitz-class nuclear carrier, and the Army was preparing the M-1 Abrams main battle tank for production. However, Carter's outright veto of the carrier and his open campaign against the B-1 poisoned his relationship with the joint chiefs. When the president proposed to withdraw troops from South Korea, the break with his commanders quickly became public.[60] Other administration initiatives proved equally unsettling to the armed services. Senior military leaders were not pleased in February 1978 when Carter announced that foreign military arms sales for that year would be less than half their 1976 level.[61]

Bridling at what they considered arbitrary and dangerous decisions, the joint chiefs retaliated by airing their views before Congress. When questioned about the adequacy of the fiscal 1980 budget, Army Chief of Staff General E. C. Meyer replied, "Right now, we have a hollow Army."[62] In their own subsequent testimony, the other service chiefs essentially confirmed the statement.[63] The timing could not have been worse for Carter, coming after the failed Iranian hostage rescue mission and amidst the 1980 presidential primary season, where Republican candidate Ronald Reagan was making American military weakness a familiar part of his speeches. More to the point, the abrupt and embarrassing candor expressed by senior officers rarely matched the rancor felt toward civilian leaders throughout the military ranks. Carter presided over decline of weapons, equipment, and material readiness, but a more basic crisis of faith in his leadership.[64]

If there was one small bright spot at end of Carter's term, it was the development of the Rapid Deployment Force (RDF). First proposed in 1977, the RDF was officially instituted in May 1980 and headquartered at Fort MacDill Air Force Base in Florida. It was initially comprised of four Army divisions and the equivalent of two Marine Corps divisions with necessary sea and airlift assets to deploy the force quickly to any point on the globe. Once in place, the RDF could serve as a barrier—a "tripwire"—to hostile aggression or be used for "horizontal escalation" to cut off supply lines in use by the Soviet Union or one of its proxies. In essence, what the Rapid Deployment Forces allowed the United States was a degree of flexibility in the spectrum of military action below nuclear conflict or conventional deployments, but in a role more substantive than that offered by contemporary special forces. A 1980 CIA report discussed the potential environment in which the RDF might deploy: "The definition of what will be considered 'vital' to us in the future is almost unpredictable. . . . In defining our 'vital interests,' we also may need to consider precedential or 'domino' effects of not protecting our interests in some countries of little intrinsic interest. In either case, there may be a wide geographical spread between the areas where we wish to project force."[65]

Even as the RDF began to coalesce, a debate roiled within the military about its exact value. One clear shortfall was in air and sealift capacity. A 1980 article in the *Washington Post* article noted that if the USSR decided to occupy the Persian Gulf area, the RDF could deploy to the Middle East in three weeks, not the "rapid" response promised by the Pentagon. Logistics were equally problematic. The absence of American bases in the Middle East clearly compounded supply problems that would arise for units fighting in the desert. Vehicles, heavy equipment, and armor would have to follow by sea and be off-loaded at a friendly port, a process that could take weeks if not months (as Operation Desert Shield later proved). This would be cold comfort to American forces facing the advance of Soviet armor and mechanized infantry. General Volner F. Warner, the commander of U.S. Readiness Command, acknowledged in an October 1980 interview that forces assigned to the RDF—the 82nd Airborne Division and a Marine brigade (35,000 personnel)—were "not too big a force to lose" if the Soviets decided to fight.[66]

Civilian critics were more pointed in identifying the RDF's other important limitations. Writing for the Institute for Foreign Policy Analysis, Jeffrey Record highlighted the fact that light forces, such as the 82nd Airborne Division, would be badly outmatched when facing armored formations in terrain suited for rapid movement. Moreover, in simple terms of equipment, comparable Soviet forces heavily outgunned their American counterparts. An airborne division in the Soviet Army (of which there were seven in 1981 compared to one in the U.S. Army) possessed 346 BMD troop carriers, each with a 73mm cannon and a Sagger guided missile system. In contrast, the American 82nd Airborne had one battalion of Sheridan M551 light tanks.[67] Given the obvious disparity in tactical firepower, as well as other deficiencies, Record concluded that "the present Rapid Deployment Force is a standing invitation to military disaster—a disaster from which the military reputation of the United States, already battered by thirty years of defeats and miscarriages, would have difficulty recovering."[68]

There also appeared to be little consensus within the White House regarding the terms and conditions that would govern the Rapid Deployment Force's actual use. While Carter and Brzezinski had approved the creation of a force that could be deployed anywhere in the world upon short notice, they were strangely reticent to use it to actively enforce American interests. In a January 1980 memorandum, the administration made it clear that the RDF were "contingency forces" as opposed to "intervention forces."[69] The distinction apparently existed in the difference between a military force that would deploy only at the request of allies and friendly governments in need of help rather than one that was an agent of unilateral American action. As a result, the RDF was essentially framed within the existing Cold War, as a potential deterrent force—a tripwire—rather than a new military option.

In terms of other initiatives related to low-intensity military affairs, the Carter administration drifted without meaningful direction until the United States suffered through the July 1979 Nicaraguan revolution, the November Iranian seizure of the U.S. embassy in Tehran, and the December 1979 Soviet invasion of Afghanistan. The cumulative impact of these events was the reversal of Carter's willingness to discard military action in favor of higher principles of international cooperation. When he announced the so-called Carter Doctrine in 1980, with its specific provision for the military defense of American interests in the Persian Gulf region, the United States formally abandoned its multilateral approach to world affairs.[70] For American allies in the Third World, this shift translated into more military aid. In 1980 the president approved Defense Department recommendations to increase the FY 1982 Military Assistance Program by $100 million over 1981 levels and to double military education and training programs (IMET) for foreign militaries.[71]

However, of all the small-scale challenges to American power in 1980, Afghanistan garnered the most attention. Brzezinski saw it as a

Soviet test "involving ultimately the balance of power between East and West." To counter what he perceived as a broader strategic problem, the national security adviser proposed a series of actions that included military aid to Pakistan, securing bases in the region, additional military exercises, and security consultations with friendly regional governments.[72]

The Afghan forces fighting Soviet occupation had a clear role in American plans. As the war unfolded, Brzezinski immediately recognized that rebel forces fighting against the Soviets were badly organized, equipped, and led. Consequently, he immediately endorsed arms shipments and "technical advice" to the Afghani resistance in December 1979.[73] For the remainder of 1980 American intelligence operatives began developing links with the anti-Soviet resistance, a collection of groups that would later collectively become known as the "mujahideen." The effort was slowed only by Brzezinski's desire for a lower profile in administration policy circles after the resignation of Cyrus Vance in April 1980.[74]

Few people knew of this early groundwork in 1980. Instead, the punctuation mark that defined military affairs during the Carter years was the failed Iranian hostage rescue mission. Operation Eagle Claw, which will be discussed in detail, typified the chronic problems that plagued the U.S. military and civil-military relations in general. The mission was, to say the least, a complex undertaking that was undercut by inadequate equipment, improper time for preparations, and unnecessary interservice rivalries. These shortcomings were exacerbated by a civilian command structure, a group dominated by Brzezinski and Carter, that constantly interfered and micromanaged the operation at nearly every stage. The ultimate failure of the mission was as much a result of its intrinsic complexities as other factors that governed Carter's relationship with the military. The president saw the rescue attempt in much the way he saw the military as a whole: as a last resort useful when better options were already exhausted. More important, it reflected a fundamental breakdown of trust that had been more than three years in the making. In the aftermath of the debacle in the Iranian desert, as political fallout engulfed the administration, it was abundantly clear within the military that the responsibility for reform would be theirs alone.

Military Reconstruction after Vietnam

Without question, the American military was a troubled institution at the start of the seventies. Historian Richard Lock-Pullen notes that in 1972 only four of the Army's thirteen active divisions were rated as ready for combat.[75] In terms of training, equipment, and overall standards, the situation in the National Guard and reserves was worse. Equally apparent was the sense that institutional morale had completely collapsed in the aftermath of Vietnam. This was evident when General William Westmoreland addressed a session of the Infantry Advanced Course at Fort Benning in 1972, promising as Army chief of staff to remove "the scum of the officer corps." He was booed off the stage.[76]

Vietnam was the fulcrum upon which American military rested in the seventies. At war's end, the service branches struggled mightily with the legacy it had bequeathed. Vietnam saw a significant expansion and deployment of American military forces, particularly with respect to those on the ground. The Army alone increased from 970,000 to 1.5 million personnel between 1965 and 1968. Overall, the total number of Army divisions grew from sixteen to nineteen at the height of the war. Defense spending also increased significantly as a result of Vietnam. Appropriations for the Army more than doubled from $12 billion in the fiscal year 1965, when major units began deploying to Southeast Asia, to nearly $25 billion for fiscal 1969.[77]

But had all this expansion been a waste of the budget windfall? A dominant theme in American military circles was a profound sense of frustration with a conflict that the institution was neither trained nor equipped to fight. By deploying a military molded around the strategic nuclear contingencies of the New Look, officers and enlisted ranks alike saw Vietnam as a massive effort that was, at its core, a tragic waste of men and materiel.

While this realization dominated the wartime debate during the sixties, once U.S. forces withdrew from Vietnam the focus shifted to a general fear that the American military would be unable to meet its basic missions. During a 1974 congressional hearing, Army Chief of Staff General Creighton W. Abrams testified that his troops had a "marginal chance of succeeding" without the use of nuclear weapons in the field.[78] His statement was significant. Immediately after American combat operations in Vietnam had ceased, senior military leaders were ready to concede in the public domain that their institution was on the brink of collapse. The basic question left was how best to rescue the United States armed forces.

The initial response to this dilemma came from within the military itself: denial. A strong contingent within the armed forces treated Vietnam as an aberration, a mistake that did not reflect internal failures of leadership, planning, or doctrine. The core of this school of thought was later articulated in Harry Summers's landmark 1982 book *On Strategy*. In it, Summers asserted that the United States had not followed necessary and well-established parameters necessary for victory. American leaders had not, for example, successfully mobilized or maintained what Clausewitz called "the trinity of war—the people, the government, and the Army."[79] Defeat in Vietnam was therefore a failure to assemble the proper set of rational, easily identified political, social, and military components necessary to win. Seemingly ignorant of the history of American wars in general, Summers maintained the argument that Vietnam was the exception to the rule that governed a balanced civil-military consensus before the United States proceeded with hostilities.[80]

More important to his audience within the armed forces, Summers also denied military culpability in losing the war in Southeast Asia. The first sentence of his introductory chapter establishes this finding very quickly: "One of the most frustrating aspects of the Vietnam War from the Army's point of view is that as far as logistics and tactics were concerned we succeeded in everything we set out to do."[81] In this denial, broadly accepted by all military ranks, was the failure to address the core problems that had resulted in defeat during the Vietnam War. Neil Sheehan assessed this profound military hubris in his Pulitzer Prize–winning *A Bright Shining Lie:* "By the second decade after World War II, the dominant characteristics of the senior leadership of the American armed forces had become professional arrogance, lack of imagination, and moral and intellectual insensitivity."[82] More to the point was the fact that the same cohort of leaders who had failed in Vietnam essentially guided, with a few exceptions, the intellectual conventional wisdom on military affairs in the seventies. Consequently, although a generation of scholars has dissected the logic of Summers's proposals since the appearance of *On Strategy,* the book represented a flat refusal to acknowledge flaws in the planning or execution of the war in Vietnam.

This logic also flowed to the inevitable conclusion that the status quo was adequate to American military objectives. As such, there was no need for doctrinal revision or institutional reform.[83] George Herring has aptly described this reasoning as "a self-conscious, collective amnesia" within the U.S. armed forces.[84]

A second military response to the Vietnam War that ran concurrently with denial was a reversion to nostalgia. From this standpoint, which mirrored to a degree Nixon's own approach to the Cold War, the service branches deliberately pursued pre-Vietnam priorities, particularly the defense of Western Europe from the Soviet conventional threat.[85] In a 1973 assessment of the American military by Creighton W. Abrams, the Army chief of staff noted that the only legitimate use of U.S. military power would be in an area of critical interest, namely defense of NATO members against the Soviet Union.[86]

By reverting to a Eurocentric vision, the American military provided itself with an institutional, doctrinal, and cultural anchor that proved not only convenient but also essential to mitigate the impact of Vietnam. The defense of Europe against a Soviet threat was something that the defense establishment and the common soldier could understand together, creating a degree of cohesion that the military found increasingly difficult to maintain in the seventies. The Soviet threat possessed traction because it provided a monolithic, conventional enemy and a linear mission that hearkened back to the days of the "good war" against Nazi Germany.[87] Nostalgia also posed few immediate risks for an institution suffering from too much internal dissent. By offering an opportunity to relearn and improve basic conventional capabilities, it created clear milestones without the additional pressure of revolutionary new doctrinal concepts. This latter quality was attractive to the administrations that followed Nixon because nostalgia would not generate pressure for military appropriations in the economic hard times of the period. James Schlesinger's preference for making nuclear weapons the keystone of European defense was not an accident. It offered the same cost-effectiveness of the New Look combined with the strategic surety of the NATO alliance, itself a bedrock Cold War institution.

Post-Vietnam military reforms were therefore notable for their lack of dynamism and penchant for retrenchment. One early beacon of the future armed services was the creation of an all-volunteer military. As president, Nixon had promised an end to the draft that would coincide with the conclusion of the war in Vietnam. Consequently, on 1 July 1973, three months after MACV was deactivated, Congress formally rescinded the authority to conscript American citizens. The decision was highly unpopular among senior officers who openly worried that without a broad base of citizenry serving a mandatory period in uniform, the American military would be "severed" from the mainstream of politics and society.[88] William Westmoreland commented in 1975: "Time has . . . demonstrated that the political maneuver by President Nixon of setting aside the draft was not in the national interest. The all-volunteer force has not produced the military posture required by the leader of the free world. Reappraisal of the ill-advised concept is essential."[89] The former MACV commander argued that without a constant infusion of short-term volunteers drawn from the whole spectrum of American social and economic classes—a common denominator for recruits throughout much of the Cold War to that point—the military might become more an introverted and cloistered subculture, lacking the fortitude that had shaped leadership and operational capabilities since World War II.

In its earliest incarnation, the all-volunteer force manifested many of these faults. After 1973, it became abundantly clear that basic recruiting standards were on the decline. A primary factor that sustained recruiting levels within the volunteer military was not patriotism or a basic desire to serve, but the economic downturn that savaged the industrial and manufacturing job force. Lacking economic opportunities previously available to high school and college graduates, many baby boomers accepted enlistment as a last resort.[90] Unfortunately, economic desperation proved to be a poor foundation for military service. Yet, even with economic recession pushing more young men into uniform, the service branches still found it difficult to meet recruitment quotas. After 1973 the Pentagon lowered basic standards for the Armed Forces Qualification Test (AFQT), hoping to recapture a broader manpower base. Consequently, the basic educational and intelligence levels of recruits began to drop significantly at a time when the military was introducing more sophisticated weapons designed to offset the Soviet advantage in numbers. The wide use of comic book–style maintenance manuals (e.g., *Preventative Maintenance Monthly*) to educate soldiers in the care and use of equipment reflected the precipitous decline in standards. This situation was compounded between 1976 and 1980, when a flaw in the AFQT allowed approximately 350,000 recruits into the military who would have normally not scored high enough for enlistment.[91]

The poor quality of recruits created a terrible ripple effect once they arrived at their first duty stations. Military service in the seventies became synonymous with drug use, crime, racial tensions, and violence against enlisted personnel and their officers. In 1971 the overall Army AWOL (absent without leave) rate was 17.7 percent and did not improve markedly in subsequent years. Retention rates in this climate were poor at best. The first-term attrition rate for soldiers in their initial enlistment was 26 percent in 1971 and peaked at 38 percent in 1974.[92]

As a lieutenant colonel commanding a battalion of the 32nd Division in South Korea, Colin Powell was faced with unit discipline in a state of chaos. At the time, it was normal practice for soldiers to openly challenge command authority and threaten or extort senior officers. The total absence of unit cohesion translated into poor unit performance only a few miles from North Korea and the demilitarized zone. Examples of strong leaders willing to challenge this destructive undertow were rare. However, as he reflected in his memoirs, when the division commander, Major General Hank Emerson, assembled his senior officers and ordered them to take back the 32nd, Powell became a true believer. Consequently, when one African-American soldier attempted to blackmail Powell, he soon found himself on a plane back to the States with an administrative discharge in his hand.[93]

As bad as the situation was in South Korea, the problem was more pronounced in Europe. By the early seventies, the U.S. 7th Army was in desperate need of reform. Originally organized as the primary American contribution to NATO, it had degenerated into a replacement center for Vietnam for most of the sixties as officers and enlisted men were randomly stripped out of standing units for redeployment to Southeast Asia. The results of these constant disruptions were predictable. At time when Saigon fell in April 1975, 7th Army was suffering from a complete breakdown of discipline and good order among the troops. In the seventies, almost 40 percent of the U.S. Army in Europe admitted to drug use and approximately 7 percent of soldiers were addicted to heroin readily available through Turkey and Afghanistan.[94]

While a significant part of the military's problems at the time were attributable to the poor quality of incoming recruits, the overall poverty of leadership in the armed forces also produced devastating results. This was most pronounced in the diminishing performance of noncommissioned officers during and after the Vietnam War. Disgusted with both civilian treatment of the military and the conduct of the war itself, many senior enlisted soldiers either opted for retirement or chose not to reenlist. The loss of these first-line supervisors, who possessed irreplaceable institutional memory and responsibility for every basic task necessary to make the military function, was devastating to the U.S. armed forces. Stopgap measures designed to address badly eroding enlisted leadership were largely inadequate to the task. The "shake and bake" NCOs who were promoted with rudimentary training and limited experience replaced the rank but not the knowledge or the wisdom of lost senior leaders.[95]

The American officer corps was more culpable for military decline in the seventies. Responsible not only for the day-to-day operations of the armed forces, but also their direction, this cohort was in disarray after Vietnam. Careerism and "ticket punching"—the jockeying for key assignments important to promotion—were endemic and reflected an institution that had begun to collapse in on itself. Junior officers at the time complained of a zero defect standard that was becoming the prototypical template for military leadership: "an ambitious, transitory commander—marginally skilled in the complexities of his duties—engulfed in producing statistical results, fearful of personal failure, too busy to talk with or listen to his subordinates, and determined to submit acceptably optimistic reports."[96] More senior officers identified similar trends. An Army War College report included a survey of 450 lieutenant colonels that identified an inflated military awards system and a general lack of accountability within the command structure.[97]

From a broad historical perspective, this type of military fugue was typical of many American postwar periods. Drastic declines in morale and the rapid onset of institutional inertia were more the rule than the exception after 1815, 1865, and 1918. As national priorities shifted from guns back to butter, the U.S. military found itself to be a bastard stepchild, bereft of appropriations and unwanted by civil society. Remediation was often a question of either a crisis or the timely appearance of leadership possessing the appropriate balance of foresight, experience, and public credibility.

The American military establishment faced just such a crossroads after Vietnam. The upheaval that typified military service was enough to provoke legions of professional soldiers to depart the service. Many endured these hard times, however, motivated not only by the idea that reform was possible but also by the notion that the war had created a crisis adequate for dramatic, systemic repairs. Not surprisingly, military publications in the early seventies—journals such as *Parameters* and *Military Review*—were filled with an active and sometimes brutally candid discussion of what ailed the armed forces, a discourse that included professionalism, doctrinal shortcomings, and fundamental civil-military relations in the United States.[98] Although this broad debate failed to immediately crystallize into a coherent reform movement within the military, it encouraged would-be critics to action and influenced a generation of officers (a young David Petraeus among them) who came of age after Vietnam.[99]

Contemporary foreign affairs furthered this process. Perhaps the most influential of these was the 1973 Yom Kippur War. The fourth Arab-Israeli conflict was, in a very important sense, a testing ground for the long-awaited clash between NATO and the Warsaw Pact. Both sides were armed with the same inventory of weapons as their respective sponsors and followed similar doctrinal principles into combat that would govern the next world war. What shocked Western military observers was both the rapidity of the war and the enormous material losses inflicted during its short duration. The Israeli air force in particular suffered under the impact of radar-controlled anti-aircraft systems introduced into Arab military units. On the ground, Israeli armor entering combat unsupported by infantry and artillery was mauled, especially in the Sinai. Overall, the number of tanks destroyed during the Yom Kippur War was roughly equal to the entire U.S. inventory at the time.[100] Israeli losses produced a new conventional wisdom that Soviet combined arms tactics were better than the U.S. military's at the time. Lastly, beyond its lethality, the war also more than drove home the point that modern nations could not afford a lengthy and prolonged mobilization for conflict. American strategists realized that the United States would have to fight with the forces that it had in place. The traditional World War II–era model of gradual, accumulating readiness, upon which much U.S. military thinking was based, would have to be significantly modified.

Combined, the Vietnam and Yom Kippur Wars provided real world traction to the barrage of criticism appearing in military journals. By framing the issue less as a case of sour grapes and more as a matter of improving military capabilities, the latter war in particular provided just the jolt that reform advocates sought. This was especially true with the confines of the U.S. Army, which was primarily responsible for ground operations. The two conflicts highlighted the need for significant reforms that ranged from combined armed tactics to strategic mobilization. But how best to enact substantial changes in the absence of civilian support and against rapidly hardening inertia within the military?

Training and Doctrine Command (TRADOC), created in 1973, was one early answer. Under the Command of General William E. Dupuy, TRADOC envisioned reorganizing the Army training system to increase its overall efficiency. More important, Dupuy believed that once the Army's curriculum and doctrine were rebuilt to address the demands of post-1973 warfare, it would have the derivative effect of improved operational readiness. The TRADOC strategy was a clear compromise with the times, a reflection of the significant economic and political limits being placed on the American military. Dupuy was proposing a revolution in quality rather than a new round of military appropriations and troop increases. Although limited in scope, Dupuy saw the creation of TRADOC as a "historic turning point in the evolution of army forces."[101]

TRADOC's most important creation was *Field Manual 100-5: Operations,* the Army's primary operations manual. Its purpose, as stated in the 1976 edition, was to "prepare to win the first battle of the next war." In practice, this meant applying the lessons of Yom Kippur to a future West German battlefield.[102] Specifically, *FM 100-5* restructured tactics, training, planning, and procurement to meet a narrowly based "Fulda Gap" scenario, one in which American and NATO forces would defend the approaches to Western Europe against an opposing force of massed Soviet armor and mechanized infantry.

At the heart of *FM 100-5* was the concept of "active defense," in which American forces would apply massed, highly accurate firepower to disrupt and destroy not only forces at the forward edge of the battlefield, but also successive echelons of combat and support units moving forward against defensive positions. In theory, active defense depended on the basic calculation that precision weaponry employed in depth would be able to overcome the inferior training and substandard equipment prevalent in the Warsaw Pact arsenal.

Despite the fact that *FM 100-5* was intended to renovate Army doctrine, it was not without its problems and provoked significant debate within the service. Critics saw active defense as unsustainable in real life. A key shortfall was logistical. While entrenched units might be adequate to blunt the first wave of a Soviet assault, neither U.S. nor NATO units possessed the personnel, ammunition, or materiel to maintain a coherent defense for any reasonable period of time.[103] Many critics also saw the active defense as a political compromise to NATO allies. By projecting a potential war from the frontline toward the Warsaw Pact, American doctrine tacitly avoided West German resistance to plans for a defense in depth. However impractical, the government in Bonn wanted no part of a strategy that would turn their entire country into a battleground and clung instead to the unlikely scenario of halting a communist invasion at the border.

As this discourse proceeded, additional reforms accompanied the publication of *FM 100-5*. In 1976 the chairman of the JCS, Air Force General George S. Brown, called for an overall modernization of U.S. forces, justifying it by the need to counter the numerical edge enjoyed the Warsaw Pact, but also reasoning that it was necessary to meet ongoing qualitative improvements apparent in the Soviet order of battle. Brown cited the new deployment of the Soviet T-72 main battle tank as one cause for upgrading American armored forces.[104] In the meantime, as the debate over *FM 100-5* continued to roil through military publications in the late seventies, senior leaders prepared to take up its modification. When he became Army chief of staff in 1979, General John Meyer advocated a major reform of active defense. Although the resulting AirLand Battle concept would not be realized until the eighties, it would revolutionize American military doctrine.

The half decade between the fall of Saigon and Ronald Reagan's election did not witness a dramatic improvement in American military fortunes. To the contrary, all the worst features of profound institutional decline characterized service in the seventies. Measured by the tangible features of the American order of battle, in terms of flyable planes, seaworthy ships, or serviceable weaponry, the story was bleak indeed. The less easily measured but more important components of armed service—morale, unit cohesion, and basic faith in the military—were more alarming.

Yet in many respects the seventies were also a crucible for those who wanted to save the American military. It was a testament to the upheaval of the times, but also the institutional tolerance present, that reform did appear in fits and starts, primarily through an intellectual debate encouraged by forward-thinking military leaders. When *FM 100-5* appeared, it was at best an intermediary step, one that the Pentagon recognized as such even when it was published in 1976. Progress would be better measured by military doctrine designed for the eighties and the future of U.S. national security. In this arena, reformers would struggle with the dichotomy of true innovation and the temptation to backslide into a more familiar Cold War status quo.[105]

American Unconventional War, 1973–1980

If American conventional capabilities declined after the Vietnam War, the country's ability to fight unconventional conflicts arguably was in even worse condition. For an important component within the U.S. armed forces, Vietnam was a blot to be erased from institutional memory. When it denied the mistakes made during the course of the war in favor of embracing the pre-Vietnam status quo, the military made the conscious decision to abandon wholesale more than a decade of unconventional operations in Southeast Asia. Historian Samuel C. Sarkesian put the matter succinctly: "For many American military men, the Vietnam outcome confirmed their view of special units. The Green Berets became the symbol of the kind of war that was fought in Vietnam and, for many Americans, a symbol of all that was wrong with the U.S. military policy and the military."[106] A potent body on knowledge and a formidable reservoir of talent became, in that instant, a liability. Celebrated as heroes a decade earlier, the special operations soldier was a liability in the new postwar order.

A similar trend was visible in the U.S. intelligence community. In keeping with the backlash generated by Watergate, the 1975 Senate Select Committee on Intelligence led by Idaho Democrat Frank Church (otherwise known as the Church Committee) began to publicly unpeel a generation of clandestine operations conducted by the Central Intelligence Agency. A byproduct of the hearings were revelations of the "family jewels," actions taken against the antiwar movement, experiments with LSD, assassination attempts and plans against Fidel Castro, Patrice Lumumba, and Rafael Trujillo.[107]

Much of this activity was well intentioned and aimed at curtailing foreign policy errors by reducing presidential prerogatives. Subsequent proposed amendments to the National Security Act of 1947 allowed Congress to request information collected by the CIA concerning "the relations of the United States to foreign countries and matters of national security, including full and current analysis by the Agency of such information."[108] Additional restrictions did not await federal legislation. The Ford administration attempted to forestall congressional action through a well-known executive order prohibiting assassination as an acceptable U.S. policy. The White House subsequently released a veritable laundry list of other prohibited actions—including domestic surveillance, opening mail, and experimental use of drugs on human subjects—shortly thereafter.[109]

The Central Intelligence Agency also cleaned house in the wake of the Church Committee investigation. Between 1975 and 1977, the CIA fired as many as 2,800 intelligence officers, many of whom were paramilitary or clandestine specialists.[110] In their place, the intelligence community increasingly relied on technological sources of intelligence gathering. During the Carter years, the CIA under the direction of Stansfield Turner did its best to abandon the ugly, albeit sometimes necessary, methodology of the old agency.

Like the military, the agency was forced into a new era of accountability that was necessary in many important ways but produced a drastic decline in unconventional capability. Clandestine service essentially became a greater institutional anathema than military special operations. The end product was the loss of hundreds of individuals with cultural and linguistic expertise as well as decades of irreplaceable field experience. Institutionally, Langley became as risk averse as the Pentagon when policy debate veered toward any form of irregular warfare.[111] While intelligence professionals no doubt understood the impact of this trend, its real impact would not be felt until the U.S. embassy in Tehran was overrun in November 1979.

Post-Vietnam special operations doctrine reflected the new climate. Terminology changed in an effort to abandon perceived past failures. Counterinsurgency itself was redefined as "international defense and development" and, later, "foreign internal defense."[112] Although the military played lip service to the idea of counterinsurgency, special operations was viewed more as an adjunct to conventional war than a primary actor with a distinct mission. Lacking institutional support, many units withered away. The overall number of Army special forces soldiers declined significantly from 13,000 in 1971 to fewer than 3,000 only three years later.[113] Units that were forward deployed around the world in special forces detachments virtually ceased to exist. The 3rd Battalion of the 7th Special Forces Group stationed in Panama was designated to train Latin America militaries in the region but dispatched only three mobile training teams during an eighteen-month period between 1977 and 1978.[114] Special operations membership in other service branches was negligible.

When the military decided to invest in special operations units, it was in a capacity directly in support of regular forces. Army ranger battalions were reintroduced in 1974 essentially as elite light infantry. Senior Army officers argued that the rangers could accomplish existing Green Beret missions—raids, reconnaissance, and target acquisition—and be more capable of integration with armored, mechanized, and other conventional units.[115] Special operations, as practiced during the Vietnam era, had become an obsolete concept.

Cognizant of the shifting tides of institutional support, the U.S. Army Special Warfare Center undertook a study in 1975 to address the special forces mission and its future role. The "Mountel Report," named for its author, Colonel Robert Mountel, offered the following summary judgment: "there is a pervasive lack of understanding, interest and support of unconventional warfare and Special Forces as a valid national response option. Based on research conducted for this study, this state of mind is nearly identical to that which existed in the mid-1950s. [The role of special forces] is generally perceived by many to be limited to the conduct of guerrilla warfare in support of conventional forces."[116] The Mountel report was candid enough to acknowledge a hard reality: in order to maintain its relevance, special operations would have to find a way to shift their doctrine, training, and missions toward conventional operations. In much the same way the military had embraced nuclear weapons when the New Look dominated strategic thinking in the fifties, special forces soldiers would compromise long-standing standards for the sake of institutional survival.

What followed was a period that alternated between crisis and hasty improvisation. From a very early point in the seventies, it became clear that threats to security had not so much diminished as evolved into new forms. One of the most prevalent was terrorism. Although it will be discussed in detail in a later chapter, the emerging series of terrorist attacks against Western European and American targets shocked the world at the start of the decade. The murder of Israeli athletes during the Munich Olympics served as a grisly cautionary tale for the United States and its European allies.

Terrorism provoked something of a special operations renaissance in the seventies. Special forces units already in existence proved adept at small, commando-type raids in hostage rescue situations. The 1976 Israeli rescue of passengers taken to Entebbe airport in Uganda became an iconic event and an international sensation. Other nations took deliberate steps to create special forces units dedicated to the counterterrorist mission. In the aftermath of Munich, the Bonn government in West Germany authorized the creation of *Grenzschutzgruppe*-9 (or GSG-9), an elite unit specifically designed to combat terrorist threats to the country. In October 1977, GSG-9 operatives successfully intervened during the hijacking of a Lufthansa airliner in Mogadishu, Somalia. The event became as famous as the Entebbe raid.

The success of these operations prompted the United States to consider forming its own counterterrorist capability. In fact, the success of the concept actually created something of an institutional bandwagon effect within the Pentagon. The Army officially created the 1st Special Forces Operational Detachment Delta (otherwise simply known as Delta) in November 1977 in the same basic vein as GSG-9. However, it also authorized an additional unit, designated "Blue Light" within the 5th Special Forces Group. In 1981, in the aftermath of the failed Iran hostage rescue mission, the Navy added its own elite unit, Seal Team Six, to the inventory of U.S. counterterrorist forces.

What is striking about U.S. special operations forces in the seventies is the inverse relationship between capabilities and need. It was clear that despite the unpopularity of the Vietnam War and military affairs in general, threats to American interests had evolved into new and disturbing forms. The Munich Olympics unveiled an enemy that was deliberate in its preparations and ruthless in the execution of the terrorist mission. This new enemy had many compatriots. Even though American leaders turned away from insurgent war, it did not abate and, in fact, had increased in many parts of the world. After the conquest of South Vietnam, fighting quickly spilled over into Cambodia. Guerrilla fighting raged throughout Africa, from Somalia to Angola and many points in between. Closer to home, guerrilla movements reappeared in Central America and challenged security forces in El Salvador and Nicaragua. As the United States focused yet again on NATO defense and nuclear strategy, violence in the Third World accumulated at an alarming rate.

However, the U.S. military essentially ignored these new forms of warfare. Faced with budget cuts, proliferating hearings and investigations, and indifferent public support, the Pentagon took the safest, most identifiable path back to its old conventional roots. Where they appeared, in remarkably small numbers, special operations forces were at best appended to outdated strategy and doctrine.

The seventies are thus notable for the absence of a coherent, multipurpose doctrine or unit that could address not only the terrorist threat but also other new missions that required imagination and operational flexibility. In his 1983 memoirs, Charlie Beckwith argued that what the U.S. military needed was a unit built in the image of the British Special Air Service, a small detachment populated by a broad cross-section of experts and capable of quick deployment. A formation of this type could fill a badly needed gap that existed between traditional American special forces and units such as Army rangers.[117] The potential for such a capability was present. But it existed within a defense bureaucracy disinterested in taking risks and before a civilian leadership intent on reasserting its authority in ways that overcompensated for past mistakes. The fragility of reform and the serious obstacles it faced would be well illustrated in smoking wreckage that stained the Iranian desert in 1980.

Operation Eagle Claw

The military history of the seventies is punctuated by the failed attempt to rescue American hostages in Iran. The event was a disaster that sadly illustrated the worst failings of American special operations and the U.S. command structure in the wake of the Vietnam War. Key leaders, particularly Secretary of State Cyrus Vance, in the Carter administration never considered a military hostage rescue a first or best option. Diplomatic measures governed Washington's approach to the crisis. In the months that followed the capture of the U.S. embassy in Tehran, Carter attempted direct negotiations as well as third-party mediation to resolve the situation. Attempts at leverage amounted to enacting progressively harsher economic sanctions once talks with the Iranian regime broke down. It was not until April 1980 that the administration reluctantly endorsed a military rescue operation. Even then, the decision marked a clear split within the cabinet, matching National Security Advisor Zbigniew Brzezinski against Vance. The very nature of this internal conflict seriously affected the undertaking from its very inception.

Delta Force was the primary American military unit responsible for rescuing the hostages. At the time of the Iranian revolution, the unit was relatively small, staffed by just 120 men in 1979. When the U.S. embassy was overrun, it had just received certification for operational readiness. Delta's embryonic form had a significant impact on the Iran mission. It lacked, for example, any organic air or sea transport. Also absent was any intelligence capability. Because it was so new, Delta was not adequately integrated into existing civilian or military intelligence agencies. In order to gain access to information in Iran proper, the unit was forced to rely on CIA assets in the country. The absence of a prior working relationship between the agency and Delta operators raised early flags because of the absolute need for reliability in the field.

In order to create a viable force capable of accomplishing the mission, the Pentagon adopted a hybrid command and operational structure that reflected both political and tactical compromises. The Delta detachment responsible for bringing the American prisoners out of Tehran remained under the command of Colonel Charlie Beckwith. However, Marine Lieutenant Colonel Edward Seifert commanded the helicopter unit responsible for transporting Beckwith's men from Navy ships stationed offshore. The commander of the Desert One refueling site—a stopover point in Iran—was Air Force Colonel James A. Kyle. Overseeing the operation was Joint Task Force 1-79 commander General James Vaught, who reported to the chairman of the JCS, the

National Security Council, and the president. As the table of organization indicates, none of the major services was willing to second itself to what was a high-risk, high-profile effort. The resulting command structure was overly redundant—with three operational commanders co-located at Desert One—and top heavy for such a small mission.

The planned division of mission responsibilities was also cumbersome. CIA assets were tasked with providing the exact location of the hostages and transportation to Tehran. With this information in hand, Beckwith's men were to handle the actual rescue mission once they arrived in the city. In the meantime, a small force of Army rangers would accompany Delta to provide site security at Desert One. The Navy, Marines, and Air Force were responsible for the various stages of transportation necessary to insert the rescue team and extract it and the hostages from Iran. In its totality, the mission required exact coordination of both military branches and civilian agencies along a very strict timetable. As a precaution, the mission plan included the option to abort at any stage, a feature that recognized its difficulty as much as its ambivalent support back in Washington.[118]

Not surprisingly, once Eagle Claw began, problems almost immediately appeared. Preparations were tainted when the Navy proved unwilling to provide the ten helicopters Beckwith wanted as a hedge against loss or malfunction (planners consider six to be the absolute minimum necessary). Marine pilots were unfamiliar with the RH53D model helicopter used in the mission and reacted poorly to sandstorms and dust that obstructed their flight path. Once the rescue force took off, bad weather and mechanical problems impeded travel to the Desert One location. Poor coordination between the CIA assets in Iran and the military marred the early stages of the mission.[119] Once American forces landed in Iran, local civilian traffic compromised the site only minutes after it was established.

On the ground, the absurdly complicated chain of command and incompatible radio equipment made quick decision making impossible. The key point of contention proved to be over the minimum helicopter transport necessary for the mission. Of the six that arrived at Desert One, only five were serviceable to fly; a sixth machine had suffered a hydraulic failure en route to Iran. Despite the obviously critical nature of this situation, none of the senior officers on the ground in

Iran had the authority to proceed or abort the mission. In his memoirs, Beckwith was adamant that it was impossible to proceed with an insufficient number of helicopters. The final decision was actually passed up to Carter himself, who concurred with Beckwith and canceled the operation.[120]

Eagle Claw's final failure is well known to any student of history. Only forty-eight minutes after the president ordered the abort, a helicopter and a C-130 transport collided while shifting positions at Desert One. The resulting explosion killed three Marines on the helicopter and five Air Force crewmen in the aircraft.[121] Grisly evidence of the collision remained behind for Iranian forces to discover. Judgment from the rest of the world was not far behind.

The failure of Eagle Claw proved to be a spectacular embarrassment for the Carter administration. Mansour Farhang, the Iranian ambassador to the United Nations, called the mission a "blatant act of invasion." From the campaign trail, Republican presidential candidate Ronald Reagan questioned why it had taken the president so long to approve a hostage rescue in the first place.[122]

The failed mission also provoked yet another round of reform efforts within the Washington Beltway. Congressional lawmakers were heartily and publicly displeased with the administration for not consulting them during the planning stages of Eagle Claw. The Pentagon's insistence on operational security, which had been largely maintained at every stage of the rescue attempt, translated into a serious political liability now that the administration was basking in public scrutiny of the disaster.[123] Senator Henry "Scoop" Jackson (D-WA), a defense hawk from Carter's own side of the aisle, complained that the news media knew more details of the rescue mission than did Congress. Senator Birch Bayh (D-IN), who chaired the Senate Intelligence Committee, called on the FBI to investigate where the press leaks had originated in the first place.[124] A particular sticking point was the War Powers Act. In order to preserve secrecy, neither the Pentagon nor the White House had directly communicated Eagle Claw to lawmakers until the mission became public. In response, Frank Church, chairman of the Senate Foreign Relations Committee, immediately authored a letter with Senator Jacob K. Javits invoking the War Powers Act, an action that was irrelevant to the mission but which typified civil-military affairs at the moment.[125]

The Joint Chiefs of Staff almost immediately convened an official review of Eagle Claw. Chaired by retired admiral J. L. Holloway, the staff released the "Holloway Report" in August 1980. In it the JCS essentially endorsed both the mission and its overall execution: "Despite all the complexities, the inherent difficulties, and the human and equipment performance required, the review group unanimously concludes that the risks were manageable, the overall probability of success good, and the operation feasible. Under these conditions, the decision to execute was justified."[126] The report summarily dismissed criticism regarding the lack of adequate helicopter assets. It also downplayed the overemphasis on operational security that many mission participants believed had hamstrung the operation.[127] However, the report acknowledged the lack of comprehensive training prior to the rescue mission and a breakdown of command and control at Desert One.

To address what it believed was largely a failure of leadership and training, the Holloway Report recommended the creation of a permanent counterterrorist joint task force within the Department of Defense. A special operations advisory panel within the JCS itself would coordinate future mission planning and execution. Both recommendations highlighted the fact that senior military leaders believed that the basic concept of an integrated, multibranch approach to special operations was fundamentally sound. All that was necessary was greater emphasis on improving the integration of existing institutions. Subsequently, the Pentagon would emphasize the Special Mission Unit concept that would lump all special operations—the ranger battalions, Delta, and the SEAL teams—into one category.[128]

The actions taken after the Holloway Report were a necessary first step toward fixing the many problems affecting American special operations in 1980. It was hard to argue against measures that addressed chronic problems in coordination and planning, faults that had handicapped Eagle Claw at important points before and during the mission. Moreover, the prospect of placing special operations within the Pentagon and JCS hierarchy was, at the very least, a deliberate attempt at inclusion within the official national security hierarchy. The authorization of Special Operations Command in 1987 reinforced this status even further.

Clearly, the attempt to integrate special operations within the Defense Department command structure produced tangible benefits.

There was an obvious need to consider communications, logistics, intelligence, and other functions in concert rather than as separate, competing entities possessed by small units. Creating an umbrella organization was an essential part of drawing together the disparate elements of U.S. special operations into a coherent whole.

How much of this thinking trickled down to the individual Special Mission Units is debatable. Owned and operated as they were by the individual service branches, the various ranger, special forces, Delta, SEAL, and other units retained their separate doctrines, training regimens, and cultures. While many of their capabilities complemented each other, redundancies and confusion persisted at the tactical level. As the eighties began, there seemed little prospect of an armed forces unification in miniature among special operators.

Conclusions

Hindsight informs the student of American military history that while the seventies were indeed a bleak period, they did not witness the final collapse of the institution. Complaints emanating from the JCS and other commanders were valid. When William C. Westmoreland and Creighton W. Abrams protested budget cuts that gutted personnel along with maintenance and training standards, they framed their objections in terms of basic military readiness. Clearly, the American armed forces witnessed a sharp qualitative and quantitative decline, at least in the short term. However, many hyperbolic warnings did not come to pass. The all-volunteer military was not a disaster. Nor was the recourse to incorporating more women into the military.[129]

Yet the military suffered as an institution nonetheless. As a country, the United States followed its historical tendency to abandon war and embrace peacetime at the expense of its warriors. It did so after 1973, but with the added public consensus that rejected Vietnam and made the military pariahs for their complicity in what was broadly accepted as a failed effort. In this context, the war was a critical benchmark for what types of military reform were possible. After leaving his post as secretary of defense in 1976, James R. Schlesinger characterized the seventies as a time when "disenchantment with Vietnam has led to the view that errors in policy, presumed to be the result of excessive strength, could be avoided through weakness."[130] In this respect, the seventies were worse than the fifties in that the country was choosing abandonment over a "bigger bang for the buck" under the New Look.[131]

Military reform existed in what amounted to a policy vacuum, a situation that severely circumscribed not only action but also the willingness to accept risk. Faced with a public that was at best skeptical of national security issues and limited by a weakening economy, it is not surprising that the armed forces returned to predictable standards. The familiar pillars of collective security and strategic nuclear planning dominated the strategic landscape, deliberately shutting off reflection on Vietnam. While many veterans of Southeast Asia continued their discourse on the war within the confines of staff studies and academic publications, the future of ground war was contained in *FM 100-5.*

At the far periphery of this stunted thinking resided American special forces. Again, hindsight is instructive in measuring the actual nature of threats to American national security. American leadership focused on the next world war at a time when low-intensity, nontraditional (e.g., terrorism) conflicts were multiplying throughout the world. It was only in the aftermath of Eagle Claw that public embarrassment finally provoked the Pentagon to act. The reforms recommended by the Holloway Report were limited in scope but emerged at an opportune time. With the arrival of Ronald Reagan to the White House in 1981, more fertile times would appear for the American military in general and special operations in particular.

3

Low-Intensity War in the Eighties

We cannot play innocents abroad in a world that's not innocent; nor can we be passive when freedom is under siege.

—Ronald Reagan, *Public Papers of the Presidents of the United States, Ronald Reagan, 1985*

Military policy in the Reagan era was built upon confrontation and the search for new forms of organized violence. The former California governor embraced the idea of recovering American strength early in his campaign for the president. During a 1978 speech Reagan articulated his vision in stark terms: "Few Americans accept the belief of some of those now in positions of importance in guiding our foreign policy that America's purpose in the world is to appease the mighty out of a sense of fear or to appease the weak out of a sense of guilt."[1] Throughout his political career, Reagan was unapologetic in his depiction of the Soviet Union as an empire dedicated to remorseless global conquest. According to his worldview, Moscow was a threat that stretched across the entire spectrum of American interests, from the nuclear arms race to hotbeds of communist aggression in Africa, Asia, and Latin America.[2] During Reagan's first term, he depicted efforts to compromise or negotiate with this enemy as naive and dangerous. Reagan's rhetorical belligerence toward communism provoked many contemporaries to compare his administration with Eisenhower's and the height of Cold War brinksmanship.[3]

But Reagan was not completely blinded by reactionary ideology. As he preached confrontation with Moscow, he also attempted to apply lessons learned from earlier stages of the Cold War. As his administration presided over the reconstruction of the American armed forces, it recalled the early sixties, when the military enjoyed a rebirth of purpose and innovation. While a Cold Warrior in terms of his rhetoric, the president also demonstrated a clear willingness to back words with concrete actions and new approaches to war.

Without question, the American military rebuilt itself in the eighties under Reagan's tutelage. This process included new forms of strategic nuclear weapons, the largest conventional forces build up since Vietnam, and a rebirth of doctrine devoted to what officials relabeled "low-intensity war." In the latter case, the U.S. military embraced not only the counterinsurgency mission but also the active promotion of small wars abroad.

The real dilemma for American strategists was how best to apply a policy of confrontation. The search for a practical use of the renovated military was analogous to capturing lightning in a bottle. Strategically, the Reagan White House saw the Soviet hand in all that was wrong in the world and sought to challenge Moscow. However, translating belligerent rhetoric into action was as difficult as it was dangerous.[4] Making the administration's hard line viable required a sea change in doctrine, training, and weapons procurement. Once created, such a military would be a sharp-edged tool that was inherently dangerous not only to the Soviet enemy, but also to global stability in general. The Reagan era, particularly the president's first term in office, was defined by a constant concerns over how quickly a war between two well-matched enemies might escalate to a thermonuclear exchange. As Richard Lock-Pullan notes, in a peacetime strategic environment that was relatively stable, military strength ironically translated into a relative weakness for American allies and nonaligned nations.[5]

At home, the prospect of a more adept and active military force remained extremely controversial. The eighties were a time in which the Vietnam syndrome dominated the public debate and placed enormous pressure on the military establishment to define specific terms and conditions for any form of military confrontation. Fairly or not, the demand for prerequisites to U.S. military deployments—specific objectives, casualty estimates, and an exit strategy—became a fixed point in policy debates regarding American military affairs.[6] Although it appreciated Reagan's patriotism, the public was consistently reticent about the potential cost of war throughout his presidency.

The prospect of small wars conducted under American auspices invited even more potential controversy. The low-intensity conflicts that Reagan contemplated in 1981 defied the clear-cut distinctions made during his presidential campaign and subsequent administration. Certain insurgent groups could not pass for what a reasonable layman considered to be "freedom fighters," no matter how well crafted the message. More worrisome were the opaque circumstances that dictated either support for or defense against insurgencies in the eighties. As a matter of practical operations, it was advantageous for American policy makers to ensure that such efforts remained covert. However, as the CIA and the U.S. military embarked on projects in areas as far separated as Central America and Southwest Asia, the aftershocks of the Church Committee hearings had not yet faded from the public domain or, more important, from Congress. When the White House and its national security team embraced the idea of fighting insurgency, they did so at a considerable risk.[7]

The New Cold War

One of Reagan's greatest strengths in the 1980 election was his promise to restore American power and fight threats to American interests. While a restored military was clearly his proposed means, equally clear was Reagan's identification of the Soviet Union as the primary threat to American global interests and world peace. Reagan used an uncomplicated template to explain international affairs. In what would become a famous articulation of his worldview, Reagan warned Americans in 1983: "to beware the temptation of pride—the temptation of blithely declaring yourselves above it all and label both sides equally at fault, to ignore the facts of history and the aggressive impulses of an evil empire, to simply call the arms race a giant misunderstanding and thereby remove yourself from the struggle between right and wrong and good and evil."[8] As president, Reagan set the tone for a philosophy that permeated policy discussions among his key staff.[9] His first secretary of state, former general Alexander Haig, echoed Reagan's sentiments almost exactly in 1981: "A major focus of American policy must be the Soviet Union, not because of ideological preoccupations but simply because Moscow is the greatest source of international insecurity today. Let us be plain about it: Soviet promotion of violence as the instrument of change constitutes the greatest danger to world peace."[10]

Even though Haig's tenure was remarkably short, truncated as it was by his own missteps after the attempted assassination against Reagan, his successor, George Schultz, proved to be just as much a cold warrior in his approach to foreign affairs.[11] Defense Secretary Caspar Weinberger initially found common cause with Schultz when he took charge of the Pentagon and openly advocated greater defense spending to regain strategic superiority over the USSR. Weinberger wanted across-the-board improvements in nuclear and conventional forces and supported increasing the total number of Army divisions along with Air Force bomber and fighter wings. He also believed that a 600-ship navy was a realistic goal under the new administration.[12]

The confrontational tone prevalent in Reagan's cabinet quickly percolated down into active diplomacy. Arms control negotiations with the Soviets became the province of individuals like Eugene V. Rostow and Richard Perle, officials who had openly opposed the SALT agreements throughout most of the seventies.[13] As the U.S. ambassador to the United Nations, Jeanne Kirkpatrick parlayed academic distinctions between totalitarian and authoritarian regimes into overt policy that supported pro-American military governments abroad.[14]

The administration made its position on small conflicts apparent in 1985 during the annual State of the Union Address. In what became known as Reagan Doctrine, the president staked out a clear position on a very specific portion of the Cold War battlefield: "We must stand by all our democratic allies. And we must not break faith with those who are risking their lives—on every continent, from Afghanistan to Nicaragua—to defy Soviet-supported aggression and secure rights which have been ours from birth."[15] Reagan Doctrine was reminiscent of Cold War policy in the fifties in that it recognized the East-West deadlock would inspire communist intrusion into the underdeveloped areas of the Third World. In a 1986 speech, Undersecretary of Defense for Policy Fred Ikle recalled the Eisenhower era: "We in the West thought that the Atlantic Alliance had checkmated Soviet expansion of the Cold War period. But . . . the Cold War was followed by insurgency and other small-scale warfare in many regions."[16] In one respect, Reagan Doctrine retained the traditionalism of previous counterinsurgency policies. The root source of conflict was consistent with the past. What changed, however, was the search for better methods to combat Soviet-inspired insurgencies. This was clearly the case in El Salvador during the eighties.

Reagan Doctrine was an important departure because it also endorsed insurgency as a means of promoting American security interests overseas. Rather than deploy regular military forces, the administration saw American-sponsored insurgents as a viable means to contest what Kirkpatrick described as the "recent acquisitions" of the Soviet empire in Afghanistan, Cambodia, Angola, and Nicaragua.[17] This particular direction appeared in U.S. national security policy as early as May 1982 with the release of National Security Decision Directive (NSDD) 32, "National Security Strategy." The document expressed the U.S. commitment: "To contain and reverse the expansion of Soviet control and military presence throughout the world, and to increase the costs of Soviet support and use of proxy, terrorist, and subversive forces."[18] As such, insurgency became an additional means toward this end for the remainder of the eighties.

There were clear advantages to a pro-insurgency policy. Cost effectiveness, another echo of the Eisenhower era, was an obvious benefit. Even at a time when American defense budgets were rapidly growing, it was easier to defer the costs of defense to allied nations and anticommunist groups.[19] The same was true with respect to the political costs of prospective casualties in these wars.

Other elements of Reagan Doctrine were subtler. Rather than simply resist local insurgency, the administration saw an advantage in fomenting rebellion. A key 1987 document, National Security Decision Directive (NSDD) 277, "National Policy and Strategy for Low Intensity Conflict," noted that the United States had the potential opportunity of "taking advantage of selected resistance movements to gain leverage against hostile regimes."[20] The same leverage could also be applied to any state that sponsored such a regime, as was eventually the case in Afghanistan. In another respect, pro-insurgency policy offered a chance to use Soviet empire building against Moscow. By raising the cost of expansion, Washington might provoke what Paul Kennedy described as "imperial overstretch."[21] Overall, American support for global insurgencies promised a case of geopolitical role reversal, wherein the United States embraced asymmetrical power in much the same way the communist bloc had in the fifties and sixties. Policy did to such a degree that in 1982 the National Security Council predicted there was a greater likelihood of war with the Soviet client state than the USSR.[22]

Reagan Doctrine eventually became the basic framework for American small wars in the eighties. One of these conflicts was in Central America, where officials contemplated the expansion of the Sandinista revolution beyond Nicaragua. Of specific concern was the fate of El Salvador. The Reagan administration, as well as Carter before him, acknowledged a direct Nicaraguan role in supporting *Frente Farabundo Martí para la Liberación Nacional* (FMLN) rebels as evidence of a larger regional problem. A January 1980 CIA report indicated that the "Sandinistas have trained, advised, and probably armed revolutionaries in El Salvador, although their commitment to export their revolution has been tempered by their preoccupation with the domestic situation in Nicaragua, confusion over political events in El Salvador, and a wish to placate antipathetic military governments in Honduras and Guatemala."[23] Later, the Reagan administration made the prevalence of Soviet aid to Nicaragua a standard part of its public talking points on Central America. The flow of economic and military assistance was presented as evidence that Moscow was actively promoting revolution and instability throughout the region.[24]

American intelligence sources believed that Soviet arms, transshipped from Nicaragua to El Salvador, might provide the critical margin of victory for the FMLN. The Central Intelligence Agency claimed that Nicaragua was providing Salvadoran insurgents not only training and modern small arms but also SA-7 and SA-14 surface-to-air missiles.[25] The potential impact of the latter was particularly serious given the Salvadoran military's use of helicopters and light aircraft for troop movement and reconnaissance. Administration officials were also concerned that Sandinista arms might spread beyond El Salvador. An October 1982 National Security Council study noted evidence of linkages between Nicaragua and dissidents in Honduras and Puerto Rico.[26]

Although the academic debate would later rage over the validity of these claims, administration officials developed a consensus that Nicaragua was a witting Soviet proxy and the region simply an appendage of the great Cold War conflict.[27] Similarly, the conventional wisdom within the military and national security policy community was that the Nicaraguan threat mandated a greater U.S. military and intelligence presence in the region.[28] Subsequent policy reflected this agreement. Released in January 1982, NSDD 17 explained American objectives in very clear terms: "U.S. policy is therefore to assist in defeating the insurgency in El Salvador, and to oppose actions by Cuba, Nicaragua, or others to introduce into Central America heavy weapons, troops from outside the region, trained subversives, or arms and military supplies for insurgents."[29]

The first real test of this policy was in El Salvador. As the eighties progressed, it became abundantly clear that the United States intended to underwrite a rapid and massive expansion of the Salvadoran military. Between 1982 and 1985, the country received $498.2 million in U.S. military assistance. The rapid infusion of American aid allowed El Salvador to expand its armed forces from approximately 10,000 troops in 1981 to 36,000 four years later.[30] These troops were rearmed with a combination of U.S., Israeli, French, and West German weaponry. The addition of helicopters to Salvadoran ground forces added an important degree of mobility for operations conducted against the FMLN.

A substantial part of American military assistance went directly to counterinsurgency programs. American special forces teams deployed to El Salvador trained three "immediate reaction" units—the Atlacatl, Atonal, and Ramon Belloso battalions—specifically to fight insurgents in the countryside.[31] Intelligence gathering efforts ran concurrently with military assistance. The U.S. country team as well as officials in Washington recognized that information was critical to counterguerrilla operations and an important means to gather popular support against insurgents. Precedents for these types of operations did not escape contemporary policy makers. A 1982 NSC memorandum titled "Reinventing the Wheel in El Salvador" recommended the following: "We should quietly establish a point of contact here in Washington which can readily draw on our Vietnam experience to help our people in San Salvador quickly solve specific counter-insurgency problems."[32] Using a methodology reminiscent of CORDS in Vietnam—the NSC memo also recommended emphasis on small unit operations, aggressive patrolling, ambushes, and night operations—the United States appeared prepared to revisit its counterinsurgency heritage in the mid-eighties.[33]

The problem facing American counterinsurgency strategy in El Salvador was not so much its tactical soundness, but its political viability back in the United States. A straightforward implementation of a program against leftist insurgents required a domestic political commitment that was simply not present at the time. Direct military assistance to Central America provoked bitter resistance from congressional Democrats. Throughout the floor debates on foreign military aid, the American public remained consistently skeptical about foreign troop deployments no matter how small in number or purpose.[34] Nicaragua was a particular lightning rod given the ill will created by deposed pro-American dictator Anastasio Somoza. Support for right-wing exiles attempting to overthrow the Sandinistas was particularly controversial. During one debate, it prompted the formidable Democrat Speaker of the House, Thomas P. "Tip" O'Neill, to claim in 1984 that "these people down there (the Contras) are marauders, they are rapists. To relocate these people with $4 million would be a disgrace to this government."[35]

When the Reagan administration won appropriations for El Salvador, they invariably came with conditions. Military assistance funds for fiscal year 1985 were tied to the successful criminal investigation of American and Salvadoran land reform workers killed in the country. Legislators also demanded consultation with the administration with respect to "death squad activities, elimination of corruption and misuse of governmental funds, development of an El Salvadoran plan to improve the performance of the military, and progress toward discussions leading to a peaceful resolution of the conflict."[36]

Reagan administration officials clearly underestimated the nature of domestic opposition to its military policies. Jeanne Kirkpatrick's distinction between "authoritarian" and "totalitarian" governments drew widespread ridicule in the media and academe. When the State Department released its white paper on communist involvement in El

Salvador in February 1981, it was universally denounced by journals like the *Latin America Weekly Report* and newspapers as diverse in their support of the administration as the *Los Angeles Times* and the *Wall Street Journal*.[37] Human rights abuses by right-wing death squads against Salvadoran union leaders, political activists, and innocent bystanders became an international scandal.[38] The vicious acts committed against the Catholic clergy in the country made an already horrifying situation worse. One group, the *Unión Guerrera Blanca* (White Warriors Union) offered the slogan "Be Patriotic—Kill a Priest" to its followers in June 1980. The subsequent deaths or expulsion of Jesuit, Maryknoll, and Benedictine clergy shocked the world.[39]

The public debate over El Salvador highlighted a more important quandary for Reagan Doctrine. It became clear as the administration attempted to move forward with plans for Central America that an inverse relationship between confrontation and public support for military action existed in the U.S. political landscape. The more administration hardliners argued for a forceful application of anticommunist policies, the more its actions generated a potential backlash.[40] The degree of public sensitivity to American military deployments became clear in early 1982 when the media reported that U.S. military advisers in El Salvador were carrying personal weapons while on duty. Special forces troops on the ground viewed self-protection in a war zone as a matter of common sense. Congressional leaders, who had prohibited the practice as a condition of approving military aid to El Salvador, did not. The ensuing scandal reverberated all the way to Caspar Weinberger's office.[41]

The prospect of courting additional controversy had a chilling effect on American small wars in the eighties. A 1985 General Accounting Office report rather blandly noted that "there was general agreement among State and Defense Department officials that U.S. military assistance is a peacetime military supply program ill-suited to the active combat situation of El Salvador."[42] Few reasonable civilian or military leaders wanted to incur the public's wrath for a real or perceived misstep.

Unfortunately, this reticence was not universal. During Reagan's first year in office, the United States began a covert program to arm and supply insurgents opposed to the Sandinista government in Nicaragua.[43] However, given the controversial nature of these forces, prompted in part by their past affiliation with the Somoza regime, lawmakers clearly restricted assistance through the Boland Amendment in December 1982.[44]

Federal law failed to prohibit further administration action. A select group of Reagan officials in the Defense Department, National Security Council, and CIA deliberately avoided congressional oversight by concocting a plan to gather funds from arms sales to Iran, initially made in exchange for U.S. hostages taken in the Middle East, for use in Central America. The proceeds of these sales, as well as donations from third parties in the Middle East, supported contra activities for a number of years.[45]

However, once this burgeoning covert effort became public, the result was politically disastrous for the Reagan administration. A series of investigations conducted by Congress in 1987 to unravel "Contragate" resulted in months of dramatic, televised testimony by key officials such as John Poindexter, Robert McFarlane, and Oliver North.[46] The subsequent indictments of more than a dozen policy makers, including one against Weinberger that was later overturned, effectively crippled the White House for much of Reagan's remaining time in office.[47]

The paradox of public antagonism amidst military recovery established an important context for American security policy in the eighties. It was easy to see in the accumulating controversies over aid to El Salvador and the Nicaraguan contras. But it produced little clarity for policymakers intent on clearly delineating the conditions that would govern future U.S. military deployments overseas.

Caspar Weinberger and senior members of his uniformed staff, such as Major General Colin Powell, wanted to create such standards. Even before the Iran-Contra scandal broke, Weinberger was moved by what he considered to be an unacceptable recklessness that inhabited American foreign policy at the time. The deployment of U.S. military forces to Lebanon, and the poorly managed campaign that had culminated in the October 1983 destruction of the Marine barracks in Beirut, exemplified the significant dangers of using military power without a coherent strategy.[48] Senior military officers like Powell took a longer view in their desire to avoid repeating the disastrous incrementalism that had crippled U.S. policy decisions during the Vietnam War. Powell would later recount in his 1996 memoir: "There are times when American lives must be risked and lost. Foreign policy cannot be paralyzed by the prospect of casualties. But lives must not be risked until we can face a parent or a spouse or a child with a clear answer to the question of why a member of that family had to die."[49]

The combined product of these two overlapping philosophies became known as the Weinberger Doctrine in November 1984 when the defense secretary made a major policy address before the National Press Club. In his speech, Weinberger posited six mandatory tests that had to be met prior to the commitment of US forces abroad:

> First, the United States should not commit forces to combat overseas unless the particular engagement or occasion is deemed vital to our national interest or that of our allies. . . .
>
> Second, if we decide it is necessary to put combat troops into a given situation, we should do so wholeheartedly, and with the clear intention of winning. . . .
>
> Third, if we do decide to commit forces to combat overseas, we should have clearly defined political and military objectives. . . .
>
> Fourth, the relationship between our objectives and the forces we have committed—their size, composition and disposition—must be continually reassessed and adjusted if necessary. . . .
>
> Fifth, before the U.S. commits combat forces abroad, there must be some reasonable assurance we will have the support of the American people and their elected representatives in Congress. . . .
>
> Finally, the commitment of U.S. forces to combat should be a last resort.[50]

As he made clear in the speech, Weinberger did not oppose any prospect of U.S. military intervention, only those without a reasonable set of preconditions necessary for success. How deeply he believed his own doctrine is debatable. In his memoirs, Weinberger later insisted that Grenada constituted a vital national interest in 1983, a fact that justified the American invasion. More likely, what justified intervention was its obvious finite timetable rather than the imminent threat of a few hundred Cuban troops occupying a small Caribbean island.

Regardless of its motives, Weinberger Doctrine placed significant restrictions on the use of conventional forces, particularly during Reagan's second term. The White House kept its bellicosity, as was the case when it responded to terrorist attacks against American citizens and military personnel stationed abroad. The protracted sparring with Libya around its "line of death" in the Mediterranean, the mission conducted against the Achille Lauro hijackers, and the air strikes against Tripoli all punctuated the second administration. However, although it may have prepared military expeditions against U.S. enemies overseas, nothing on the scale of the Lebanon peacekeeping mission or the Grenada invasion occurred again.

Applied to American strategic thinking, Weinberger Doctrine magnified many of the worst aspects of previous Cold War decision making. The lengthy list of prerequisites to U.S. military action hearkened back to Dwight Eisenhower's deliberate effort to prevent a nuclear strike against the Viet Minh to save the French war effort in 1954.[51] Moreover, implicit in Weinberger Doctrine was the faith that conflict could be clinically managed from afar, an approach that recalled Robert McNamara's attempt to apply systems management to the war in Vietnam.[52] Military historian Brian McAllister Linn notes that Weinberger's statement of the uses of military power reflected "the propensity to view war as an engineering project in which the skilled application of correct principles could achieve a predictable outcome."[53]

Importantly, Weinberger Doctrine did not address the use of special operations forces for specific missions (e.g., terrorism or counternarcotics) or counterinsurgency as a whole.[54] However, this absence did not connote a greater degree of operational freedom. If anything, the doctrine was a blanket statement that conflated both conventional and unconventional military operations. More to the point, because special operations sometimes existed in what could be best defined as a gray area concerning legality, if not public disclosure, the standards set by Weinberger Doctrine were often prohibitively high.

Consequently, small wars did not escape the restrictions placed on larger conventional conflicts by the Defense Department, Congress, or public opinion in general. Some of these proscribed activities were very precise. Federal lawmakers limited the number of U.S. advisers in El Salvador to fifty-five and specifically dictated their duties while deployed in country.[55] Later, congressional leaders would attempt to control assistance to "democratic resistance forces within Nicaragua" with similar guidelines but significantly less success.[56]

The Reagan Military

Ronald Reagan's primary objective for his military was as straightforward as his approach to the Cold War in general. Defense policy during his presidency, particularly in the first term, was designed to move America's military standing with the Soviet Union from strategic parity to superiority. Significant increases in defense spending supported his intent. Between 1981 and 1988, the Department of Defense budget nearly doubled from $157.5 billion to $290.4 billion.[57] In historical terms, the Reagan years represented one of the three peak periods for federal spending for national defense after 1945, alongside the Korean and Vietnam wars.

Within the benefices of the new administration, the American military sought to recover lost ground. When Weinberger first offered additional spending to the Joint Chiefs of Staff in 1981, the separate services revisited long-deferred wish lists of weapons systems stalled or sidetracked by Carter. These included a host of big-ticket items such as upgraded strategic nuclear missiles, the M-1 tank, the B-2 bomber, and the Trident submarine.

The Reagan administration's support for defense produced an immediate impact on the American military. The proportion of the defense budget dedicated to weapons procurement, research and development, and construction rapidly increased in the early eighties. Research and development proved to be the fastest growing component of the defense budget, growing as a percentage of expenditures from 9.3 percent in 1981 to 12.9 percent by 1988. This new priority was reflected in investment for strategic missile defense systems (under the Strategic Defense Initiative, or "Star Wars"), stealth technology for a new generation of Air Force fighters and bombers, and the like.

The Defense Department spent additional resources on military pay, housing, and benefits. As a result, the U.S. military retained more personnel and reenlistments improved throughout the decade. The

Pentagon also dedicated new funding for conventional forces. All branches benefited from equipment upgrades and additional training time. The overall higher quality of American forces was reflected in experience, technical expertise, and overall readiness.[58] It was clear by 1990 that the qualitative decline within the American military had been substantially reversed.

These glory days largely lasted until the final two years of the Reagan administration, when spending cuts began to impinge upon training, maintenance, and unit deployments. Once Frank Carlucci replaced Weinberger as secretary of defense in 1987, he introduced new austerity measures that interrupted some programs, such as the deployment of the new HMMV, in midstream.[59] In general, however, the military kept its positive improvements into the nineties and was largely prepared for deployment to Saudi Arabia and Operation Desert Storm.

New doctrine coincided with additional defense funding in the eighties. The time period was important in that it witnessed a significant shift in American military thinking, specifically as it applied to ground forces. As discussed in the previous chapter, by the late seventies the Army had begun to move away from active defense and toward war fighting built around maneuver and depth on the battlefield. One author, Army Colonel Wayne A. Downing, described the active defense as "a general warfare doctrine that is bankrupt," one that emphasized "almost mechanical methods of fighting—or applying firepower."[60]

The response to this shortfall became known simply as the AirLand Battle Doctrine. It approached potential ground combat by applying the concept of geographical depth to both friendly and enemy forces, but also included factors such as time, distance, resources, intelligence, and the contributions of other service branches, particularly with respect to tactical airpower. Ironically, these reforms were essentially advocating the adoption of the Soviet combined arms concept by the American military. Like the Soviets, the new doctrine focused on maneuver and joint action between war fighting units at all tactical levels. Unlike the Soviets, however, AirLand Battle emphasized individual initiative and command flexibility wherever possible.[61]

The latter feature was particularly important. American military planners recognized that the modern battlefield comprised a rapidly changing mix of components necessary to defeat an enemy force that were themselves being compressed into an increasingly rapid tempo of operations. In order to succeed, the soldier in the field and the institution as a whole had to adapt in order to survive and prevail.

Despite the improvements introduced by the AirLand Battle Doctrine, it remained limited in scope. The American military was better prepared to fight in the eighties, but its focus remained on conventional war in Western Europe. This was clearly evident when the Army opened the National Training Center (NTC) at Fort Irwin, California. Beginning in 1982, regular and reserve units rotating through the center practiced a simulated form of advanced armored war against an opposition force of Krasnovians who dutifully replicated standard Soviet battle tactics. The Joint Readiness Training Center (JRTC), later established at Fort Chaffee, Arkansas, focused on light infantry training. The overall purpose of NTC and the JRTC was to present units with a worst-case scenario that tested small unit cohesiveness and junior leaders under the most realistic conditions possible at the time. Both centers emphasized conventional environments and tactics. Although the JRTC did include insurgents as part of its regimen, they were utilized to harass units rather than to offer specific training in counterinsurgency.[62]

The ongoing renovation of both military budgets and doctrine had clear implications for American special forces and their ability to fight small wars.[63] Throughout the eighties, U.S. special operations forces benefited from two distinct and mutually supporting trends. The first was the fact that the AirLand Battle Doctrine identified them as an important adjunct to conventional operations. With this restored relevance, these units presented an unmistakable opportunity to rebuild and progress beyond the doldrums of the seventies. Secondly, and more broadly, civilian policy makers saw the special forces as a critical component of proxy wars that they planned to conduct against communism around the world. Integration into the military establishment was solidified further with the passage of the Cohen-Nunn amendment to the 1987 Defense Authorization Act. The amendment instituted within the Pentagon the assistant secretary of defense for special operations and low-intensity conflict. The creation of this office reinforced the trend toward inclusion of special forces in the senior command structure begun after the 1980 Holloway Report.[64] In 1987, the Defense Department also created Special Operations Command (SOCOM), an action that effectively integrated special forces units from all service branches under a single umbrella organization and elevated their function within the defense bureaucracy. Although SOCOM did not enjoy peer status with other theater commands (e.g., CENTCOM), special forces no longer existed on the periphery of the organizational system after 1987.

Special Operations in the Eighties

During the Reagan years, the special forces option enjoyed a significant renaissance. This was evident when American operatives were deployed to countries as far dispersed as Angola, Cambodia, Afghanistan, and Nicaragua. More to the point, the conventional military wisdom of the period began to coalesce around low-intensity warfare as a plausible policy option. This was evident when the Defense Department began to support conferences on the topic and invite acknowledged experts in the field. When the Low-Intensity Warfare Conference met in 1986, one of its guest speakers was R.G.K. Thompson, architect of British counterinsurgency in Malaya in the fifties, who provided many of the basic concepts that the American military later applied in South Vietnam. Newer members of the academic and policy communities, such as Sam Sarkesian and Robert Kupperman, also contributed significantly to the discussion.[65]

The emerging intellectual consensus focused on a number of basic conclusions. The first was that the underdeveloped nations of the Third World were particularly vulnerable as they struggled with what Sarkesian called the "problems of modernity."[66] This context was dominated by social, economic, and political systems in a state of flux, conditions that made countries as well as entire regions ripe for Soviet exploitation.[67] An effective American counterinsurgency policy had to incorporate these nonmilitary factors in order to not only remove the preconditions for Soviet success but also to effectively combat existing insurgencies.[68] Contemporary theorists understood that none of these conclusions were necessarily new. Many could be traced back to conflicts fought in Central America and the Caribbean after World War I. Moreover, much of what was proposed simply revisited doctrines and methods forged during the Vietnam War.[69] However, what this school of thought collectively re-created was a sense of confidence that the United States could fight and win low-intensity conflicts on a global scale.[70]

Much of this academic discourse eventually translated into new doctrine. When the Army revised *Field Manual 100–20: Low Intensity Conflict,* it included many of the basic precepts of multicausal theory. The military, in other words, came to many of the same conclusions that it had when counterinsurgency doctrine was created in the sixties—namely, that neither the cause of nor the solution to guerrilla war could be found in any single quality of war. Instead, effective counterinsurgency required "a carefully balanced combination of economic, political, informational, and military instruments."[71] Low-intensity warfare, as practiced in the eighties, increasingly reverted back to its earlier incarnation in Vietnam under Robert Komer and William Colby.

The operational tempo of special forces deployments increased in concert with reconstructed doctrine. This trend was notable in the deployment of military mobile training teams (MTTs). In 1978 Army special forces maintained 53 MTTs worldwide, a reflection of their diminishing importance and support during the Carter administration. In contrast, by 1986, 260 mobile training teams were conducting training in thirty-five countries.[72]

Unfortunately, the new wealth of attention and commitment produced its own problem: overexpansion. A senior officer within the special forces community, Colonel Charles M. Simpson, noted at the time: "There is a pervading dearth of maturity and experience. . . . The A Detachments consist primarily of E-3s and E-4s, some commanded by second lieutenants. There are some experienced NCOs in A Detachments, though too little detachment training to compensate for inexperience takes place. When there is a mission, they scrape together what experienced personnel there are and send them off, thus wearing out the old hands and leaving the newer soldiers still not fully trained or experienced."[73]

Special operations units were showcased in the two major deployments of American military forces in the eighties, during Grenada (1983) and the invasion of Panama (1989). Results were mixed. The Army ranger assault on the Port Salinas airfield went according to plan for the most part, although anti-aircraft fire inflicted a number of casualties.[74] In contrast, Navy SEAL teams sent to reconnoiter Point Salinas suffered unnecessary deaths due to poor planning of their initial drop zones. The relatively small size and light equipment organic to special forces units created additional problems. SEAL operatives dispatched to rescue British Governor General Sir Paul Scoon found themselves under siege by better-equipped Cuban forces. Similarly, when SEAL units were dispatched to secure the Punta Paitilla airfield during Operation Just Cause in 1989, heavy casualties offset their initial success once local Panamanian Defense Force units counterattacked.[75]

In the aftermath of Operation Urgent Fury, the institutional assessment within the military tended to be on interservice communications, intelligence, and logistics. One official history, written in 1997, recorded that Grenada had revealed a need for greater command control to alleviate the problems experienced during the invasion. Military operations in Panama were a different story. The 18th Airborne Corps commander, Lieutenant General Carl W. Stiner, spoke for many senior officers in a February 1990 *Army Times* interview: "JUST CAUSE . . . validated that what we are doing is right . . . that the training program . . . is exactly as it should be. . . . We expect tough, realistic training of our troops, and this includes live-fire and night operations. Our training program paid off in spades in Panama and that's the reason you saw the discipline, the efficiency, the effectiveness and the proficiency that was demonstrated by our troops."[76] Noticeably absent from critiques of both Urgent Fury and Just Cause was any acknowledgment of special operations. Difficulties experienced in Grenada were perceived as peripheral to the overall mission's success. Much the same was true in Panama, even though the consensus was that Just Cause was a success.

In sum, although special operations forces expanded and were increasingly included as part of conventional missions during the eighties, they remained essentially split from the mainstream military. Funding grew significantly, particularly during the overall surge in defense spending between 1981 and 1985. During that time period official special operations budgets almost tripled from $441 million to $1.2 billion. Personnel growth followed suit. By 1985 the total number of operators in all military branches was 14,900, up from 11,600 four years earlier.[77]

Growth within special operations was less than uniform, however. The Army officially activated its ranger regiment in 1985 and headquartered the unit in Fort Benning, Georgia. The increase in the number of ranger battalions from two to three bolstered the overall number of special forces personnel then in service. In contrast, the Air Force cut its special operations funding by 40 percent in fiscal year 1985. At the time, Military Airlift Command placed special operations at fifty-ninth in its official priority list for transportation. As the Special Operations Forces (SOF) ground complement grew, air assets failed to keep pace, restricting both training opportunities and overall readiness for deployment.[78]

Training standards were also a concern, not only as a function of the relative inexperience of many special forces soldiers, but also in their basic goals and methods.[79] Army rangers, while superbly trained, remained essentially tied to their World War II–era mission as a raiding force. As noted earlier, they could accomplish this task with aplomb, as was the case at Port Salinas airfield or the Omar Torrijos airport in Panama. However, they did not move much beyond the airfield seizure mission in the eighties. Norman Schwarzkopf's reluctance to incorporate ranger units into Operation Desert Storm reflected in part his skepticism regarding their narrow capabilities. Similarly, Army special forces training retained a strong adherence to OSS standards established by Aaron Bank and other World War II veterans who first codified doctrine in the late forties. Candidates for special forces qualification were taught the fundamentals of cultivating local popular forces along lines that would have been familiar to OSS operatives building contacts with partisans in France before D-Day. Unfortunately absent from this training was the intricacies of counterinsurgency or counterterrorist training then being crafted by Sarkesian or other policy planners.[80]

These shortfalls were readily apparent to the public and policy makers alike, particularly after the problems experienced during the invasion of Grenada. Consequently, only a few short years after Urgent Fury, congressional leaders began to argue for another round of reforms within U.S. special forces. A letter from Sam Nunn (D-GA) and Barry Goldwater (R-AZ) to Caspar Weinberger in January 1986 addressed the issue of aircraft available for special operations when it noted: "We are particularly concerned that six years after the tragedy at Desert One, we appear to have made few significant improvements in this [special operations] capability."[81] In 1986, Nunn, along with

Maine Republican William S. Cohen, proposed a number of reforms in an amendment to the 1987 defense authorization bill. The legislation called for basic institutional improvements that included a unified special operations command, an Assistant Secretary of Defense for Special Operations and Low-Intensity Warfare, and a special operations command slot at a four-star rank. It also required greater integration of special operations within the Defense Department and the National Security Council.

Although the Defense Department resisted the amendment, the Pentagon eventually accepted a watered-down version of the Nunn-Cohen proposal. A three-star rank was created for the officer in charge of U.S. Special Operations Command (SOCOM), effectively preventing advocacy on par with other commands. Operationally, SOCOM would be seconded to theater commanders and the JCS itself. The first assistant secretary of defense for special operations and low-intensity conflict was Ambassador Charles S. Whitehouse, a foreign service officer with experience in neither area.

Within Special Operations Command, the Nunn-Cohen amendment offered more positive changes. When SOCOM was officially established on 23 April 1987, its mandate was to integrate the existing hodgepodge of special operations missions—foreign internal defense, unconventional war, and intelligence gathering—into a more cohesive whole. Organizationally, this meant that special operations units scattered around the country—the 23rd Air Force at Hurlburt Field, Florida; the Naval Special Warfare Command at Coronado, San Diego; and the 1st Special Operations Command at Fort Bragg, North Carolina, as well as assorted civil affairs and psychological operations units—were now the single domain of Lieutenant General James J. Lindsay, the first SOCOM commander. His mission was to integrate the overall function of these units and draft future doctrine that would eventually guide their actions as a whole.[82]

SOCOM's first real test came in the Persian Gulf during Operation Earnest Will. Responding to an escalating series of Iranian attacks on international shipping, the Reagan administration deployed special operations units to the region between 1987 and 1989. As this small-scale war unfolded, SEAL teams equipped with shallow-draft patrol boats and helicopters battled Iranian fast-attack craft and minelayers.[83] The so-called tanker war revealed a number operational problems and some ingenious solutions. As American special operations forces fought Iranian sea assets and fixed facilities, it quickly became evident that there was no existing logistical network in the region. SOCOM remedied the difficulty by leasing two civilian oil-servicing barges that were placed in international waters, neatly avoiding a formal request for base rights from local Arab nations.[84]

Operation Earnest Will reflected a maturing American special forces capability that was far better prepared for its mission than it had been at the start of the decade. By 1989 it was clear that special forces had evolved beyond peripheral inclusion into the convention forces structure and doctrine. Special operations at the end of the Reagan administration were better funded and better organized than at any time since the Vietnam War. For all its limitations, the Nunn-Cohen amendment was significant because it established a more secure niche for special operations within the Pentagon bureaucracy. Moreover, it was clear that by promoting an improved special forces capability, congressional leaders were also tacitly granting their approval of the special forces mission, something that had clearly been lacking prior to 1980.[85] Collectively, many of the actions taken in the eighties both improved American special forces and raised expectations in the policymaking community regarding their use.

Case Study: Supporting the Mujahideen

American involvement in the Middle East and its environs was dictated by a single interest that remained consistent throughout the twentieth century. Policy documents produced during the Reagan years retained the same emphasis as the Carter administration and its predecessors in that the primary American policy objective for the region was to "maintain continued access for the U.S. and its principal allies to Gulf oil."[86] When the Soviet Union invaded Afghanistan in 1979, Washington interpreted it as a deliberate effort to control this strategic resource. Conversely, the Reagan administration also believed the insurgency following the Soviet occupation of Afghanistan presented a unique opportunity to weaken Moscow. The Afghan resistance, while disorganized and poorly equipped, had proven tenacious even against the unrestricted firepower of the Red Army. Although few leaders in the White House or the Pentagon believed that the mujahideen, as they became known, would prevail, their resistance offered the United States the prospect of sponsoring a war of attrition against the Soviets. In Afghanistan, as was also the case in Central America, low-intensity warfare doctrine presented an opportunity for success.[87]

In reality, the pro-insurgency approach to Afghanistan originated under Jimmy Carter. The administration first considered aid to Afghan rebels in March 1979, just as Soviet fortunes in the country began to unravel. In July of that year, the White House authorized the Central Intelligence Agency to spend $500,000 on nonmilitary assistance to the rebels fighting against the Moscow-backed government in Kabul.[88] On 17 December 1979, based on initial signs of success in the field, the NSC Special Coordinating Committee expanded American aid to the mujahideen.[89]

American interest in the Afghan rebels took a major step forward after the Soviet invasion in December 1979. Unbeknownst to most people at the time, U.S. aid to the insurgency became one of the first active expressions of Carter Doctrine in 1980.[90] Although the United States did not directly confront the Soviet Union to protect the integrity of the Persian Gulf region, it did so with willing proxies in the mountains of Southwest Asia.[91]

American funding constructed a transportation network that brought weapons to Pakistan for storage and shipment across the border into Afghanistan. Direct transfers of weapons and equipment began in 1980. The first armaments consisted of obsolete World War II surplus. One early delivery contained bolt action .303 caliber British Lee Enfield rifles from Greece and India. Later, Afghan insurgents received more modern small arms as well as mortars, rocket-propelled grenades, and launchers from sources as disparate as communist China, Egypt, Turkey, and Israel. The quality of these arms drastically varied from country to country. Chinese-made weapons were better than materiel obtained from Egypt. Weapons and ammunition procured from Cairo were often dirty, corroded, and unusable once they arrived in Pakistan. A 1985 shipment of 30,000 82mm mortar rounds were so swollen and damp they would not fit in the tubes to fire.[92]

The Reagan administration significantly expanded the scope and the scale of operations in Afghanistan. During Reagan's first term, the White House hosted numerous lobby groups intent on making a positive case that Afghan freedom fighters needed better support from the United States. Members of the Afghan Relief Committee, the Committee for a Free Afghanistan, and the Afghan Youth Council all met with the president in February 1983 as part of a highly publicized push for greater funding. In the Congress, Representative Charlie Wilson of Texas became one of the mujahideen's most formidable supporters, successfully lobbying for hundreds of millions of dollars in additional aid during both Reagan terms.[93]

Collectively, the mujahideen lobby enjoyed great success in the eighties. Between 1981 and 1984 alone, American assistance to the rebels increased from $30 million to $200 million. More significant was an ongoing pledge from Saudi Arabia to match U.S. support, a policy that effectively doubled these amounts for most of the decade.[94] By 1983 a U.S. intelligence estimate noted that rebel forces were increasing their hold on Afghanistan and that the insurgency constituted "a continuing—but bearable—drain on Soviet resources."[95]

Aside from the Soviet refusal to abandon their occupation of Afghanistan, the next most pressing obstacle to American pro-insurgency efforts was Pakistan. From 1979 onward, the pipeline for the military assistance to the rebels ran through Pakistan and the government of General Mohammed Zia-ul-Haq. In turn, the primary Pakistani agency responsible for governing aid to the mujahideen was the Inter-Services Intelligence (ISI).

The ISI acted as an intermediary between the United States and the Afghan rebels. Central Intelligence Agency field officers and Defense Department personnel provided American funding to the Pakistanis, who, in turn, purchased the weapons and shipped them to Afghanistan. The relationship allowed the U.S. government distance from direct links to the war and plausible deniability. For its own part, the arrangement also gave the ISI and the Pakistani government direct control over the tempo of aid going into Afghanistan.

In practice, the system provided Pakistani officials with ample opportunities to siphon off U.S. aid for its own purposes. More important, it allowed the ISI to designate what specific guerrilla groups would receive aid. As the war against Soviet occupation unfolded, Pakistani intelligence demonstrated a specific tendency to grant support to fundamentalist mujahideen groups at the expense of more moderate rebel leaders. One ISI officer later conceded that between two-thirds and three-quarters of military aid went to these particular factions but argued that it was military effectiveness and not ideology that drove this decision.[96]

At the time, American officials underplayed Pakistan's role as a sanctuary and support base for the insurgency. The CIA argued that it was "not essential" to the war effort. In the absence of support across the border, the agency believed that Afghan rebels could garner weapons and equipment from a Soviet-backed national army. Moreover, because the mujahideen controlled significant portions of the country, they had adequate territory for their own bases.[97]

By the second Reagan term, it was clear that the scope of insurgent operations in Afghanistan had begun to change. In March 1985 National Security Decision Directive 166 proposed a distinct shift from supporting a guerrilla war of attrition against the Soviet Union in Afghanistan to an effort designed to actively drive them out of the country. To support this new approach, the administration increased aid to Afghan insurgents. American military assistance subsequently peaked at $400 million in 1987 and 1988. Additional funding paid for an increasing array of sophisticated weapons systems. When U.S. officials traveled to Egypt to purchase arms, they considered a long list of options, from ammunition, to anti-aircraft guns, to specialized munitions for use in urban terrorism. As was the case in earlier years, one important limiting factor was the actual condition of the weapons. CIA officers found stocks of Soviet SAM-7 missiles so poorly stored that they were unusable.[98] The decision to adopt American-made Stinger missiles, first fielded in September 1986, instead of their Soviet counterparts became one of the best-known examples of the increasing tempo of the war in Afghanistan.[99]

The shift to more aggressive operations was partially successful. Soviet losses accumulated more rapidly after 1985, reflecting the growing effectiveness of Afghan insurgents. By 1989 an estimated 15,000 Soviet troops had been killed by the mujahideen and as many as 1,000 fixed and rotary wing aircraft lost. When the last Red Army departed the country in February 1989, the total cost to the Soviet treasury was sixty billion rubles, or ninety-six billion in 1990 U.S. dollars.[100] Perhaps more important, the immediate costs of the Afghan war served to highlight Soviet exhaustion at the end of the eighties and the pressing need for fundamental political, economic, and diplomatic reforms then being proposed by Mikhail Gorbachev.

American military success in Afghanistan was not without consequences for its protagonists. After the collapse of the Soviet Union in 1991, Southwest Asia continued to be a disturbingly consistent source of violence. Former Afghan guerrillas served as proxies in Pakistan's ongoing dispute with India over Kashmir. Veteran rebel fighters also appeared in the Balkans after the collapse of Yugoslavia and served in the region throughout much of the nineties. For more than a decade before 9/11, India suffered through a series of terrorist incidents that many scholars considered to be prototypes for the attacks on the United States.[101]

The United States shared responsibility for these problems. Flush with victory after the collapse of the Berlin Wall and the end of Soviet communism, American leaders gave precious little attention to a post-Soviet Afghanistan or a demobilized mujahideen. The specific consequences of this lack of vision were alarming. Although the United States and its allies had funded the purchase of hundreds of millions of dollars in weaponry, after the war there was little energy spent on recovering them. This was particularly true with respect to Stinger missiles. During the last few years of the Afghan insurgency, approximately 1,000 of these weapons were shipped to the mujahideen. According to available sources, about 340 were used between 1986 and 1989. However, after the last Soviet units departed in 1989, the rebels refused to return the remainder, forcing the CIA to purchase them back in 1991 at a cost of between $50,000 and $100,000 for each missile. Even after American field officers spent additional millions of dollars, as many as 200 Stingers remained in Afghan hands.[102]

Ascertaining the physical accountability of high-tech surface-to-air was the veritable tip of the iceberg in the post–Cold War world. American operatives managed to return most of these highly dangerous weapons systems. The same could not be said of the mundane, but probably more deadly, small arms and ammunition lavished on the Afghan insurgency. They remained behind and, as later authors would reflect, posed an even greater threat to the stability of "failed states" and "cusp nations" in the region and around the world.[103] The men trained in their use, who had outlived its usefulness at the end of the Cold War, would haunt the next decade.

Conclusions

By the end of Reagan's term, American military policy had promoted victory, but at a cost not fully comprehended at the time. The late eighties are notable for the fact that Reagan was able to achieve a form of détente that Ford or Carter could not.[104] The Berlin Wall fell. Eastern Europe was freed. Soviet communism died in 1991. However, the consequences of this vacuum rippled through the world for years. Similarly, American military power was restored to a degree not witnessed since the early sixties. Yet it became increasingly evident after the Cold War was over that military power was losing its traditional relevance.

Unfortunately, even rediscovered military prowess had its own costs. Venezuelan president Carlos Andrés Peréz provided a glimpse of this in the aftermath of the December 1989 invasion of Panama: "We have witnessed a new and unfortunate humiliation inflicted on our people with the invasion of Panama. I have the authority to say this because I have been a firm critic of the shameless Panamanian regime and have eagerly sought a Latin American consensus to find a peaceful and democratic solution in Panama. . . . Meanwhile the United States has resorted to the ancient and objectionable practice of military intervention."[105]

For a comparatively pro-American country (at the time) like Venezuela, the invasion was an indicator that U.S. political pressure and economic sanctions—in fact, American leadership in general—had failed miserably. Thus, while the invasion was comparatively easy, to many Operation Just Cause represented a blunt instrument that caused far more damage to American standing than anything the country gained through military expediency. The Panama invasion was indicative of a trend that would be reinforced less than a year later when Iraq invaded Kuwait and faced the U.S.-led coalition in Operations Desert Shield and Desert Storm. While decisive, war no longer produced clarity. The nineties presented the paradox of unparalleled American military power made irrelevant by political and social conditions it was not trained or prepared to meet.

The forces created and sponsored by the United States to prosecute low-intensity wars around the world were another legacy of the eighties. Jorge Dominguez has argued that America's pro-insurgency military policies supported neither the moral nor strategic goals of US policy. Amidst the procession of successful, U.S.-backed insurgencies, it was difficult to justify basic principles of American foreign policy—the rule of law and transparency—while supporting violent alternatives to them. Moreover, supporting armed factions within or against a nation-state was likely to fragment it and undermine the end goal of long-term stability. Thus, pro-insurgency doctrine was a failure when measured by both liberal and conservative yardsticks.[106]

This basic failure was more pronounced when the Cold War ended. Once their mission was complete, American proxies in the fight against communism were summarily abandoned in place. Nicaraguan contras suffered a fate very similar to the mujahideen in Afghanistan.[107] When the Sandinista government was successfully overcome in the 1990 national election, Nicaragua dropped off the American policy radar screen. The aftereffects of a ten-year war against Nicaragua remained, however, further contributing to the country's suffering and regional instability.[108] The impact of this abandonment was more pronounced in Afghanistan. Once the last Soviet troops departed the Friendship Bridge in 1989, the vacuum that they left behind provided ample opportunity for the Taliban to coalesce into a national government. In the final analysis, American "victory" in the Cold War would provide many of the basic elements for its next round of small wars in the nineties and beyond.

4

The First Gulf War and the New World Order

You see, as the Cold War drew to an end we saw the possibilities of a new order in which nations worked together to promote peace and prosperity.

—President George H. W. Bush, "The Possibility of a New World Order: Unlocking the Promise of Freedom," *Vital Speeches*

Someone has to make a decision here. Do we shoot someone for looting a bag of rice? Or trying to?

—Major Martin N. Stanton, "After Action Report: Wanwaylan Incident, 30 December 1992"

The final collapse of Soviet communism in 1991 offered unprecedented opportunities and dangers to the United States and the world. When the Iron Curtain fell, Eastern European markets, culture, and governance lost their old shackles. It was a story repeated throughout the globe that was, for the first time in generations, now free from the Cold War.

The world's sole remaining superpower did not escape this period of transition. As John Lewis Gaddis noted in 2005, the global upheaval that followed after 1989 caught all major powers by surprise.[1] Without the Soviet enemy, American military, diplomatic, and intelligence services collectively lost what had been their primary reason for being. The impact was perhaps most pronounced at the Pentagon.

The question confronting the military and its civilian leadership was as simple as it was profound: what purpose did power have in a dawning era of global peace?

The future of American military affairs at the end of the century was predicated on an ability to answer this question and adapt to new circumstances. Hindsight indicates that military relevance rested upon jettisoning Cold War standards in constant practice for almost fifty years. Yet, interestingly, this was not a prevailing judgment at the start of the nineties.

America's war against Iraq in 1991 briefly provided a respite from the future. In what was the largest deployment of U.S. military forces overseas since Vietnam, the remarkable success of Operation Desert Storm seemed to cement the validity of the Cold War model. Rather than alter institutional practices and doctrine already in place, American military leaders were tempted to believe that their existing conventional armed forces already possessed the flexibility necessary to prevail in the new world order.

Translating this concept into actual military readiness proved much more problematic in practice, however. The deployment of American forces to Somalia in 1992 immediately tested the limits of American military might in an environment much different that the Kuwaiti desert. Operation Restore Hope illustrated a new framework for American military policy in the new era. As U.S. forces struggled to regain order in the streets of Mogadishu, their efforts reflected two factors that became guideposts for military action in the nineties: the severe limits of domestic support for long-term deployments and, perhaps more important, the problem of fighting an enemy who did not belong to any identifiable country. How would the United States, as one author put it, conduct "war among the people"?[2]

The Bush Administration and the End of the Cold War

As president, George H. W. Bush had the apparent foreign policy credentials that his predecessor lacked, combined with a more careful and pragmatic approach to the world. With service as U.S. envoy to China and director of the Central Intelligence Agency, Bush's career reflected a degree of substance in foreign affairs that was relatively rare for presidents after 1945. Although not a peer of Dwight Eisenhower on this count, he clearly was better prepared for the world than either Lyndon Johnson or Jimmy Carter.

Bush was also a cautious leader, a style that initially suited the fluid climate of international relations at the time. Throughout his life, he had always shined more as a team player than an innovator. His acceptance of the Republican National Committee chairmanship at the height of the Watergate scandal illustrated his belief in party before personal ambition. When he appointed James Baker, former Reagan chief of staff and treasury secretary, Bush chose a trusted insider who would not challenge his worldview. National Security Advisor Brent Scowcroft also echoed his president's basic approach to foreign affairs. Reflecting on the First Gulf War in 1998, Scowcroft claimed that "from an American foreign-policymaking perspective, we sought to respond in a manner which would win broad domestic support and which could be applied universally to other crises. In international terms, we tried to establish a model for the use of force. First and foremost was the principle that aggression cannot pay. If we dealt properly with Iraq, that should go a long way toward dissuading future would-be aggressors."[3]

The statement recalled the standards set down by Caspar Weinberger more than a decade earlier. Scowcroft's stance, and that of U.S. foreign policy in general during the first Bush presidency, was built on the principle that force was allowable only after a careful series of preconditions were met. Like Weinberger Doctrine, the overall purpose of American national security policy was to mitigate risk. Unlike the policy that framed American military action in the eighties, however, it was based not on the dangers of the past (Vietnam) or the present (escalation against the Soviets), but the unknown future. The Bush Doctrine of the early nineties emphasized careful consideration rather than bold changes to the status quo. At its core, American foreign policy reflected a conservative approach that fit poorly with the rapidly changing and fluid nature of world events after 1989.[4]

The collapse of the Soviet Union provided Bush with his first major policy challenge. It also rather quickly illustrated the conceptual limits of American policy at the time. As the USSR finally began to collapse, Bush's primary emphasis was to limit potential instability rather than embark upon any dramatic initiatives. In July 1991 he presided over the START I nuclear arms reduction treaty, a leftover from the Reagan administration dedicated to addressing the already obsolescent concept of a superpower arms race. While traveling through the city of Kiev on his way back to the United States, Bush cautioned his audience against the temptation of post-Soviet radicalism: "Freedom is not the same as independence. Americans will not support those who seek independence in order to replace a far-off tyranny with local despotism. They will not aid those who promote suicidal nationalism based upon ethnic hatred."[5] While well intentioned, the message clearly was out of step with the times. Local Ukrainian leaders were taken aback by Bush's stern warning, seeing it as a message for Russian interests rather than democratic principles.[6] Conservative pundits back in the United States savaged Bush for his timidity in what became known as the "Chicken Kiev" speech.[7]

The administration's approach to national security was not wholly uniform. This was especially true with respect to Bush's Secretary of Defense Richard Cheney. Appointed after John Tower's nomination for the post failed, Cheney had no military experience entering his new position but was an experienced bureaucratic soldier with impeccable Cold War credentials. When charged with implementing a response to the Iraqi occupation of Kuwait in 1990 and 1991 (see below), Cheney proved to be an adept and aggressive advocate for the American military. However, once victory was complete, the defense secretary found little time or consensus to construct new, post-Soviet military doctrine. Instead, Cheney ironically devoted a disproportionate amount of time overseeing the deconstruction of the American military in the nineties.

In the aftermath of the Gulf War, American strategic planning was defined by the public debate over the post–Cold War "peace dividend." In part, this was the function of an American public primed to shift from defense to domestic affairs, a point driven home by an economic recession that began in 1991. The rapidity by which this overtook the Bush presidency surprised Republican political operatives. The same was not true among Democrats. James Carville's admonishment in the Clinton campaign's war room that the election was about "Change vs. More of the Same, The Economy, stupid," and "Don't forget health care," captured the conventional political wisdom of the moment.[8]

American military preparedness subsequently appeared to be an archaic concept that represented Cold War dogma rather than contemporary reality.[9] In the budget debates that followed the First Gulf War, maintenance of the existing military, much less attempts at "force modernization," became indefensible positions, particularly in the wake of endlessly repeated images of the Berlin Wall coming down or coalition armored columns entering Kuwait City. Administration arguments that the B-2 bomber and the mobile MX ICBM system were essential to the future of strategic arms control were almost universally rejected by law makers and the public alike.[10]

Military budget retrenchment thus became the standard for the nineties. As early as February 1992, the House Armed Services Committee passed resolutions that called for between $15 billion and $208 billion in real spending cuts to defense by mid-decade. Senate proposals ranged from $78 billion to $208 billion during the same period.[11] Federal legislators projected military savings into a number of potential areas, from tax cuts, to deficit reduction, to additional spending for infrastructure, education, AIDS prevention, health care, and social security.[12] Between 1990 and 1995, actual annual American defense spending decreased from $306.1 billion to $277.8 billion.[13]

Public opinion regarding foreign affairs was as problematic as the military budget debate. The American people were not reflexively opposed to the use of military force in the nineties. In fact, one of the emerging attributes of the period was greater media access to all manner of tragedies. In the aftermath of the Cold War, a constant barrage of information available on both cable television and the emerging Internet made human suffering—the student uprising in Tiananmen Square, starvation in Somalia, or "ethnic cleansing" in the Balkans—impossible for policy makers to avoid. Moreover, when Bill Clinton became president, leading an administration centered on its willingness to express empathy, the new age offered abundant opportunities to establish American commitments to basic principles like democracy and human rights.

The confluence of public concern and presidential inclination did not guarantee a blank check to defend the new world order, however. While the First Gulf War exorcised many of the ghosts of Vietnam, long-term military commitments abroad were an entirely different matter. The American public of the nineties had precise expectations regarding policy objectives and the means to accomplish them. Support for overseas military operations subsequently tended to be more finite and based on specific situations. Initial public support for the Somalia intervention in late 1992 was very high, upward of 70 percent, but limited to the parameters of a humanitarian mission. Later efforts to apprehend Mohamed Aideed and to involve the United States in nation building saw popular support collapse to 47 percent even before open warfare erupted in Mogadishu in October 1993.[14]

The context for military operations in the early nineties consequently represented an important paradox. As the sole remaining superpower, the United States appeared prepared to accept greater (and as yet unclarified) responsibilities for global stability. At the same time, the country seemed equally if not more invested in the idea that it should enjoy a hard-won "peace dividend" after the Cold War. The military's charge thus combined accomplishing highly limited objectives with almost surgical precision while avoiding the potential for quagmires in parts of the underdeveloped world that had already declined into anarchy. Bitter experience would soon prove the fallacy of these assumptions.

The Legacy of the First Gulf War

The American-led coalition war against Iraq in 1991 was an early sign that the Cold War's constraints on military action were all but gone. The invasion of Kuwait by Saddam Hussein in August 1990 resulted in the most important U.S. diplomatic and military effort since the Vietnam War. The multinational coalition that gathered in Saudi Arabia was comprised of major European allies in addition to large cohorts of Arab military forces. Overall, the size and scope of Operation Desert Shield/Storm would have been unthinkable only a handful of years earlier.[15]

For the American military, Desert Storm vindicated a generation of military reform. The rapid and unexpected success following the invasion of Kuwait in 1990 provided clear evidence that new tactics, doctrine, and weapons worked. Desert Storm was celebrated as a case study in the decisive use of both strategic and tactical airpower. The carnage inflicted by the U.S. Air Force along the Basra road seemed indicative of the potency of precision bombing.[16] The Gulf War became a starting point for advocates of "brilliant" weaponry, who saw in these new devices the ability to destroy the "strategic core" capabilities of an enemy's infrastructure, as well as for attrition against their forces on the ground. Although the Air Force was very careful to offer caveats regarding the actual effectiveness of the air campaign—the goal of achieving a 50 percent attrition rate for the Iraqi army was never achieved—policy makers endorsed the concept of decisive air power.[17]

The history of small unit operations and specials forces during the First Gulf War was a much less auspicious story. As CENTCOM commander, General Norman Schwarzkopf resisted using special forces because he believed they would interfere with rather than supplement conventional operations. Consequently, he placed special operations assets directly under his control in CENTCOM, stripping them away from Special Operations Command Central (SOCCENT), the theater special operations command. For much of Operation Desert Shield, Schwarzkopf forbade special forces units from crossing into Iraq. He was also very slow in scheduling the deployment of other specialized units to the theater of operations. As a result, civil affairs and psychological operations detachments—which proved highly useful during Desert Storm—arrived very late to the Persian Gulf.[18]

CENTCOM also took great pains to carefully delineate the special forces mission into four areas: coalition liaison and warfare support, special reconnaissance, coordination of combined special operations area forces, and training.[19] Each conformed to the basic parameters of the AirLand Battle Doctrine. An additional mission, the search for Iraqi ground-launch missiles, the so-called Scud hunt, was not introduced until later in the war.

The coalition liaison and warfare support mission hearkened back to the days of the Vietnam War when American special forces advisers teams worked directly with indigenous military units. During Desert Shield/Storm, U.S. Navy SEALS contributed a twenty-man element and a Special Boat Unit that eventually included 260 personnel. For the most part, however, the Army was primarily responsible for special forces operations in Saudi Arabia and, later, Kuwait. During the U.S. deployment to the Persian Gulf, 109 detachments from 5th Special Forces Group were present in five Arab divisions within the coalition, providing instruction in areas that ranged from basic rifle marksmanship to airmobile movement.[20]

The special forces training mission was more rudimentary. American advisers became wholly responsible for reconstructing Kuwaiti ground forces prior to Desert Storm. Special operations instructors trained four brigades of light infantry, an armored brigade, a motorized infantry brigade, and a special forces battalion. The latter effort was limited by the fact that the unit initially attracted only sixty volunteers.[21]

"Special reconnaissance" occupied an increasingly important role as CENTCOM began the transition from Desert Shield to Desert Storm in late 1990. Special operations teams sought out information on the enemy order of battle, as well as Iraqi army main supply routes for later air strikes. Highway 8 was a particular target of interest due to its value as a main artery for Republican Guard counterattacks against the impending coalition invasion. Long-range reconnaissance missions proved difficult to execute, however. Special forces teams inserted into the Iraqi countryside were often immediately spotted by the local population and were extracted by air, sometimes under fire.[22]

"Direct action" missions were a variation of special reconnaissance intended to prepare the way for conventional forces. In these instances, special forces units marked either high-value targets, such as Iraqi radar sites, for destruction by the coalition air units or attacked these themselves. When Iraq began launching missiles against Israel, special operations units actively sought out Scud units for destruction.[23]

In essence, Desert Storm was the last great hurrah for special forces based on the traditional Cold War model. This was most apparent in the teams scattered throughout Saudi Arabia that were advising and building what were mostly conventional Arab military forces. Yet, even within the limited scope of this model, a number of key special operations units found themselves largely excluded from the Gulf War by CENTCOM. There were, for example, no direct-action missions designated for the Army rangers as part of Desert Storm. A plan to rescue U.S. diplomats who remained behind in Kuwait City (Operation Pacific Wind) was quietly abandoned after they were released in December 1990. Similarly, the Army special forces did not receive permission to create a "guerrilla warfare operational area" or attack high value military and civilian targets despite seemingly ideal sources of potential recruits in Kurdistan and the restive region of southern Iraq. Both CENTCOM and the White House opposed this mission in deference to a short, decisive war. Other command resistance to special operations is more difficult to explain. Throughout the fall of 1990, Schwarzkopf and his senior commandeers initially equivocated on the use of psychological operations forces in the Persian Gulf, specifically the 4th Psychological Operations Group. However, it was not until very late in Desert Shield that "psyops" units were directly integrated into both air and ground war planning. During the buildup to Desert Storm, they were responsible for dropping 29 million leaflets over Iraqi lines. As the ground campaign unfolded, it became readily apparent that a combination of threats and enticements effectively prompted the surrender of thousands of Iraqi soldiers.[24]

It was clear in the aftermath of Operation Desert Storm that the "big war" had overshadowed small unit operations in their entirety. In the early planning stages of the Kuwait invasion, the tacit inclination toward conventional operations was absolute. Moreover, the relatively short span of the American deployment and subsequent combat also undercut any long-term investment in constructing relationships with coalition military partners. When the "hundred hour war" ended, troops redeployed to their home stations around the world. Relationships forged during the short months in 1990 and 1991 were largely lost. Insofar as Iraq proper was concerned, the Bush administration policy that limited Desert Storm to the liberation of Kuwait stymied conventional and unconventional operations alike. Although the White House publicly endorsed the idea of a popular revolt in Iraq to topple Saddam Hussein, it offered little in the way of military support.[25]

In a larger and more important strategic sense, the First Gulf War endorsed a conventional wisdom regarding post–Cold War deterrence and its military foundation. When George H. W. Bush and his national security adviser, Brent Scowcroft, claimed that the value of the war was its ability to dissuade "would-be aggressors," they believed that appropriate military power would be adequate to promote American principles and interests. For all intents, Desert Storm presented a seamless application of the same principles used against Soviet communism to new challengers to U.S. hegemony. Unbeknownst, or perhaps unrealized at the time, was the potentially open-ended nature of this commitment, reflecting as it did the belief that American power in the new world order could be applied universally to all challenges. Regardless,

Desert Storm established a trajectory in American policy that vastly underestimated the degree to which global instability would grow and how tentative the application of military power would become.[26]

The Nature of World Conflict in the Nineties

As the nineties unfolded, there developed a gradually hardening consensus among policy makers and academics that the absence of structure created by the Cold War ultimately led to global upheaval. What Steven Kobrin described in 1998 as the "deintegration" of the world had created renewed forms of conflict based on race, religion, ethnicity, access to resources, and a host of other accumulating problems no longer held in check by the threat of thermonuclear escalation.[27] Jessica Matthews noted in 1997 that of the nearly 100 conflicts fought after the end of the Cold War, nearly all were intrastate affairs. Lacking the superstructure of bipolar power or the traction afforded by communist and anti-communism ideology, national allegiances in many parts of the world collapsed along fault lines determined by blood ties or religious beliefs.[28] In the nineties, small wars became the rule rather than the exception.

There were many sources of this new world disorder. Primary among them was ethnicity. Samuel Huntington argued that in periods of drastic change and uncertainty, civilizations gravitate toward more fundamental sources of identity: language, history, customs, and local institutions. Huntington believed that cultural characteristics were "less mutable and hence less easily compromised than political and economic ones."[29] The penchant for ethnic identity was also an assertion of self-determination after the demand for assimilation or conformity was removed. Self-determination originally had been enshrined in the United Nations charter as a means to preserve the sovereignty of the nation-state after World War II. However, as Daniel P. Moynihan pointed out in his 1993 work *Pandaemonium: Ethnicity in International Politics*, ethnicity had devolved into a destructive starting point that demanded local identity at the cost of national stability.[30]

In this context, the 1991 Gulf War was important not only for restoring Kuwaiti territorial boundaries; it also normalized international intervention to preserve ethnic sovereignty when a multinational force deployed to assist Kurdish refugees. Subsequent NATO intervention in the former Yugoslavia accomplished a similar task.[31]

Religion complemented ethnicity as a cause for conflict and as a means to resist the centrifugal forces of modern socioeconomic and political change. Faith was fundamental to identity and stability in a world with fewer barriers to cultural and moral intrusions. In an effort to reshape the post–Cold War world, the Vatican attempted to foster collective religious efforts for peace. These largely failed to produce a consensus, much less collective action. As Western religion foundered, non-Western alternatives grew. Martin van Creveld observed in 1991 why Islam was the fastest growing religion in the world: "While there are many reasons for this, perhaps it would not be so far fetched to say that its very militancy is one factor behind this spread. By this I do not mean to say merely that Islam strives to achieve its aims by fighting; rather that people in many parts of the world—including downtrodden groups in the developed world—are finding Islam attractive precisely because it is prepared to fight."[32] Fundamentalist Islam in particular offered a response and a haven to encroaching modernity that drew boundaries for neither countries nor mores. Consequently, a new Iron Curtain between Christianity and Islam emerged in which, to use Huntington's term, the "fault lines" between countries were drawn by faith and not politics.[33]

The newest version of the information age accelerated conflicts over ethnicity and religion. The rapidly expanding Internet, not ubiquitous but novel at the time, confronted local tradition with the imminent diffusion of alien ideas and technology. Indigenous cultures subsequently became islands in a sea of intruding global communication. The proximate ties that bound many societies together either eroded or failed under the onslaught of a homogenous global culture and the pressures created by worldwide economies of scale.[34] Social, religious, or ethnic identity, as measured by centuries of practice, shrank under their combined weight.[35] One author in 1998 compared the time to the Middle Ages, when change required individuals to assume overlapping loyalties to region, king, church, and family.[36] Those who refused to succumb to this division became the new recruits in the small wars of the nineties.

The cumulative effect of cultural and religious conflict was the increasing frequency of disruptions to life and stability as the decade wore on. Samuel Huntington agreed that the primary actors in the world remained nation-states, but added the important caveat that the "fault lines between civilizations will be the battle lines of the future."[37] Nativism and xenophobia became a new common element of conflict. The Western world did not escape the trend. The visceral response in Scotland that followed the premier of the movie *Braveheart* (1995), the Los Angeles riots, and the amount of vitriol spilled over illegal immigration during the 1992 U.S. presidential election covered a spectrum from absurd to tragic.[38]

The final product of all these trends was what Francis Fukuyama described as "the end of history."[39] It was a time defined by profound pessimism regarding the failure of modern political, economic, and intellectual institutions to meet expectations for prosperity and security. It marked the return of reactionary fundamentalism based on misguided nostalgia for a past that did not exist. Even in cases where liberal democracy spread, Fukuyama saw the paradox of new discontent expressed in a more tolerant environment.[40] Robert Kaplan was even less sanguine than Fukuyama, describing a future comprised of the internecine conflict between haves and have-nots. He noted in 1994 that "while a minority of the human population will be, as Francis Fukuyama would put it, sufficiently sheltered so as to enter a 'post-historical' realm . . . an increasingly large number of people will be stuck in history . . . where attempts to rise out of poverty, cultural dysfunction, and ethnic strife will be doomed by a lack of water to drink, soil to till, and space to survive in."[41]

Beyond their diverse expression of instability, these multiple sources of conflict cumulatively posed an increased threat to U.S. national security interests after the Cold War. Failed states in possession of tools left over from the old conflict—nuclear, biological, and chemical arms—increased the risk of proliferation in an environment governed by fewer restraints. The first attack on the World Trade Center in 1993 and the release of nerve gas into the Tokyo subway system by domestic terrorists two years later indicated that this was not simply a perceived threat, but one prepared to evolve into ever more dangerous forms.[42]

Ironically, these weapons of mass destruction were not a primary cause for concern. In the nineties, American policy makers also confronted the prospect that weaponry from the lowest part of the technology scale posed the greatest threat. Massive stocks of conventional weapons left over from the Cold War, particularly small arms, constituted the most disruptive element of the new world order. The period witnessed a radical change in the nature of military and civilian casualties. Where approximately 5 percent of casualties in World War I were civilian, by the late eighties, estimates indicated that the percentage stood closer to 90 percent.[43] Small arms accounted for the vast majority of nearly 4 million deaths in global conflicts in the nineties.[44] Michael Klare described the time as "The Kalashnikov Age," noting that "when Charles Taylor invaded Liberia, he unleashed the most deadly combat system of the current epoch; the adolescent human male equipped with an AK-47 assault rifle."[45]

A simple reality in the post–Cold War world was the fact that relatively poorly equipped forces were now capable of creating havoc. The arsenals necessary to accomplish task were widely available. Enormous Cold War–era weapons stocks remained scattered around the world long after the Berlin Wall fell. Academic sources estimated that as many as 125 million automatic weapons were available worldwide in 1999. Even with this enormous reservoir, global weapons sales continued.[46] It was a small wonder that in 1995 UN Secretary General Boutros Boutros-Ghali called for "micro-disarmament."[47]

A prime focus of this collective global discontent was the United States and its interests. Ralph Peters observed in 1999 that, in the midst of global torment, people began to seek out the myth of a lost "golden age" that would provide stability. This search became the root source of religious and ethnic revivalism and their diametric opposite, a future defined by modernity.[48] America was central to both concepts, for the former in terms of what it threatened, for the latter in the unreachable example that it demonstrated to an increasingly poor and crowded world.[49]

In more practical terms, the world's sole remaining superpower confronted the simple reality that there was a shrinking array of modern governments able to function for their intended purposes. Built upon a foundation of transferable technical skills, truly participatory political systems, and a common social purpose, many Western countries prospered in the post-1991 era. Most countries around the world, however, did not. States were rendered incompetent or impotent by demographic pressures, the collapse of resource bases, backward educational and economic systems, and the proliferation of weapons left behind by the Cold War. The nature of global power in the nineties was consequently much different than it had been in previous decades. Lacking a U.S. or Soviet framework, the first tier of nations comprised modern, prosperous, and stable countries, wherein economic power was the primary attribute of global status. The second tier of nations existed on the "cusp" between governability and collapse. The third tier, or "Third World," under this newly defined hierarchy, comprised what Steven Metz described as "the ungovernables."[50]

Moreover, it was clear that America would not exercise uncontested power in the new era. By the outset of the nineties, nonstate entities were increasingly important actors in international affairs. Nongovernmental organizations (NGOs) with greater access to information over the World Wide Web were a particularly important addition. Near the end of the decade, the nonprofit Association for Progressive Communications provided 50,000 NGOs in 133 countries with access to the Internet for the price of a local call.[51] Beyond the NGO, other international entities appeared ready to fill the vacuum of traditional power. Multinational corporations spread into previously uncharted areas of the world after the disappearance of old Cold War tripwires and exploited new global economic opportunities. Trade agreements such as NAFTA (1993) established a new standard in the nineties, one dedicated to removing national trade barriers that retarded "neoliberal" development.[52] Unrestricted investment subsequently flowed to pursue profit in dangerous areas of the world that offered new markets or, more important, access to abundant natural resources. Proven reserves of oil and natural gas drew investors to Saharan Africa and Central Asia, neither of which could be described as stable at the time. Regardless, overall trends were clear. Investment grew in the forty-four poorest countries from an average of approximately $1 billion in 1987–1992 to almost $3 billion by 1998.[53]

More important to American security interests was the emergence of other global actors not intent on providing government oversight or legitimate economic growth. Criminal organizations flourished in the new world order. In Eastern Europe, the breakdown of communist police states opened the doors to organized crime. NAFTA proved a mixed blessing as open borders facilitated both narcotics and weapons trafficking. Whatever their location or activity, criminal syndicates benefited from ready access to technology, weapons, and First World affluence.[54] During the nineties, a number of these organizations became powerful enough to openly challenge some national governments.

Overall, both weak and powerful countries struggled to find their proper place in the post–Cold War era. On one end of the spectrum, "cusp nations" and failed states fought not for relevance but for survival as small wars challenged or overcame their authority. For the United States, the dilemma was different. At the outset of the nineties, American policy makers faced a new series of demands for growth, stability, and all the broadly held global expectations of peace that followed the Soviet collapse.[55] Divining a clear and tangible means to achieve these goals would bedevil the White House and, more specifically, the Pentagon, when it became increasingly apparent that the new world order was anything but orderly.

Strategic Priorities in the New World Order

During his only term in office, George H. W. Bush had the opportunity to bask in the afterglow of victory twice. The decline and fall of the old Soviet enemy and the consequent, clear-cut use of American military power in the Persian Gulf appeared, for all intents and purposes, to be harbingers of a new future. This hope was reflected in Bush's somewhat glib prediction regarding American power in 1991:

> Twice this century, a dream born on the battlefields of Europe died after the shooting stopped. The dream of a world in which major powers worked together to ensure peace; to settle their disputes through cooperation, not confrontation. Today a transformed Europe stands closer than ever before to its free and democratic destiny. At long last, Europe is moving forward, moving toward a new world of hope.
>
> At the same time, we and our European allies have moved beyond containment to a policy of active engagement in a world no longer driven by Cold War tensions and animosities. You see, as the Cold War

> drew to an end we saw the possibilities of a new order in which nations worked together to promote peace and prosperity. I'm not talking here of a blueprint that will govern the conduct of nations or some supernatural structure or institution. The new world order does not mean surrendering our national sovereignty or forfeiting our interests. It really describes a responsibility imposed by our successes. It refers to new ways of working with other nations to deter aggression and to achieve stability, to achieve prosperity and, above all, to achieve peace. . . .
>
> It springs from hopes for a world based on a shared commitment among nations large and small, to a set of principles that undergird our relations. Peaceful settlements of disputes, solidarity against aggression, reduced and controlled arsenals, and just treatment of all peoples.
>
> We also recognized that the Cold War's end didn't deliver us into an era of perpetual peace. As old threats recede, new threats emerge. The quest for the new world order is, in part, a challenge to keep the dangers of disorder at bay.[56]

Bush, as well as many of his fellow countrymen, saw a time defined by the ascendancy of liberal democracy and free-market capitalism. Both embodied a future universalism under American leadership, a revisited Pax Americana even greater than that which defined the post–World War II era. Democracy and capitalism, as Francis Fukuyama reflected, were, if not the best systems available, at least the ones that had survived where communism, fascism, and socialism had not.[57] However, as much as he believed in the triumph of fundamental American principles, Bush remained cognizant of pragmatic limits to U.S. power. His controversial decision to halt coalition forces short of the Iraqi border in 1991 and preserve the Hussein regime for the sake of a regional balance of power expressed the true limits of his new world order.[58]

In fact, Bush had already recognized these limits long before the First Gulf War. In March 1989, as part of its initial review of military strategy, the administration acknowledged that the factors that had justified and supported U.S. defense policy were already diminishing in relevance. However, the report also noted that "it would be reckless to dismantle our military strength and the policies that have helped to make the world less dangerous, and foolish to assume that all dangers have disappeared or that any apparent diminution is irreversible."[59]

Thus, despite the obvious decline of the Soviet Union, the administration's focus remained on potential conventional threats. Both the Pentagon and the national security community retained what was essentially a Cold War outlook. After 1989, official documents reflect a consistent, almost ingrained conceptual framework that identified nation-states as the primary threat to U.S. security interests. Policy guidance regarding intelligence capabilities as well as counterintelligence and security countermeasures remained on very familiar ground. American strategists focused on traditional political, military, and economic sources of information and the potential threats posed by "foreign intelligence sources."[60] Policy debates and decisions moved in a similar direction. The Bush foreign policy team was notable for its willingness to pursue a series of potential strategic threats left over from the Cold War. The administration attempted to finish the strategic arms reduction treaty (START), pursue international nonproliferation agreements, and reduce conventional forces in Europe.

The attraction of humanitarian relief stood separately and in contrast to traditional strategic planning. Again, the First Gulf War served as a starting point. While the conflict clearly embellished American confidence in its military power, it also had created a concurrent disaster for the people of Iraq and the surrounding area.[61] The fate of over nearly 2 million refugees, primarily Kurds in northern Iraq displaced into Turkey and Iran, depended on the outcome of the war when they rebelled against Baghdad and soon found themselves bearing the brunt of Iraqi retaliation alone.[62] In the aftermath of Desert Storm, American officials estimated that as many as 400 to 1,000 refugees, mainly children, were dying each day, primarily as a result of unsanitary conditions and disease.[63]

Rather quickly, particularly within the National Security Council, humanitarian relief also became conflated with U.S. strategic goals in the Persian Gulf. NSC officials saw in any proposed mission to northern Iraq potential leverage to influence Iraqi compliance with postwar disarmament and other wartime treaty provisions.[64] Moreover, in simple domestic political terms, a relief mission to support the beleaguered Kurds had the added advantage of assuaging domestic criticism that the Bush administration halted the war too early. Consequently, as a result of genuine concerns over the fate of the Kurds and clear opportunism, Operation Provide Comfort was launched in early April 1991. Interestingly, once the Defense Department assumed primary responsibility for the mission, it became clear that neither the Pentagon nor the National Security Council understood the exact methodology of humanitarian relief. Harry Rowan, the Assistant Secretary of Defense for International Security Affairs, confessed in a March 1991 memorandum that the mission was "a new drill for us" and was not exactly clear on the source of funding available or its total amount.[65] By the time the actual mission began in April, the Department of Defense had determined that it was authorized to spend an initial amount of $25 million for "disaster assistance" from a $75 million appropriation made for that purpose each year under the Foreign Assistance Act. Most of the funding would go toward rudimentary supplies such as military rations, basic medicines, and tents.[66] After other federal agencies made their own separate contributions, approximately $53 million was designated for Provide Comfort. In the first ten days of the operation, Western military units airlifted 1,350 tons of supplies to refugee camps along the southern Turkish border.[67]

From the start, the relief mission was a military operation with the United States, Great Britain, and France providing the bulk of air transport and units on the ground. However, the Bush administration's intent was to have as many countries participate as possible. Defense Department planners placed specific emphasis on countries that could support their own military deployments. According to a joint State-Defense communiqué issued on 18 April 1991: "We are not/not looking for dozens of small, unsupported, unfunded units from around the world. Rather, we want a dozen or so countries, primarily from Europe, with a minimum of one or two each from Asia, Africa, and the Americas to contribute to the operation."[68] Special emphasis was placed on engineering, medical, and civil affairs units, as well as military police. The Defense Department asked specifically for light infantry to provide security in a mountainous region that made the use of heavy vehicles and armor next to impossible. Eventually, more than thirty countries contributed forces to the mission, although the 12,000 personnel deployed by the United States were by far the largest contingent.[69]

A second explicit component of Operation Provide Comfort was the United States' insistence that it become a civilian-led operation once the refugees' immediate needs were met. Numerous organizations such as the International Red Cross/Red Crescent, as well as Oxfam, UNICEF, the World Food Program, and Medecins sans Frontieres (Doctors without Borders) were already active in Iraq and Turkey. The expressed intent, therefore, was to have military units survey sites for refugee camps, initiate operations, and leave longer-term management of relief and resettlement to civilian agencies. On 7 June, slightly more than two months into the operation, the United Nations High Commissioner for Refugees formally took over responsibility for the mission from the military.[70]

American special forces units played a key role in both halves of the relief mission. The entire 10th Special Forces Group was deployed to the Kurdish region in support of Provide Comfort. Special forces soldiers were particularly useful in establishing and maintaining contacts with tribal leaders ("agas") and opening up a dialogue with the many civilian NGOs that were also actively involved in the relief effort. The unique linguistic and cultural skills possessed by 10th Group detachments proved critical in winning local trust in the early stages of their deployment. A situation report from the relief task force captured the spirit of the mission on 17 April: "By providing the refugees with ample and timely delivery of lifesaving goods, a confidence has been established that should grow through the next few days. If so, the air delivery will progress more rapidly and the threat of accidental loss of life through chaos and panic will significantly diminish."[71]

The latter relationship with civilian agencies was particularly important to the extent that they took a long-term view necessary for recovery and offered the American military an exit strategy that would allow military operations to be finite in nature.[72] To this end, Provide Comfort was completely successful. Coalition military forces began redeployment in July 1991, less than four months after the operation had begun.

Taken as a whole, Operation Provide Comfort was a success that established a precedent for future U.S. humanitarian relief missions in the nineties. The product of a collective effort with finite objectives, it responded to human suffering on par with what Desert Storm had been to unsanctioned aggression. The Kurdish relief mission reinforced the understanding that standing forces had the ability to address post–Cold War upheaval without long-term commitments or debilitating political controversies at home. Just as the United States was entering the new world order, it appeared that it possessed the proper doctrine and know-how necessary to accomplish great things.

Maintenance of a limited commitment did not necessarily mean that Kurdistan was trouble-free after 1991. American intelligence reports from May 1991 indicated that the Hussein regime was moving clearly and decisively to settle Arab populations in the portions of northern Iraq vacated by Kurds. It was clear that Baghdad intended its own version of "ethnic cleansing" before the term became popular in the Balkans a few years later. Perhaps more important, the Iraqi government intended to keep a firm grip on crude oil fields located around the city of Kirkuk.[73] As much as Provide Comfort illustrated the potential assistance American leadership could render, its clear limitations were a signpost to the significant complexities inherent in later humanitarian relief missions.

American Military Reforms after Desert Storm

In the aftermath of Operation Desert Storm, the American military as an institution was brimming with a sense of confidence unrealized for a generation. There was a clear note of triumphalism contained in both the public statements issued by American military leaders and in postwar studies of Desert Storm. CENTCOM commander Norman Schwarzkopf's press conferences were notable as celebrations of the "bravura performance" of American arms, particularly its guided weapons systems.[74] When the Department of the Army produced its official history of the conflict in 1993, it saw fit to call it *Certain Victory: The United States Army in the Gulf War.* William DePuy expressed this new conventional wisdom in the following terms: "there is emerging a distinctive American style of warfare, a style that is essentially joint, drawing on the unique capabilities of each service via centralized planning and decentralized execution. This jointness, plus an amalgam of surprise, discriminate use of overwhelming force, high operating tempo, and exploitation of advanced technology, has led to a whole new order of military effectiveness. This is the 'revolution in military affairs.'"[75]

The consensus that the U.S. military had reached an unparalleled aptitude in the art of war was not universal, however. Many saw post-1991 celebrations as premature at best. One officer, Lieutenant Colonel Robert Leonard, spoke candidly when he stated that "the U.S. Army that led coalition forces to success was not a good army. It was simply better than its opponent."[76] Leonard and others warned that, in the aftermath of public adulation, needed scrutiny of the many problems and mistakes experienced in Kuwait might slip away. For example, the brevity of the war could not mask the basic problems of fighting a large-scale mobile conflict in terrain without reliable roads. Despite months of preparations, transportation shortages affected logistics during both Desert Shield and Desert Storm, particularly with respect to sea lift capability for heavy weapons systems and bulk cargo. So-called smart weaponry did indeed perform well, but difficulties with unit intermingling during the war had resulted in avoidable friendly fire casualties. Nor did CENTCOM commander Norman Schwarzkopf escape attention. Although celebrated by the public and the American media, Schwarzkopf's penchant for abusing his subordinates and his attempts at micromanaging tactical operations reflected poorly on "the revolution in military affairs."[77]

Most of all, the naysayers following in the wake of Desert Storm warned against hubris and the onset of "victory disease," both of which might lead to complacency and institutional inertia.[78] Some basic realities supported this conclusion. Postwar studies of Desert Storm revealed many of the same conclusions produced in the aftermath of the 1973 Yom Kippur War. The war against Iraq made it very clear that the same form of overwhelming industrial attrition America had brought to bear in previous conflicts was no longer a supportable option. To be truly effective, future American military doctrine had to integrate the near-term lethality of "brilliant" weaponry with the significant logistical preparations necessary to mobilize and deploy troops, factors that placed a premium on forces in place.[79] Moreover, in future wars

American military leaders had to be cognizant of the fact that despite the decisive nature of tactical operations in Desert Storm, "war termination" was a much more complicated process that involved economic and political stabilization operations after fighting ceased. The First Gulf War and Operation Provide Comfort had moved the issue of properly executing an exit strategy from theory to actual practice. It seemed that military units responsible for postwar stability operations—special forces primary among them—might gain new traction within the Defense Department as a result.[80]

Work on the 1993 revision of *FM 100–5: Operations* reflected the internal institutional struggle to translate the lessons of Desert Storm and Provide Comfort into a viable doctrine. The manual's wording illustrates the difficulties of expressing military action in a post-Soviet environment. Hairsplitting distinctions abound, between "synchronization" and "simultaneity," for example, to explain an integrated approach to combined arms warfare, a type of "AirLand Battle Plus."[81] The result was overcomplicated and cumbersome. The difference between an "area of operations" and "battlespace" may have made sense in a clinical staff environment, but it translated poorly for real-world, operational use at the platoon and company level.[82] The manual represented more a list of principles created by a well-meaning but disconnected community of academics than tools useful for a rapidly moving, modern battlefield. One innovation that *FM 100–5* added was a new category of military action that fell short of conventional war or other types of combat: operations other than war (OOTW).[83] The new classification focused on a host of new missions then being adopted by the United States and its military, from disaster relief to peacekeeping and counterterrorism operations. They also included:

Noncombatant evacuation operations
Arms control
Support to domestic civil authorities
Humanitarian assistance and disaster relief
Security assistance
Nation assistance
Support to counterdrug operations
Combating terrorism

Peacekeeping operations
Peace enforcement
Show of force
Support for insurgencies and counterinsurgencies
Attacks and raids

Policy makers in the Pentagon expected that the bulk of these new missions would fall to conventional units, although some seemed ideally fitted for American special forces. In many respects, *FM 100–5* was a small godsend for Special Operations Command, which had undergone extensive budget cuts after the First Gulf War and struggled for relevance after 1991. Once *Operations* was published in 1993, American special forces adopted a laundry list of new missions to bolster the already formidable roster contained in the manual. "Counter Proliferation" and "Ecology and Biodiversity" were added in 1994. "Humanitarian Demining" appeared in 1996. The counterproliferation mission became particularly important after the Soviet downfall, when U.S. officials rightfully worried about the spread of technology and weapon's grade nuclear material outside the former communist bloc.[84]

Unfortunately, even as the Defense Department recognized the potentially diffuse nature of post–Cold War military conflict, doctrine proved no clearer with respect to conventional units. *FM 100–5* attempted to provide guidance for small unit operations in this new environment, recognizing that "a diverse group of forces—military units, international and national relief groups, police and fire departments, local government agencies, and others—integrate their efforts and cooperate to achieve specific objectives."[85] Clearly, a new doctrine reflected the military's experience with NGOs and other elements during Operation Provide Comfort and other "war termination" efforts. However, recognizing a need did not necessarily translate into a command structure willing or able to effectively include civilian interests that were often antagonistic to the United States or its military into an effective plan. *FM 100–5* recognized this dilemma: "In such operations, other government agencies will often have the lead. Commanders may answer to a civilian chief, such as an ambassador, or may themselves employ the resources of a civilian agency. Command arrangements may be only loosely defined, causing commanders to seek an atmosphere of cooperation rather than command authority to achieve objectives by unity of effort. Military commanders consider how their actions contribute to initiatives that are also political, economic, and psychological in nature."[86] With that rather vague flourish, *Operations* acknowledged the dilemma facing the post–Cold War America military. It offered no guidance as to how an actual commander on the ground might successfully resolve fundamental problems confronting civil-military cooperation or relief missions as a whole. The real-world viability of U.S. doctrine would soon be tested in the midst of another human tragedy on the Horn of Africa in 1992.

The Somalia Intervention

Operation Provide Comfort provided a precedent that later prompted U.S. intervention in a worse humanitarian disaster in eastern Africa. American interest in the area preceded the First Gulf War and the Bush administration by decades. Within the logic of the Cold War, Somalia and the surrounding region were valuable for their port facilities and access to the Persian Gulf.[87] Arms, advice, and interference from both Moscow and Washington followed and became a normal component of local affairs for years.

Once the Cold War ended, the superpowers departed but left behind a formidable arsenal with little to offset its potential impact on stability. When Somalia collapsed after the overthrow of the Mohammed Siad Barre dictatorship in January 1991, a functioning national government ceased to exist.[88] Local warlords, armed with potent stocks of primarily Soviet bloc weapons, filled in the vacuum, but only to the extent that they defended their clan or tribal affiliations. In truth, chaos reigned supreme.

Initially, the tragedy garnered little attention outside the academic community. This situation soon changed, however, when the unfolding crisis became a worldwide sensation in the Western media, which descended upon Somalia to record human suffering for emerging cable news networks.[89] In this context, the problem was less about a failed state than the immediate needs of millions on the brink of starvation. Between 1991–1992, approximately 300,000 Somalis died of famine and an additional 1.5 million remained at risk of the same fate. Overall, nearly 4.5 million suffered from severe malnutrition and disease, as many as 70 percent of all Somalis, according to the International Committee of the Red Cross.[90]

As this message spread, framed in both figures and horrific images, demands at home and abroad for U.S. intervention grew. In a letter to national security adviser Brent Scowcroft, the vice president of the interim Somali government described the situation as "hell on earth."[91] The United Nations leadership also vented its frustration to Washington. Although the UN had successfully brokered a ceasefire between the major factions in March 1992, it could do little to reconstruct order. "Technicals"—a generic term for the armed militias controlled by various Somali factions—regularly looted relief supplies.[92] Writing to George Bush in November 1992, UN General Secretary Boutros Boutros-Ghali noted that

> in the absence of a government or governing authority capable of maintaining law order, Somali "authorities" at all levels of society compete for anything of value in the country. Armed threats and killings often decide the outcome. Looting and banditry are rife. Amidst this chaos, the international aid provided by the United Nations and voluntary agencies has become a major (and in some areas only) source of income, and as such is the target of all the "authorities," who may sometimes be no more than two or three bandits with guns.[93]

Someone, according to the general secretary, needed to break the "cycle of extortion and blackmail."[94]

These same calls echoed through the halls of Congress and the White House that fall season. Letters demanding American action in Somalia arrived from constituencies that stretched from the Northeastern Pennsylvania Synod and the American Jewish Committee to the Black Business Association of Los Angeles.[95] Congressional voices shortly thereafter joined the chorus. Senator Carl Levin (D-MI) called for "creative solutions and immediate action." The House Select Committee on Hunger noted in December that "we cannot just stand by and wash our hands of the horror in Somalia. Knowing that this is the most pressing humanitarian tragedy in the world, we feel it is imperative that the U.S. do its utmost, in concert with other countries willing to try again, to push for negotiations for at least a partial ceasefire."[96] Newt Gingrich (R-GA) offered his strong support for a relief mission but counseled the president that "immediate contact with the local population should be done by other countries, particularly Third World countries whose troops are more used to dealing with these situations and who are more likely to blend into the population." He worried, however, that "we will end up in a quagmire without end, on a constantly changing mission."[97]

The case for global intervention was further bolstered by a number of key precedents. One of the important latent effects of the 1991 Gulf War was the fact that military intervention in the furtherance of UN goals became normalized policy. UN Resolution 688 (5 April 1991) allowed for member nations to intervene in cases of humanitarian need. The policy, applied at the time to Kurdish and Shiite refugees in Iraq, paved the way for action in Africa the following year.[98] On 5 December 1992, UN Resolution 794 was adopted for action in the case of Somalia. When Operation Restore Hope was launched, it had a clear mandate at home and within the international community.

Still, when Bush administration officials began planning for the Somalia intervention, it did not assume that because the UN Security Council had reached an accord on action, an international mandate would translate into an open-armed welcome once U.S. forces arrived in country.[99] Official guidelines for the U.S. contingent were established in National Security Directive 74, "Peacekeeping and Emergency Humanitarian Relief Policy," on 24 November 1992. These guidelines dictated placement of American combat, engineering, and logistical units at UN disposal. The American military made significant contributions to strategic air transportation, communications, and medical support. However, Bush made it equally clear that individual nations would determine the exact degree of their own participation in the relief mission.[100]

The United States joined the Unified Task Force (UNITAF) at the end of 1992 and was one of forty-two countries that eventually deployed more than 20,000 troops for the relief mission. According to the UN mandate, they were authorized to use "all necessary means" to secure the delivery of humanitarian aid to Somalis.[101] Publicly, Bush repeatedly claimed that mission objectives were limited in nature. America's primary goal was to "create security conditions which will permit the feeding of starving Somali people and allow the transfer of this security function to the UN peacekeeping force."[102]

The 1st Marine Expeditionary Force and elements of the 10th Mountain Division were the first major contingent of American forces to arrive in Somalia.[103] In the early stages of the operation, conventional units secured Mogadishu and the basic infrastructure—port facilities, roads, and warehouses—necessary to distribute relief supplies. Throughout, American forces appeared whenever they could in large numbers as a massive demonstration of force. Lieutenant Colonel Tom O'Leary, who commanded "Team Tiger," a 700-man Marine unit bound for Baidoa, Somalia, with relief supplies, told *Time:* "You have to use overwhelming force. That's the only way you can go in smiling and waving."[104] Thus, the assumption followed that Somali gunmen, when confronted with an overt display of American and coalition firepower, would simply surrender the field to UNITAF forces.

American special operations forces were deeply involved in Operation Restore Hope. They provided early reconnaissance of landing and deployment sites, gathered intelligence on enemy movements, and established contacts with tribal leaders. Special forces psychological operations teams were also dispatched to broadcast UN intentions to the population and counter claims by local warlords that the relief effort was designed to recolonize the country or desecrate the Somali religion.[105] In the later stages of Restore Hope, special operations units interdicted illegal arms shipments and assisted coalition forces in confiscating large caches of arms, including heavy weapons.[106]

Conventional troops proved adequate to the task of protecting the humanitarian relief network and distribution of aid. Unfortunately, the broader problem of stability in Somalia made the mission more tenuous than originally recognized. In December 1992, the NSC received reports that after U.S. and French forces delivered relief supplies to the town of Baidoa, gunmen began immediately looting them.[107] Despite these reverses, high-ranking American officials were confident that coalition forces would prevail. A January 1993 memo written by Colonel

Daniel E. Brown, chief of the Combined Arms Assessment Team in Somalia, noted that through the "graduated use of force" American units would able to control the tempo of conflict.[108] Brown's memo reflected the general consensus that a show of force would be more than adequate to cow Somali warlords into submission. More important, policy makers believed that a precise application of power would allow them to retain the initiative in Somalia.

The situation looked much different on the ground. Faced with the desperate scrambles for food that followed wherever coalition forces distributed aid, riot control became a problematic exercise for American units. Most marines and 10th Mountain Division troops lacked either the training or the experience to quell civil disorder. A clash with Somalis at Wanwaylan in late December 1992 revealed significant gaps in equipment or even basic rules of engagement. Infantry units called upon to break up riots over food distribution resorted to fixed bayonets and shots fired into the air to push back the mass of people crowded around the relief site. For a brief moment, the small American contingent walked an extremely fine line between halting violence and being overrun by an angry mob. The latter would have been likely in a matter of minutes, according to the after-action report. The document itself perfectly captured the U.S. dilemma: "Someone has to make a decision here. Do we shoot someone for looting a bag of rice? Or trying to?"[109]

As Restore Hope continued into 1993, it became apparent that neither the United States nor its coalition partners were willing to address the deeper problems plaguing Somalia. Food aid was not followed by efforts to restore the economy. Perhaps more important, foreign troops failed to disarm warlords directly, instead relying on the March 1993 Addis Ababa Accords, which allowed the various factions to voluntarily turn in their arms. Politically, the forces on the ground had no mandate or ability to reconcile Somali factions ruling disparate parts of the country.[110] At best, the commitment of thousands of soldiers and considerable resources had proved capable of barely bringing Somalia back from the brink of disaster. The type of nation building necessary to resolve more systemic problems was on an order of magnitude far beyond what U.S. officials envisaged when Restore Hope began.

This stance changed when Restore Hope transitioned to Operation Continue Hope in June 1993. Gone was the limited focus on basic famine relief first envisioned six months earlier. Replacing it was a more intrusive and deliberate effort at nation building, a process contemporary observers and later scholars would describe as "assertive multilateralism."[111] Consequently, Continue Hope became the largest peacekeeping mission in UN history, involving a total of 28,000 troops and 2,800 civilian staff at its peak.[112]

In practice, the primary objective of Continue Hope was the pursuit of armed militias and the restoration of basic order to Somalia. This meant establishing "credible police forces in large cities and towns," according to an August 1993 speech by Defense Secretary Les Aspin.[113] Although conceptually simple, it was an ambitious program. Nothing resembling a national police force or regular military existed in Somalia at the time. Moreover, coalition forces tasked with defeating tribal militias to create order confronted an enemy that had no resemblance to a conventional opponent. Efforts to "find and fix" one of the primary groups operating in Mogadishu under Mohamed Farah Aideed proved frustrating. American intelligence agencies were unable to consistently glean information from a clan system that relied more heavily on blood ties than satellite transmissions. When American forces clashed with the militias, the outcomes were predictable. The "technicals" suffered from superior U.S. weaponry, but firepower risked civilian casualties and normally succeeded in stoking Somali xenophobia.[114]

The shift to more conventional operations also created blind spots. Significantly absent from Continue Hope was the same level of psychological operations capability that had characterized the earlier coalition effort. Where the original Operation Restore Hope had 150 military personnel assigned to information dissemination through a radio station and a Somali-language newspaper in early 1993, United Nations Operation Somalia II (UNOSOM II) reduced this number to five.[115] Without the ability to either articulate the nature of the new mission or blunt criticism from Aideed and the clans, the upgraded military effort lost ground in Somalia even as it attempted to take back the streets of Mogadishu. In this context, the confrontation between American forces and Somalis in October 1993 was more a punctuation mark than a new departure.

As many scholars and policy makers have since observed, the Somalia mission had a profound impact on America's approach to military intervention in the nineties. In the wake of the controversy that surrounded the Battle of Mogadishu, post-1991 applications of Desert Storm's methodology proved to be problematic exercises at best. Washington learned, as one author put it, that there was no such thing as a "humanitarian surgical strike."[116] A thoughtful study that appeared when the United States withdrew from Somalia in 1994 questioned even the adequacy of peacekeeping operations in general. Ramesh Thakur noted that the UN force deployed to Somalia "fell between two stools," in that it was insufficient for the purposes of coercive enforcement but "extravagant" for peacekeeping duties.[117] The mission failed not just because member nations in the coalition lacked the political will or military cohesiveness to prevail; more simply, they had the wrong tools for the job.

The American response to Somalia was a mix of retrenchment and reassessment. A clear signal came when Presidential Decision Directive 25 (PDD-25), "U.S. Policy on Reforming Multilateral Peace Operations," appeared on 3 May 1994. The document indicated a substantial change in American policy, specifically curtailing U.S. military participation in humanitarian missions. In the event future American forces did deploy, the Clinton administration adopted new criteria for participation in peace operations. PDD-25 delegated overall responsibility for these missions to the United Nations, recommending it reorganize the management of military deployments and reduce U.S. contributions in personnel, equipment, and funding. The White House also added a long list of preconditions for American support entitled "Supporting the Right Peace Operations," which addressed the advancement of U.S. interests, the legal mandate for action, and domestic and Congressional support for intervention.[118] In many respects, PDD-25 was an updated version of the Weinberger Doctrine—although rather than establish clear parameters for American military policy, it seemed more intent on precluding their risks.

In 1993 American military intervention in Haiti established the tone for this new reluctance. When U.S. forces aboard the USS *Harlan County* initially attempted to weigh anchor at Port-au-Prince in October 1993, a mob waiting on the docks actually managed to forestall the landing. Later, when the 10th Mountain Division finally arrived in country, it adopted an extremely aggressive and risk-averse approach toward operations on the island. The division's mandate, expressed in its after-action report, was clear: "Every movement outside a compound is a COMBAT OPERATION."[119] It was common practice for soldiers to travel only in heavily armed and armored convoys. Contact with the Haitian people was kept at a hostile distance. Special forces soldiers who accompanied the 10th Mountain and other regular forces to Haiti argued that the absolute desire to avoid casualties actually inhibited peacekeeping operations by alienating not only the people but the local military as well.[120] Yet this type of behavior during deployments to the underdeveloped world became standard practice for the remainder of the decade.

A year after American forces left Somalia, it was also clear that the military was ambivalent as to how it might apply many of the lessons learned from Restore Hope/Continue Hope. A 1995 report by the Army Combat Training Center reflected the belief that conventional forces were more than adequate to the new missions then being adopted by the United States military: "A good combat soldier equals a good peacekeeper/peace enforcer. You have to be well-grounded in the basics. You have to be skilled in order to handle the many dilemmas that you are going to face on the decentralized OOTW battlefield."[121] Despite this perhaps misplaced faith, the Pentagon did attempt to incorporate the Somalia experience into an updated version of *FM 100-5: Operations* (1993). By introducing the concept of OOTW, peacekeeping, peace enforcement, and a host of other nontraditional missions were introduced into mainstream military thinking.[122]

There were derivative benefits to this step. Operations other than war received greater attention for the purpose of planning and coordination. Reflecting the relevance of civilian aid agencies, the Pentagon created the Civil Military Operations Center (CMOC) to better coordinate activity between nongovernmental organizations and deployed military units.[123] The later additions of *FM 100-23: Peace Operations* and *FM 100-23-1: Multiservice Procedures for Humanitarian Assistance Operations* in 1994 were further attempts to articulate the means by which America pursued its growing portfolio of overseas missions.[124]

Conclusions

In 2001 John Lewis Gaddis observed that, with the benefit of ten years' perspective, Americans could understand how dangerous the prospects for the world were at the start of the nineties and how inadequate American power was to ensure security.[125] Hindsight is always generous in that respect. Time grants the ability to understand the difficulties inherent in the momentous events of the period, to make distinctions as Ian Roxborough also observed in 2001, between instability and meaningful change.[126]

What America enjoyed after 1991 was a rare opportunity to shape the world, an opportunity potentially greater than the one witnessed immediately after World War II. Lacking the imperatives inherent in the U.S. and Soviet rivalry, the post–Cold War was an era of "discretionary policymaking," especially for the side that won.[127] The nineties started as a celebration of all the qualities—free-market capitalism, tolerance, and democracy—that defined the West and, more specifically, the United States. Fresh from its victory against Iraq, the military enjoyed an endorsement of its own particular qualities, qualities that had prevailed over evil in a very short war.

Success proved to be one the largest obstacles to military adaptation in the nineties. The unquestioned victory of Desert Storm made reform all that much more difficult to advance over old habits and institutional inertia.[128] Even as defense budgets withered, military leaders remained optimistic that forces in place were adequate to the new tasks of the new world order. Operation Provide Comfort appeared to prove that Powell Doctrine could be applied to humanitarian relief. Wars could be kept small, or even relatively peaceful, if policy makers applied the proper restraint.

Somalia destroyed that sense of complacency and prompted a period of necessary introspection. New doctrine, cognizant of the limits of military force and an understanding of the many actors involved in peacekeeping and peace enforcement slowly emerged. Conceptually, OOTW envisaged conflict on an order of magnitude broader and more complex than at any time since the Vietnam War. Unfortunately, an intellectual and organizational leap of this type required time to gel. As the nineties progressed, time was at a premium as the American military faced additional burdens when it deployed with increasing frequency to hot spots around the world.

5

"Peace," Nation Building, and the New World Disorder

> *The longing for the preservation or resurrection of an old order, real or fantastic, is the key to understanding much of the world's disorder. Even when our enemies are not personally motivated by the fear of change, it is the fears of their neighbors that grant those enemies opportunity. . . . Demagogues capitalize on the sense of trust betrayed and the "evil" of the new. They are geniuses of blame. All of their failures, and the failures of all of their followers, will forever be the fault of someone else.*
>
> —Ralph Peters, "Our New Old Enemies"

> *One way or another, we are in for it, and the only real question is whether we will realize it in time.*
>
> —Madeleine Albright, "The Testing of American Foreign Policy"

America began the post–Cold War era with a new world and new leadership. As was the case with Mikhail Gorbachev only a few years earlier, Bill Clinton represented a generation whose coming of age postdated World War II. As a "new" Democrat, Clinton remade his party's approach to domestic affairs. Similarly, with respect to American foreign policy, the White House actively sought out a model that would move beyond the ossified lines of the old world order. Candidate Clinton had been highly critical of the Bush administration coddling countries that endorsed repression, particularly communist China.[1] He proposed that, in the future, the United States would promote standards around the world that embodied its democratic principles.

Much as Jimmy Carter had done at the start of his presidency, Clinton embraced a high-minded desire for the United States to become a primary sponsor of global economic, political, and social progress. However, lacking foreign policy credentials, Clinton exhibited two unfortunate characteristics during his time in office. One was a tendency to conflate the foreign and domestic sides of his policy making. This trait allowed him to dovetail his diplomatic portfolio with a successful political campaign and allow him to speak about diplomacy with some degree of authority. As president-elect, Clinton claimed that "in this new era, our first foreign priority and our first domestic priority are one and the same: reviving the economy. An anemic, debt-ridden economy; the developed world's highest rates of crime and poverty; an archaic education system; decaying roads, ports, and cities; all undermine our diplomacy, make it harder for us to secure favorable trade agreements, and compromise our ability to finance essential military action."[2] Unfortunately, what meant rhetorical sense did not translate well in reality. Despite his efforts to lend gravity to American foreign policy, Clinton's lack of depth in foreign affairs distanced him from foreign service professionals and the Pentagon, making the practical application of his ideas difficult.[3]

A second tendency was Clinton's penchant for delegating responsibility for foreign policy. To alleviate the gap between his experience and policy demand, Clinton relied heavily on a small group of key cabinet level officials: Secretary of Defense Les Aspin, Secretary of State Warren Christopher, and National Security Adviser Anthony Lake. Collectively, they were idealists, combining foreign credentials with a general frustration about the status quo bequeathed by the Bush administration, in addition to an academic faith in sound international relations theories.[4] When he left the State Department after Ronald Reagan's election, Christopher called for a "new compact" between the president and the Congress, emphasizing "foreign-policy decision making based on mutually reinforcing commitments and mutually accepted restraints."[5] In 1984 Tony Lake wrote at length, along with

Leslie Gelb and I. M. Destler about the pitfalls of American policy making. The article recalled Henry Kissinger's belief in policy designed for global realities and suggested a new consensus that moved the country away from "organizational disarray," inconsistency, and the self-inflicted wounds of political partisanship.[6]

At its core, American foreign policy in Clinton's first term was fundamentally reactionary, responding to the real and perceived shortfalls of the Reagan-Bush era. Moreover, the new foreign policy team and the president tended to focus on process rather than policy objectives in an effort to derive a new consensus from common practices (e.g., neoliberal economic policies) rather than common agreements. Unfortunately, without clear objectives, the administration suffered in its first term, particularly when it traveled in the wake of previous decisions. Such was the case in Somalia in 1993. What the White House required was time to formulate an effective and, perhaps more important to a president who was fixated on opinion polls, a politically palatable approach to the world.[7]

While the civilian leadership struggled to find its feet, the American military shouldered the burden of escalating deployments to small conflicts around the world. American intervention in Kurdistan and Somalia, as well as the prospect of imminent entry into the chaos that was the former nation of Yugoslavia, had taught hard lessons and placed a premium on new methods of military action bearing little resemblance to the Cold War. The split between military and civilian was clear from the first day Clinton entered office, although it had little to do with his military service or approach to military culture. As civilians prevaricated, the Pentagon embarked upon another major revision of U.S. military doctrine. The military confronted the difficulties of diplomatic principle as well as the degrees of impartiality and noncoercion required to win compliance (if not victory) between actors who no longer represented nation-states.[8]

The Need for Engagement

There was little question that the new national security team assuming power in 1993 recognized their place at a key moment in history. Secretary of Defense Les Aspin, sounding much like George Bush two years earlier, made note of this during his confirmation hearings:

> The Cold War world that emerged from global conflict is no more. The Moscow-led Warsaw Pact military alliance that threatened Western Europe and the peace of the world has crumbled. The 70-year experiment in the repression at home and ideological export abroad that was the Soviet Union has failed and dissolved.
>
> In sum, the bi-polar world of military and ideological competition that shaped our security thinking in nearly every way is now gone. The world that will replace it is being re-created, and it will be re-created by all of us here in this room.[9]

As it marked the end of one era, the new administration issued a warning that the United States could not afford any form of isolationism. History was often brought forward to serve this claim. During Clinton's first term, it was popular for members of his team to make reference to the failed potential of Woodrow Wilson as he struggled with American foreign policy after the First World War.[10]

Instead of obsolete Cold War paradigms or a retreat from the world stage, policy makers articulated their take on U.S. policy in terms of assertive multilateralism. In general, this meant that the United States would seek cooperation as a central pillar of its foreign affairs, particularly through older institutions such as the United Nations and newer venues like the North America Free Trade Agreement (NAFTA), the General Agreement on Tariffs and Trade (GATT), and Asia-Pacific Economic Cooperation (APEC).[11] In a statement delivered before the Senate Foreign Relations Committee in November 1993, Secretary of State Warren Christopher cited "economic security" as America's first strategic priority.[12]

The approach focused primarily on nonmilitary methods of cooperation: democratic institutions, free-market economies, and the peaceful, diplomatic settlement of conflict. All became part of a familiar mantra during the Clinton years. The argument for assertive multilateralism proceeded from the starting point that spreading democratic institutions, coupled with open markets, would spawn cooperation between traditional enemies and isolate "backlash states." Political and economic cooperation together would carry over into security affairs by eliminating the root causes of conflict. This conventional wisdom argued that economic integration could break down old regional rivalries in favor of material and ideological progress. Contemporary U.S. policy makers pointed to the March 1991 Treaty of Asunción that integrated the southern cone economies of South America. The explosion of trade from $4 billion in 1990 to over $20 billion by 1997 was subsequently followed by greater diplomatic cooperation between Argentina, Bolivia, Chile, Uruguay, and Brazil.[13]

The nineties thus became a decade of great diplomatic summitry. Many traditional areas of interest, such as strategic nuclear arms reduction and international trade, remained at the forefront of negotiations. Joining them were new discussions on climate change, humanitarian relief, and European unification. Clearly, it seemed as if a new era of cooperation had begun.[14]

Within the confines of this new worldview, military affairs occupied what could best be described as a peripheral role. Collective security, the backbone of American military defense abroad after 1945, was reinterpreted to support multilateral cooperation. In this new context, military training between nations had utility because it supported "confidence building measures" between regional or international rivals.[15] Similarly, in 1997 Christopher's replacement, Madeleine Albright, promoted NATO expansion in Eastern Europe as a means to spread democracy. She touted the entry of Poland, Hungary, and the Czech Republic into NATO as "an irreversible affirmation of their belonging within the democratic community of the West."[16] Clearly, the old methods and goals of military policy no longer had the same traction as they had in a more rigid, bipolar world.

With this new approach to international relations, the United States contemplated nation building on a global scale. National Security Adviser Anthony Lake compared U.S. post–Cold War obligations to those of the Marshall Plan more than fifty years earlier. In 1990, he wrote: "Today, it may be hubristic to try to design new economic or political patterns in Third World nations, and even to try to apply new technologies, when there were important cultural and environmental reasons for the old. But in many areas we consider here, there may be no real choice."[17] Albright echoed the same note eight years later when she maintained that the United States "must fortify the international system by helping transitional or otherwise troubled states become full participants." She saw it as a multifaceted approach that involved economic development, political reform, improved law enforcement, and diplomatic intervention.[18]

Armed with these convictions when approaching the many unstable parts of the post-1991 world, American policy makers focused almost entirely on infrastructure, development, and technical aid. They emphasized in particular the idea that "market democracies" could provide the basis for future political liberalization and stability.[19] Even when recognizing the risks inherent in restoring political and economic order to disparate parts of the world, officials habitually left very little room for security planning.[20]

The first real sticking point, among the many that would emerge over time, had to do with nations that refused to conform to the priorities of the new world order. Iraq, Iran, North Korea, Libya, and Cuba, countries that National Security Adviser Anthony Lake described as "backlash states," all at one point or another simply refused to acquiesce with world opinion as it applied to nuclear nonproliferation or officially sanctioned terrorism.[21] More problematic were the various ethnic factions and tribal entities that also defied international agreements. These lacked the fundamental structure amenable to diplomacy or susceptible to economic sanctions.

The consistent intransigence of these state and nonstate actors eventually returned American (and Western) attention to the prospect of effectively using military power. As the nineties moved forward, multilateral agencies such as NATO and the United Nations failed rather spectacularly to secure stability in numerous regions overwhelmed by internal turmoil. The collapse of Yugoslavia at the start of the decade and its subsequent descent into bitter ethnic and religious factionalism became a case study in failed assertive multilateralism. Similarly, the complete absence of effective regional security arrangements in Sub-Saharan Africa resulted in hundreds of thousands of deaths and immeasurable human suffering.[22]

As global instability worsened, American leaders began to reconsider the utility of military institutions to the world condition. Rather than place national militaries on the periphery of global affairs, the argument followed that they were the anchor for both internal stability and national development. Thus, Madeleine Albright's reasoning for NATO expansion—that indigenous military institutions were essential to democracy—took on a more central importance. Because they represented repositories of technical expertise and professional culture, militaries around the world were presented as an essential transitional means toward a reformed future, one in which they would actively promote democracy rather than simply protect it. It was a tremendous leap of faith, but one that would restore the American military to a central position in post–Cold War policy making.[23]

As the U.S. military emerged victorious from the Cold War, a stance burnished by Desert Storm, the American armed forces became the exemplar for global reform. In practical terms, this meant an expansion of purpose beyond the conventional functions of the AirLand Battle Doctrine that the military had performed so well in Kuwait. New times required a new flexibility that promised to significantly multiply the number and types of missions delegated to the Pentagon.[24] These new missions conflated American interests and principles. Anthony Lake noted in 1996: "we face situations that do not threaten our nation's vital interests—yet do still affect our interests and the character of the world in which we live. It might be conflict, such as Bosnia, that produces terrible suffering and jeopardizes stability in a region of vital importance to our nation. Or it might be a brutal coup, like the one in Haiti, that endangers democracy in our hemisphere and prompts thousands of desperate refugees seeking sanctuary on our shores."[25] In real terms, this meant military commitments of unprecedented scope and complexity at a time of increasing public ambivalence regarding foreign interventions. Despite this, senior civilian officials were optimistic. Lake argued that OOTW provided valuable experience for future combat operations because they would "catalyze innovation."[26]

The restored relevance of the American military was further reinforced by Madeleine Albright's appointment as secretary of state. Her arrival at the start of Clinton's second term marked a clearer recognition of global military threats and a corresponding American willingness to confront them. Albright embodied a growing impatience with unresolved conflicts in the Balkans, as well as a rising drumbeat of criticism against Russia for its military actions in Chechnya, Georgia, Moldova, Azerbaijan, and Tajikistan.[27] Albright's service as the U.S.

ambassador to the United Nations was notable for her interest in using or threatening to use military power. As secretary of state, she made note in 1998 that "obvious Cold War threats have been replaced by a viper's nest of more subtle perils—from poison gas to ethnic violence to disruptions in the global economy." Her itinerary after 1995—confronting Iraqi intransigence regarding weapons inspections, stability in the Balkans, NATO enlargement, approval of the Comprehensive Nuclear Test Ban Treaty—was an interesting reversal of priorities from 1993.[28]

Albright clearly took a much more aggressive approach to American foreign relations than Warren Christopher. She defined a key component of foreign policy as "spine," a quality "which dictates that we honor our commitments, back our words with actions, bear essential costs, and take necessary risks."[29] Without question, Albright reinvigorated interest in the use of force to supplement diplomacy, as later military actions in the Balkans, Africa, and Afghanistan indicated. It was also clear that the new secretary of state established a more aggressive conventional wisdom within the Clinton policy team. During a June 1996 speech, even Tony Lake endorsed the idea of "diplomacy backed with force," citing the positive examples of Haiti, the Persian Gulf in 1994, and Bosnia.[30]

Although Albright lent a certain cachet to military intervention, her approach suffered from a number of deficiencies. One clear limit was its Eurocentrism. When the secretary of state considered military action, she tended to focus on NATO as a key agent of American policy. This applied to the bombing campaign against Serbia and democratic expansion into the former Soviet bloc. More broadly, as vested in international relations as Albright may have been, a European perspective also significantly shaped her worldview. Like George H. W. Bush, she drew her historical lessons from the World War II era and tended to see a lack of resolve and compromise as appeasement. When State Department spokesman James Rubin asked her to soften the U.S. line on Serbian policy, Albright responded, "Jamie, do you think we're in Munich?"[31] Lastly, despite a public persona built around forcefulness, Madeleine Albright could not escape Clinton's skittishness about deploying ground troops to combat missions after Somalia. When the United States did decide to wield the military stick, it was generally accomplished with air power. In the case of Kosovo in 1999, tactical restrictions placed on U.S. forces severely hampered their effectiveness.[32]

In many respects, the transition witnessed from the first to second Clinton terms—from idealism to realism—was typical of modern American diplomacy. It recalled the passage from the universalism embodied in the Bretton Woods Conference (1944) to the Truman Doctrine three years later.[33] In a more recent context, the Clinton administration resembled more closely that of Jimmy Carter, which saw idealism founder upon geopolitical realities.

Madeleine Albright appeared at a point in which American policy makers discovered the limits of peaceful multilateralism. Even so, her concept of cusp nations applied primarily to either the remnants of Yugoslavia or post-Soviet countries of Eastern Europe, both of which could be addressed by NATO. Outside of this arena, where potential failed states were not so much former communist nations as simply unstable ones, Albright lacked a coherent alternative. Nonstate actors were less amenable to confrontation or deterrence in either a diplomatic or military form. Consequently, the accumulating small wars of the former Third World received only periodic attention, usually in the form of air strikes, as was the case after the 1998 terrorist attacks on two U.S. embassies in Africa.

Domestically, the obstacles to effective American diplomatic and military policy again recalled the post–World War II period. The late nineties witnessed a remarkable time of prosperity on the home front, one which saw the Dow Jones industrial average grow from 2,588 in 1991 to 11,722 in 2000.[34] Celebrating an era of plenty, few Americans were interested in or cognizant of conflict growing ever closer to their country. Overlaying the post–Cold War boom was a degree of political partisanship unseen since the second Red Scare. Scandal became an endemic part of Washington political culture in the late nineties. Overlapping layers of controversy successfully cocooned the White House and eventually led to Clinton's impeachment in 1998. With more than two years in office, the president had not lost his title but most of the credibility that came with it.[35] Even when the administration attempted to respond to terrorist attacks on Americans, action was subsumed by partisanship. Cruise missile strikes against terrorist targets after the African embassy bombings and the bombing of Iraq at the end of the year almost immediately drew cries of "wag the dog" from critics.[36]

As the nineties concluded, it appeared that the United States was prepared to make limited progress in the area of small wars. The initial effort to emphasize peaceful cooperation diminished significantly by the time Clinton's first term was complete. Madeleine Albright's arrival marked a more belligerent approach to world affairs that outshone both National Security Adviser Tony Lake (and, later, Sandy Berger) as well as Secretary of Defense William Cohen. Conversely, the limits of this more aggressive take were equally clear. Hamstrung by an unwillingness to replicate the debacle in Mogadishu and increasingly distracted by domestic affairs, the Clinton administration placed significant restrictions on the actual and potential use of military force. Nevertheless, as its actions in the latter half of the decade indicated, the American military's approach to small wars both matured and expanded in scope and scale, something civilian leadership's did not.

The Search for a New Military Doctrine

The American military after 1991 was a victim of its own success. Absent the strategic pressures of the Cold War, it had lost its Soviet enemy and a fundamental reason for being. Edward Luttwak framed the problem well when he observed in 1996 that "the strategic culture of the Cold War combined great eagerness to accumulate weapons with great caution in their use."[37] Without this standard, the very utility of the American military as an institution was uncertain when applied to accumulation or use. As discussed in the previous chapter, this basic realization kicked off the debate over the so-called peace dividend. While it was obvious at the time that the military would persist as a factor in American life and policy making, it was equally obvious that the armed forces would have to undergo significant changes to regain their relevance.

Military leaders recognized that they were about to enter a period in which the "industrial" standards for war were nearing an end. No longer could militaries rely on mass and mechanization as they had in the past.[38] The heavy formations of armored vehicles, carrier battle groups, and bomber formations were, at best, obsolescent as the country approached the new millennium. Conceptually, the days of "trinitarian war" that Clausewitz helped form, one that combined the power of a state monopoly over the practice of war with a professional military and a mobilized citizenry, where fast disappearing. The key challenge for American military leaders was to find productive ways to modify twentieth-century standards of military power—technological aptitude, industrial output, strength of institutions, and individual leadership capabilities—without disrupting the institution they were attempting to reform.[39]

A simple but significant obstacle to reform was inertia. As an institution, from private soldiers to the Joint Chiefs of Staff, habit and long practice prevented the U.S. armed forces from altering doctrine to suit new missions. Fifty years of history, three major wars, and innumerable large and small-scale deployments combined to create a visceral resistance to change. Luttwak asserted that the Cold War had gone on for so long that there was no substitute point of reference.[40] The embedded habits associated with combating the former Soviet Union partly explained the military's unbending insistence on outdated readiness requirements. The Pentagon retained most Cold War weapons systems after 1991 regardless of their applicability to contemporary missions. One admiral argued in 1999 that twelve carrier battle groups were inadequate to cover global deployments. Similarly, the Navy believed that fifty submarines were too small to support subsurface operations.[41]

Just how prevalent these attitudes were within the armed forces was revealed in a survey of more than 500 midlevel career officers attending professional military command and staff schools. Published in 2000, the survey indicated that most agreed that low-intensity warfare (terrorism stood out as the number one response) was the most likely threat to American interests. However, paradoxically, these same officers resisted the idea of active involvement in this type of conflict. Their preference was not simply a reflection of military combat specialty or the desire for decisive conventional military action. These young leaders, representing the future of the military, were also well versed in the significant absence of civilian support for prospective small wars.[42]

The civil-military divide that characterized much of the nineties clearly retarded meaningful reform within the American armed forces. Former Army officer Ralph Peters spoke for many of his civilian contemporaries when he described the military as "ponderous and grossly inefficient."[43] Unfortunately, many saw the end of the Cold War as the death knell of a culturally obsolete institution. The 1991 Tailhook scandal set the tone for the period as advocates attempted to reform the military culture from within.[44] Consequently, the discussion shifted from readiness to social equity.[45] Public debate became more embittered when Bill Clinton altered the military's policy on gay service members in 1993.[46] Senior officers took little heart when a former congressman and critic of the military, Les Aspin, was nominated to be secretary of defense. It was a small wonder that Madeleine Albright became a guiding light of national security policy from the State Department.

The cumulative effect of inertia and controversy was to retard meaningful attention to low-level conflict. As late as August 2001, an article in *Defense Analysis* commented on the minimal doctrinal progress undertaken for OOTW.[47] As was the case in the years following Vietnam, the political environment created an atmosphere averse to risk, particularly with respect to casualties. Substituting technology for soldiers was an alternative popular for civilian and military leaders alike. Within the Pentagon, the emphasis on weapons systems satisfied the military desire to retain older components of the Cold War. For civilian leaders, precision-guided munitions promised what one expert called a lower "casualty exposure index."[48]

A review of the strategic policy documents produced during this period reflects an attempt to navigate a path between institutional preference, civilian priorities, and domestic ambivalence toward war. One early statement produced by the Joint Chiefs of Staff in January 1992, the *National Military Strategy of the United States,* is indicative of this search. In its introduction, the JCS recognized the need for a "flexible strategy which is more regionally oriented and capable of responding decisively to the challenges of this decade."[49] Essentially, the Pentagon's response to the post-Soviet era was to downgrade its geographical purview while keeping most of the methodology of the Cold War. Deterrence is a constant theme in the document. It is applied to nuclear proliferation, stability, and, most important, regional actors who threatened U.S. interests and those of the global community.[50] To meet these challenges, the JCS endorsed a "forward presence" of U.S.

forces that would be prepared for "crisis response" to ensure regional stability. Again, as the strategy recognized, forces in place could accomplish these missions in the same manner that they had while practicing containment against the Soviet bloc. In a nod to contemporary reality, the Pentagon recognized that U.S. forces on hand would shrink considerably as the country pursued a "peace dividend." Moreover, new priorities emanating from the administration, specifically the need to "mediate economic and social strife," were also included in the military's list of new missions.[51] Overall, however, the policy is notable for the absence of dramatic change to American military thinking.

The Bottom-Up Review followed the *National Security Strategy of the United States* in 1993. Initiated by Les Aspin that year, it echoed many of the topics introduced earlier by the JCS. The review again marked a point of demarcation between the Cold War and "An Era of New Dangers." More specifically, the most important threat to American security was the persistent danger of nuclear weapons. This was followed by the problems of ethnic and religious animosity, state-sponsored terrorism, and subversion.[52]

Despite this growing list of threats, the review counterintuitively argued that fewer military forces were necessary to protect vital U.S. interests: "Today, there is the promise that we can replace the East-West confrontation of the Cold War with an era in which the community of nations, guided by a common commitment to democratic principles, free-market economics, and the rule of law, can be significantly enlarged."[53] Accompanying the sense that greater international cooperation would obviate the need for Cold War–era standing forces, Aspin also believed that the scale of future conflicts would be much smaller. The review asserted that U.S. military readiness should be dictated by preparation for two major regional conflicts (MRCs), specifically against Iraq and North Korea. If the United States was adequately prepared for these smaller wars, the defense secretary believed these would be an accompanying benefit to deterrence: "History suggests that we most often deter the conflicts that we plan for and actually fight the ones we do not anticipate."[54]

The *Bottom-Up Review* basically proposed that the United States prepare for a second version of Desert Storm while committing to the defense of South Korea. Both were essentially warmed-over versions of Bush-era war plans with the added expectation that available

American forces would be much smaller in the future. The potential Iraq war scenario, circa 1993, is illustrative of the many compromises contained in the plan. Forces committed to a regional crisis point were significant in their limited size; one combat brigade's worth of equipment was positioned forward in Kuwait with additional units rotating through the country each year. More interesting to note, with the hindsight provided by Operation Iraqi Freedom (2003), are the forces designated for "Phase Four" of a major regional war—that is, for "post war stability." These included "a division or less of ground forces, and special operations units."[55]

In terms of potential small wars in the myriad other unstable places of the world, the *Bottom-Up Review* offered precious little attention. It designated a fraction of standing forces, 50,000 combat and support personnel, to "peace enforcement and intervention operations."[56] More important was the priority awarded these types of deployments. The review was careful to note that low-level interventions could not be attempted at the same time as preparing for or fighting the two major regional conflicts.

The basic purpose of the *Bottom-Up Review* was to justify massive cuts in U.S. military personnel. Active duty ground forces declined precipitously in the nineties. Between 1989 and 1995, for example, the regular Army shrank from 780,000 to just 510,000 service members.[57] Aspen's report was, in the political reality of the time, a rearguard action to preserve the status quo, in terms of not only doctrine but also funding priorities. In the wake of Desert Storm, the Pentagon agreed to abandon the land-based Midgetman nuclear missile and the W-88 warhead for Trident II missiles. It kept in development the C-17 cargo aircraft, the V-22 Osprey transport, and the F-22 fighter, as well as an additional nuclear aircraft carrier.[58]

While it maintained political traction and budget relevance, the *Bottom-Up Review* was a poor strategic template. Derived from Cold War methods and objectives, it was a sop to the status quo within the Pentagon but wholly inadequate to future small wars. The designation of resources to regional "Iraq equivalent" or "Panama equivalent" conflicts did not account for the long-term nature of conflict and new, complex demands on military capabilities, particularly postconflict stability operations.[59] The absolute commitment of forces to a future postinvasion Iraq scenario characterized policy thinking more intent on retrenchment than a realistic approach to modern warfare.

Despite the limitations of Pentagon thinking at the time, leaders within the American military did pose alternatives to the *Bottom-Up Review.* One of the most important came from Special Operations Command (SOCOM) itself. As noted in the previous chapter, SOCOM wanted to avoid falling victim to the post–Cold War syndrome of budget cutting and worked hard to adopt missions that would maintain its relevance. More to the point, senior leaders, particularly SOCOM commander Lieutenant General Carl W. Stiner, believed that American special operations forces were tailor made for the new conflicts awaiting the U.S. military. Stiner's argument rested on the twin foundations that special forces were vital to a balanced defense posture, both as a response to provocation and as a means to create stability. Special forces possessed high levels of training and aptitude and could be deployed to trouble spots with greater precision and flexibility than conventional formations. Their ability to cover a vast spectrum of missions, from war fighting (Operation Desert Storm) to humanitarian relief in places such as Bangladesh (Operation Sea Angel), was not simply theoretical but a matter of a large and expanding record.[60]

To demonstrate this utility, SOCOM issued a series of internal publications that focused on instability in the underdeveloped world. Africa was a particularly popular and relevant topic in the nineties.[61] At the same time, Stiner reached out to the major regional military commands in an effort to build institutional and political momentum for his case. To the commander of U.S. Pacific forces, he wrote in December 1992, "There is a definite need to keep SOF forward based to counter potential threats and take advantage of opportunities." Stiner stressed the skill level that special forces brought to the various regional commanders, emphasizing their military training, language capabilities, and cultural expertise. Cumulatively, special forces units offered a "low visibility, non-intrusive presence that clearly signals U.S. resolve and commitment."[62]

Stiner's campaign for relevance had a mixed impact. It did not result in a new round of long-term deployments to the former Third World. Sadly, in areas that likely could have benefited from U.S. intervention, such as Africa at mid-decade, the Clinton administration remained extremely reticent about the prospect of potential military casualties. SOCOM efforts did bear fruit in other areas, however. By maintaining the argument for flexibility and a focus on the implications of force on indigenous culture, Stiner and his special operations cohort were able to influence American thought and action in the rare moments the White House did commit to peacekeeping and peace enforcement. Perhaps more important, SOCOM and like-minded elements within the military continued the trajectory toward improving America's treatment of small wars even as civilian leadership succumbed to the impeachment process at the end of the nineties.

Balkan Deployments and the Search for Flexibility

The history of the Balkan conflicts of the early nineties was a combination of long-standing grievances given new life in the aftermath of the Cold War. The long-term trigger for war was the death of Josef Broz Tito, whose communist regime had held together the disparate ethnic and religious elements present in the region since the forties. By 1991 his successors were no match for the centrifugal forces that tore apart Yugoslavia. That year, Slovenia and Croatia declared independence and were subsequently recognized by the European Community. Serbia, which represented the largest faction of the former Yugoslavia, went to war in an effort to regain lost territory, punish the upstart new republics, and deter future losses. Over the next four years, the United Nations, the European Union (EU), and NATO attempted to broker cease-fire agreements and largely failed to restore any semblance of order in the Balkans. "Ethnic cleansing" and all its attendant tragedies entered the common parlance. One French political analyst, Pierre Hassner, noted at the time, "the new world order of George Bush died in Sarajevo."[63]

Even as the consequences of the Balkan wars worsened, it was equally clear that there was no international consensus on humanitarian intervention. Neither the United Nations nor NATO possessed adequate doctrine even after peacekeepers were deployed to the region.[64] In the face of mounting international condemnation, Serbian forces remained defiant. This situation reached a low point in May 1995 when 350 UN personnel were taken hostage to forestall air strikes.

The Clinton administration contributed to this problem for nearly two years as it wrestled with the prospect of intervention. Public opinion consistently indicated that troop deployments were unpopular at home, a fact not lost on a White House that took polling extremely seriously.[65] Moreover, because he had committed American foreign policy to multilateral diplomacy, Clinton was reluctant to divorce himself from ongoing efforts to peacefully resolve the situation. Unfortunately, Washington's reluctance to offer ground forces to enforce a ceasefire undercut the West's resolve toward this end.

By 1995 the United States finally committed to military force to the Balkan conflict. A number of factors accounted for this change. In part, Serbian intransigence had finally provoked a number of key nations—most notably, France under Jacques Chirac—to consider more direct military action. The Serbs further inflamed the West in July when their forces seized the town of Srebrenica, which had been declared a "safe zone" by the United Nations. The massacre of thousands of Muslims in the wake of this operation prompted renewed calls for intervention.[66]

Consequently, American air units joined in the NATO bombing campaign in August and September 1995, which finally drove Serbia to the peace table. Two months later, Serbs, Croats, Bosnians, and representatives of the UN, EU, and associated nations (including France, Russia, and Germany) met at Wright-Patterson Air Force Base near Dayton, Ohio, to work on the details of a settlement that would end the conflict.[67] The Dayton Peace Accords, signed on 21 November 1995, formalized the partition of contested territory under armed international supervision.[68]

The initial U.S. military contribution of ground troops to a Balkan peace began at the end of 1995, when it joined the UN Implementation Force (IFOR) that would oversee a ceasefire and political partition of the region. As part of the Dayton Accords and subsequent agreements in Paris at the end of the year, the United States agreed to dispatch 20,000 soldiers to Bosnia. These would join a NATO contingent numbering 60,000 personnel under Operation Joint Endeavor.[69]

The primary American unit deploying to the region was the 1st Armored Division, which arrived in Bosnia as part of Task Force Eagle. Under the general heading of "peace enforcement operations," Task

Force Eagle's portfolio during its first six months in Bosnia included the surrender of heavy weapons, mine removal, monitoring of police equipment and vehicles, and prisoner release. However, the number one priority issued by its headquarters was "force protection," a function that stressed the safety of U.S. personnel stationed in Bosnia above all other missions.[70] This included not only a high level of operational security while conducting field operations, but also additional precautions to ensure the safety of troops from accidental death or injury. Years after returning home, Lieutenant Colonel Jeffrey W. Hammond, commander of the 4/29th Field Artillery, reflected on the simple dilemma of his troops carrying loaded weapons on a daily basis for the first time. Accidental misfires, whether they were found to be negligent or not, had the potential to end an officer's career.[71]

In a larger sense, the Army's interest in personnel security reflected deep reservations within the Pentagon regarding American participation in Joint Endeavor.[72] The massive force dispatched to Bosnia signaled a clear-cut effort to deter additional bad acts on the part of Serbia. In this respect, it made a good deal of clinical, logical sense in the environs of the State Department and NSC. Military leaders knew better, however. U.S. forces placed amidst the three contending sides, along with their French and British counterparts, faced a divisive and dangerous environment in which attempts to disarm or hold any faction accountable for its actions posed serious risks. Senior military officials understood that American soldiers at the sharp tip of the IFOR spear would enjoy little if any clarity once their various peacekeeping and peace enforcement missions began in earnest.

Pre-deployment planning within the 1st Armored Division demonstrated this ambivalence. The division leadership struggled with the uncertainty of what their deployment might bring once the unit entered into the religious and ethnic morass that was Bosnia at that time. In an interesting document entitled "Beyond D+120: Tasks We Don't Want, May Get," Task Force Eagle contemplated involvement in securing mass grave sites, controlling black market activities, the apprehension of war criminals, providing civilian medical care, and security operations during elections.[73] In 1995 the Army had barely begun to incorporate stability operations into its basic practices. Field commanders rightly worried that the gap between training and new missions might have disastrous consequences, as it had in Somalia only two years earlier.

Still, the Defense Department made rudimentary efforts to prepare deploying troops that demonstrated a greater degree of sophistication than Restore Hope had in 1992. A sixteen-page pocket guide was issued to American personnel prior to their departure that offered a brief synopsis of Bosnian history, politics, and key phrases with pronunciation keys. The booklet also provided guidelines for individual soldiers' personal conduct when talking to the media. Under the section entitled "Religion and Sensitivities," it recommended the following: "Remember, these people are the product of more than 1,000 years of history and culture. They can be easily insulted when they perceive any disrespect of them or their culture. Simply act in a respectful and considerate manner at all times."[74]

Throughout the division's deployment to Bosnia, a number of key leaders on the ground raised concerns regarding the size and scope of their mission. One intelligence officer noted that Army doctrine was inadequate for peacekeeping and peace enforcement operations: "20 brigades belonging to the three former warring factions in addition to police forces, criminal elements, and ethnic transnational terrorists" had overwhelmed existing intelligence gathering capabilities, presenting "an infinitely expanding field of targets which never die."[75] Similar points were made regarding the task force's intelligence gathering capabilities. Although the division had the ability to identify and track items normally included in a conventional order of battle—armored vehicles, heavy weapons, communications facilities—as it had during Desert Storm, it lacked key information that was critical to a peacekeeping mission, mainly human intelligence. In a February 1997 official review of the unit's deployment, Colonel Gregory Fontenot, the first brigade commander, noted the significant lack of intelligence on the local population and Bosnia, Serb, and Croat military units.[76]

Many predeployment worries were justified once Task Force Eagle arrived in Bosnia in 1996. As the year proceeded, the division commander recorded an increasing array of problems associated with hostile armed factions and their civilian supporters. Units sent to over see the exhumation of mass graves and the apprehension of war criminals frequently were required to intervene in violent conflicts between displaced refugees on all sides. Moreover, the freedom of movement provisions in the Dayton Accords that allowed refugees to return home regularly resulted in attacks upon people and property throughout the task force's area of operations. Such confrontations were not limited to civilians. Task Force Eagle personnel often found themselves obstructed by Bosnia and Croat military units when conducting weapons inspections. Faced with this interference, American commanders found it difficult to convince Serbian police units to patrol resettled areas.[77]

While Western intervention ended the worst parts of war in the Balkans, American hopes for a short-term military commitment proved premature. U.S. military forces remained in the region despite a pledge by the White House that they would remain in Bosnia for only a year.[78] Once its tour was complete, the 1st Armored went home. Other regular units and, later, reserve and National Guard forces, would maintain the Dayton agreement.

In order to create a military balance, the United States began the Train and Equip Program, a $100 million effort to modernize the Bosnia-Herzegovina Federation Army.[79] However, although American military advisers worked within the project, the bulk of the responsibility for planning, training, and equipment fell to private contractors. These new actors, who were appearing with increasing frequency (one in ten Americans stationed in Bosnia were employees of private military corporations), allowed the Pentagon to delegate direct involvement with the factions at hand and preserve distance from risk.[80] As will be discussed in a later chapter, it was a tempting option that grew in scope and frequency over the next decade.

It is clear that American military intervention in Bosnia benefited from the experiences gained in the nineties. As was the case with the initial deployment of forces to Somalia in Operation Restore Hope 1992, the United States acted as one contributor, albeit a large one, to an acclaimed multinational effort. Unlike Somalia, the mission objectives, established at Dayton, remained transparent and consistent.[81] The American military learned its own lessons equally well by 1995. When the United States sent the 1st Armored to Bosnia in 1996, it did so as part of a decisive, large-scale deployment of reliable, largely Western European military forces. IFOR ground units, backed by

NATO airpower, were more than adequate to the task of quelling ethnic violence and restoring the degree of order mandated by the Dayton and Paris accords. Where intervention required more intimate involvement in Balkan affairs, the Pentagon could delegate functions to civilian contractors or newly established agencies such as the International Criminal Court.

In the final analysis, even though the American mission to Bosnia largely succeeded, it provided a poor precedent for U.S. military action in small wars. In terms of structure and weaponry, the various Balkan factions, particularly the Serbs, more closely resembled a debased version of the old Warsaw Pact than true irregular forces to be found in Somalia, Afghanistan, or other portions of the underdeveloped world. Nevertheless, by committing conventional forces to a mission that defied conventional doctrine and training, Operation Joint Endeavor vindicated advocates within the Defense Department and civilian policy making community who wanted an American military that was more adaptable to an increasingly diverse array of threats to national security.

Tentative Changes to the Status Quo

It was evident in the latter half of the nineties that the American military was under considerable pressure to adapt to both new global circumstances and a new set of missions. Caught between the contradictory pressures of shrinking budgets and increasing deployments, the Pentagon sought more than simple relevancy in foreign policy. In some respects, the period resembled the time after Vietnam when the American military embarked on a fundamental debate regarding its purpose as an institution. The critical departure in the intellectual discussion in the late nineties was its basic assumptions. Many Vietnam veterans remained in the upper echelons of the military. Their younger contemporaries, in contrast, had risen through the ranks during the eighties, a time when Reagan administration policies had rebuilt confidence and capability. Operation Desert Storm, not the fall of Saigon, punctuated their experience. Consequently, the future leadership of the American armed forces tended to focus more on aggressive adaptation to war fare than to simply contemplating retrenchment and renovation.[82]

Doctrinally, the American military took an increasingly abstract approach to identifying threats and responses. Some of the methodologies discussed at the time read like a college course catalog and included such academic disciplines as sociology, theology, and anthropology.[83] Advocates argued for the abandonment of conceptual straightjackets created and maintained by the Cold War. Modern soldiers had to incorporate social, economic, ethnic, and religious factors into basic decisions by the whole spectrum of military leadership, from the Pentagon to combat units in the field. In essence, the American military had caught up to arguments raised by Carl Stiner and SOCOM at the start of the decade.[84]

Military policy documents produced during this period followed a similar trajectory. The 1995 revision of the *National Military Strategy of the United States* made "flexible and selective engagement" a key prerequisite for action. Peacetime missions included a laundry list of functions such as "improve military capabilities, promote democratic ideals, relieve suffering, and enhance regional stability." While the strategy reaffirmed the commitment to fight and win two regional wars, more than two-thirds of national military objectives were dedicated to "peacetime engagement" and "deterrence and conflict prevention."[85]

Two years later, a new revision of the *National Military Strategy* found the Pentagon groping its way toward articulating both the ends and means of military policy. The document acknowledged that, "in all cases, the commitment of U.S. forces must be based on the importance of the US interests involved, the potential risks to American troops, and the appropriateness of the military mission." Primary threats broke down into "regional dangers" from Iraq, Iran, and North Korea; "asymmetric challenges," such as those posed by terrorists; the "transnational dangers" presented by such problems as ethnic strife; and the "wild cards" that might produce threats from unanticipated sources. The prescribed responses were an interesting mélange of vague ideas such as "promoting stability" and "confidence building" measures offered by joint training exercises and exchange programs. A reliance upon deterrence runs throughout the 1997 document. The JCS suggested that American allies could be backstopped by military assistance and enemies given pause by a display of power and resolve. However, this Cold War device was highly problematic when applied to regional threats, the very "rogue" nations mentioned by Anthony Lake, terrorist organizations, or sources of transnational instability, which, by definition, would not observe the same rules as rational actors.[86]

Despite the fact the American military was prepared to accept new approaches to doctrine, old habits were hard to lose. This was evident in *Joint Vision 2010,* a 1996 publication that the Pentagon presented as "the conceptual template for joint operations and warfighting in the future."[87] *Joint Vision 2010* was formed around four fundamental concepts: dominant maneuver, precision engagement, dimensional protection, and focused logistics. Its goals were ambitious, promising "a joint force—pervasive in peace, decisive in war, preeminent in any form of conflict."[88]

However, a close reading of *Joint Vision 2010* reveals that nuclear and conventional forces remained at the center of U.S. military doctrine.[89] Many proposed reforms were simply managerial in nature. The JCS promised technological innovations to eliminate redundancy, with the ultimate goal being "information superiority" that would guide the four fundamental concepts of American military power. Along the same vein, "connectivity" would allow American forces to act with "decisive speed and tempo" and result in "positional advantage" against future enemies.[90]

To its credit, *Joint Vision 2010* acknowledged the fact that computer technology was the new frontier of warfare in the modern era.[91] The potential threat of "cyber war" had indeed become very serious as the United States joined the rest of the world in its embrace of electronic data collection and the Internet. Media sources noted in 1999 that as many as 120 groups or countries were developing information warfare systems and twenty-three nations had specifically targeted the United States.[92] The need for a new capability to address these challenges was self-evident.

Unfortunately, even as cyber war joined the lengthy list of new military endeavors, technology mattered most as a means to improve existing forces. In this context, military strategy became an exercise in technological superiority, wherein the Pentagon sought out increasingly elaborate systems to deliver munitions and control the flow of tactical information on the future battlefield. The Army adapted the Land Warrior system that promoted the concept of "angular speed," which loosely translated as the ability to outthink the enemy and maintain the combat initiative.[93] All branches of the armed forces placed increasing emphasis on automation and miniaturization. Each service, for example, pursued research and production of drone aircraft for use in the field.[94]

Whether applied to the Internet or the modern battlefield, the U.S. armed forces subsequently adopted the Revolution in Military Affairs (RMA). Built around America's comparative advantage in technology, the RMA posited the belief that superior organization and coordination could overwhelm an enemy, not with mass but with the precise application of information. Historian Steven Metz wrote in 1997 that "simultaneous operations across one or more military theaters might soon be possible. At the same time, the relationship between accuracy and distance in the application of military force might change as extremely precise, standoff strikes become the method preferred by advanced militaries. The RMA could relegate the close-quarters clash of troops to history."[95] Utilizing the pinpoint accuracy afforded by global positioning systems and "brilliant" weaponry, the United States was essentially projecting cyber war into the real world. By deliberately attacking command, control, and communication infrastructure, U.S. forces could effectively paralyze an enemy, creating a man-made "fog of war" that would result in victory with minimal casualties.[96]

The real beneficiary of this thinking was the U.S. Air Force. In a situation reminiscent of the fifties, the Air Force offered the balance between affordability and precision while emphasizing technological advantage. It was a "bigger bang for the buck" in the new age. More broadly, *Joint Vision 2010* and the revolution in military affairs were highly appealing to the American military because, updated phrasing aside, they were warmed-over versions of old, Cold War practices that did not require a major revision of doctrine. Plans to decapitate an opposing forces command structure, for example, could be traced back to Strategic Air Command plans in the late forties. The RMA was also attractive to national security policymakers. It did not require the same massive application of force (or need for basing rights and third-party cooperation) that had been necessary in the First Gulf War. What it did call for was basically warfare by remote control, as demonstrated by cruise missile strikes against suspected terrorist targets after the African embassy bombings in 1998 and the campaign against Serbian forces threatening Kosovo in 1999.[97]

Fortunately, as American strategists were burnishing past doctrine, they devoted much-needed attention to small wars on the ground. By the mid-nineties, the Defense Department began publishing a series of documents that articulated the specific components of conflict at the lowest end of the spectrum. These manuals included *Joint Tactics, Techniques, and Procedures for Peacekeeping Operations* (1994), *Joint Doctrine for Military Operations Other Than War* (1995), and *Field Manual 100-20: Stability and Support Operations* (1996).[98] The latter publication was described as a "mature expression of U.S. theory and doctrine for limited conflict as it has evolved over the last 35 years."[99]

Special Operations Command added to this growing catalog in 1996 with the publication of *SOF Vision 2020.* SOCOM saw itself as ideally positioned to meet new demands placed upon the American armed forces after the Cold War. It could address a broad spectrum of threats, such as "subversion, terrorism, global environmental degradation, illegal drugs, information-based warfare, and other challenges to international stability and prosperity."[100] *SOF Vision 2020* went on to claim that "U.S. success in the crises of 2020 will largely hinge on small, mature, and when necessary, lethal forces to assist those in need, to stabilize flashpoints, or to pursue aggressors."[101] Subsequent special forces deployments—such as Safe Passage, an operation to train local forces in mine-clearing operations in Afghanistan, Eritrea, and Ethiopia—stressed this expanded portfolio of missions.[102]

To put these concepts into common practice, the U.S. military created the Army Combat Mission Training Center (CMTC). Located in an old training area near Hohenfels, Germany, the CMTC was a simulation of contemporary operational conditions in Bosnia. It included five complete towns with the "appropriate religious and ethnic mix of people," simulated warring factions, and a variety of nongovernmental organizations.[103] It was designed to acclimatize conventional formations to the unexpected difficulties they might encounter in urban terrain densely populated with civilians, the media, and international observers. Later, these same functions were introduced at the JRTC, located at Fort Polk, Louisiana.

By the end of the nineties, it was clear that the American military had shifted some of its training and doctrine to more closely suit operations other than conventional warfare. However, the sum of a weighty body of new scholarship and field manuals did not translate into a revolution in military affairs for small wars. By and large, the armed forces, particularly the U.S. Army, clung to the basic idea that the existing force structure, weapons, and training were adequate to the task of new OOTW missions. Units on peacekeeping deployments tended to focus on conventional readiness standards defined by the mission essential task list (METL) mandated for all units. Consequently, the day-to-day methods used for Operation Joint Endeavor in Bosnia were translated through the METL into dismounted patrolling and static defense rather than the more subtle practices taught at Hohenfels.[104] Through this type of lens, unit commanders saw peace enforcement operations as an opportunity to reinforce conventional training. Colonel Alan W. Thrasher, the artillery commander for the 1st Armored Division in Bosnia, noted in his official correspondence that Joint Endeavor offered unique opportunities to cross-train with British, Russian, Turkish, Danish, Estonian, and Finnish units serving in the region, but not to develop his unit's aptitude for small wars.[105]

In reality, the training programs established at the CMTC and the JRTC had a limited impact on units rotating through the facilities. A simple reason was expediency. Rather than completely retrain large formations in the art of low-intensity war, the Defense Department largely adapted skills already present in the conventional portfolio. Consequently, peace enforcement was reduced to sniper and countersniper tactics, small unit operations, urban patrolling, armor-infantry operations, security, checkpoint, and convoy operations, a playbook that read like a warmed-over version of Cold War–era doctrine. Appended to this list was training to improve "situational understanding" and efforts devoted to "engaging the locals."[106]

Just how much of this latter training was internalized became apparent during the Mountain Eagle training exercises conducted at the CMTC. One of the primary problems, according to a 1998 Army report, were failed attempts to train soldiers in the *Joint Military Commission Handbook,* the rules of engagement, and the graduated response matrix (GRM). Neither individual soldiers nor their commanders fully understood the dense, complicated guidelines contained in the matrix. As the Center for Army Lessons Learned later noted: "Many commanders simply repeat verbatim the GRM they receive from higher headquarters. Consequently, leaders fail to fully grasp the purpose and use of the GRM during operations; hence, they cannot explain it to subordinates. Leaders often show the GRM as a flow chart in the hope that soldiers can easily decipher it themselves. Yet one leader confessed that he would need an advanced degree in calculus to fully comprehend the flow chart himself."[107]

In many respects, Mountain Eagle represented both the final fruition of small wars doctrine and its next generation of new dilemmas. By the end of the nineties, there is no question that the U.S. armed forces made considerable progress with respect to low-intensity conflict. A host of detailed studies, based on years of reflection and the applied lessons of multiple deployments, now graced the shelves of the Pentagon, SOCOM, and conventional units stationed around the world. The Defense Department had also taken the next logical step in creating dedicated training areas like the JRTC and the CMTC to introduce new practices into the standard training regimen of units destined for stability and support operations. Completing this process was a problem of a different order, however.

Reshaping conventional small unit practices to fit the GRM proved to be difficult for two primary reasons. The first was simple habit. Regardless of specific branch or specialty, the combat arms mission is straightforward: to close with and destroy the enemy. In peacetime, unit evaluation standards and individual promotion are predicated on the successful completion of these tasks. In wartime, the premium on survival creates its own litmus test. Units trained in combat missions lacked the finesse necessary to cultivate relationships within an arena comprising many actors, most of them civilian. Simply breaking down large conventional units into small subcomponents did not automatically create the flexibility necessary to cope with a potpourri of new, unexpected, and confusing elements. In fact, by relying most heavily on small unit leaders, Charles C. Krulak's "strategic corporal," the U.S. military was placing enormous responsibilities on its least experienced personnel, company-grade officers and junior noncommissioned officers.[108] While this may have worked within SOCOM, in regular units it was problematic.

A second obstacle was conceptual. Stability and support operations are complex. Integrating as they did a host of cultural, political, and economic issues, the most well-intended guidelines could quickly overwhelm soldiers on the ground, as the Army learned during Mountain Eagle. In order to address this problem, the military needed to devote additional time to allow units to internalize the practices necessary to successfully prosecute small wars. Given the Pentagon's desire to retain nuclear and conventional forces at the core of its strategic thinking, this proved difficult. Unfortunately, the tragic events of the new century would allow for even less reflection and preparation.

Conclusions

Global events and domestic preference established sharp boundaries for military affairs in the Clinton era. As late as January 2000, the administration publicly maintained a national security policy that restricted military action even as military commitments grew. In "A National Security Strategy for a New Century" (2000), the White House announced: "American engagement must be tempered by recognition that there are limits to America's involvement in the world, and that decisions to commit resources must be weighed against the need to sustain our engagement over the long term."[109] Recognizing these limits, the Clinton administration argued for the "selective" use of armed force and set the bar very high before considering it. The document asked: "Have we explored or exhausted non-military means that offer a reasonable chance of achieving our goals? Is there a clearly defined, achievable mission? What is the threat environment and what risks will our forces face? What level of effort will be needed to achieve our goals? What are the potential costs—human and financial—of the operation?"[110] Consequently, even as the U.S. military developed a more precise method for treating small wars, national security officials produced their own more precise limitations on military action.

Later, these self-imposed limits would be overtaken by more conventional priorities. Domestic prosperity proved to be a major distraction just as the military finally embarked upon meaningful reform in the late nineties. Deploying ground forces for peace stability operations, as Kosovo proved, was next to impossible in the climate of the time. However, the impact of political partisanship on national security policy making proved to be an even greater drag on overseas commitments. Former Secretary of Defense William Cohen commented in a 2001 article on the "corrosive effect of partisan discord seeping into the national security arena."[111] Once the impeachment proceedings were concluded, Clinton's capacity to lead effectively ended with more than two years left in his term.

The military establishment was also complicit in blocking reform. Even as it endorsed the next generation of small wars doctrine, the Pentagon remained largely focused on its conventional and nuclear missions. Although the separate branches reoriented a limited number of units and training to smaller conflicts, the core of the internal discussion was whether or not the United States could maintain forces adequate for two major regional wars.[112] Viewed within this context, stability and support operations suffered as an opportunity cost of more important strategic priorities.[113] Consequently, as the decade moved forward, military leaders became prone to what Richard Haass defined as "minimalism," a reversion to smaller and smaller actions designed to retain discretion.[114]

In the end, military and civilian leadership moved along parallel and complementary paths with respect to small wars. Regardless of their motives, they successfully, if not intentionally, promoted the contradictory results of better preparedness for low-intensity conflicts coupled with a reduced commitment to them. When the Bush administration took this military to war in 2001, it found an institution largely defined by these contradictions.

Early peacekeeping. U.S. Marines on patrol in Beirut, Lebanon, 1983.

OPPOSITE:
Above: Preparing for the big war in Europe. U.S. armor during REFORGER exercises, West Germany, January 1985.
Below: The war on drugs at sea. U.S.S. *Taurus* stops a merchant ship during a drug interdiction patrol, 1989.

TAURUS
PHM-3

Armed intervention in Latin America. American armored personnel carriers on the Pan American Highway enroute to Panama, 1989.

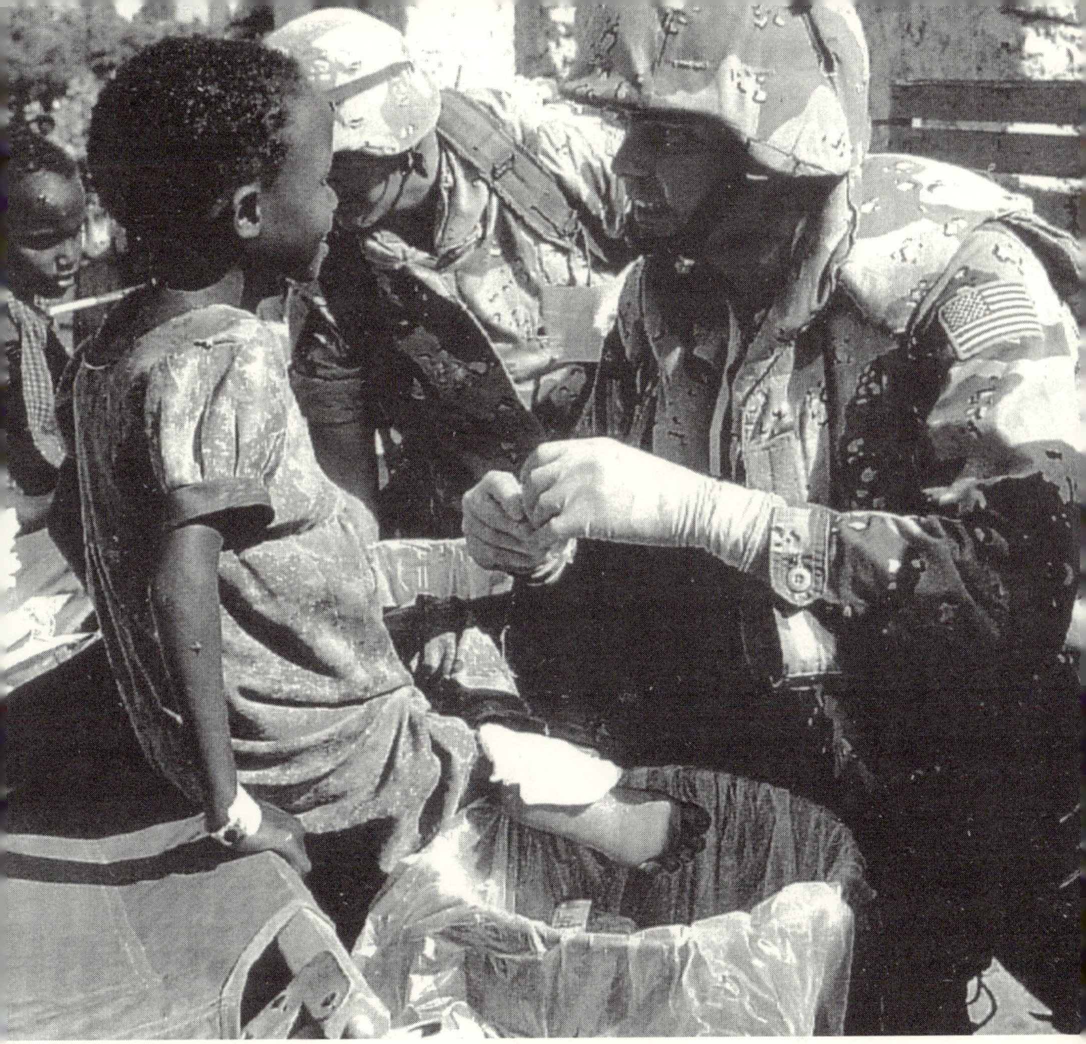

Early stages of humanitarian intervention. U.S. Navy corpsman treats Somali girl, January 1993.

OPPOSITE:

Above: American power in the New World Order. Iraqi MIG-25 destroyed on the ground during Operation Desert Storm, 1991.

Below: New American responsibilities. Iraqi Kurds awaiting relief supplies during Operation Provide Comfort, 1991.

6

The Drug War

Others may want to quibble or dispute my terms. But what matters is that the President act and not be acted upon. Leadership. Let's go.

—William J. Bennett in a memorandum to John Sununu

It has become a truism in drug policy research that the illicit cocaine and heroin industry resembles a balloon filled with air or water. If this "balloon" is squeezed by law enforcement, that air or water, i.e. the coca or opium poppy fields, cocaine and heroin production sites, and trafficking routes, simply shift elsewhere.

—Cornelius Friesendorf, "Squeezing the Balloon? United States Air Interdiction and the Restructuring of the South American Drug Industry in the 1990s," *Crime, Law & Social Change*

On 2 December 1993 Pablo Escobar Gaviria, head of the Medellín drug cartel, was shot dead on a rooftop by Colombian security forces. Police and intelligence officials celebrated the end of one of the country's most notorious criminals. A *Time* magazine story noted that the once powerful figure had died barefoot as he fled: "Pablo Escobar exited his life in a fashion antithetical to the spirit in which he lived: desperate and vulnerable."[1]

Many leaders in both the United States and Colombia were convinced that Escobar's death was a significant victory in the ongoing "war on drugs." Older, more experienced observers knew better, however. The vacuum created by the destruction of Escobar's cartel was soon filled by smaller, more agile organizations. As one senior Drug Enforcement Administration (DEA) official commented shortly after Escobar's death, "The bottom line is that the cocaine business is bigger than ever."[2]

In many respects, the circumstances surrounding the Medellín cartel's downfall were emblematic of the high hopes and hard realities of another type of small war fought by the United States over the course of forty years. While the Vietnam War raged, illegal drugs were primarily a domestic policy problem shaped by rising public concerns over crime, addiction, and a breakdown of basic social standards. At the end of the sixties, the issue rose to national prominence and prompted the creation of cabinet level agencies dedicated to treatment and law enforcement.[3] By the eighties, the Reagan administration intruded upon these civilian domains by deliberately committing the Pentagon to counter the flow of narcotics into America. Once Soviet communism collapsed in 1991, the United States needed another raison d'être to be in Latin America. Many authors claim that drugs simply became a new surrogate for communism.[4]

Presently, the drug war is directly linked to the U.S. war on terror. Since 2001, the United States has constructed a problematic linkage between narcotics trafficking, regional insurgencies, and terrorism. While the three factors no doubt intertwine at points, discerning their exact relationship presents a significant dilemma for American policy makers. So has the increased degree of U.S. military intervention in Latin America. In its attempts to combat the flow of drugs into the United States at its source, Washington risks disrupting the very stability it seeks in the hemisphere. Referring to Colombia in 2003, one historian noted that American policy "has severely distorted some basic democratic mechanisms, abducting them from public deliberation and creating reserved domains that are not only undemocratic, but also allow the growth of authoritarian tendencies within the state."[5]

Over four decades, the American commitment to this "war" has grown and spread into both foreign and domestic policy making. When it began in the late sixties, efforts to counteract illegal drugs were dominated by a discourse that addressed domestic laws and programs. For the most part, public officials concerned themselves with policies contained within the medical community and the criminal justice system.[6] Moreover, as the public commitment to fighting illegal drugs grew, the drug war also became a fixed point in American politics. Because it so readily drew media attention and evoked public fears, a candidate's particular stance on drugs was a critical electoral litmus test. Consequently, combating drugs became as much a function of real policy making as it was a function of tough-sounding rhetoric.

By the seventies, as public consumption of controlled substances increased, the drug war also became a significant foreign policy issue. Initially, the root source of the problem was Southeast Asia. Recent scholarship has argued that drug use within the American military in Vietnam, and the subsequent public outcry over what one periodical in 1971 described as the "specter of weapons-trained, addicted combat veterans," provoked the Nixon administration into action. To counteract the purported threat, the White House requested that millions be appropriated for drug treatment programs in the military. At the same time, the United States rapidly escalated counternarcotics efforts in South Vietnam, Laos, and Thailand.[7] The same mix of domestic and foreign initiatives would come to dominate policy debates regarding Latin America, where a cocaine and marijuana boom quickly became an integral component of regional politics and military affairs. Tens of millions of illicit dollars were a dangerous temptation to weak governmental systems. Narcotics also provided cartels with formidable resources to threaten the rule of law, police agencies tasked with its enforcement, and even national military institutions.[8]

Positioned as it was between the foreign and domestic policy arenas, American counterdrug programs were often confusing and contradictory. In part, this was a product of the tension between treating drug addiction (demand) and punishing drug traffickers (supply). In another more important sense, problems also became more pronounced as U.S. officials progressively militarized counternarcotics policy.

Military force was a tempting way to satisfy the red meat rhetoric that policy makers regularly offered on the topic of law and order. Using American armed forces to fight the threat of drugs invited, by definition, political superlatives. It was the toughest of tough options. The substance of military participation in the drug war was equally attractive.

In policymaking terms, military force was tempting because it offered decisive action. When American military forces were introduced into the drug war, it was an article of faith that constructing security was necessary before political, social, or economic reform could begin. This conventional wisdom was a latent feature of the Cold War repeatedly applied to the Third World, including Latin America during the Alliance for Progress and afterward. It would retain its relevancy when the focus shifted from anticommunism to counternarcotics.[9]

The transition from treatment and law enforcement to successive military campaigns in the hinterlands of South America was anything but immediate. However, the root elements of militarization were present once the Nixon administration identified illegal drugs as a threat to the American polity. Military power was a reflection of the importance placed on defeating the threat at a time when it was not uncommon to frame a domestic policy process (e.g., the War on Poverty) in these terms. The application of graduated levels of military power also revealed the temptation to find tangible progress in what hindsight recognizes was a dynamic and increasingly intractable problem.

The Forty Years' War

As a presidential candidate, Richard Nixon ran hard on the issue of law and order.[10] A major plank of the 1968 Republican campaign was his response to significantly increasing instances of murder, rape, robbery, and assault. Equally troubling were widespread protests on hundreds of university campuses that offered a disturbing counterpoint to urban riots ravaging the country. In his first year in office, Nixon warned of the "cultural calamity" that awaited the country unless quick and decisive steps were taken.[11]

Action was not long in coming. To test its point and the limits of American jurisprudence, the administration introduced legislation for the District of Columbia that included such provisions as "no knock" warrants and "preventative detention" (holding criminal suspects up to sixty days before trial). Both were successfully challenged in the courts as flagrant violations of due process. In the longer term, they set out clear public markers regarding Nixon's stance on law and order and established the overt limits of federal policy.[12]

Nixon took a similar rhetorical approach to illegal drugs, which he considered to be a component of the larger crime problem. In a special message to Congress on 17 June 1971, the president declared drug abuse "public enemy number one in America."[13] But rather than institute a radical approach to attacking the drug problem with the blunt instruments introduced to the District of Columbia, the administration adopted a broader and more constructive approach. Starting in 1971, the White House initiated an extensive series of policy initiatives that were designed to limit consumption at home and constrict supply abroad. Interestingly, the Defense Department became an early beneficiary of federally sponsored treatment programs. In the latter years of the Vietnam War, military personnel were experiencing an increasing incidence of substance abuse and addiction. To address this problem, the Pentagon received $50 million to begin Operation Golden Flow, a urinalysis-testing program for active-duty service members.[14] Civilian initiatives also followed in 1972. The administration created the Office of Drug Abuse and later combined it with the Bureau of Narcotics and Dangerous Drugs to form the Drug Enforcement Administration a year later. As part of his budget for 1973, Nixon won $420 million in appropriations for drug control, eight times federal spending before he became president.[15]

While these projects unfolded, it became evident that the administration's primary intent was not a hard line on law enforcement but a greater emphasis on drug treatment programs. This was clear in Nixon's budget proposals, where approximately two-thirds of the funding requested focused on prevention and treatment under the guidance of the National Institute of Drug Abuse, itself a 1971 creation of the administration.[16]

Regardless of his emphasis on law enforcement or treatment, Nixon permanently established drug abuse and prevention as a national policy issue. Moreover, the proliferation of programs and new federal offices charged with either assistance or interdiction created a growing bureaucratic infrastructure in Washington and in field offices around the United States. As this process unfolded, Nixon fostered the basic public expectation that Washington would construct affirmative policies to arrest the annual increase in domestic drug consumption and counter the social and economic problems that followed in its wake. His successors could challenge these expectations at their own political risk.[17]

Nixon also deliberately linked the problem of illegal drugs to U.S. foreign policy. In addition to State and Justice Department programs in Southeast Asia, he expanded attention to Latin America, reflecting the growing importance of the region to the drug trade. Under Operation Cooperation (1969), for example, the United States trained 500 narcotics police in Mexico and provided helicopters and surveillance equipment for counternarcotics operations.[18] In relatively short order, American allies discovered that compliance in the drug war was a key litmus test for U.S. assistance.

Unfortunately, American counternarcotics programs did not escape the systemic corruption and conflicts of interest that embodied so much of the Nixon era. Law enforcement officials active in Southeast Asia discovered direct CIA complicity in the regional drug trade. In 1976, a Justice Department investigation directly linked the Central Intelligence Agency with the opium trade in the "Golden Triangle" region of Laos. Corruption also plagued the Drug Enforcement Administration in its early years. A 1975 Senate investigation of the DEA verified media claims that the agency had covered up the illegal activities of Robert Vesco, a heroin dealer who had donated $200,000 to Nixon's campaign fund. Its final report noted that the DEA's "environment was conducive to corrupt and irregular practices."[19]

The remainder of the seventies reflected what could best be called a lull in federal activity. Representing a shift in the public debate toward greater tolerance, Jimmy Carter called for decriminalizing marijuana during his campaign and supported proposed federal legislation to reach this goal by 1977.[20] Once Carter assumed office, his administration also pressed for policy reforms that would make distinctions between heroin, cocaine, and marijuana use. Officials considered efforts to curtail coca cultivation as problematic at best. The 1978 annual report of the White House Office of Drug Abuse Policy commented that "there are serious problems in attempting to reduce coca cultivation. Coca is legally grown in Peru and Bolivia, is a part of the Indian history and culture and has extensive legitimate local use. In addition, the coca bush is extremely hardy, easy to grow and harvest, and lives for nearly 40 years. Both major producing countries are poor, and coca is a principal cash crop for many of the people. Obviously, we cannot expect instant changes."[21]

After downgrading the threat posed by marijuana and dismissing the likelihood of progress against cocaine cultivation, policy makers focused their specific attention on heroin. Heroin was arguably a more dangerous narcotic than cocaine and, in policy terms, a major threat to public health as well as law enforcement. Although its use had increased, it was a comparatively more isolated problem than the other two drugs. Consequently, the White House endorsed the decision to essentially ration federal spending and manpower to address what policymakers believed was the greater threat.[22]

Although there was initial public sympathy for Carter's approach to the drug problem, it did not last. The public saw the separate treatment of marijuana and other drugs as a contradiction rather than the application of logic. As the debate over muddled policy priorities evolved, it was followed by a backlash against what a growing number of parents' organizations considered to be the administration's permissiveness regarding illegal substances. Disinterested in fine distinctions, a growing number of Americans were deeply disturbed by the proliferation of drugs throughout the country. According to a 2006 study, U.S. drug use peaked in 1979, with 25 million Americans, or 14.1 percent of the population, regularly consuming illegal substances.[23]

Carter's efforts to halt the flow of drugs did not help his case. When the administration requested aid for projects abroad, officials found themselves quickly enmeshed in congressional conditions restricting its use. In the post-Vietnam period, lawmakers consistently asserted their prerogative to control general policy decisions as well as the specific types of equipment purchased with U.S. funding, such as helicopters, patrol vessels, and transport vehicles. Much of this difficult and counterproductive debate was exemplified in the controversy over the Mexican government's use of the herbicide paraquat. A congressional amendment to the International Security Assistance Act of 1978 prohibited its use for fear of the potential health risk to marijuana smokers in the United States. While the amendment reflected the concerns of health advocates in America, it provoked outrage in Mexico, which was attempting to combat drug trafficking at its source. They were not alone. Countries that had embraced Nixon's aggressive approach only a few years earlier now found themselves at odds with American law. Speaking of the general climate at the time, one diplomat remarked in 1980: "It's like asking someone to build a house by telling him he cannot use any hammers, saws, or nails. These guys in Congress are like janitors playing brain surgeons."[24]

At the start of the eighties it appeared that the public and policy makers alike had reached the consensus that counternarcotics policy was adrift and in need of a new focus. The increasing incidence of drug use in America reinforced their case. By 1979 more than 35 percent of high school seniors admitted to using some type of illicit drug, according to an annual survey entitled *Monitoring the Future.* As the eighties proceeded, there was increasing evidence of drug use in major cities such as Washington, Los Angeles, and New Orleans. Drug-related illnesses were also reported with an increasingly disturbing frequency in hospital emergency rooms. The introduction of crack cocaine into the American market was a major source of the problem. As crack addiction wreaked havoc in the health care sector, its rapid growth in popularity also prompted a subsequent increase in crime and violence across the country. Narcotics arrests surged in their wake. In 1986 the DEA reported $370 million in drug seizures, more than double the previous year.[25]

By the end of the decade, Americans identified drugs as the number one problem facing the nation. A 1988 *New York Times*/CBS poll indicated that 48 percent of those surveyed believed that drug trafficking was America's most important foreign policy problem, ahead of Central America (22 percent), arms control (13 percent), and terrorism. Americans believed that stopping the flow of drugs was more important than confronting communism by a ratio of 3–1 (63 percent to 21 percent).[26]

Lawmakers were quick to respond. In many respects the inflamed rhetoric of the period recalled the anti-Soviet bromides of the fifties. Representative Arthur Ravenel Jr. (R-SC) called for the U.S. military to shoot down suspected drug-trafficking aircraft on sight. Reflecting the consensus of the day, Tom Clancy popularized the idea in his best-selling 1989 novel *Clear and Present Danger.*[27] The Anti-Drug Abuse Act of 1986 promised a series of programs for education, treatment, and rehabilitation, and greater emphasis on tougher enforcement policies and lengthier prison sentences. Federal outlays for these programs also increased, from $2.2 billion in 1986 to $3.9 billion the following year.[28]

As Nixon had done, the Reagan administration expanded its efforts to attack the source of illegal drugs but produced problematic results at best. American agencies spent significant amounts of time and funding on simply destroying crops on the ground. In Peru, the Special Project for the Control and Eradication of Coca in the Upper Huallaga (CORAH), subsidized by USAID, eliminated 5,000 hectares of coca fields in 1985. However, that same year an additional 12,000 hectares of new fields were brought into cultivation.[29]

The mid-eighties represented an important turning point in the drug war. Clearly, a consensus had emerged regarding the nature of the threat to American interests, although the public largely construed this threat in domestic terms. Congress was more than ready to jump on this bandwagon by meting out harsher federal penalties for drug trafficking and greater funding for a host of programs at home and abroad. However, the difficulties in finding traction against the drug epidemic in the United States and a significant lack of success within the supplier nations of South America called for even stronger measures, both as a matter of policy and public rhetoric. At the time, the advantages of militarizing the drug war seemed self-evident.

The Reagan administration's initial response to this idea took the form of National Security Decision Directive (NSDD) 221, "Narcotics and National Security," in April 1986. A portion of the document provides important context for the period: "Of primary concern are those nations with a flourishing narcotics industry, where a combination of international criminal trafficking organizations, rural insurgents, and urban terrorists can undermine the stability of the local government; corrupt efforts to curb drug crop production, processing, and distribution; and distort public perception of the narcotics issue in such a way that it becomes part of an anti-U.S. or anti-Western debate."[30] What the finding makes clear are the linkages between local insurgencies and terrorist groups that used drug money to smuggle weapons.[31] By framing narcotics trafficking in terms that affected American allies and their stability, the administration established the necessary prerequisite for direct military intervention.

Consequently, the White House directed the Defense Department to "enable U.S. military forces to support counter-narcotics efforts more actively, consistent with the maintenance of force readiness and training." Military assistance provided intelligence collection, analysis, and dissemination for counternarcotics operations. The administration mandate also included the planning and execution of large-scale operations to interdict drug trafficking into the United States. In countries that provided the bulk of cocaine and marijuana, American military missions added counternarcotics to their portfolio of foreign military assistance.[32]

The Pentagon contributed formidable resources to interdict inbound narcotics shipments, particularly those smuggled through the air. In 1983 alone, the U.S. Air Force estimated that 4,000 flights brought contraband into the United States, transporting approximately 11,000 tons of marijuana and between 54 to 71 metric tons of cocaine. To counter this deluge, a host of air assets, including E-3 AWACS, AEROSTAT blimps, B-52s, P-3Bs, and HC-130N/Ps, were deployed to close off radar gaps along the southern border of the continental United States. It was an expensive proposition. According to the Air Force, it cost as much as $4,400 for each hour flown by one AWACS aircraft. Overall, the air cordon cost between $75 million and $310 million a year depending on the degree of coverage.[33]

The Defense Department also contributed substantial assets to attacking the sources of drugs in Latin America. The primary locus of the cocaine trade was the Andean region. In 1987, Peru, Bolivia, and Colombia accounted for virtually all of the 120 tons of cocaine arriving in the United States that year.[34] To address this problem, U.S. special forces became actively involved in training paramilitary police in both Bolivia and Peru during the late eighties. Operation Blast Furnace, launched in 1986, was the direct product of American assistance. Involving six Black Hawk helicopters and 160 troops, it briefly paralyzed the cocaine industry in Bolivia. Between 1987 and 1988, the Defense Department also provided over 15,000 hours of airborne surveillance to counternarcotics in Latin America proper. American military helicopters saw use in the Caribbean during Operation BAT (Bahamas and Turks). Ground radar units were also deployed along the Arizona-Mexico border as part of Operation Groundhog.[35]

What these efforts accomplished was at the very least debatable. Balanced against the hundreds of millions of dollars spent, the Pentagon claimed overall drug seizures totaling $2.8 billion between November 1985 and February 1986.[36] However, balanced against the sheer volume of drugs entering the United States in the eighties, one author described military efforts as "only marginally effective."[37] As will be discussed below, neither the U.S. military nor the host countries involved in the drug war were able to destroy the cartels or reduce the flow of drugs.

A number of factors account for this failure. The first involved priorities. Although charged by the civilian leadership to join the war of drugs, the military did so only reluctantly and with the clear sense that counternarcotics operations were a distant second to other national security priorities. American military decision making in Central America illustrates this trend. Throughout the decade, U.S. Southern Command maintained Manuel Noriega as an asset despite the knowledge that the Panamanian Defense Forces were actively involved in the drug trade. The same applied to individuals who provided arms for the contras and transported narcotics to the United States. Although allegations that the CIA created the so-called crack epidemic proved false in subsequent investigations, the agency was aware of its operatives' links with Latin American drug cartels. Throughout much of the undeclared war that raged in Central America during the eighties, it was also apparent that drug smuggling transcended ideology. At various times Fidel Castro, Manuel Noriega, and the Sandinista government of Nicaragua were directly involved with the cartels. Former Southern Command (SOUTHCOM) commander General Paul Gorman put the matter bluntly: "If you want to move arms or munitions in Latin America, the established networks are owned by the cartels. It has lent itself to the purposes of terrorists, saboteurs, of spies, of insurgents and subversives."[38]

Military reluctance was also shaped by the fact that senior leaders consider counternarcotics to rightly be the province of domestic law enforcement agencies. Commanders at all levels were well aware of the provisions contained in the Posse Comitatus Act of 1878 that specifically prohibited the use of military forces in law enforcement. Although the original act had been subsequently modified, military officials remained leery of the potential gray areas that might ensnare their institution. One method devised to deflect calls for additional military engagement in the drug war was to recommend the use of the National Guard. Deployed at the behest of state governors, these units purportedly had better training and, more important, a clearer understanding of local conditions that reduced the risks of violating state and federal law.[39]

Despite these reservations, demands for military participation in the war against drugs continued unabated into the presidency of George H. W. Bush. In a May 1988 campaign speech, Bush claimed: "The logic is simple. The cheapest and safest way to eradicate narcotics is to destroy them at their source. . . . We need to wipe out crops wherever they grow and take out labs where they exist."[40] Bush's drug czar, William Bennett, issued an impromptu call for action only a few months after the new administration began. In an April 1989 memorandum to White House chief of staff John Sununu, Bennett urged with his characteristic impatience that "it is time to cut through the analytic morass. . . . Others may want to quibble or dispute my terms. But what matters is that the President act and not be acted upon. Leadership, Let's go."[41]

The administration did move forward, preserving much of Reagan's domestic law enforcement initiatives but shifting the primary focus of overseas programs. After 1989, U.S. aid was directed toward halting the flow of narcotics from the Andean region, specifically Bolivia and Colombia. While the United States maintained interdiction programs in countries such as Peru, the main effort was in the former countries. During the Bush years, the administration provided Bolivia and Colombia funding for military assistance, law enforcement, and intelligence programs designed to disrupt drug trafficking at its source.

Under a series of national security directives issued between June and August 1989, the Defense Department was directed to expand military aid for counternarcotics programs.[42] Much of this work fell to the ground forces. The Army, for example, deployed Tactical Assistance Teams to Peru and Bolivia in 1989. Made up of special forces and military intelligence personnel, they assisted the host militaries in developing networks of informants as well as collecting more sophisticated sources of technical information from electronic monitoring. Special forces advisers were active on the ground in training small units for operations in rugged mountain and jungle terrain where the cartels normally hid their airstrips, processing labs, and storage areas. They also served as liaisons with the local armed forces and police, as well as the U.S. Drug Enforcement Administration.[43]

An unexpected byproduct of military participation in the drug war was the tangle it produced between law enforcement and intelligence collection. Although the *posse comitatus* limits did not apply to overseas operations, administration officials raised significant concerns regarding the potential conflict between the use of classified intelligence sources and an individual's right to confront an accuser in court.[44] The attorney general's office expressed concerns about deploying military personnel against drug traffickers, not only as a matter of law, but also for the impact that it would have on federal officers pursuing cases outside the United States. At Langley, the CIA leadership rejected a proposal that they share responsibility for filing legal notices barring discovery or "staying a civil proceeding where necessary to protect an ongoing investigation, prosecution, or national security operation."[45] In the end, allowing host countries to retain the right to prosecute cases against alleged drug traffickers largely solved this dilemma. A few high-profile cases, Manuel Noriega is perhaps the most notable, did make their way to American courts. However, these represented a very small percentage of individuals tried at the time.[46]

In the meantime, the American military role in the drug war grew. By virtue of the 1989 National Defense Authorization Act, Congress made the Department of Defense the primary agency responsible for monitoring illegal drug trafficking into the United States. The policy reflected the reasonable assumption that the vast scale of the drug trade was overwhelming civilian law enforcement agencies in detail. The Defense Department thus served as a counterbalance to this David and Goliath battle, providing the means to integrate intelligence, surveillance, and communications on a substantially upgraded scale. As was the case in the eighties, the military was authorized to use its surveillance and interdiction capabilities to augment law enforcement.[47] To support this new plan, lawmakers appropriated significant resources: $300 million in fiscal year 1989, $450 million in 1990, and $1.1 billion in fiscal year 1991.[48]

Once given formal leadership of the drug war, the Pentagon largely reverted to already established practices. Specific functions were delegated to regional and special commands. The Navy commander in chief of the Atlantic Command was responsible for the Atlantic Ocean, the Gulf of Mexico, the Caribbean, and parts of the Eastern Pacific. The commander in chief of the North American Aerospace Defense Command controlled surveillance operations along U.S. land and coastal borders. The military coordinated its activity with civilian law enforcement agencies through a series of joint task forces (e.g., JTF-4 in Key West, Florida) located near the major military commands.[49]

On the ground, the U.S. military largely conflated counterinsurgency and counternarcotics doctrine. The relatively small numbers of military personnel assigned to the Andean region saw the problem in terms of providing local military and police units with better equipment and training. Ideally, American influence would produce more professional and apolitical security forces, although this derivative benefit was often sacrificed for better military performance. In the countryside, the U.S. military emphasized civic action programs to woo the native peasantry away from coca production and loyalty to the cartels in much the same way CORDS attempted to win rural peasant support in South Vietnam in the late sixties.

While drug use initially declined as a result of these combined efforts, it rebounded by the end of the Bush presidency. According to a 1993 General Accounting Office (GAO) report, estimated cocaine production increased from 845 to 1,050 metric tons in 1989 to between 955 and 1,170 metric tons in 1991.[50] The report characterized Defense Department efforts to assist in the drug war as "negligible."[51] However, despite the apparent lack of progress, the administration clung to the model that emphasized attacking the sources of narcotics instead of reducing domestic demand. As late as September 1992, the Office of National Drug Control Policy argued that treatment programs could not reach hard-core users. Officials believed that greater attention needed to be spent on interdiction, particularly in Colombia.[52]

When he first assumed office, Bill Clinton folded the drug war into his larger domestic policy agenda, initially focusing on the sources of the problem at home while at the same time downplaying it as a priority. Most of his work instead addressed poverty, health care, unemployment, issues that dovetailed better with the 1992 election campaign.[53] Military efforts in Latin America continued but received scant attention by the administration. When they were addressed, it was largely within the context of the peace dividend debate. A September 1993 GAO report was notable for highlighting the inefficiencies of military drug interdiction: "Sensors designed to detect large supersonic aircraft and nuclear-powered submarines are less proficient against low-flying planes and small wooden boats."[54]

By the mid-nineties, Clinton could no longer maintain a passive approach to the drug war. Policy reversals in Africa and the Balkans placed a premium on decisive action. So too did the Republican surge in the 1994 election that resulted in their control of Congress and a subsequent endless drumbeat of criticism directed against the White House.[55] Both factors produced renewed interest in interdiction efforts in Latin America. Publicly, policy makers expressed a desire to attack the so-called air bridge that allowed traffickers to move their product from South America to the United States.[56] More deliberate approaches were also in the making. In fact, as early as 1993 the administration had ordered a "controlled shift" from interdiction back to a direct attack on drug production in Colombia, Bolivia, and Peru.[57] Presidential Decision Directive 14 (PDD-14) returned American attention to "source countries" much in the same manner as the Reagan and Bush administrations before it. Consequently, American bilateral military support to the Andes accelerated, as did joint operations such as Operation Green Clover (1995), in which 300 American military personnel joined the counternarcotics efforts of Peru, Colombia, Ecuador, Panama, Costa Rica, and Venezuela.[58]

In Clinton's second term, the administration accelerated both funding and overseas projects. Between 1996 and 2000, U.S. assistance for counternarcotics grew from $266.1 million to a formidable $2.4 billion.[59] Much of this money went to "international narcotics control" training, as well as to the maintenance and repair of equipment, intelligence gathering, and aerial and ground reconnaissance.[60] American programs also emphasized increasing regional and local military cooperation. Taking the concept of integrating the counternarcotics effort to its logical conclusion, U.S. assistance attempted to include Latin

American military and police into a more strategic approach to the drug war.

Under Clinton, American military officials sought additional derivative benefits to their policies that went far beyond simply combating drugs. What policy makers wanted was a basic reform in civil-military relations in Latin America. A Defense Department official explained this goal in 1991: "Currently, in SOUTHCOM's view, the U.S. military's part in promoting democracy . . . is neither to work for a reduction in Latin American military forces nor to attempt to delimit the role of the armed forces in Latin American societies. Rather, the U.S. military role is to continue to strengthen military capabilities on the assumption that democratic values will be transmitted."[61] It was an objective that hearkened back to the School of the Americas during the Alliance for Progress years in the sixties. Yet, within the context of the nineties, military adherence to the rule of law was at a premium on par with international scrutiny over human rights abuses.

The stress on democratic values and cooperation was an important feature of Clinton era counternarcotics policy. In one respect, it translated military policy into terms more readily understandable to a president whose political mandate and personal tendency were to view foreign policy problems through a domestic policy lens. For the American military, the opportunity to add counternarcotics and counterinsurgency under the umbrella of nation building was unavoidable, particularly at a time when the armed forces struggled with post–Cold War relevancy. By placing the drug war in a context framed by military subservience to civilian authority, the Pentagon's approach echoed that of Secretary of State Madeleine Albright in 1997 when she argued that NATO expansion into Eastern Europe was the critical component of democratic reform.[62] In the case of Colombia, the recipient of the vast majority of American attention and resources, reality would be much different.

Clinton's legacy to the incoming administration of George W. Bush was its justification for eliminating the boundaries that surrounded counternarcotics policy. Well before the terrorist attacks of September 2001, a succession of presidents and congresses had eroded the line between military action and law enforcement. In the nineties, whether contained by statutory limits to policy or not, renewed military attempts to disrupt the drug pipeline resulted in combining counterinsurgency technique with counterdrug action. The next step toward conflating drugs with terrorism was a short one. Clinton's drug czar, former general Barry McCaffrey, acknowledged the need to abandon in practice what he considered an arbitrary policy distinction in 2002: "There was always an artificiality to this policy that endorsed helping a democratically elected Colombian government against drug criminals, but refused to help them when they are threatened by people who are blowing up oil pipelines, murdering mayors, and kidnapping politicians."[63]

The year following Bush's declaration of a global war on terror proved to be a key turning point in the story. In March 2002 an emergency budget outlay of $28.9 billion for the war on terror included a provision for "a unified campaign against narcotics trafficking [and] against activities by organizations designated as terrorist organizations."[64] That November, Secretary of Defense Donald Rumsfeld met with Latin American defense ministers to discuss the sources of instability in the hemisphere and the dangerous prospect of individual nations losing what he described as "effective sovereignty."[65]

Within this policy, the small war portfolio in Latin America increased to include, drugs, insurgency, and terrorism. The U.S. ambassador to Colombia, Anne Patterson, made this point abundantly clear in November 2002 when she addressed the Colombian Cattlemen's Federation: "The U.S. strategy is to give the Colombian government the tools to combat terrorism and narcotrafficking, two struggles that have become one. To fight against narcotrafficking and terrorism, it is necessary to attack all links of the chain simultaneously."[66] The American approach to the drug war thus became one of combination rather than a specific focus. Perhaps more important, although it continued to include provisions for developmental assistance (i.e., nation building) the inclusion of counterterrorism and counterinsurgency projects began to skew American action increasingly away from law enforcement and toward military operations.

A host of journalists and scholars have roundly criticized the Bush administration's combination of drugs and terrorism. They have argued that the United States arbitrarily grafted terrorism onto its regional security plans for the sake of justifying additional aid. However, at the time, public support for nearly any action taken against terrorism remained strong, at least for the first few years of the global war on terror.[67] Moreover, American action did have a reasonably sound endorsement from the international community. In September 2001, UN Security Council Resolution 1373 recognized that "the close connection between international terrorism and transnational organized crime, illicit drugs, money-laundering, illegal arms-trafficking, and illegal movement of nuclear, chemical, biological and other potentially deadly materials, emphasizes the need to enhance coordination of efforts on national, subregional, regional, and international levels to strengthen a global response to this serious challenge and threat to international security."[68]

The Bush administration committed resources to the war against drugs/insurgency/terror that dwarfed the Clinton years. Between 2004 and 2009, military and police aid to Latin America totaled $5.9 billion. Among the top recipients were Colombia ($3.1 billion), Mexico ($912.7 million), Peru ($332.2 million), and Bolivia ($240.7 million).[69] The Defense Department rapidly increased training programs throughout the hemisphere to a degree unmatched since the sixties. Between 2001 and 2005, 85,820 Latin American military personnel trained in the United States.[70]

In addition to supporting regional military and police forces, the American military presence in Latin America also grew. Base closures in Panama and the formal relinquishment of the canal zone in 1999 forced the Pentagon to open "Forward Operating Locations" in alternate countries. Consequently, the United States built new bases in Ecuador, Aruba, El Salvador, and Curacao to handle intelligence collection, logistics, training, and other functions related to the new military effort in Latin America.[71]

As the U.S. military buildup increased, so too did official rationales for American involvement. Throughout the first Bush administration, professional journals and official documents added to the list of direct and derivative benefits of conducting small wars in Latin America. A 2004 edition of the U.S. Naval Institute *Proceedings* cited the political utility of improved Latin American military ties with the United States. By augmenting hemispheric military capabilities, the author argued that aid was a means to maintain order and stability in an increasingly dangerous region. When it bolstered host militaries, the United States was not only halting the prospect of revolution but also arresting the growth of the radical Latin American Left, particularly the influence of Venezuelan leader Hugo Chavez.[72]

SOUTHCOM offered its own take on the objectives and methods of U.S. policy in 2007 when it published *Command Strategy 2016*. Immediately discernable was the degree to which American actions represented continuity with the past. Although written in a twenty-first century atmosphere, the document recalled toppling dominoes and the Cold War in its first few pages. *Command Strategy* made it clear that SOUTHCOM's primary purpose was "the forward defense of the United States by defending its southern approaches."[73] It did acknowledge the diverse nature of threats, a list that included terrorism, weapons of mass destruction, as well as "narcotics connections to terror networks and other terrorism support activities."[74] Moreover, the methodology proposed to meet these challenges was a departure from tradition. *Command Strategy* is notable for its recognition that nonmilitary factors—crime, poverty, corruption—were major contributing factors to Latin American instability. It further noted that the U.S. military had a duty to cooperate with host nations as well as civilian agencies. The same emphasis on relevant nonmilitary influences also appeared in the 2008 revision of *Field Manual 3-0: Operations,* the Army's primary doctrinal guide.[75] Both documents reflected a newly found optimism in fighting small wars. *Command Strategy* concluded that "the synergistic effect of these efforts will harness the power of the entire U.S. Government to work with partner nations to enable peace and prosperity throughout the Western hemisphere."[76]

Beyond the official optimism pronounced in the updated doctrine, there were numerous and profound reasons for concern regarding the overall trajectory of U.S. policy and its particular application to the drug war. One departure was the changed nature of military influence within the larger policy community. A 2008 study by the Center for International Security noted that the SOUTHCOM policy statement set the radical precedent of imposing military priorities over what traditionally had been a civilian domain. The authors believed that it was laudable to include issues like poverty, crime, and economic development into military action. However, stripping them away from civilian agencies also eliminated bureaucratic balance. Without civilian agencies to counteract SOUTHCOM or the Pentagon, or to assert traditional civilian primacy in policy decisions, the United States risked warping its foreign affairs toward military ends.[77]

The hard data generated to measure the success of the drug war was equally worrisome. In September 2008 a Department of Health and Human Services report noted that an estimated 19.9 million Americans were current (within the past month) illicit drug users. Although rates had remained stable since 2002, the total number was significant.[78] Compared with overall consumption a generation earlier, fewer Americans overall and as a percentage of the total population consumed illegal substances. However, regular users still numbered almost 20 million, with national demand further augmented by millions of casual consumers.

The cost of achieving these gains was astronomical. The Defense Department possessed sophisticated surveillance and communications capabilities. However, these assets, particularly air units, were extremely expensive. Between 1989 and 1993, Department of Defense "operational tempo" (flying or "steaming" hours by air and naval units) funding increased by 300 percent, representing a four-year expenditure of $3.3 billion on detection and monitoring alone. Yet the increased military effort, according to a 1993 GAO report, "does not appear to be providing a reasonable return." Further, the GAO noted that the Defense Department's contribution to the drug war would likely diminish as smugglers developed new methods to defeat U.S. surveillance capabilities.[79]

Despite the expense and upgraded effort, the U.S. military failed to achieve its stated goals. The original 1989 National Drug Control Strategy, created by the Office of National Drug Control Policy, called for a 10 percent reduction in cocaine shipments to the U.S. in two years and a 50 percent reduction in ten years. According to DEA estimates, the actual reduction in global cocaine shipments might have been 5 percent between 1989 and 1992.[80] As will be discussed, none of the steps in the trafficking process, from the total acreage being used for coca production to the final street price of cocaine, were much affected by American efforts.

Just how effective the military's role in training, surveillance, and interdiction was remains an open question today. The quantitative approach to drug seizures in the eighties and nineties became the new "body count" of the era but did a poor job of measuring Pentagon's overall impact on the drug war.[81] One American intelligence officer explained in February 2000: "I don't think we can make any progress on the drug issue by escalating our military presence in Colombia. As in Vietnam, the policy is designed to fail. All we're doing is making body counts, although instead of bodies, we're counting seizures—tons of cocaine, kilos of heroin."[82] A more difficult dilemma lay in quantifying the increasing effectiveness of U.S. training efforts in Latin America. Measuring the degree to which Latin American security forces internalized principles such as subordination to civilian authority or the acceptance of the rule of law remain highly opaque exercises.

Not all problems were strictly American in nature. A simple, ongoing difficulty for the United States was the commitment of individual host nations to the drug war. In a situation reminiscent of Vietnamization, successive administrations struggled with the question of how best to impart a sense of purpose to their Latin American client. Internal corruption was a massive obstacle to progress. A Peruvian colonel noted in a conversation with a U.S. border patrol agent in 1992: "I have the opportunity while I'm here to make $70,000 by looking the other way at certain times. You have a family, they are protected in the United States, you have a proper pension plan. My family is not protected and I don't have the proper pension plan and I will never have the opportunity to make $70,000 as long as I live. I am going to make it."[83] More experienced observers also made it clear that corruption was not simply a matter of individual choice. It represented a systemic problem within Latin America. One analyst noted in 1994: "While the cocaine industry has substantial economic, political, and military clout to challenge the authority of legitimate governments throughout the region, it also represents and economic and social linchpin, preventing economic stagnation, debt and unemployment in these poorer nations."[84]

More important, none of these qualities were limited to the Andean region proper. One of the unfortunate impacts of U.S. counternarcotics operations was to displace the traditional flow of drugs to new locations. By the nineties, with Manuel Noriega overthrown and a new multilateral presence in Haiti, Central American nations such as Guatemala and Nicaragua developed into a nexus for northbound shipments of narcotics. Caught in the wake of hundreds of millions of dollars, corruption soon became epidemic. In Guatemala, hard-line army officers dissatisfied with the peace accord reached with guerrillas transitioned into a well-organized criminal cartel. As one author observed shortly after the September 2001 attacks, the cocaine trade created "a dangerous synergy between political terror and drug trafficking."[85]

At the writing of this book, the forty-year war against drugs proceeds relentlessly toward an unachievable goal. Four decades of domestic imperatives and a gradually accumulating portfolio of military responsibilities have resulted in billions spent and a U.S. military institution permanently ensconced in a conflict it is still poorly prepared to wage. By militarizing what started as a law enforcement and social welfare task, the United States has gained some traction. Success has come at a considerable cost, not only in terms of dollars but also at the expense of a process skewed away from civilian control. This process cost the United States a sense of balance in terms of policy. In the nations where the drug wars have raged for decades, the price has been much higher.

Narcotics, Insurgency, and Terrorism in Colombia

The primary "front" in the war on drugs has been and remains the nation of Colombia. In terms of legitimate trade, it is an important partner for the United States, ranking twenty-fifth overall and fourth among its Latin American neighbors.[86] Legal commerce aside, Colombia is the primary source (80 percent) of cocaine for American and European consumption. The country has suffered for this dubious honor. Narcotics have wreaked political and economic havoc while inflicting a worse human cost. By 2002 Colombia had the third highest number of internal refugees in the world after Angola and Sudan.[87]

Much of Colombia's modern-day history is defined by internal instability. La Violencia (1948–1965) left a profound mark on the country decades after its conclusion. The civil war that broke out between liberals and conservatives resulted in the deaths of approximately 160,000 people. The endemic bloodletting effectively destroyed constructive political dialogue in its aftermath and retarded anything resembling the reconstruction of basic social institutions.

The mid-sixties brought little relief. During the heyday of the Alliance for Progress, American assistance improved Colombia's ability to resist a Cuban-inspired revolution. Counterinsurgency programs focused on internal stability but failed to identify the dividing line between political dissent and subversion, a line already blurred by the two major parties during La Violencia. Consequently, American aid supported the formation of irregular civil defense groups designed to aid the state in prosecuting the war against insurgents. These paramilitary organizations were the genesis of the United Self-Defense Groups of Colombia (Autodefensas Unidas de Colombia, or AUC) that dominated the country a generation later. In response, the Colombian left armed itself. One offshoot of this effort was the creation of the Fuerzas Armadas Revolucionarias de Colombia (FARC) in 1964. As was the case with many embryonic Marxist and leftist organizations of the time, armed force demonstrated solidarity with the Cuban revolution. Perhaps more important, it became a necessary component of self-preservation and the promotion of a political agenda in a country where open discourse had failed.[88]

American military assistance prevented Castro's *foquismo* from gaining a foothold in the sixties, but at a long-term cost to the country's political institutions. Rather than allow breathing space after La Violencia, American-sponsored security policy prolonged violence between divergent political factions. State-supported violence sharpened the already problematic nature of politics by marginalizing or eliminating parties outside the traditional Liberal and Conservative axis of domestic politics. The two-party system thus became more entrenched and less accountable to the Colombian people. Much of Colombia, particularly at the regional and local level, fell outside the national political dialogue. Ironically, as the state readied itself for a politically motivated insurgency, the body politic atrophied overall.[89]

Violence became the most common currency of Colombian politics. It has successfully stymied meaningful attempts at reform or compromise. In 1984, for example, the FARC arranged a ceasefire with the government and created a new political party, the Union Patriotica (UP), through which it could engage in open debate and submit candidates for public office. The UP enjoyed some early successes in mayoral and local elections, but it came under almost constant attack by right-wing paramilitaries sponsored by the Colombia military. Over the course of nearly twenty years, some 3,000 of its members have been assassinated.[90] They were not alone. The campaign of violence extended to labor organizers, human rights organizations, and other groups considered subversive by the military and its allies.[91]

The drug war is thus a more recent chapter in a much longer history of violence. This was particularly evident during the "extradition wars" that raged between national government and the cartels from 1984 to 1991. Provoked by deliberate attempts to bring traffickers to justice in Colombia and the United States, the cartels unleashed a wave of assassination attempts and attacks on police, the judiciary, and other public officials. Thousands were killed and wounded in the process.[92]

Colombian authorities responded in kind. The dramatic death of Pablo Escobar on a Medellín rooftop in 1993 highlighted what was a successful police and military campaign against the Medellín and Cali cartels. However, the defeat of two larger organizations did not result in a victory in the drug war. In relatively short order, the two cartels were replaced by hundreds of small organizations that learned to, according to one Colombian publication, "export a little, earn a lot, and make little noise."[93]

Recent economic and social trends have not alleviated conflict in Colombia. Free-market reforms adopted in the early nineties had a severe and negative impact on the country. The 1992 decision to reduce tariffs on imported agricultural products (from 31.5 percent to 15 percent) very quickly resulted in the collapse of small and medium farms.[94] Disconnected from traditional agriculture, thousands of indigent farmers quickly gravitated to coca production. A coca tree, on average, matured in only eighteen months and remained productive for thirty to forty years. Coca leaves, which sold for $1.50 a kilogram in 2001, were far more profitable than any other legal substitute crop.[95] Work in legitimate manufacturing industries has also suffered in the recent past. Colombian textiles kept pace with the world market from the forties until the seventies until foreign competition shuttered many businesses.[96]

Residency patterns have profoundly changed in the last fifty years. After World War II, approximately 70 percent of the country lived in rural areas. By the end of the century, this percentage declined to approximately 25 percent of the population. Many are attracted by higher wages or the prospect of better public services in cities like Medellín. Others have simply escaped failed farms or encroaching violence. Urban migration has largely failed to meet many of these expectations. The massive shantytowns surrounding Colombia's major cities are rife with disease, primitive living conditions, unemployment, and underemployment.[97] Rather than serve as a brake against criminal enterprises, they are often a haven for crime, from petty theft to the cartels themselves.[98]

Exacerbating the problems of a society in flux has been the breakdown of traditional social controls. Notable in the modern era is the diminishing authority of the Roman Catholic Church in Colombia and elsewhere in Latin America. Long-standing church doctrines are routinely dismissed by the lay public. Colombia's declining birth rate (from 4.4 percent in 1970 to 1.8 percent by 1998) indicate increasing acceptance of birth control, once considered a social taboo.[99]

Both insurgents and drug traffickers have thrived in a socially fragmented and economically desperate country. Neighborhoods, individual towns, or, in some cases, entire regions were prepared to grant their loyalty to any entity that might provide a safe haven in an era defined by almost constant turmoil. Consequently, by 1997 there were an estimated 132 guerrilla factions and 100 paramilitary groups operating in approximately 300 Colombian municipalities.[100]

Such as it was, a combination of factors facilitated Colombia's evolution into the primary source of cocaine in the Western Hemisphere. Chronic internal instability created a political, economic, and social vacuum that the cartels readily fill. At the same time, increasing U.S. and Western demand facilitated the transfer of millions (and later billions) of dollars. In 2007, the UN Office on Drugs and Crime estimated that Colombia produced 600 metric tons of cocaine with a "farm-gate" value (i.e., the wholesale value of coca leaf and paste) of $934 million.[101] It is a small wonder that government officials have found it difficult to circumvent "narco-dollars" from affecting the police, military, and judiciary.

Circumstances have also facilitated an alliance between the *narcotrafficantes* and Colombia's traditional insurgent movements. The FARC in particular has benefited from this relationship. Although it continued its guerrilla campaigns well after the sixties, the Frente was never able to successfully adapt its Marxist-Leninist platform to Colombia politics or society. Popular support proved fleeting if not impossible to obtain over the long term. Militarily, the FARC was wholly unable to defeat U.S.-backed national security forces. As a consequence, it declined to about 1,000 fighters by the early eighties.[102]

The drug trade essentially rescued the movement from oblivion. When the Medellín and Cali cartels retreated under U.S. and Colombian pressure, the FARC filled a specific vacuum, providing security for smaller, emerging drug traffickers in exchange for cash.[103] The actual amounts were staggering. By the late nineties, academic sources estimated that narcotics provided as much as half of guerrillas' $500 million to $1.5 billion in annual income.[104] The financial boon allowed FARC strength to increase to approximately 15,000 by 2000. It has also reportedly financed connections with organized crime in Chechnya, Russia, Ukraine, and Uzbekistan.[105] These relationships improved the market for Colombian cocaine and granted traffickers ready access to vast stores of Cold War–era weaponry. Both the cartels and smaller Colombia syndicates have similarly benefited from outside expertise. Lacking the ability to construct truck bombs in 1993, Pablo Escobar simply contracted out the work to the FARC rival, the Colombian National Liberation Army (ELN).[106]

It is important to point out that the "narcoguerrillas" are not a homogenous unit. In some cases, a simple division of labor articulates the relationship between insurgent and cartel. Certain traffickers continue to maintain separate security at their own airfields and labs, whereas the guerrillas protect acreage under cultivation. While the FARC has grown closer to large and small cartels, it retains its traditional role as an advocate for peasant interests. Frente forces protect small peasant farms from large-scale cultivators, whether legal or not. The FARC also maintains a progressive tax structure that exempts small producers. In the public domain, for example, the organization has assisted demonstrations against aerial fumigation of crops.[107]

Right wing forces in Colombia are also partnered with the cartels. Ironically, it appears that they may enjoy a more natural alliance than existing insurgent groups. As Robert Filippone observed, the cartel leadership has always professed an ideology—pro-Colombian, procapitalist—that placed it much closer to the military.[108] The organization Muerte a Secuestradores (MAS) exemplifies this relationship. The 1981 creation of 223 drug traffickers, MAS retaliated for kidnappings conducted by the rebel group M-19. Because it enjoyed direct contacts with the Colombia military, MAS obtained training, weapons, and intelligence information that it wielded against insurgents. Over time, MAS became a useful extralegal ally of the military and was responsible for the deaths of insurgents and a lengthy list of political dissidents and activists. The open campaign of violence against the FARC and its civilian representatives in the Union Patriotica resulted in more than 200 UP leaders assassinated in 1988 alone.[109] A year later, Colombian president Virgilio Barco went so far as to declare that right wing paramilitary groups were "terrorist organizations" in themselves.[110]

Despite official condemnations from within and outside Colombia, the relationship between the government, right-wing paramilitary groups, and drug traffickers continued unabated. The AUC, a product of the self-defense organizations sponsored by U.S. counterinsurgency efforts in the sixties, remained closely linked with both the military and cartels. In September 2001, in the midst of its antidrug surge in Colombia, the United States placed the AUC on the list of foreign terrorist organizations.[111]

It comes as no surprise that, bolstered by allies within Colombia and an enormous flow of foreign revenue, narcotics traffickers enjoyed an extremely strong position for much of the last quarter century. During the early nineties, it was clear that the Colombian government was in full retreat. The military suffered a series of defeats at the hands of rebels. At Las Delicias in 1996, the FARC captured over 100 soldiers. Two years later, military units were decimated in the departments of Caquetá, Guaviare, and Vaupés.[112] Legitimate investments, particularly in key areas of the economy, also suffered. Between 1986 and 1997, attacks on the petroleum industry cost an estimated $1.4 billion.[113]

By the end of the decade, the national government attempted to end conflict with a conciliatory strategy. President Andrés Pastrana gave the FARC a "demilitarized zone" in south-central Colombia approximately the size of Switzerland. The secession of territory, known as the *despeje,* was intended as a sop to further ongoing peace talks with the insurgents.[114] The effort failed. Within a very short period of time, it became obvious that the FARC was using the demilitarized zone as a logistical marshalling area from which it could mount coordinated strikes against Columbian military forces. More ominous were disturbing signs that the organization had moved to "bulk buying" its weapons from increasingly diverse sources within and outside Latin America, a group that by 2000 included communist China.[115]

In contrast, as the FARC and other groups consolidated their strength, most Colombian police and military units were scattered throughout the country. According to one estimate in June 2000, less than a third of the Colombian army was available to use against the FARC and ELN; 20 percent was deployed to guard key locations and provide VIP protection, 25 percent was in training, and 25 percent was devoted to logistical duties.[116] Lacking adequate troop strength, the government was forced to withdraw from significant sections of the countryside outside the *despeje*. At the start of the new century, it was abundantly clear that the government had lost the initiative.

The primary focus of U.S. aid at the time was to restore what had been lost to both insurgents and drug traffickers. American military assistance expanded accordingly. Between 1987 and 1994, the United States provided half of the $320 million in arms purchased by Colombia.[117] Beginning in 1990, the United States provided military sales for counternarcotics operations in the amount of $15.4 million. This quickly increased to $58.1 million by 1992.[118] Military training under American auspices also significantly grew. Colombia provided the largest contingent trained under the International Military Education and Training (IMET) program. A total of 7,618 personnel, or more than a third of those trained in Latin America, received instruction in the United States and military facilities scattered around the hemisphere.[119]

Although the Reagan, Bush, and first Clinton administrations devoted considerable time and resources to the drug war in Colombia, it received an additional boost in the late nineties when American policy makers officially adopted what became known as Plan Colombia. Originally developed by the Colombian government in 1999, it was a $7.5 billion strategy that promised an integrated national effort: "to meet the most pressing challenges confronting Colombia today—promoting the peace process, combating the narcotics industry, reviving the Colombian economy, and strengthening the democratic pillars of Colombian society."[120] Toward these ends, the United States provided $1.3 billion in assistance. Many existing projects were subsequently upgraded with new funds. The American military expanded its system of ground-based radar installations to close holes in surveillance previously exploited by smugglers using small aircraft. To improve tactical mobility, the United States provided 84 UH-60 and UH-1H helicopters between 1999 and 2003.[121] U.S. intelligence agencies also worked more closely with the police counternarcotics division (DIRAN) to improve the flow of information regarding insurgent and trafficking organizations.[122]

On the ground, the United States expanded its training programs. In order to win back the initiative in the countryside and make full use of improved air mobile assets, U.S. advisers assisted in the creation of the Fuerza de Despliegue Rápido (Rapid Deployment Force) in 1998.[123] American military personnel were responsible for creating three special forces battalions dedicated to counternarcotics operations in the southern departments of Caquetá and Putumayo. American assistance was also instrumental in forming a Riverine Brigade as part of the Colombian Marine Corps to patrol the waterways of Putumayo, Guaviare, Guainía, and Magdalena Medio.

Specific training, managed through IMET courses and the SOCOM Joint Command Exchange Training Initiative, focused on the military skills most useful to fighting drug traffickers and insurgents deep in rural Colombia. By 2001 the most frequent subjects taught were light infantry tactics, riverine operations, and coastal patrolling.[124] In these training programs it is apparent that the U.S. conventional wisdom regarding small wars in Colombia was consistent with contemporary practice in the nineties. As was the case with the Balkans, the Pentagon believed existing conventional doctrine was more than adequate and adaptable to meet the new hybrid threat of narcotics and insurgency.

Prior to the attacks on the World Trade Center, American military support for Colombia operated under a number of policy and legal restraints. The ongoing distinction between counternarcotics and counterinsurgency remained fixed until 2001.[125] Moreover, the number of U.S. military personnel deployed to the country was strictly limited by federal statute to four hundred, with additional allowances for four hundred private military contractors.[126] Both contractors and military advisers were additionally prohibited from directly participating in combat operations. Despite these constraints, American involvement in

Colombia, and the military's share of it, continued unabated into the new century. By 2000, at approximately $289 million, Colombia was the third largest recipient of American military aid in the world.[127]

The increase in American military assistance coincided with the arrival of a new Colombian president. In his 2002 campaign, Álvaro Uribe Velez promised "democratic security" for a population grown weary of concessions to guerrillas and traffickers. The Oxford and Harvard-trained leader appeared ready to personally endure the consequences of his aggressive stance against the cartels. Uribe managed to survive four separate assassination attempts by the time he entered office.[128]

The Uribe administration also produced a blueprint to combat the cartels in 2003 when the Defense Ministry published *Democratic Security and Defence Policy*. The plan articulated an approach to counterinsurgency that encompassed both narcotics and terrorism. The introductory passage from the president strikes a hard note from the very start, stating in simple terms: "There can be only one response to terrorism: its defeat."[129]

According to the document, Colombia's key problem was a chronic lack of personal security that undercut the authority of the state and produced constant instability. Consequently, the government's primary mission was to reconcile individual and national security. The policy notes that: "Democratic Security is what is required to guarantee the protection of the citizens. If the State protects all its citizens equally and without discrimination, all Colombians will be able fully to enjoy their rights." Uribe rejected the concept of security based on "ideological hegemony and political exclusion" and offered instead a universal policy of political tolerance.[130] To achieve this end, he offered an ambitious, comprehensive package of political, legal, financial reforms designed to consolidate power once it had been won back by the Colombian military.

The military portion of *Democratic Security and Defence Policy* was its most important. Before other types of reforms could begin, it was necessary to regain control of the country from "illegal armed groups," a category that included drug traffickers as well as the FARC and the AUC.[131] To achieve this task, the military devoted a combination of conventional, special operations (noted above) and local forces to purge the countryside of these groups. Regular forces were deployed to provide basic security. Mobile units became responsible for searching out sanctuaries enjoyed by insurgents and their allies. Perhaps the most important innovation was the addition of 20,000 troops (Soldados de mi Pueblo), who served as an all-volunteer local counterinsurgency militia. Working in concert with the national military, police, and a series of economic and social development plans, the intent was to provide both security and a better standard of living that would win grassroots support to the government's cause. Contemporary scholars compared the Colombian plan to successful counterinsurgency efforts in Thailand, the Philippines, and Peru.[132] From a longer historical perspective, the program also closely resembled American efforts in South Vietnam after 1968 and British actions in Malaya a decade earlier.

However, even as the government in Bogotá adopted a "softer" approach to small wars, attempting to reconcile civil-military relations, the post-9/11 climate was anything but conducive to this policy. The U.S. global war on terror essentially eliminated the barriers separating narcotics trafficking, insurgency, and terrorism. Programs to counter real and potential terrorist threats to Latin America—and Colombia, in particular—accelerated significantly after 2001. Between 2002 and 2009, Colombian security forces received $50.7 million in U.S. antiterrorism assistance and training. Some of this money, specifically $10 million, went to protect oil infrastructure in Arauca. Other projects included training light units to combat terrorists in Colombia. American assistance created sixty-four 150-man mobile *carabinero* units—based on the U.S. Army Rangers—to patrol rural areas in search of guerrillas and terrorist cells.[133]

Measured in terms of budgets and equipment transfers, the actual impact of terrorism on Colombian military affairs appears to be very small. The numbers speak for themselves. In the five years following the terrorist attacks on the United States, only $50.7 million went into counterterror programs in the country, a tiny fraction of billions spent for military aid. Training statistics reinforce the pattern. Of the 26,923 Colombians instructed by the United States between 2004 and 2006, only 653 received specific courses in counterterrorism.[134]

More important to the Colombian approach to internal security were military attitudes regarding the end purpose of U.S. assistance.

A comment by a Colombian general in 2000 illustrates the point: "We were caught by surprise, because we had American doctrine. The American approach taught us there were two types of war, conventional and unconventional, what you call 'war' and 'other than war' (OTW). This is a mistake. This is your view, but it is not correct for us. Actually there is only one conflict, going from guerrilla war through mobile war to conventional war. It's all integrated. And we must be able to fight at all levels."[135] In other words, the fine distinctions made within the Pentagon and the confines of the National Security Council were largely irrelevant to the Colombian military. American military assistance was useful to the extent that it helped combat enemies of the state. To this end, Bogota was willing to incorporate a broad-spectrum approach to internal stability, as evidenced in *Democratic Security and Defence Policy*. However, execution and prioritization remained in Colombian hands. Consequently, the precise balance of military and nonmilitary methods promoted by U.S. assistance became incidental to the war in Colombia.

Since 2001, and clearly since the start of the Uribe administration, military power has outweighed civilian prerogatives. This is readily apparent in terms of the rule of law. Special emergency powers have normalized military action outside the bounds of the Colombia constitution.[136] The sheer size of the current Colombian military has also increased its institutional standing. By 2008, the army alone was comprised of more than 200,000 soldiers. Moreover, between 2000 and 2008, the defense budget has nearly doubled from $3.7 billion to $6.6 billion.[137] Bolstered by foreign aid and domestic spending, the military currently overshadows most other civilian components of the national government.

The broad militarization of Colombian public affairs is no doubt aided by the nature of the war itself. Guerrillas, drug traffickers, and right-wing paramilitaries rarely demonstrate an inclination to negotiate in good faith. In the late nineties, the FARC used the "truce" negotiated by the Pastrana government to consolidate its control over the *despeje* and prepare for urban war. Similarly, as the national military struggled with conditions in the cities and the countryside deteriorated, the AUC gained additional relevance and leverage in the public domain.[138]

Moreover, for all the effort devoted to defeating guerrillas and traffickers on the battlefield, the news is equally bad. Despite the rapid uptick in U.S. aid under Plan Colombia, the FARC matched American funding almost dollar for dollar. In 2000 the FARC secretariat instructed its various fronts to increase tax collection and other fund-raising to $600 million a year, roughly equal to the 2003 American military and counternarcotics aid package of $624 million.[139] With money available on this scale, guerrillas and traffickers advanced their purchases of sophisticated weapons and maintained their hold on Colombian officials, who remained susceptible to bribery and intimidation.

The root source of this wealth and influence, coca, has proven extremely resilient to U.S. and Latin American counternarcotics programs. This is because of the simple, albeit unfortunate, reality that the drug trade provides hard currency that South American nations depend upon. Burdened by poor conventional economic growth, high inflation, and economic austerity programs demanded by the international banking community, countries like Colombia have turned to narcotics for revenue and as means to employ hundreds of thousands of its citizens. Efforts to encourage alternative agriculture have largely failed to achieve traction. In July 2001, for example, 37,000 families in Colombia's Putumayo department—approximately half its population—signed "social pacts" with the government pledging to eradicate the coca crops in exchange for assistance to grow more traditional products. By April 2002, fewer than a quarter of these families had received their promised aid.[140] Poorly conceived and implemented projects that are completely overshadowed by the military leg of Plan Colombia are unquestionably part of the reason for failure.

Larger economic considerations are probably more to blame than simple incompetence or an overemphasis on things military. The foremost dilemma in the drug war is the simple earning power of coca. A peasant in Peru's Upper Huallaga Valley cultivating coca for the drug industry made between $8,000–50,000 a year in 1988. No other cash crop came close to this kind of wealth. Fernando Garcia Arganaras observed the same situation in Bolivia in the late nineties: "The new peasant farmer was thus the child of his time, in which coca cultivation was the alternative to urban unemployment and the purveyor of some empowerment. The preservation—if not expansion—of coca cultivation was, therefore, his early cry."[141] It is small wonder that a national leader of coca farmers, Evo Morales, rose to become president of Bolivia in December 2005.[142]

As a consequence of these factors, the drug war has taken on the appearance of a quagmire in Colombia and elsewhere. Despite the massive investment of time and treasure, as well as the increasing subordination of civilian law to military contingency, progress is tentative at best. Violence has spilled into Ecuador, Panama, Peru, and Venezuela. In the meantime, drug trafficking has expanded into the less regulated areas of Central America and the Caribbean.[143]

Conclusions

During the latter stages of the drug war in Latin America, the United States spent unprecedented amounts on military and police aid, more than $7.3 billion between 1997 and 2007. Colombia, Bolivia, Peru, and Mexico all joined the ranks of America's primary foreign aid recipients. Most assistance was designated for counternarcotics training, equipment, and operations in the field, although the global war on terror added a new layer to American aid after 2001.[144]

But what has this massive effort gained? Outside of Colombia, the drug war has not resulted in a renaissance of U.S. influence in Latin America. In the last ten years, Latin America has experienced a leftist renaissance in countries such as Nicaragua, Venezuela, and Bolivia, primarily as a direct consequence of Washington's increasingly heavy-handed approach to the hemisphere. Successful U.S. policies have been distinctly nonmilitary in nature. NAFTA and CAFTA-DR possesses greater potential to cultivate more important ties with America's neighbors. Similarly, ongoing debt restructuring is more likely to gain more traction with Latin American nations than weapons transfers or military training.[145]

The direct results of the war on drugs have also been dubious. The flow of drugs into the U.S. southern border has remained relatively stable. Mexican authorities seized 25 metric tons of cocaine in 2004, double the amount in 2002, but lower than 2001.[146] Drug production has proven difficult to stamp out. During the Clinton years, the total number of hectares under cultivation in Colombia alone grew from 39,700 in 1993 to 122,500 in 1999.[147] Eradication programs initiated after 2001 were able to reverse this trend. However, near the end of the decade, cultivation had rebounded from 78,000 hectares in 2006 to 99,000 hectares in 2007, a 27 percent increase.[148] Potential cocaine production also remains high. According to the United Nations Office of Drugs and Crime, Colombia produced 600 metric tons of cocaine in 2007, down from the peak of 695 metric tons in 2000 but almost double the total of 350 metric tons in 1997.[149]

Quantitative measurements aside, there is a more important blind spot within U.S. counternarcotics policy that remains unresolved. Overlaying decades of American projects and programs has been the confusion of efficiency for effectiveness.[150] The Pentagon, the Department of Justice, and the myriad U.S. agencies charged with "winning" the war on drugs have unquestionably been effective in accumulating tons of contraband and thousands of arrests. More pertinent to both the systemic factors underpinning drug production and their long-term solutions has been the qualitative impact of American decisions.

The most important byproduct of America's many small wars against drugs is the distortion of legitimate defense policy and the progressive militarization of Latin American domestic affairs. In order to attain quantitative victories in the drug war, the United States has chosen what one observer described as "unholy alliances" with the internal security forces of Latin American nations.[151] Rather than promote transparency, respect for civilian leadership, and the many constructive tasks cited in documents like Colombia's *Democratic Security and Defence Policy,* the United States and its Latin American clients have sacrificed principle for debatable empirical progress.

Moreover, the many small wars fought against drugs, insurgencies, and terrorism have badly skewed civil-military relations in Latin America.[152] Both official and, in particular, extralegal government actions have decimated the body politic along with meaningful political discourse. National military institutions and their right-wing paramilitary allies are blunt instruments of state-sponsored terrorism rather than agents of grassroots reform.[153] The confluence of military and political activity undercut state legitimacy as a result. Media revelations regarding the so-called "parapolitical" scandal, in which paramilitary leaders worked with pro-Uribe candidates to ensure their victory, dominated Colombian politics after 2006. By 2009 more than sixty members of the Colombian Congress were in jail or under investigation.[154]

In the end, the drug war has failed because it is a conflict unredeemable by military means. The drug industry, indeed the entire process by which drugs are grown, processed, and distributed, lacks what the military terms "a center of gravity." This was clear when the destruction of the Medellín and Cali cartels simply resulted in new networks that easily filled a vacuum created by the Colombian government. This basic reality applies to South America as a whole, wherein the decentralized nature of drug cartels makes the war analogous to squeezing a balloon.[155] Even as Plan Colombia has advanced, success has not followed at the same rate in Peru or Bolivia.

7

The War on Terror

If only we are prepared to look, we can see a revolution taking place under our very noses. Just as no Roman citizen was left unaffected by the barbarian invasions, so in vast parts of the world no man, woman, and child alive today will be spared the consequences of the newly-emerging forms of war.

—Martin van Creveld, *The Transformation of War*

Today's terrorists don't want a seat at the table, they want to destroy the table and everyone sitting at it.

—R. James Woolsey in National Commission on Terrorism, *Countering the Changing Threat of International Terrorism*

Without question, the September 2001 attacks on the United States focused the country and its leadership on the nature of terrorism and its real threat to American interests. The very label "global war on terror" became an embedded element of U.S. policy and the common lexicon for years. In daily life, in public places, and in major decisions used to justify new wars abroad, terrorism occupied a permanent and important place in American thought and action.

Often lost in this discourse is the lengthy history of terrorist activity during the modern age, particularly after World War II. Although relatively rare in the Soviet Union and many Western nations for decades, terrorism flourished in what was known as the Third World. Scholars have focused on the complex economic, cultural, and political sources of this violence, attributes encouraged and, in some cases, manipulated by the United States and Soviet Union.[1] Once the Cold War ceased to be, the motivating factors behind terrorism remained largely intact and enjoyed a second life after 1991. Many academics revisiting terrorism in "cusp" nations throughout the world noted a broad array of root causes, a field ranging from religious and ethnic animosity to socioeconomic pressures brought about by Western-style capitalism. However, while the driving force behind terrorism remained relatively consistent, its use did not. Contemporary conflict is notable for the vast disparities of power between modern nations and their nonstate adversaries. Actors with no chance of matching their enemies in conventional warfare now regularly resort to terrorism as a more effective means of prosecuting conflict.[2] Al Qaeda, as David Kilcullen observes, possesses "postmodern capabilities but a premodern structure." It cannot hope to defeat the United States in a traditional conflict and instead opts for a strategy of exhaustion that will sap America's will and means to fight.[3]

Regardless of cause or method, it is readily apparent that terrorism has drawn closer to Western and American interests in the last forty years. By the early seventies, the cushion separating affluent, industrialized nations from terrorism began to disappear. The resurgence of "troubles" in Ireland, the hostage crisis at the Munich Olympics, and an increasing drumbeat of assassinations, airline hijackings, and kidnappings quickly brought home the realization that no Western, industrialized nation was safe from groups that deliberately ignored the separation between civilian and soldier.

As was the case with narcotics trafficking and other challenges to the security of the modern state, the United States and, more specifically, its armed forces, struggled with the prospect of waging war against a dangerous and divisive enemy that recognized no boundaries to conflict. History was not on its side. In Vietnam, Americans had routinely experienced the types of actions that later generations would immediately identify as terrorism.[4] The war in both the South Vietnamese countryside and its major cities witnessed degrees of brutality that badly scarred U.S. service members and the military institution. One of the clear motives for American military reform in the seventies was the deliberate desire to leave this form of conflict behind.

Yet, despite its reticence, the U.S. military was forced to confront this new enemy and a new form of war. Like the war on drugs, it would enter the conflict reluctantly and tentatively. However, as the years wore on, national security policy and military contingency planning became inextricably linked with terrorism. Although they displayed great reluctance to embrace conflict with a terrorist enemy, the U.S. armed forces eventually accepted the new mission and pursued it with increasing frequency. This evolving process is an important part of understanding America's small wars today.

Terrorism in the Modern Era

Terrorism was a natural byproduct of the Cold War. Without recourse to conventional conflict, the use of force by other means became standard operating procedure for both sides in the years following World War II. Car bombings, assassinations, as well as terror attacks against civilian and military targets were all common devices. Reliable studies of U.S. activity in Iran, Guatemala, and Cuba describe an array of methods utilized to intimidate and terrorize both real and perceived threats to American security.[5]

By the seventies, the growth of international terrorism accelerated even beyond Cold War standards. The attack on Israeli athletes at the Munich summer Olympics captivated and horrified a global audience. Similarly, when a civilian airliner was hijacked and diverted to Entebbe, Uganda, in 1976, the world again held its breath and celebrated when a daring Israeli rescue attempt succeeded in rescuing the hostages. However, above and beyond the newsworthy highlights and the international drama was increasing evidence of terrorist activity. International terrorist incidents rose alarmingly from 50 in 1968 to over 400 by 1982. Attacks focused on individuals and individual targets in Western Europe, the Middle East, and Latin America.[6]

At the start of the seventies, the nexus of terrorism was the Middle East, specifically the state of Israel. Israel's unexpected resilience against the Arab world in a succession of wars had led to its controversial occupation of the Sinai, West Bank, Golan Heights, and Gaza. Seemingly undefeatable by conventional assaults on its territory, Israel became a prime target of terrorist groups intent on reducing the country by other means.[7] In the early seventies, American intelligence focused in particular on the Palestine Liberation Organization (PLO), Fatah, and associated groups such as the Black September Organization.

Despite the growth of these groups, fueled by the teeming refugee camps that surrounded Israel and an ample supply of foreign sponsors, U.S. policy makers dismissed them as a long-term threat. A September 1972 CIA report described Middle East terrorist groups as a "disunited, uncoordinated, and crumbling movement" that was struggling for relevancy.[8] The various Palestinian terrorist organizations were not, however, prepared to accept their demise. Instead, they embraced even greater violence against a larger spectrum of international targets. Organizations such as the PLO established a pattern of contacts and support for terrorism throughout the world. As the seventies progressed, this network included the Red Army Faction, the Turkish Peoples' Liberation Army, the Eritrean Liberation Front, and European terrorist factions such as Baader-Meinhof. All of these organizations enjoyed overt and covert assistance from the Soviet Union and communist China.[9]

As the threat of terrorism spread, American policy makers debated their next steps. A clear and necessary decision was first defining the nature of the problem. A March 1973 cable written by the U.S. embassy in Tel Aviv is notable for its insights:

> Any country or group fighting for what it thinks are fundamental interests judges weapons at its disposal not on their own merits but in terms of justification of the cause in which they are employed. Honorable professional military conduct in accordance with the protocols of warfare is a luxury of the past, or of opponents not too different from each other who fear in defeat nothing catastrophic or final. As the cause approaches desperation, and the consequences of defeat or even of failure to attain victory appear more and more final, cataclysmic and dishonorable, groups and nations have shown that they will use any

> means at their disposal to gain their ends and will feel fully justified in doing so.[10]

In short, officials closest to the terrorist threat against Israel understood that it defied the conventional wisdom applied to war. Perhaps more important, they realized that actions taken to counter terrorism offered the prospect not of a clear victory, but a paradoxical outcome that would likely produce an enemy possessing even greater resolve.

Unfortunately, American leadership at the time lacked the luxury of contemplating either terrorist motives or a response equivalent to the complexity of the threat. What the Nixon administration did accomplish was the creation of the Cabinet Committee to Combat Terrorism in September 1972. Chaired by the Secretary of State William P. Rogers, its mission was to "coordinate, among the government agencies, ongoing activity for the prevention of terrorism."[11] The committee comprised ten cabinet-level members and ten federal agencies that included the FBI, the Department of Transportation, and the Federal Aviation Administration. The Department of Defense and the Central Intelligence Agency were also included as participants. The committee issued its first comprehensive report on 27 June 1973. Its primary, somewhat axiomatic, finding was that the United States required policies designed to protect Americans abroad. Moreover, as a superpower, the United States had an obligation to assume "an international leadership role in pursuit of multilateral remedies."[12]

From the start, the State Department–dominated policy applied to the problem of terrorism. In the aftermath of the Munich tragedy, the guidance from Secretary of State Rogers was to convince the Arab world that sponsorship of terrorist organizations like Black September had left their image "badly tarnished" and was ultimately working against their best interests.[13] To this end, American policy makers primarily pursued diplomatic and legal devices to mitigate terrorism. The United States sponsored the Convention for the Prevention and Punishment of Certain Acts of International Terrorism in September 1972. The agreement narrowly defined a terrorist as "anyone who unlawfully kills, causes serious bodily harm or kidnaps another person commits an act of international significance."[14] It excluded acts of terrorism committed by individuals within their own borders or acts of civil violence. More tellingly, the convention also excluded attacks on military personnel from its final language.[15]

The Committee to Combat Terrorism assigned primary operational responsibility for domestic and international counterterrorism to the Federal Bureau of Investigation. Actual enforcement of U.S. policy such as it was would be the responsibility of a civilian agency. The committee did recognize, however, that some tasks, particularly those overseas, might transcend FBI capabilities. In November 1972, the attorney general wrote to Secretary of Defense Melvin Laird requesting the "loan of military equipment and/or weaponry, or members of the services functioning in a technical but not law enforcement capacity."[16] Laird concurred with the request, maintaining the practice that the military would have a tertiary role in counterterrorism, following after diplomatic efforts and civilian law enforcement.

Despite its circumscribed role, the Defense Department adopted counterterrorism as part of its portfolio in the seventies. Interestingly, the U.S. Air Force led the way when it came to developing military contingencies to combat terrorism. According to one RAND study, the Air Force Office of Special Investigations published 90 percent of all government intelligence on terrorism in the early seventies. Civilian and military students alike attended the "Dynamics of International Terrorism" course offered at the USAF Special Operations School at Hurlburt Field, Florida.[17] Over time, these efforts would be included with a growing number of studies dedicated to understanding terrorist origins, motives, and actions.[18]

By the time Gerald Ford became president, a number of initiatives had been translated into concrete action. During the mid-seventies, reflecting growing concerns about their vulnerability to terrorism, federal officials increased airport security measures in major terminals throughout the country. Precautions included an embryonic electronic system created to check passenger luggage. These steps were accompanied by tighter visa, immigration, and customs procedures. In 1975 the United States also reached a bilateral agreement with Cuba to deter its use as a safe haven for hijackers.[19]

The Cuba initiative reflected the administration's continued treatment of terrorism as a legal and diplomatic problem. Rather than pursue terrorist groups outside the United States, policy makers argued for better preparedness and deterrence. A February 1975 State Department memorandum to Ford stated very clearly: "Our principle desire is to deter a terrorist from striking by placing legal, physical, and other barriers before him. Should he strike, we seek to apprehend him and ensure that he pays a sufficiently high penalty to discourage other potential terrorists."[20] Thus, while officials recognized the growing epidemic of kidnapping in Central and South America, and ongoing conditions of poverty and violence that were ideal for terrorist recruitment, the conventional wisdom focused on improving communications between federal agencies.[21] A more proactive approach to the problem seemed unnecessary.

Jimmy Carter's arrival to the White House was accompanied by a temporary decrease in terrorism around the world. With the decline of the threat went any sense of urgency. New initiatives were rare at the start of Carter's term. Regardless, the American intelligence community was not sanguine regarding existing trends. Threats to U.S. citizens abroad remained significant. According to a 1978 CIA report, North Americans (42.6 percent) and Western Europeans (32.6 percent) comprised the significant majority of terrorist victims.[22] The most common form of attack suffered by these targets was an explosive device or an incendiary bomb, a methodology that guaranteed groups of victims rather than individuals.[23] More disturbing was the evolving nature of terrorist organizations and methodology. The CIA report noted that terrorist groups had adopted smaller, more fluid structures that were more adaptable to security countermeasures. These were designed to avoid direct confrontation with the military or police. Moreover, although kidnapping, hijacking, and hostage incidents represented a very small proportion (13.1 percent) of terrorist incidents between 1968 and 1977, the CIA warned against cultivating high expectations if the country attempted to pursue a vigorous antiterrorism policy. Direct action—on par with the Israeli rescue at Entebbe in 1976—came with risks: "the government's desire for international prestige together with domestic pressure may lead to a rescue attempt in inappropriate circumstances, yielding counterproductive results."[24] The National Security Council concurred with this particular assessment: "Unreasonable expectations are another problem. One should not be carried away by the success of the Israeli rescue operation at Entebbe or the German operation at Mogadishu. The Israelis and Germans not only had well-trained military units; they also had a great deal of luck."[25] Yet, direct action was becoming increasingly necessary as terrorist groups experimented with new methods to attack targets. The CIA predicted that one such means might be "standoff weapons," such as heat-seeking missiles, to avoid "direct confrontations with authorities."[26]

When the Carter administration embarked on its own counterterrorism policy, its actions reflected cognizance of the threat, but also a sense that dramatic action carried unacceptable risk. Consequently, policy makers tinkered with the existing structure rather than substantive reform. In keeping with Nixon and Ford, the White House continued to categorize terrorist actions such as hijacking, kidnapping, and extortion as criminal acts under the jurisdiction of the civilian justice system.[27] One organizational change that Carter did make was to place responsibility for terrorism policy within the NSC as part of a Special Coordinating Committee (SCC). Below the SCC was the Executive Committee on Terrorism, chaired by the State Department, and the Working Group on Terrorism, chaired by the Department of Justice.[28] The military remained in its nominal supporting role for the diplomatic and law enforcement communities.[29] This was essentially the system in place when revolution overwhelmed Iran.

From 1979 onward, the Iranian revolution and the subsequent hostage crisis defined the remainder of Carter's presidency and its approach to terrorism. The hostage takers themselves were, for all intents and purposes, acting without the official sanction of the Iranian government. Their status as nonmilitary actors fit the basic definition of terrorists at that time, as did their actions. The administration's initial responses to the crisis were equally consistent with U.S. policy. With the State Department as the lead agency, the United States attempted a regimen of diplomatic initiatives and, when these failed, a series of economic sanctions designed to successfully resolve the standoff with Tehran.[30] The 1980 rescue mission was invoked only as a final recourse and with great reluctance. The schism it caused with Carter's cabinet, which led to the eventual resignation of Secretary of State Cyrus Vance, represented the depths of disagreement over any action that militarized the hostage crisis.

The Iran situation aside, Carter's term ended on a bleak note regarding global terrorism. A 1979 report by the CIA National Foreign

Assessment Center marked that year as the worst in terms of casualties since the agency began keeping records in 1968. More ominous was the specific judgment: "The increase in casualties and casualty-producing incidents—particularly in light of the notable rise of assassinations—is especially alarming. Although operations deliberately intended to result in mass casualties have been rare, terrorists believe that a larger number of casualties are now necessary to generate the amount of publicity formerly evoked by less bloody operations."[31] In sum, what the Tehran hostage crisis represented was a mere glimmer of the future, one in which American policy and capabilities were wholly inadequate to the task.

Ronald Reagan became president in part because of the Iran hostage crisis. It allowed him to portray Carter as a weak, vacillating leader and provided the former California governor with a chance to make a clean break with what the public perceived as failed policy. Once in office, Reagan was true to his campaign rhetoric. After 1981, official U.S. policy framed terrorism under the category of "low-intensity conflict," placing it in the same category as insurgency and illegal drug trafficking. While it did not pose a direct threat to the United States by definition, the administration saw the primary danger of terrorism in the potential "cumulative nature" of problems it could cause, specifically the isolation it might create between America and its political allies and major trading partners.[32] In what was a modernized version of the domino theory, policy makers believed that the United States was compelled to confront terrorist attacks before they escalated further. The new conventional wisdom was, for example, that the successful 1981 abduction of Brigadier General James L. Dozier by the Red Brigade terrorists would inevitably encourage other terrorist groups to attack NATO allies.[33] A 1985 National Security Council report put the matter bluntly when it said: "In short, the perception that terrorism succeeds must be erased."[34]

From the White House's perspective, terrorism was a component of the larger Cold War conflict with the Soviet Union. Consequently, when it identified the sources of terrorism, the administration focused specifically on host governments known to be supporting terrorist groups. American policy responses thus applied to the Soviet Union, which policy makers believed was using terrorists as Cold War proxies.[35] They also applied to other nations, such as Libya, a country that openly sponsored terrorist attacks against the West. The latter nation would occupy significant American attention in the eighties.

A multiplying series of attacks against the United States and its citizens seemed to provide evidence of these suspicions. The bombing of the Marine barracks in Beirut in October 1983, killing 241 service members, sent a shockwave through the country. Smaller, no less deadly terrorist attacks continued against U.S. military personnel stationed overseas. In August 1985, a car bomb exploded at the U.S. Rhein-Main Airbase in West Germany, killing two. That November, another car bomb detonated at a military shopping center in Frankfurt, West Germany, resulting in thirty-four wounded.[36] In April 1986, Libyan and Palestinian terrorists attacked a West Berlin nightclub frequented by American military personnel.[37]

American civilians living and traveling abroad suffered a similar litany of violence in the eighties. The shockingly brief period between June 1985 and December 1988 witnessed the hijacking of TWA Flight 847 to Beirut, terrorist assaults on airports in Rome and Vienna, the capture of the *Achille Lauro,* and the midair explosion that destroyed Pan Am Flight 103 over Lockerbie, Scotland. In the meantime, kidnappings of American citizens in Lebanon became a routine occurrence.[38]

Hard data on terrorism drove home a trend regularly illustrated by the media. A 1986 report by Robert Oakley noted that globally there were on average 500 terrorist attacks each year between 1979 and 1983. By 1985, this number had reached 780. Casualties also increased from 1,279 (41 U.S.) in 1984 to 2,200 (198 U.S.) the following year.[39] The U.S. Office of Counter-Terrorism and Emergency Planning predicted a broader spectrum of likely victims, including businessmen, clergy, and journalists, in addition to usual military and diplomatic targets.[40] The rising tempo of attacks put U.S. public opinion on edge. The tragic death of Leon Klinghoffer on the *Achille Lauro* and the murder of U.S. navy diver Robert Stethem on TWA Flight 847 struck a chord with the American people. A Roper poll taken in the summer of 1985 showed that 78 percent of Americans believed that terrorism was one of the most serious problems facing the country.[41]

The policies crafted during the Reagan era reflect this sense of urgency. As early as January 1981 the National Security Council convened to address the problem of terrorism. Policy makers discussed a series of broad-based questions that challenged nearly a decade of counterterrorism doctrine. They addressed the rules of engagement for embassies under attack, the potential utility of a central "clearing house" for intelligence sharing, and the prospects for new diplomatic antiterrorist conventions. Explicit throughout the meeting was a consensus that there was a need for a better, more direct approach to the terrorist threat.[42]

New policy arrived in the form of National Security Decision Directive (NSDD) 30, "Managing Terrorist Incidents," on 10 April 1982. As one of its guiding principles, the document noted the need for "a rapid, effective response, immediate access to institutional expertise, and extensive prior planning." However, despite the rhetorical commitment to reform counterterrorist policy, what distinguished NSDD 30 was the absence of real change. Like the previous three administrations, the State Department remained in charge of a multiagency coalition (CIA, DOD, FBI, DOJ, FEMA) that was simply given the new title of the Terrorist Incident Working Group. Domestic terrorist incidents fell under the purview of the FBI, while responsibility for airline hijacking resided with the Federal Aviation Administration.[43]

The assistance programs designed to address terrorism also largely fell under civilian agencies during the first Reagan administration. In 1983 the State Department created the Anti-Terrorism Assistance Program, which provided training in crisis management, bomb detection, and airport security. By the end of 1984, the program included personnel from the Department of Transportation, the Bureau of Alcohol, Tobacco and Firearms, and the State Department Office of Security, who conducted training for police and security officials from over fifty countries.[44]

In keeping with past practice, the administration also continued to define terrorism as a criminal act under the jurisdiction of federal law enforcement. As late as January 1986, National Security Decision Directive (NSDD) 207, "The National Program for Combatting Terrorism," used this very definition and declared that the United States would follow a "no-concessions policy" regarding potential negotiations with terrorists in order to protect the greatest number of people. The policy explicitly stated: "The USG [U.S. government] will pay no ransoms, nor permit the release of prisoners or agree to other conditions that could serve to encourage additional terrorism."[45]

However, by the time NSDD 207 was released, the antiterrorism policy status quo was no longer viable. As the frequency of attacks increased, the American public became increasingly restive and doubtful of any approach considered too lenient. Congressional pressure to enhance U.S. counterterrorist capability also grew. In 1984 Senator Arlen Spector (R-PA) proposed changes to U.S. policy that would permit the "forcible apprehension" of terrorists.[46] To assuage these concerns, in July 1985 Reagan authorized Vice President George H. W. Bush to lead a task force to address more aggressive measures against terrorism.[47] Public officials also ratcheted up U.S. rhetoric regarding terrorism and stronger countermeasures. When the White House announced the Bush task force, Secretary of State George Schultz endorsed the idea of an active defense against terrorism. Additionally, Schultz called for a "preemptive capacity" to "deter terrorism by way of raising the price or 'ante' of terrorism activities."[48]

The search for a more aggressive methodology inevitably led policy makers to the U.S. armed forces. Each branch subsequently pursued its own improved counterterrorism capability. In January 1984, the Navy authorized OP-06D, the "Red Cell" unit, to identify vulnerabilities on ships and installations.[49] The Red Cell was the institutional counterpoint to Seal Team Six, which served as the Navy's primary antiterrorist unit after 1981. The other service branches followed a similar path. In 1987 the Army published *Field Manual 100-37: Terrorism Counteraction* as a primer for commanders to prevent terrorist attacks.[50] The manual accompanied the development of the Army Delta Group, which served as that service's equivalent of a Seal Team. Congress unified these separate activities with the creation of the Special Operations Command in 1986, mandating that American special forces were responsible for the "immediate and primary capability to respond to terrorism."[51]

Despite the improvements in military counterterrorism capability, the Pentagon and civilian officials remained reluctant to commit conventional or special operations units.[52] When the National Security Council discussed potential responses to five Americans taken hostage in Lebanon, the military option was restricted to retaliation by naval air power deployed from carrier battle groups stationed in the Mediterranean.[53] At no point did senior officials seriously consider a hostage rescue mission utilizing Delta or Seal Team Six ground units. Perhaps the best-known counterterrorist action taken by the Reagan administration was air strikes against Libya in April 1986. Otherwise, the White House sought out alternative diplomatic and economic means to isolate Libya for its support of terrorism. According to NSDD 205, "Acting Against Libyan Support of International Terrorism," this obliged the United States to pursue policies that "demonstrate resolve in a manner that reverses the perception of U.S. passivity in the face of mounting terrorist activity."[54]

The larger question during the Reagan years was how best to demonstrate this resolve. Military options were clearly limited once they were pried away from the aggressive rhetoric typical of the time. It was impractical to begin military operations in areas where terrorist attacks occurred since many of these nations (e.g., West Germany) were American allies already tentative about increasing Cold War tensions. Deploying military force against the sources of terrorism was equally problematic. The choice to use ground or air units inside Iran, Libya, or Syria contained significant military as well as diplomatic risks. Even when the United States acted within international waters or airspace, as was the case with Libya's "line of death" across the Gulf of Sidra in 1986, it drew inevitable criticism that the United States could not use international principles—such as Article 51 of the UN Charter that allowed for self-defense—to legitimize military force so far from home.[55]

At the one point the Reagan White House attempted a decisive, sustained effort on the ground, it seriously handicapped the administration's ability to wage small wars against terrorism or any other threat. Declassified documents have since revealed that American support for Nicaraguan contras was essentially a proterrorism project.[56] Regardless, when the scandal broke in 1986, it was a major distraction for all programs foreign and domestic. In a June 1987 letter to the president, Vice President George Bush referred to the "temporary reduction in credibility" that the Iran-Contra investigation was causing the administration.[57] While it had promised dramatic action against the terrorism, the Reagan (and Bush) administrations were enveloped in multiple indictments and investigations that finished out the decade.

Under the Clinton administration, the post–Cold War period served as a new context for terrorism. In the absence of direct U.S.-Soviet conflict, policy makers attributed terrorist actions to a greater diversity of motives that, in retrospect, were obviously present during the period after 1945, but were more plausible as threats once the Cold War dichotomy was gone. Consequently, the national security establishment gave increasing credence to ethnicity, religion, and other factors as the driving forces behind terrorist activity. Both public officials and scholars recognized that although these presented more difficult features for analysis than political ideology, they were nonetheless powerful motivators. Perhaps even more important, as terrorism became more closely linked to the intangible features of faith and cultural identity, it also became less discriminate in its objectives and far less predictable.[58] A 1985 RAND study had alluded to this eventuality with the following prediction: "Warfare in the future may be less destructive than that in the first half of the twentieth century, but also less coherent. Warfare will cease to be finite. The distinction between war and peace will dissolve. Armed conflict will not be confined by national frontiers."[59]

In terms of the raw number of terrorist attacks, the nineties promised to be a dangerous time. According a 1991 CIA report, strikes against U.S. interests hit a historical high in 1990. Chile had the largest number of incidents in the world, followed by Peru and Bolivia. The agency attributed these attacks in part as a response to Operation Desert Shield in Saudi Arabia. The CIA also argued that past American support of dictatorships, particularly the Pinochet government in Chile, had made it a popular terrorist target.[60] By 1997 American citizens and facilities worldwide made up 40 percent of terrorist targets, up from 25 percent the preceding year.[61]

This period was punctuated by a series of devastating attacks against American interests abroad, as was the case with the Khobar Towers bombing in 1996 and at home. The first attempt to destroy the World Trade Center in 1993 and the Oklahoma City bombing in 1995 brought home the realization that the United States was not immune from spreading global instability, regardless of its source. As violence against the United States continued, two interrelated trends appeared in the architecture of terrorism in the nineties. The first was related to the institutions that had begun to flourish in the aftermath of the Cold War—a complex, fragile web of electronic infrastructure, commercial systems, and a public driven by readily accessible media information. These institutions, typical of a modern, affluent, and vulnerable world, allowed terrorist groups a much easier point of purchase to further their particular goals. A second trend was the rampant proliferation of a broad spectrum of weaponry—from small arms to nuclear, biological, and chemical weapons of mass destruction—that could be used against "soft" civilian targets.[62] In sum, terrorism in the last decade of the century was as much a product of more vulnerable potential victims as it was the product of deadly new capabilities.

The Clinton administration's approach to this threat was consistent with history. For the most part, the president and his national security team reverted back to the treatment of terrorism as a diplomatic and legal problem, a standard expressed in the June 1995 Presidential Decision Directive (PDD) 39, "U.S. Policy on Counterterrorism." The document made it clear that American policy on terrorism was dedicated to "deter and preempt, apprehend and prosecute, or assist other governments to prosecute, individuals who perpetrate or plan to perpetrate such attacks."[63] This intent was later echoed by Madeleine Albright, who publicly endorsed the need to "bring suspected terrorists before the bar of justice."[64] The lead agency for policy and international incidents was again the State Department. One of its first actions was sponsoring the "Summit of Peacemakers" at Sharm al-Sheik in 1996, which produced a pledge from twenty-nine countries to commit greater resources to fight terrorism.[65] As an adjunct to diplomacy and legal prosecution, the Clinton administration also embraced economic sanctions as a key measure to deter violence against the United States and its interests.

This approach produced what could be best described as mixed results. When the FBI attempted to investigate the Khobar Towers bombing in Saudi Arabia, local authorities refused to grant it equal jurisdiction, seriously impeding any progress.[66] However, in some instances, American officials were able to win cooperation overseas. Between 1993 and 1998, ten suspected terrorists were extradited back to the United States for trial.[67] Organizational problems also appeared after PDD 39 became official policy. The division of labor between the State Department and the FBI created its own unexpected blind spots. As a matter of bureau policy, the FBI regularly conflated domestic and international terrorism into what was essentially the same category. In its 1998 annual report, for example, the FBI lumped together abortion clinic bombings, white supremacist group activity, and overseas attacks on U.S. diplomats.[68] This classification standard did little to establish a reasonable sense of priority for analysis or action. Lastly, while economic leverage became a common recourse in the nineties, it had a minimal impact. In January 1995, Clinton issued an executive order threatening sanctions against any person or group who supported terrorism.[69] This policy was later extended specifically to the Taliban in 1999 after the embassy bombings in Kenya and Tanzania proved that the original sanctions had been ineffective.[70]

The 1998 African embassy bombings were a clear turning point for U.S. counterterrorism policy. The massive explosions, which struck the American embassies in Nairobi, Kenya and Dar es Salaam, Tanzania, on 7 August 1998, killed 252 people (12 U.S. citizens) and wounded more than 5,000. The Islamic Army for the Liberation of Holy Sites, a group led by Saudi millionaire Osama bin Laden, claimed credit for the attacks. Initially, the U.S. response was carefully consistent with previous policy. President Clinton quickly signed an executive order freezing assets owned by bin Laden.[71] The FBI launched a massive investigation of the two attacks. More than 900 special agents deployed overseas, the largest operation of that type in bureau history. By the end of 1998, eleven indictments were handed down in federal court and four suspected terrorists were in custody.[72] Reconstruction and embassy defense received particular attention after the attacks. The State Department budgeted $677.5 million to rebuild in Kenya and Tanzania. Congress appropriated an additional $748 million for embassy security upgrades worldwide. By 1999 the State Department security budget was more than six times larger than the previous year.[73]

After the 1998 embassy attacks, the administration also launched a series of military operations against known and suspected terrorist targets. Specifically, the administration ordered strikes against terrorist bases in Afghanistan and a "pharmaceutical" plant in Sudan. At the time, these attacks were made against terrorist organizations rather than specific individuals. Moreover, they were intended not only to be retaliatory for the embassy bombing, but also preemptive to the extent that they would disrupt terrorist activity, at least over the short term.[74]

The military actions taken against terrorist targets in 1998 were reminiscent of the more militarized American policy in the eighties. However, they were not a simple reaction to more adverse circumstances. In fact, a series of new federal laws in the mid-nineties had begun to shift a greater burden for counterterrorism to the U.S. armed forces. The 1996 Defense Against Weapons of Mass Destruction Act made the Defense Department directly responsible for preparations against these attacks on the United States.[75] Broader authority followed the same year. Specifically, the 1996 Antiterrorism and Effective Death Penalty Act authorized: "The President should use *all necessary means, including covert action and military force,* to disrupt, dismantle, and destroy international infrastructure used by international terrorists, including overseas terrorist training facilities and safehavens."[76] In May 1998 Presidential Decision Directive 62 created a National Coordinator for Security, Infrastructure Protection and Counter-Terrorism within the National Security Council.[77] This latter action marked a clear shift from the domain of law enforcement to that of national security. The presidential order recognized that the scope and scale of terrorist attacks had grown as the decade ended. The African embassy attacks made it clear that terrorists' primary objective was to cause massive civilian casualties without regard for specific political goals. More telling was the increasing frequency of American intelligence reporting of the likelihood that a weapon of mass destruction would be used against the United States.[78]

9/11

The first months of George W. Bush's presidency were replete with predictions of an impending terrorist attack. As declassified documents later proved, clear warning signs were present throughout his first months in office.[79] However, the same claims regarding a serious threat to American security also appeared as early as June 2000 in a report of the bipartisan National Commission on Terrorism. It was a remarkably candid document, which suggested that the United States was drifting away from combating state-supported terrorism. The report's authors believed that U.S. policy was generally too passive and overly focused on defeating the bin Laden network. Among its recommended reforms were removing existing limitations on the recruitment of CIA counterterrorism informants and, importantly, that the Defense Department become the lead agency in the event of a "catastrophic attack on U.S. soil."[80]

The September attacks permanently removed the issue from the realm of speculation. For its own part, the Bush administration depicted the immediate post-9/11 period as a sea of change in the American understanding of war and national security. Vice President Dick Cheney asserted this point of view in 2003: "The strategy of deterrence, which served us so well during the decades of the Cold War, will no longer do. Our terrorist enemy has no country to defend, no assets to destroy in order to discourage an attack. Strategies of containment will not assure our security either. There is no containing terrorists who will commit suicide for the purposes of mass slaughter."[81] However, as much as the administration portrayed the situation in 2001 as a clear point of demarcation, it was in reality the culmination of a generational war against terrorism. In this context, the attacks on New York and the Pentagon were part of the inheritance of Munich, Entebbe, the *Achille Lauro,* the USS *Cole,* and the embassy bombings in Africa. Historian Melani McAlister noted in 2002: "With the memory/forgetting of captivity and rescue behind us, it became time for Americans to win the thirty years' war—by pretending it had just begun."[82]

In more practical terms, 9/11 was an event that ripped the Bush administration away from its election promises and significantly challenged basic strategic decisions made in 2001. During his presidential campaign, candidate Bush had signaled a retreat from many Clinton-era commitments, specifically those involving overseas military obligations. Early in his term, he supported a miniscule, $4.5 billion, annual increase in defense spending.[83] The lion's share of debate and commitments in the 2000 campaign went to domestic policy issues such as Social Security and Medicare.

Two years after the election, Bush's approach to national security affairs was profoundly more assertive. Gone was the reticence regarding overseas deployments and the prospect of military casualties. When it was finally published in 2002, *The National Security Strategy of the United States of America* established a new template for military policy: "It has taken almost a decade for us to comprehend the true nature of this threat. Given the goals of rogue states and terrorists, the United States can no longer solely rely on a reactive posture as we have in the past. The inability to deter a potential attacker, the immediacy of today's threats, and the magnitude of potential harm that could be caused by our adversaries' choice of weapons, do not permit that option. We cannot let our enemies strike first."[84] Equally important was the place occupied by the terrorist threat. Although the document would indicate the importance of freedom, "human dignity," and regional alliances—allowing a degree of continuity with Clinton—its core goal was the ultimate destruction of terrorism by military means.[85] This basic standard would define American wars abroad for the remainder of the decade.

The Global War on Terror

The year 2001 was filled with contrasts for the U.S. military. In the aftermath of the 2000 election, the armed forces seemed almost resigned to financial retrenchment and a future defined by limited strategic goals. When the Pentagon began internal discussion of the 2001 Quadrennial Defense Review, it essentially revolved around doing more with less. The JCS and their respective branches focused on the demands for greater flexibility and mobility in the post–Cold War environment. Yet continued force reductions were an ongoing reality. In early 2001 the Defense Department considered reducing the Army by two divisions.[86] Moreover, at a time when all the services wanted additional personnel, equipment, or both, cuts in the surface fleet and bomber and fighter groups remained on the table. Strategically, these factors translated into a serious discussion as to whether or not U.S. military should abandon the two "major theater wars" doctrine set a decade earlier.[87]

When the final version of the *Quadrennial Defense Review* was released on 30 September 2001, the change in its approach to U.S. security and military affairs was jarring. While it retained the more traditional references to nuclear strategy and conventional readiness, readily apparent in the document is the sense of imminent danger to the United States and its interests. In this new world order, chemical, biological, radiological, nuclear, and "high-yield explosives" (CBRNE) wielded by international terrorists constituted the primary threat to American security.[88] In order to meet this new threat, the QDR called for the rapid transition of military training, unit organization, and doctrine for domestic security as well as "contingency operations" abroad.[89]

Omitted from proposed reforms was a call for any serious increase in standing forces. Rather than rely on additional conventional or special operations forces, the Defense Department emphasized "developing transformational capabilities," which, stripped of its jargon, meant that the U.S. military would thereafter supplement existing units (redefined as "legacy forces") with new technologies that would improve their capabilities.[90] In part, the new doctrine was an updated version of *Joint Vision 2010,* originally proposed in 1996.[91] Its key difference, however, was a much more explicit integration of advanced technologies at the tactical level. Theoretically, the revolution in military affairs, circa 2001, would apply "cyberwar" to the entire spectrum of conflict—from a conventional invasion of part with Desert Storm to small unit operations in the underdeveloped world.

During the latter months of 2001, the American military transitioned rapidly from theory to action. As will be discussed in the following chapter, the United States and its coalition allies invaded Afghanistan (Operation Enduring Freedom) in October 2001. In March 2003, a full-scale invasion of Iraq—Operation Iraqi Freedom—began with the expressed intention of overthrowing the Hussein regime. Although neither conflict could be considered a "small" war, special forces figured prominently in both invasions, particularly Afghanistan. As late as 2003, the Pentagon was optimistic that more conventional force commitments were unnecessary. The deployment and use of special operations units, in concert with CIA paramilitary officers, proved to be a decisive element in the war against the Taliban. As Operation Enduring Freedom unfolded in 2001, it seemed that a very small contingent of Americans, supplemented by precise tactical bombing and indigenous allies, had redefined the art of war. Many civilian leaders, most importantly Secretary of Defense Donald Rumsfeld, in fact preached that the "revolution in military affairs" was here.[92]

With respect to the counterterrorism mission, special operations forces were a natural fit. Operating as they did in small detachments, special forces were at once more precise and deliberately less intrusive than conventional formations. It was common to have a significant degree of linguistic and cultural expertise among these units as well as advanced training for working with indigenous, irregular forces.[93]

Because of their obvious utility after the 9/11 attacks, U.S. special operations forces accumulated an increasing amount of autonomy and institutional support in waging America's small wars against terrorism. After 2001 SOCOM became a "supported" as well as a "supporting" organization, which translated into a greater degree of operational autonomy, sometimes removed from regional commands like CENTCOM.[94] SOCOM also gained a greater share of the defense budget. Its fiscal year 2007 funding of $6.6 billion was an 81 percent increase over pre-9/11 levels.[95]

Bolstered with these resources, the number of special forces operatives within the U.S. military expanded well beyond their prewar levels. By the end of fiscal year 2006, special operations units of all types included 52,846 personnel.[96] Approximately 742 soldiers were directly added to A-teams (550 regular, 192 to National Guard). SOCOM also created a new SEAL team in 2006 and another in 2008.[97] The Marine Corps, a longtime skeptic of elite forces, initiated its own prototype special operations unit, authorizing an eighty-six-man detachment that deployed with Navy SEALS to Iraq in 2004.[98] The Defense Department will increase SOCOM by an additional 15 percent by 2013, a number that also includes 3,700 new civil affairs and psychological operations personnel.[99]

SOCOM's counterterrorism mission grew considerably after 2001. Mobile training teams visited dozens of countries to teach new tactics and familiarize host militaries with new technology. Large multicountry events became more common. SOCOM sponsored Sovereign Challenge in 2005, in which military attachés from eighty-two countries were invited to exchange off-the-record information on terrorism.[100] By mid-decade, SOCOM also assumed paramilitary functions that were previously the province of the Central Intelligence Agency. In 2005, Congress appropriated $25 million specifically for intelligence gathering and the cultivation of nonstate indigenous groups around the world.[101]

One of the most important battlefields in the war on terror was in the Philippines. American special operations forces were already actively training the Philippine military prior to the September attacks.[102] By the end of the year, they had expanded operations to include counterinsurgency and counterterrorism. This was the case when special operations forces were deployed as part of Exercise Balikatan 02-1 in November 2001. Follow-up missions continued until late 2003 in what was heralded at the time as the "second front" in the global war on terror.[103]

The initial focus of the Balikatan operation was Basilan Island, located in the southern Philippine province of Mindanao. Its primary target was the Abu Sayyaf Group, a Philippine terrorist organization that had been active in the region for years before September 2001. Later military operations extended throughout southern Mindanao and the Sulu Archipelago.[104]

The primary U.S. contribution to the campaign against Abu Sayyaf came from elements of the 1st Special Forces Group. American personnel were responsible for training ten infantry battalions in the Philippine army. Additional missions included base camp improvements on Basilan and medical support missions for civilians living in the area. Navy Special Boat Teams, an Air Force Special Operations Squadron, and Military Information Support Teams (MIST) also lent their expertise to improve local sea interdiction capabilities and nighttime tactical air operations. MIST units were a concession the Pentagon saw as necessary to counter Abu Sayyaf propaganda.[105]

Overall, the American "second front" against terrorism operated under significant limits. A "force cap" imposed by Pacific Command initially prohibited civil affairs units from deployment to the Philippines and allowed Abu Sayyaf the opportunity to frame American involvement as an attack on the people and their beliefs. MIST teams were a late response to this shortfall. The greater priority granted special operations in Iraq, and Afghanistan also handicapped American logistics in the Philippines. When the 1st Special Forces Group arrived, it was wholly dependent on the U.S. embassy for secure communications.[106] For their own part, the Philippine government placed its own specific limits on American forces. Manila initially rejected the deployment of psychological warfare specialists, given past abuses by these units under the Marcos government. Since the first American advisers deployed in 2001, their hosts have forbidden them to participate in combat operations.[107] The Philippine national authorities have also prohibited action against specific rebel groups. The Moro Islamic Liberation Front (MILF) was protected from counterterrorist operations while government officials negotiated a peace agreement with the group. This policy continued despite the fact that the MILF enjoyed close cooperation with Jemaah Islamiyah and Abu Sayyaf and provided them with de facto sanctuaries from military sweeps through the region.[108]

Much of the U.S. military effort in the Philippines reflected traditional counterinsurgency rather than the counterterrorism mission originally envisioned by SOCOM. American actions remained wholly dependent on the host nation, which placed significant restrictions on operational flexibility, a critical ingredient in fighting terrorists. Once limited operations began, American planners faced the problem of sustaining them over the long term. After U.S. units departed Basilan Island, terrorists grew increasingly active. Clashes with Philippine marines in June 2007 left fourteen government personnel dead. Renewed fighting at the end of the year killed five more soldiers and wounded an additional twenty-four. Despite years of effort, experts pointed out that many of the root problems that formed the basis for terrorist recruitment—endemic poverty and claims of discrimination against Muslims—remained largely unchecked by Manila.[109]

After September 2001, Africa attracted renewed American attention in the global war on terror. Conditions within many parts of the continent—highlighted by widespread poverty, disease, and instability—made it almost ideal ground for recruitment, even more so given the fact that 50 percent of the population is under the age of fifteen.[110] In September 2005, the State Department named the Africa-based Salifist Group for Call and Combat, a terrorist threat on par with Al Qaeda. In practice, African terrorism extended far beyond the continent. According to official U.S. estimates in 2006, as many as one-quarter of the foreign fighters in Iraq (5,000–8,000) were African. It was common for these fighters to gain combat experience against coalition forces in the Middle East and to return home to train new terrorist recruits.[111]

To address this challenge, the Defense Department created the Combined Joint Task Force–Horn of Africa, stationed at Camp Lemonier in Djibouti in 2002. At the time, the facility was home to 1,200 personnel and was the only permanent U.S. base on the entire continent.[112] It marked a significantly increased American military presence designed to combat terrorism at its root source. In June 2005 the

United States launched Operation Enduring Freedom–Trans Sahara. It was the largest deployment of U.S. forces to Africa since World War II, involving a total of nine countries, and was the most important commitment of military units since Operation Restore Hope in Somalia more than a decade earlier. As was the case in the Philippines, the operation utilized both civic action projects and military training. After 2005, American advisers drawn from both SOCOM and the regular military fanned out across Africa as part of the Trans-Sahara Counter Terrorism Initiative.[113] Training was accompanied by direct military action. The United States began routinely sharing intelligence with the military in Chad as it conducted counterterrorist strikes. U.S. special forces soldiers accompanied Ethiopian forces into Somalia in December 2006 to assist with intelligence dissemination and tactical air support.[114]

The United States solidified its commitment to Africa in 2007 with the creation of a major military command (AFRICOM). However, the initiative ran into widespread trouble almost as soon as it was launched. Nigeria, South Africa, Algeria, and Libya immediately opposed the measure, claiming that it had been made to counter growing Chinese influence in the hemisphere. South African Defense Minister Mosiuoa Lekota went so far as to publicly demand in 2009 that none of the African Union's fifty-three member nations host a permanent U.S. base.[115] Although Liberia and Botswana briefly considered sponsorship of the post, at the end of 2009 AFRICOM headquarters remained in Germany and the search for a base was "completely off the table," according its commander, General William Ward.[116]

As noted in the previous chapter, the global war on terror has substantially changed American military operations in Latin America. This has been particularly true with respect to Colombia. After 2001, U.S. military assistance shifted from counternarcotics to counterterrorism, which, in turn, was conflated with counterinsurgency. Throughout, American military officials and the intelligence community emphasized suspected links between the FARC, the cartels, and Iran.[117]

While the United States broadened its military strategy beyond interdicting narcotics, assistance addressed a growing array of security needs in Colombia. Programs that improved the physical security of key strategic resources gained in importance. In late 2001 the Pentagon considered a plan to train a new Colombian army battalion specifically responsible for infrastructure, such as the Caño Limon oil pipeline in the northeastern part of the country.[118] The following year, the United States committed $100 million to train a much larger unit, the 18th Brigade, for this very purpose.[119] Other programs have gone into training elite forces with a skill set flexible enough to be appropriate for counterterrorism. The Colombian military subsequently trained a commando unit in 2003 based on the model of a U.S. Army Ranger battalion, but with the capability to collect intelligence as well as execute small unit operations. A counternarcotics brigade previously organized with U.S. assistance additionally was broken up into smaller, more mobile units.[120] To take away guerilla infrastructure near Bogotá, Boyacá, and the Valle del Cauca, the Colombia military also created a number of "high mountain battalions" that used, like their sister units, an array of satellite imagery, listening stations, ground-based radar, and surveillance aircraft to pin down the FARC and other insurgent groups.[121] The total cost of these programs in 2004 alone was $574.6 million. Approximately 320 U.S. military personnel, along with 400 civilian contractors, provided the necessary expertise for the transition from fighting drugs to combating what the White House described as terrorism in Colombia.[122]

When the Colombian military gained new effectiveness in the countryside, the FARC increasingly embraced urban terrorism. Insurgents began large-scale bombings in public areas and against the military. A massive explosion in January 2002 that killed twenty-nine troops in the southern town of El Dorado recalled the methodology of the Provisional Irish Republican Army. Later that year in September, a series of FARC mortar attacks in Bogotá proper revealed an increasing degree of sophistication within the insurgency. Contemporary media reports noted that militants possessed a complex urban support network of safe houses, weapons caches, and escape routes to support attacks against the national government.[123]

As the decade drew to a close, it was clear that the Colombian military had successfully placed significant pressure on insurgent forces generally classified as "terrorist," but it was reaching the limits of its effectiveness. The FARC, other active rebel groups, and their sometime allies among the cartels could not operate with the same impunity as they had in the early nineties when Andrés Pastrana was president. As they have lost ground, the guerrillas and the cartels have reverted to a smaller-scale presence that is augmented by outright acts of terrorism.[124] Small wars in Colombia have grown less frequent, but more deadly, particularly with respect to civilians caught between government security forces and terrorism made indiscriminate by design.

Conclusions

In some important respects, the American global war on terror has been a victim of its own success. Nearly ten years of operations against terrorism in general as well as specific terrorist groups have yielded a number of important victories. The American military and its allies around the world have successfully disrupted terrorist organizations and their sanctuaries. Neither countries (Afghanistan) nor particular regions (Mindanao, southern Somalia) offer terrorists the safety they once enjoyed before September 2001.

But victory is incomplete and has resulted in a threat that is now more diffuse and difficult to combat. American military operations successfully disrupted Al Qaeda and other groups to the point where they are no longer easily identifiable. A small war against terrorism has thus become smaller. An increasingly decentralized enemy now finds sanctuary in great expanses of difficult geography—as is the case along the Afghanistan-Pakistan border or in Indonesia—or within the crowded urban sprawl of the underdeveloped world.

The terrorist enemy has also proven to be adaptable. After the initial phase of "shock and awe," terrorists are proving extremely resilient in the face of American efforts. Terrorist networks that survived the onslaught of 2001–2003 have adopted revised tactics to new locations to protect their viability. Ironically, many reappeared in the very western nations that the global war on terror was originally supposed to protect. The increased incidents of militant Islamism in Europe, specifically in England, Spain, and Denmark, indicate a deliberate plan to attack vulnerable populations while enjoying a legal shield from direct military action or covert operations. It is highly unlikely that any member of the European Union would tolerate American special operations missions within their borders.[125] While international cooperation has been a general principle, many affected countries increasingly have reverted to their own internal military and police agencies.[126]

As the war against terror progresses, it also reveals the limits of direct military action. Over the long term, the term “global war against terror” has proven to be a misnomer. In actual practice, this type of small war obliges the United States to address the underlying causes of terrorism rather than simply its command structure or order of battle.[127] Without question, it demands a more subdued, patient approach focused on ideology, propaganda, and recruitment patterns, factors that have as much to do with socioeconomic and cultural challenges as military ones.[128] Since 2001 the military has incorporated social science into its arsenal of responses to terrorism. Counterterrorism has become a highly sophisticated form of counterinsurgency.[129]

In the end, even well-designed and precisely applied methodologies will likely reach a point of diminishing returns.[130] Conventional military units have been able to incorporate many of the missions and doctrine currently employed by special forces. Civil affairs, psychological, and information operations are now a normal part of military practice. The U.S. military has proven adaptable even when the counterterrorist mission requires greater degrees of across-the-board training and interconnectivity. Yet, despite this progress, preventing terrorism has reproduced the same prerequisites that the military realized during the Vietnam War; success is ultimately dependent on the strength and resilience of the host nation and its own institutions. This final end phase of the global war on terror is highly problematic for many reasons: the high degree of training necessary for military forces and the complex balance of force and encouragement necessary to make true counterterrorism work.[131] Early indicators of the U.S. withdrawal from Iraq and the 2009 “surge” in Afghanistan are subject to much scrutiny and debate. It is likely that it will take many additional years to assess the true nature of success or failure in these key countries and other areas affected by the war.

8

Iraq and Afghanistan

We cannot kill our way out of this endeavor.

—General David Petraeus, "Multinational Force-Iraq Commander's Counterinsurgency Guidance"

War followed the September 11 attacks on the United States, rapidly in the case of Afghanistan, but also in Iraq after a prolonged and controversial public debate. The two conflicts were the first large-scale, sustained U.S. military efforts since Desert Shield/Storm more than a decade earlier. While both were dramatically successful in their early stages, practically no one in the upper echelons of civilian or military leadership, much less the public at large, fully comprehended the precise nature of the conflicts they began.

The initial stages of each war offered an important degree of foreshadowing to the future of modern war. In both Afghanistan and Iraq, the conventional phase of each respective invasion was short. American ground forces, augmented by absolute air superiority and precision guided munitions, proved decisive and successful in overwhelming the Taliban and the Iraqi military. However, while conventional military victory was simple, postwar occupation was not. When tasked with reconstruction, the American military discovered a new set of dilemmas in administering occupied territory. After May 2003, when the president declared an end to major combat operations, American soldiers encountered an open Pandora's box of new, growing, and seemingly intractable problems.[1]

American civilian and military leaders struggled mightily to resolve the challenges of instability and insurgency as well as their root causes in both occupied countries. Iraq descended into lawlessness and sectarian war. In Afghanistan effective national sovereignty was largely limited to major cities. As the two wars lengthened and grew more costly, policy makers faced the political consequences of eroding public and congressional support.

Meaningful doctrinal reform did not appear for almost four years, when Lieutenant General David Petraeus first made his argument for a troop "surge" to resolve some of the difficulties plaguing Iraqi stability. Until then, the American military underwent the trials of a bloody, indecisive war that sapped its resources and sense of purpose. Petraeus' eventual contribution was not limited solely to producing success in Iraq and the pretext for an American withdrawal. It also served as an indicator of just how drastically the U.S. military was willing to evolve in order to restore itself and the global war on terror.

Operation Enduring Freedom

The clamor for a military response to the attacks on the World Trade Center and the Pentagon began before their aftershocks had completely passed through America. Benefiting from a wealth of intelligence accumulated before and after the disaster, U.S. national security officials readily targeted the Taliban government in Afghanistan as one of the primary sources of the assault.[2] Planning for a counterstrike rapidly translated into action.

Air attacks commenced on 7 October 2001. From its inception, Operation Enduring Freedom was a test of a new Pentagon theory that a massive, conventional invasion of Afghanistan was unnecessary. Secretary of Defense Donald Rumsfeld was particularly adamant on this point, rejecting the early drafts of invasion plans as "unimaginative" and too similar to Desert Storm. He exhorted CENTCOM commander Tommy Franks to abandon existing doctrinal standards in favor of a new and more radical approach to fighting that eschewed a large commitment of ground troops. Rumsfeld was essentially asking Franks and the military establishment to abandon the operational template forged by the First Gulf War in 1991.[3]

In reality, the debate over Operation Enduring Freedom came at the end of a more general argument within the Pentagon over the future direction of the American military. It centered on the basic conclusion that existing weapons, doctrine, and force structures were simply outmoded and unable to provide effective security in the twenty-first century. More specifically, Rumsfeld and his cohort rejected the idea that a lengthy interval of preconflict mobilization could be an integral part of American military planning. National security mandated rapidity of mobilization, deployment, and action. Where Desert Storm represented a traditional, almost plodding approach to war, Rumsfeld demanded the type of military operations discussed within the Pentagon since the 1973 Yom Kippur War.[4]

From this premium on speed, the concept of "rapid decisive operations" (RDO) or, using the definition that became popular with the American media during the invasion of Iraq, "Shock and Awe" was born. The core concept behind rapid decisive operations was an outgrowth of the 1993 version of *Field Manual 100-5: Operations.* In an updated format, RDO continued the previous emphasis on integration of military action within a defined "battlespace."[5] However, what was better understood by 2001 was the idea that asymmetrical actions could be taken by a conventional American force against an enemy. Rapid decisive operations thus essentially married the pro-insurgency warfighting doctrine of the eighties with the technology of the First Gulf War.[6] In the latter case, "kinetic" or "effects-based outcomes," translated into substituting precision munitions for "boots on the ground." Precisely delivered airpower offered the prospect of disrupting and overwhelming an enemy with minimal U.S. exposure to casualties. The appeal, both in terms of economy and American public support for war, was obvious.[7]

When American ground forces entered Afghanistan in 2001, they did so primarily in the form of military special operations forces and CIA paramilitary units. These small contingents of specialists operated directly with local Afghani tribes, themselves loosely grouped under the title of the "Northern Alliance" and numbering approximately 20,000 poorly armed fighters. Working in concert with these tribes, American operatives very effectively used sophisticated target acquisition equipment to call Air Force strikes against conventional Taliban units that decided to resist the U.S. invasion.[8] The November 2001 assault on Mazar-e-Sharif illustrated the effectiveness of this tactic. American special forces teams, accompanied by nearly 900 tribesmen under the command of Abdul Rashid Dostum attacked a Taliban force of 9,300 soldiers equipped with armor, field artillery, and surface-to-air missiles. The decisive factor in this instance was global positioning system (GPS) equipment that allowed American observers to guide bombs into Taliban positions with pinpoint accuracy.[9]

It was a pattern repeated for the next few weeks as Operation Enduring Freedom unfolded. At Bishqab, U.S. special forces soldiers were able to call in precision munitions at a range of over eight kilometers.[10] Devastated by unseen air strikes that overwhelmed all efforts at defense, Taliban strong points rapidly succumbed to American and coalition forces. By mid-November, Herat, Kabul, and Jalalabad had all fallen. In contrast, the actual commitment of U.S. ground troops remained small as major operations wound down. The largest unit deployed to Afghanistan at the time was a one thousand-man Marine Expeditionary Unit, which joined American and coalition special operations forces at RHINO, a base sixty miles south of Kandahar.[11]

For all intents and purposes, the first months of Operation Enduring Freedom seemed to vindicate Rumsfeld's assertion that a massive commitment of conventional forces for victory was indeed obsolete. Writing for *Foreign Affairs* in 2002, Michael O'Hanlon called the operation "a masterpiece of military creativity and finesse."[12] The significance of the moment, although clearer with hindsight, was not lost at the time. Within policy-making circles, Rumsfeld's credibility was at its apex.[13] The same was true with respect to his public standing and his relationship with the American media. Rumsfeld became a celebrated—and feared—figure that dominated the political and policy-making landscape.[14] In military terms, the secretary's growing clout translated into accelerating plans for another application of rapid decisive operations; this time against the Hussein regime in Iraq.

A thoughtful observer of American military operations against the Taliban at Tora Bora in 2002 would have discovered many flaws in

Rumsfeld's argument.[15] Located in a mountainous region some twenty miles south of Jalalabad, Tora Bora served at the time as one of the last redoubts for Taliban forces in Afghanistan. Honeycombed with hundreds of miles of tunnels and chambers containing food, water, electrical, power, and munitions, Tora Bora offered the survivors of Operation Enduring Freedom a sanctuary and, perhaps more important, a series of escape routes leading into Pakistan.

American commanders on the ground understood the value of Tora Bora to a future insurgency against coalition forces in Afghanistan. Yet they remained reluctant to commit significant U.S. forces to clear the region of Taliban fighters. In keeping with the RDO concept, CENTCOM and the Pentagon believed that a large contingent of conventional American units was unnecessary to defeat the Taliban. Moreover, officials also asserted that a large U.S. military force might alienate the Pashtun tribes that dominated the region. Consequently, the United States and its coalition partners entered Tora Bora with a minimal number of foreign troops. The bulk of the ground war was left to the "Eastern Alliance" of supposedly loyal tribes who would fight with American special operations forces.[16]

Operation Anaconda was launched in the Shah-i-Khot Valley near the Afghanistan-Pakistan border on 2 March 2002. According to the plan, American and coalition military units—forces that included elements of the 10th Mountain Division and the 101st Airborne Division, as well as American and allied special forces—would establish blocking positions in the eastern and southern portions of the valley. Afghan forces, led by American special operations personnel, would then push retreating insurgents into the awaiting coalition units. Initial intelligence estimates had the number of enemy combatants at several hundred, although as many as a thousand would join the battle once it began.[17] To counterbalance potentially difficult resistance on the ground, coalition planners could rely upon an overwhelming advantage in tactical airpower.

Unfortunately, as Operation Anaconda unfolded, a number of serious problems immediately became apparent. Afghan forces designated to support the American operation proved unreliable and unwilling to pursue offensive operations against Taliban positions. Conversely, the enemy proved surprisingly resilient. Al Qaeda and Taliban forces supplemented their defensive positions with crew-served weapons, including recoilless rifles, Soviet-made DShK heavy machine guns, and mortars, which were all used to good effect. American forces were also surprised to discover that the Tora Bora defenders possessed night-vision goggles identical to the type used by the United States. Despite stiff resistance, coalition forces were able to inflict substantial casualties on Taliban and Al Qaeda fighters. By 6 March, U.S. commanders were reported to have killed as many as 400 to 600 total insurgents.[18] Air strikes figured significantly in the Shah-i-Khot Valley. B-52 heavy bombers regularly dropped 250- and 500-pound bombs on fortified positions blocking coalition forces. At one point, a B-52 strike was called in on a single Taliban mortar position. More advanced ordnance, such as 2000-pound thermobaric bombs designed to eliminate oxygen from cave complexes and suffocate the enemy, also saw use during the operation.[19]

Ultimately, Operation Anaconda failed to break either Al Qaeda or the Taliban. Violence in Afghanistan continued, along with increased coalition military deployments to the country. By mid-2003, U.S. and allied forces numbered 12,000 and were drawn from a total of nineteen foreign nations. Between 2003 and 2005, the basic concept of operations in Afghanistan was identical to Iraq: destroy Al Qaeda and Taliban insurgents in the country while reconstructing the Afghan military. To reach that goal, coalition military forces conducted a series of raids, described specifically as "counterterrorist" missions, to kill or capture Taliban and Al Qaeda personnel and destroy their infrastructure within Afghanistan. American and allied military units routinely entered urban neighborhoods and rural villages in search of suspected terrorists. Their consistent ignorance of local history or the particular dynamics of tribal rivalries often soured relations between the Afghan people, the United States, and its coalition partners.[20]

Not surprisingly, reconstruction projects, conducted by individual military units and outside contractors, tended to have very limited impact on Afghanistan. The primary obstacle to substantive progress was the lack of contact with and support from the local population. American forces attempting to conduct standard counterinsurgency operations regularly violated any number of cultural taboos.[21] An American soldier entering an Afghani dwelling uninvited for any reason brought shame upon its owner. Similarly, if American forces wanted the Afghan army or police to fight during Ramadan, they had to obtain an exemption from local mullahs in the same manner as the Taliban.[22] In a country that lacked a coherent national or even regional government, American forces found themselves directly tied to tribes, councils (shuras), and religious leaders in order to prosecute the war in Afghanistan.

Over time, American officials attempted to include some of these basic realities into their plans for Afghanistan. By late 2003 a reformed approach to fighting the Taliban and Al Qaeda placed the Afghan people at the "center of gravity" of U.S. operations, much like the Iraqi "surge" a few years later. American commanders were encouraged to emphasize a "light footprint" that placed priority on winning popular support rather than destroying insurgents.[23] Concurrently, the United States included international and multilateral actors into reconstruction and counterinsurgency efforts. NATO, the United Nations, and nongovernmental organizations (NGOs) were all incorporated into nation-building programs to a degree that surpassed Operation Provide Comfort in Kurdistan after the First Gulf War. In the case of NGOs, ground commanders found it difficult to maintain the "unity of effort" envisaged in *FM 100-5* given the adversarial stance sometimes taken by civilian organizations against the military. Overall, coordinating the bureaucratic requirements of foreign volunteer agencies, coalition military forces, and the various official national and multilateral organizations working in Afghanistan proved complex and frustrating. The U.S. Agency for International Development, for example, delegated 90 percent of its reconstruction projects to private contractors, who had no obligation to cooperate with military authorities.[24] Missteps like these seriously impeded American progress in the years following the invasion.

Consequently, despite increasing attention to the root causes of Afghan insurgency, internal stability steadily worsened after the first phase of Operation Enduring Freedom. By the end of 2006, more than 26,000 troops (12,000 U.S.) occupied the country. Additional "boots on the ground" produced little in the way of security. Suicide attacks jumped from only 2 in 2003 to 139 three years later.[25] Old problems also returned to haunt Afghanistan. Absent stringent Taliban sanctions against narcotics trafficking, activities familiar to the Golden Crescent roared back to life after the coalition invasion. Heroin production in 2003 alone was estimated at 3,600 tons.[26]

This situation prevailed until 2009, when the incoming Obama administration began its own version of a troop surge to bolster Afghan stability and win a concrete withdrawal plan for U.S. forces. By the fall of 2009, the administration announced its intention to deploy a total of nearly 100,000 American troops who would be responsible for reducing Taliban and Al Qaeda–controlled areas in Afghanistan while training a 134,000-man Afghan national army capable of assuming full responsibility for internal security. According to the American plan, U.S. forces would begin a full-scale withdrawal from the country as early as 2011.[27]

Early returns on this policy were mixed at best. At the start of 2010, U.S. forces engaged insurgents in sustained combat operations throughout the country, particularly in Helmand Province. In February the American commander, General Stanley McChrystal, noted "real progress" was possible that year.[28] The degree of actual success in training the Afghan National Army was more problematic. As late as 2009, shortages of equipment, training facilities, and instructors handicapped American efforts. Ethnic cleavages also worked against developing a cohesive force capable of securing the country. Despite these formidable obstacles, the U.S. officer in charge of the training program, Lieutenant General Richard Formica, believed the goal remained "difficult, but achievable."[29]

If Afghanistan was the first real application of Rapid Decisive Operations, it serves as an illustration of the strengths and weaknesses of the doctrine. Although RDO was wildly successful in overturning Taliban control of Afghanistan, it proved completely inadequate to some of the traditional, fixed realities of war. Over the long term, weather conditions, terrain, particularly Afghanistan's rugged mountains and dense urban areas, and the tenacity and innovativeness of the Taliban and Al Qaeda, all made rapid decisive operations a questionable device. In sum, "shock and awe" largely has failed since almost its first inception in 2001.

In Afghanistan, it is clear that the U.S. military had to relearn some of the bitter lessons of Somalia. H. R. McMaster and other authors note, for instance, that American enemies are generally not "awed" for long. Both the Taliban and Al Qaeda adopted simple countermeasures to high-tech warfare, from masking internal communications to fortifying and dispersing their bases against attack, as demonstrated in the Tora Bora tunnel complexes in 2002. Moreover, the recurring absence of human intelligence handicapped American efforts for years. Adequate linguistic and cultural expertise necessary to understand the motives and goals of both potential allies and enemies is only a recent addition to the U.S. portfolio of military options.[30]

Operation Iraqi Freedom

Even as American forces attempted to consolidate their hold on Afghanistan, the Bush administration began preparing the ground for the invasion of Iraq. Some of these efforts were diplomatic in nature. UN Security Council Resolution 1441, adopted on 8 November 2002, formally censured Iraq for its failure to comply with previous United Nations mandates on weapons inspections, weapons of mass destruction (WMDs), and long-range missiles.

Military mobilization for a war against Iraq also proceeded apace. Like Afghanistan, preparations for the invasion reflected a prolonged debate within the Pentagon. Secretary of Defense Donald Rumsfeld advocated a minimal application of ground troops to an Iraqi operation, citing the success of Operation Enduring Freedom as evidence of the soundness of his plan. CENTCOM commander General Tommy Franks was skeptical and eventually reached a compromise that stood between Rumsfeld's minimalism and a Desert Storm–type of invasion.[31] The crux of Franks's proposal, codenamed OPLAN 1003V, was what he dubbed the "Running Start" concept.[32] It contained two basic elements: the massive use of air units against Iraq forces in a manner similar to 2001 operations in Afghanistan, and, secondly, the incremental inclusion of forces to combat as they arrived in the Iraq theater, essentially without the massive buildup that had preceded Operation Desert Storm. American troop deployments were already under way by the fall of 2002 in the guise of training missions to Kuwait, Qatar, Oman, Jordan, and Saudi Arabia. By 15 February 2003, 128,000 troops were in place for the invasion. The four Operational Iraqi Freedom operational phases were as follows:

Phase I—Preparation
Phase II—Shape the Battlespace

Phase III—Decisive Operations
Phase IV—Stability Operations

The Pentagon expected that the early stages of Operation Iraqi Freedom would be short. Planners estimated that the actual ground invasion, "Phase III—Decisive Operations" under OPLAN 1003V, would take only ninety days. Once U.S. and coalition forces successfully overwhelmed the Iraqi military, the expectation was that minimal occupation forces would be necessary for what Defense Department officials dubbed "Phase IV—Stability Operations."[34] Contingencies for a postwar occupation reflected a consensus amongst both civilian and military leaders in charge of the Iraq war. As noted in chapter 5, the 1993 Defense Department *Bottom-Up Review* had posited a similarly small force for occupation once a conventional war ended.[35]

Operation Iraqi Freedom began on 20 March 2003. It was comprised of a two-pronged attack originating from Kuwait and Turkey. The southern portion of the invasion was intended to proceed to Baghdad and destroy or capture major military facilities, as well as the headquarters of Saddam Hussein's Ba'ath Party. The mission went to the Army V Corps, commanded by Lieutenant General William Wallace and comprising the 3rd and 4th Infantry Divisions, the 101st Airborne Division (Air Assault), and the 2nd Brigade of the 82nd Airborne Division. The 1st Marine Expeditionary Force, under Lieutenant General James Conway, which included the 1st Marine Division, the British 1st Armored Division, and Task Force Tarawa, accompanied V Corps on the assault.[36]

The northern tier of Operation Iraqi Freedom was designed to seize control of Kurdistan and the massive oil fields that dotted the region. In contrast to the conventional units streaming out of Kuwait in March 2003, this mission was largely the province of American and coalition special forces. Thus, while conventional units were concentrated on a north-south axis of advance leading from Kuwait to Baghdad, special operations forces were active in nearly every other part of the country. It was a remarkable contrast to Operation Desert Storm.

Prior to invasion, special operations units were extensively engaged in Phase II activities known within the military community as "shaping the battlespace." Translated into layman's terms, this meant psychological operations, raids on key Iraqi facilities, deep reconnaissance, and establishing contacts with the significant numbers of dissidents who populated the country. In southern and western Iraq, operational detachments from the 5th Special Forces Group secured known SCUD missile launch sites and captured key airfields and oil facilities. Special forces operatives preceded larger combat elements into Iraqi cities to prepare entry points and convince local military units to surrender. Small special forces contingents provided reconnaissance for the 3rd Infantry Division before it reached the Karbala Gap south of Baghdad, for example. Similarly, these units preceded British and American forces before their advance into the southern city of Basra. During Operation Iraqi Freedom, Army Rangers finally had an opportunity to fight. In March, elements of the 75th Ranger Regiment undertook raids against suspected chemical and biological research centers such as Al Qadisiyah in western Iraq.

Coalition special forces were even more instrumental to the invasion in northern Iraq. This was clearly evident in the Kurdish region of the country. Elements of the 10th Special Forces Group infiltrated into northern Iraq and made contact with *peshmerga* fighters belonging to the Kurdish Democratic Party (KDP) and Patriotic Union of Kurdistan (PUK). By March 2003, when the invasion began, a total of fifty-two operational detachments were working alongside approximately 60,000 Kurdish militia in much the same way as American forces had in Afghanistan. Their mission was to pin down three Iraqi corps—a total of 150,000 troops—before regular coalition units entered Iraq from the north. American and Kurdish forces were also tasked with the destruction of the Ansar al-Islam terrorist base on the northeastern border with Iran.

Overall, the northern portion of Operation Iraqi Freedom proved to be successful. Special forces soldiers were able to offset the disadvantage in numbers and heavy equipment by calling in air strikes against Iraqi units. In April, B-52s were instrumental in reducing enemy positions around the city of Mosul before the Kurds liberated it.[37] Special operations troops, working in conjunction with *peshmerga* militia also prepared landing zones for the 173rd Airborne Brigade when it jumped into Bashur Airfield on 26 March 2003.[38]

When president George W. Bush declared an end to major combat operations on 1 May 2003, the same problems that had surfaced in Afghanistan reappeared with respect to "shock and awe" in Iraq. Professional military journals, while lauding the rapidity of victory, pointed out numerous failings evident even as coalition forces were eliminating the last pockets of Iraqi resistance. A specific criticism focused on the fact that the air war seriously outpaced the deployment of ground forces to Iraq. Unlike Operation Desert Storm, the tactical air plan was not adequately coordinated with the spearheads moving toward central Iraq. Other authors made the case that the heavy formations were the truly decisive actors in Operation Iraqi Freedom. According to this argument, the 3rd Infantry Division, the British 7th Armored Division, and the Marine Expeditionary Force carried the brunt of the fighting, while lighter divisions—the 82nd and 101st as well as special forces, largely operated on the periphery of the war.[39]

More alarming than these particular shortcomings was the almost total absence of postwar planning. Recent studies have made it abundantly clear that "stability operations" were, at best, an afterthought within CENTCOM and the Pentagon. Not surprisingly, immediately after coalition units stood down from combat, Iraq suffered a systemic breakdown of law and order. Widespread looting followed in the wake of coalition advances throughout the country. No institutions, whether schools, hospitals, or museums, were immune. A member of the U.S. Army 422nd Civil Affairs Battalion recalled the looting of a bank in Baghdad: "Eventually they got some dynamite and were able to blow a small hole in the top of the safe, through about two feet of concrete and rebar, then the steel. It was big enough to get a small child in there. So they had lowered a small child in there, and he was coming and giving them money. We think they probably got away with about $2 million."[40] As civil order collapsed, so too did basic public services, particularly police, fire, and electrical power. Baghdad and most other Iraqi urban centers quickly became focal points of crime and violence.[41]

Many early policies promoted by the Bush administration and the Coalition Provisional Authority made a bad situation worse. Senior policy makers in the Defense Department, including Donald Rumsfeld and Paul Wolfowitz, believed that the Iraqi population would rally to coalition forces as liberators, that civilian police and other government agencies, once purged of Ba'ath Party members, would effectively govern the country, and that the need for occupation forces would be minimal. Wolfowitz testified before Congress in February 2003 that the Defense Department believed the U.S. presence in Iraq could be reduced to 30,000–40,000 troops within six months of the initial invasion.[42]

Without an imperative for action or even a clear recognition of the problems at hand, U.S. policy drifted. A number of American agencies, the State Department, USAID, and the Defense Department, did prepare plans for postwar occupation. However, their efforts were poorly coordinated and did not reflect a consensus amongst civilian or military leaders. The resulting mishmash of organizations that appeared in 2003 was created too late and with too little influence to affect the postwar occupation of Iraq.[43]

The primary agency emerging from this morass was the Coalition Provisional Authority (CPA) under L. Paul Bremer. When he became a permanent envoy to Iraq in May 2003, Bremer had broad powers to address economic, political, social, and security policies. Unfortunately, Bremer did a poor job of coordinating CPA activities with coalition military commanders and the intelligence community. The CPA's most significant mistake came soon after Bremer's arrival, when he abruptly announced the decision to demobilize the Iraqi army. Bremer assumed that Iraqi police forces would replace the military in maintaining civil order. However, neither he nor most of his staff understood that the military had been primarily responsible for domestic police functions. More important, once thousands of demobilized Iraqi troops left the military, they had virtually no prospects in the shattered civilian economy. Many quickly joined a growing insurgency against the United States and its allies. A 2008 RAND study noted: "Because Iraq's own police and military evaporated shortly after Saddam fell, ordinary Iraqis lived in a basically lawless society for months, during which, among other things, insurgents, terrorists, and criminal gangs assembled with impunity. And because U.S. forces have had to focus on providing security for their own personnel (both military and civilian) as much as for Iraqis, the buildup of coalition forces did not bring the degree of safety and security it might have brought had order been imposed from the start."[44]

Local and sectarian militias easily filled this security vacuum and eventually became among the primary determinants of internal security. Based in the slums of Sadr City in northeastern Baghdad, Muqtada al-Sadr, backstopped by his "al-Mahdi Army," refused to recognize the coalition-appointed Iraqi Governing Council or the legitimacy of foreign troops he labeled as occupiers. After 2003, al-Sadr's rise became emblematic of the larger difficulties of internal instability and postwar American attempts to arrest Iraqi decline.

American military efforts between 2003 and 2006 offered little reason for optimism. For a period of roughly three years, CENTCOM and Pentagon officials devoted their attention to dual, theoretically mutually supporting objectives already applied to Afghanistan: defeating the insurgent threat and creating an Iraqi military adequate to maintain stability. Thus began a war of attrition against the insurgency. American and coalition forces subsequently conducted major operations against insurgent strongholds in Baghdad and other important cities such as Balad and Fallujah.

Operation Phantom Fury, which encompassed the Marine Corps assault on the city of Fallujah at the end of 2004, typified American military action during this period. After cordoning off the area, conventional units, supported by tactical airpower and artillery, retook Fallujah one block at a time. In the process, Marine units discovered substantial limitations in contemporary urban warfare tactics but readily adapted to their circumstances. By the end of December 2004, the city was declared secure and major combat units began their withdrawal.[45]

While ultimately successful, Operation Phantom Fury was costly, particularly with respect to long-term stability. Combat operations eliminated a major insurgent presence, but extensively damaged residences, mosques, and other buildings necessary to life after the conclusion of military operations.[46] Moreover, while operations like the one in Fallujah certainly disrupted insurgent and terrorist activity in Iraq, they failed to address sectarian violence, which significantly worsened by 2006. In order to remove American forces from the potentially disastrous consequences of this situation, the Pentagon made the conscious decision to withdraw U.S. forces into forward operating bases and other well-defended facilities.

By this point in the Iraq War, the conventional wisdom had shifted to reflect the belief that American forces were an irritant provoking instability rather than deterring it. By 2006 a creeping sense of defeat was palpable as the initiative passed to guerilla cells around Iraq. One U.S. officer quoted by *Time* magazine in September 2005 captured the mood when he claimed: "We have not broken the back of the insurgency. The insurgency is like a cell phone system. You shut down one node, another somewhere else comes online to replace it."[47]

In the meantime, the reconstruction of Iraqi police and military forces proceeded slowly at best. Staff shortages of both military personnel and private contractors inhibited the training of police, border guards, and regular military units. Despite the fact that there was something on the order of 203,000 total Iraqis assigned to security duties, attempts to hand off responsibility to the host nation failed repeatedly in the years following Operation Iraqi Freedom.[48] A 2008 *Military Review* article summed up the situation succinctly: "In the wake of *shock and awe,* we faced disenfranchised populations neither shocked nor awed by our presence. We failed them in many ways, and much of our focus remained on applying the lethal and destructive aspects of our military might rather than the nonlethal, constructive capabilities so vital to success in operations conducted among the people. Our inability to exploit time effectively ceded the initiative to a course of events already spinning out of control. We won the war, but were quickly losing the peace."[49]

It was not until 2007 that the American leadership in Iraq began to craft a strategy adequate to postwar Iraqi reconstruction and stability. Loosely described in the U.S. media as the "surge," it comprised successfully applied counterinsurgency techniques then emerging from some of the most hotly contested portions of Iraq. Although these took time to mesh into a coherent doctrine, what mattered most at the time was the fact that U.S. officials understood that the status quo was a recipe for failure.

One of these places was the city of Tal Afar, located in the northwestern portion of the country near the Syria border. Tal Afar was first "cleared" of insurgents by the 14th Armored Cavalry Regiment in November 2004 and again by the 3rd Armored Cavalry Regiment, the 2nd Battalion, 325th Airborne Infantry Regiment, and the 3rd Iraqi Army Division in September 2005. It was during the 3rd ACR's rotation through Tal Afar under the command of Colonel H. R. McMaster that a number of key doctrinal changes were introduced to combat insurgents.

Code-named Operation Restoring Rights, McMaster's unit developed and executed a detailed, painstaking methodology that combined intelligence gathering, combat operations, and stability programs to reconstruct coalition control of the city literally one neighborhood at a time.[50] The initial phase of Restoring Rights involved collecting data on local culture to determine the specific locations of insurgent infrastructure. Over time, American forces gradually came to understand the influence that the Iraqi Ba'ath Party retained in Tar Afar after decades of efforts to co-opt the Turkoman population. Understanding this history, the United States realized how the insurgency manifested itself and spread once the Hussein government collapsed in 2003.[51]

To undercut this core of resistance, U.S. and available Iraqi forces cordoned off sections of the city and created controlled entry points. After an area was secured, coalition forces conducted an extensive house-by-house search for weapons, munitions, and intelligence information. Legal residents were interviewed and registered by the military, creating a database to track the local population. One key point of departure from previous operations involved the simple expedient of leaving forces behind in neighborhoods to create a permanent security presence and cultivate popular support. American troops assigned to individual neighborhoods conducted foot patrols throughout their area of responsibility, engaged insurgents where necessary, and restored basic public services. When combat did occur, U.S. units issued claims cards to residents so that they could obtain compensation for property damage.[52]

American officials also made it clear to local residents of Tal Afar that their presence in the city was temporary. As Iraqi police and military units were trained to a satisfactory level, American units conducted joint operations and eventually relinquished control of security operations so that local forces could assume the mission alone. In the meantime, U.S. military commanders negotiated with local sheiks to encourage refugees to return to their old neighborhoods. It was a complex process that required a degree of trust from both the sheiks and coalition forces. In exchange for safe transit back into Tal Afar, returning men were allowed to keep AK-47s for personal defense.[53]

Although Operation Restoring Rights was subject to misunderstandings and open manipulation, it was successfully implemented between 2005 and 2006. Minor tribes like the Marhat and Jolaq were sometimes able to forge individual deals with coalition forces, much to the resentment of long-standing local ethnic elites.[54] However, American forces were able to maintain an effective balance among competing local interests. Subsequent analysis of the success in Tal Afar attributed it to better U.S. military training, equipment, and communications and, more important, a cognizance of earlier mistakes made in deployments to the underdeveloped world—such as Somalia—more than a decade earlier.[55]

In 2006 the U.S. military formalized many of the techniques used at Tal Afar in *Field Manual 3-24: Counterinsurgency* and the 2008 update of *Field Manual 3-0: Operations*. The former document was the first comprehensive revision of American doctrine in two decades. The overall degree of detail present in *FM 3-24* is impressive. After providing an overview of the salient characteristics present in insurgencies, it goes on to discuss both the traditional (intelligence gathering) and nontraditional (cooperation with civilian agencies) methods effective against a low-level threat. Historical examples are included throughout the narrative in addition to appendices covering information gleaned from Iraq and Afghanistan. In particular, the manual addresses linguist support, the productive use of airpower, and, in a reflection of ongoing difficulties defining the rules of engagement in both wars, "legal considerations."[56] For its own part, *FM 3-0* reflects the new premium placed on fighting counterinsurgencies abroad. The initial chapter, addressing the "operational environment" of 2008, placed "instability and persistent conflict" at center stage.[57] While many elements of *FM 3-0* recognize the more traditional components of the U.S. military (leadership, command, and control functions), the stress on counterinsurgency is apparent throughout. Unlike 2003, "stability operations" figure prominently, as does the constant stress on providing local populations with a "safe and secure environment" from which substantive reconstruction can proceed.[58]

By the end of the decade, a new conventional wisdom with respect to counterinsurgency and small wars began to take hold in the American military. In a fall 2008 article for *Military Review*, the U.S. commander in Iraq (and eventual CENTCOM commander), General

David H. Petraeus, spoke of the Iraqi people as the "decisive terrain" in the war. In order to secure their loyalty, he emphasized a constructive "nonkinetic" (noncombat) methodology designed to preserve reconciliation and civil stability.[59] Essentially, Petraeus was asking the military to embrace a doctrine that combined contradictory practices into its basic mission. American forces simultaneously were tasked to "pursue the enemy relentlessly" while at the same time building support within the civilian community.[60]

Applied to the circumstances present in both Iraq and Afghanistan, the doctrine made a good deal of practical sense. The single-minded directive for American forces to get out of their vehicles and conduct dismounted foot patrols from bases located in urban neighborhoods reversed the bunker mentality that grew up inside sequestered forward operating bases. Similarly, American military operations predicated on local intelligence gathering made them much less clumsy than the large-scale cordon and sweep tactic common after 2003.

However, even the best-structured doctrine faced difficulties in practical application. The logical order dictated by *FM 3-0*, like that of the doctrines published in the early nineties, often ran afoul of the complex cultural, political, and economic circumstances present in the towns and villages of the Middle East and Southwest Asia.[61] Local preferences and idiosyncrasies consistently defied deliberate attempts at compartmentalization. American ignorance also inhibited new doctrine. The constant rotation of U.S. forces, as well as the significant qualitative differences between regular, reserve, and national guard units, inhibited the type of precise understanding of human terrain necessary under new doctrine. A final concern was the nature of the respective host governments in Iraq and Afghanistan. The U.S. military could and did defeat the insurgents in both countries, but it could not provide an effective substitute for public services or law and order that were the responsibilities of Baghdad and Kabul. Neither elicited much confidence in the early stages of the Iraq surge or, later, in Afghanistan.[62]

When coalition forces applied the lessons of Tal Afar to Iraq as a whole, it reshaped the entire U.S. approach to the country. After he moved to CENTCOM, Petraeus worked in concert with Lieutenant General Raymond Odierno, who took command of the Multi-National Corps–Iraq in December 2006. Both commanders spent months carefully preparing the Iraqi "battlespace" for newly arriving U.S. combat brigades by collecting intelligence, organizing logistics, and coordinating their efforts with the Iraqi government and the U.S. embassy. Ambassador Ryan Crocker proved instrumental in constructing a Joint Campaign Plan that would guide the surge and its various military and civilian components. It was a remarkable departure from the ongoing hostility that existed between L. Paul Bremer's Coalition Provisional Authority and American military officials only a few years earlier.

Applied within the confines of Iraq, the surge strategy fit well with many conventional military precepts. Odierno treated the insurgent network as a conventional structure dependent on its own communications and logistical support. Consequently, his campaign directly attacked the insurgent "lines of operation," operating from the standpoint that they could be disrupted and defeated in the same manner as a support network on a linear, conventional battlefield.[63] Odierno's contribution to the surge was not his tactical insights but the effective coordination of coalition efforts across Iraq. Yet, working in concert with the new CENTCOM commander, the two generals proved to be a formidable pairing: Petraeus responsible for the operating concept, Odierno the "synergy," to use the military term.[64]

Although the surge applied to Iraq as a whole, the primary area of operations was around Baghdad. Initial counterinsurgency operations were designed to dislodge insurgents from the safe houses, IED "factories," weapons caches, and command posts. Once coalition forces secured a particular section of Baghdad, it was handed over to Iraqi security forces and civilian reconstruction agencies. An explicit goal was permanent reoccupation by the Iraqi government, eliminating the necessity to repeatedly reconquer urban areas, as had been the case since 2003. Odierno, Petraeus, and Crocker also understood the importance of initiative when executing the surge. When Operation Fardh al-Qanoon (Enforcing the Law) began to secure the Baghdad metropolitan area in February 2007, it was quickly accompanied by operations against rural sanctuaries in July and August.[65]

As 2007 proceeded, the surge picked up momentum. Success bred success. As U.S. and coalition forces created stable areas before handing them off to the Iraqi government, more people proved willing to cooperate with the effort. By the end of the year, U.S. officials estimated that 75 percent of Baghdad was under government control, as opposed to 8 percent only a year earlier.[66] Thousands of Iraqis joined "concerned local citizen" (CLC) units, later renamed "Sons of Iraq," to man checkpoints and provide intelligence information to coalition forces. By 2008 Iraqi police and military personnel numbered 566,000, a threefold increase from 2005.[67] The overall quality of Iraqi units, while not up to U.S. standards, had also improved. The Iraqi military had its own special operations brigade, and Iraqi police possessed their own specialized counterterrorist units (ISWAT) in nine provinces.[68]

In his April 2008 report to Congress, Petraeus noted "significant but uneven security progress in Iraq."[69] Clearly, there was much cause for optimism. When Petraeus made his statement, most insurgent activity centered in the north, around the city of Mosul. Former hotbeds of terrorist activity, such as Anbar Province, had been successfully incorporated into coalition security planning. The "Awakening Movement" invited local militias and their leadership into the military infrastructure, where weapons and hard cash purchased intelligence information and security. By the beginning of 2008, as many as 70,000 Iraqis were on the American payroll, earning on average about $300 a month, a substantial income in the country's ravaged economy.[70] As one senior enlisted soldier assigned to the 3rd Infantry Division made clear: "We're paying them not to blow us up. It looks good right now, but what happens when the money stops."[71]

Over the longer term, the surge was complicated by the problem of public expectations in Iraq and the United States. Improvements in local security spurred additional demands for the restoration of other basic public services like electricity and potable water. These basic needs became exponentially more difficult when refugees displaced by the war—estimated in 2008 at 2 million within Iraq and 2 million outside the country—began returning to their former towns and cities.[72] In the United States, collapsing public support for the war counterbalanced any pretense of success the surge may have had. Just as the doctrine gained traction in Iraq, a March 2008 poll by the *Washington Post* and ABC news reported that 63 percent of Americans believed that the war in Iraq was not worth fighting.[73] More critical to long-term U.S. policy was how this rejection translated in the voting booth. Candidates promising an end to American overseas military deployments—a keynote to Democrat campaigns in 2006 and 2008—gained significant support during the midterm and presidential elections. One of Barack Obama's most important appeals during his own victory was the explicit promise to reverse the military decisions of the preceding administration.

Conclusions

Small unit operations were decisive in both Afghanistan and Iraq during the early stages of the war against both countries. American forces, augmented by vastly superior technology, wreaked havoc on the battlefield. This was true throughout the first months of Operation Enduring Freedom. Facets of the war in Afghanistan were later applied to good effect, particularly in Kurdistan, at the start of Operation Iraqi Freedom. However, as military analyst Anthony Cordesman commented in 2002, the conditions in Afghanistan at the time of U.S. invasion were unique and the rush to endorse the "revolution in military affairs" was premature at best.[74] As the global war on terror unfolded, military operations additionally suffered familiar problems created by poor intelligence and limits on the application of technology. Operation Anaconda proved that rugged terrain could overcome the most sophisticated remote surveillance platforms or firepower.

The profound difficulties of postwar stability again placed a premium on small unit operations as the conventional phase of both invasions wound down. Once the Taliban and Hussein regimes fell, "shock and awe" ceased to have any utility. Unfortunately, a doctrine necessary to articulate "stability operations" largely did not exist. Although the United States had developed plans for humanitarian assistance and peace enforcement prior to the September 11 attacks, none were sufficient for what was essentially an exercise in nation building.[75] What filled this vacuum between 2001 and 2006 were, generally, improvisations vulnerable to ethnic and religious factionalism and local manipulation. Once the lessons of Tal Afar were applied on a national level, the United States had a workable counterinsurgency doctrine for Iraq. While initially successful, at the time of this writing, such doctrine remains vulnerable to Iraqi stewardship and American public impatience with the war on terror.

The strategic shift of U.S. resources to Afghanistan since 2009 has reduced the focus on Iraq at the risk of future stability. Successful counterinsurgency operations in Iraq are now the province of the host government. Iraqi military and police have at their disposal an arsenal of weapons and doctrines provided by their American sponsor. True stability, however, will result from not only military security but also the basic features—education, employment, the rule of law—that a modern nation must possess. If the actions taken by Nouri al-Maliki's government are any indication, the record for all these issues is already problematic.

Even as it winds down operations in Iraq, the success of the "Petraeus Doctrine" has left a significant imprint on the American military. After reaching its nadir in 2005 amidst sectarian war in Iraq and a subsequent deluge of public criticism, the American military institution recovered and proved itself adaptable to its new circumstances. The Pentagon and the separate service branches appear amenable to the concept that military operations must be directed by effects-based objectives rather than traditional measurements of success. Similarly, the U.S. military is more broadly cognizant that intangible factors such as culture and popular support must guide doctrine and current operations.[76] This change is perhaps best illustrated in the reconstruction of the NTC, located at Fort Irwin, California. Formerly the prime training site to reinforce skills necessary for armored combat in Western Europe, the NTC shifted emphasis to counterinsurgency after 2003 to focus on sophisticated counterinsurgency training.[77]

There is reason to believe that the surge doctrine envisaged under *FM 24-3* must undergo another revision in Afghanistan. Clearly, the operating environment is significantly different than Iraq. Mountainous terrain, particularly along the eastern border with Pakistan, does not support "clear and hold" operations reminiscent of Tal Afar or Anbar Province. Moreover, the widespread narcotics trade in Afghanistan will also likely severely inhibit stability operations. These limits and others are evident as NATO and U.S. forces attempt to transition police and military missions to their Afghan counterparts. At the start of 2009, American teams advising the host army were at half their authorized strength. Units responsible to mentor police units were at one-third strength.[78] A multitude of problems plague Afghani mobilization as well. Illiteracy remains a chronic difficulty, as do desertion and corruption. Of the 170,000 police trained since 2002, only 30,000 remained on duty in 2010. An unceasing stream of complaints against these forces, including extortion, rape, and assault, has yet to be effectively addressed by either Kabul or Washington.[79] The road ahead, already difficult in the face of stubborn Taliban and Al Qaeda resistance, will not be helped by these factors.

9

Private Military Corporations in the New Century

We fight the war, and they do the shit work.

—Senior U.S. officer quoted in Joshua Hammer, "Cowboy Up"

We live in a time of postmodern international relations. Since the end of the Cold War, basic features that once consistently defined national sovereignty and legitimate conflict have been changed almost beyond recognition. Individual nations now exist in a global environment that contests basic exercises in power, particularly war. In 2002 Lawrence W. Serewicz discussed two particular forces that mitigate the power of the traditional sovereign state. One is the product of multilateral organizations, like the European Union, that undercut individual national authority by vesting political and economic decision making in a collective structure.[1]

Conversely, individual nations are also challenged by what Serewicz describes as "sub-state military actors," which attack the nation-state's legal monopoly on violence.[2] The "warlord," an actor recognizing neither conventional authority nor practices that divide combatant from noncombatant, is a normative part of post–Cold War international relations today. Once an aberrant factor in terms of military conflict, organizations such as Al Qaeda, the FARC, or Abu Sayyaf, are now ubiquitous enemies of traditional stability. Faced with this type of threat, both individual nations and their transnational counterparts often respond with armed force that is too large and clumsy to be effective or too unwilling to embrace a cause that is perceived as vague or peripheral.

Part of this failure can be simply explained by declining military capability. When the Cold War concluded, it eliminated the justification for massive standing armies. Almost without exception, most major European and American military institutions declined significantly after the collapse of Soviet communism. France reduced its armed forces from 547,000 in 1987 to 381,000 in 1997; England from 319,000 in 1987 to 214,000. The former Soviet Union, desperate to cut the costs of military mobilization, followed suit, cutting its total active armed forces from 5.2 million in 1987 to 1.2 million a decade later.[3] The United States did not escape this trend. After 1991, the country indulged in the so-called peace dividend and oversaw a precipitous drop in active duty forces.[4] The U.S. Army alone declined from 711,000 service members in 1991 to 487,000 in 2003.[5] The mass exodus of soldiers has cost global militaries in important ways. Conventional formations that cased their colors for the final time lost years of accumulated training and expertise, often obtained at great expense. Losses among special operations personnel, whose very qualities were most needed to address unconventional conflict in the new world order, were perhaps even more dearly felt in the nineties and beyond.

Another part of declining military capabilities may also be attributed to a failure of will. Martin van Creveld has observed that the larger and more complex the modern state becomes, the less likely individual citizens are directly linked to national security priorities. This is clearly the case in the United States, wherein mainstream society is largely disconnected from active participation in the military.[6] Thus, although the military as an institution is held in high regard, actual membership in it remains at near record lows. The shock of the September 11 attacks did not result in a sea change in public attitudes toward military service. Contemporary media sources recorded increasing reenlistments, but no concurrent clamor from the uninitiated to volunteer. A military draft was one of the most controversial issues of the 2004 presidential campaign, with both candidates going to great lengths to make it clear conscription was not forthcoming.[7]

The combination of multiplying challenges and declining means has placed enormous strain on the existing cohort of stable, modern nations. The world since the fall of the Berlin Wall and Soviet communism has been defined by upheaval rooted in race, religion, ethnicity, or access to resources, among many other factors.[8] Discerning a proper context to exercise power has proven difficult, particularly for the United States. Multilateral consensus-building, a strategy embraced by the Clinton administration, poses the problem of sacrificing national interests for the sake of global cooperation. A more unilateral approach, typical of the Bush administration circa 2003, risks a decline into pariah status.[9]

In the recent past, many nations have turned to an emerging, and powerful, ally to restore a semblance of stability to the global system: the transnational corporation. Like the multinational agencies mentioned above, private enterprise has become a ubiquitous feature of contemporary international relations. Susan Strange describes corporations that have joined the nation-state in the "new diplomacy" of the modern age: "The governments of states may still be the gate keepers to the territory over which other states recognize their authority. But if no foreign firms want to go through their gate, their countries have a slim chance of keeping up with the competition from other, more welcoming governments for world market shares.[10] Individual countries, particularly those in the underdeveloped world, increasingly find themselves negotiating with corporate entities on equal footing. Some of these relationships are subject to simple dependency measured not only in terms of trade or finance, but also in terms of material and cultural sovereignty.[11]

Some of this dependence on corporate prerogatives extends into military affairs. The small, vulnerable "cusp" nations that maintain marginal stability are increasingly reliant on private support to backstop their slippery hold on power. This is a scenario prevalent in Africa. When the government of Ethiopia required replacement aircraft for its air force, it directly contracted a wing of SU-27 jet fighters from the Russian Sukhoi company, a deal that included the pilots, flight crews, and staff necessary to maintain and use them.[12]

In this postmodern environment, private military corporations (PMCs) have grown in concert with the spread of economic globalism. The collapse of Iron Curtain and the disappearance of old Cold War sanctions have revealed opportunities in previously untouchable regions. Neoliberal capitalism gratefully filled subsequent economic vacuums, in some cases as a matter of private entrepreneurship; in others, as a result of deliberate trade policy. A key characteristic of the nineties-era diplomacy was its penchant for free-trade agreements like NAFTA that celebrated free-market initiative.[13] Unfortunately, many of the opportunities presented during this period were compromised by the fact that they were often located in extremely dangerous parts of the world. Profits from oil and mineral wealth were possible if corporations could invest in areas such as the Republic of the Congo or Colombia.[14]

Increasing attention to corporate security was a natural product of this environment. Stability dictated demand. In Algeria, oil companies spend 8–9 percent of their annual budgets on security. Rapidly increasing demand also generated new corporations whose sole purpose is providing security. Consultancy firms such as Control Risks Group, a company started by former CIA officers and British commandoes, specifically market themselves to corporate customers deliberately targeted by terrorists and organized crime.[15] Whether defined by kidnappings in Latin America or assassination attempts in the Middle East, risks to life and limb have sadly become part of the price of doing business.[16] Nor has the developed world escaped this trend. The first bombing of the World Trade Center in 1993 was indicative of increasing attacks on private sector buildings, a problem that grew to include nonprofit organizations in the nineties. Recent studies indicate that more Red Cross workers were killed in that decade than soldiers of the U.S. Army. Faced with this sort of operating environment, the World Wildlife Fund solicited a bid from the private security company Saracen in 2004 to protect its personnel in the Democratic Republic of Congo.[17] Presently, there is a serious discussion regarding the use of private contractors for peacekeeping duties in lieu of United Nations troops.[18] A clear attraction is their relative cost effectiveness. When the PMC Executive Outcomes conducted operations in Sierra Leone over a twenty-one-month period from 1995 to 1997, their contract cost $35 million. In contrast, the annual price for UN peacekeeping forces deployed to Sierra Leone under Operation UNAMSIL (1999–2005) was $600 million.[19]

In the twenty-first century, the changing nature of global power posed a significant challenge to state sovereignty, but it also provided a potential means to cope with it. With the Soviet Union departed from the world stage and no nation—save a rapidly emerging communist China—prepared to take its place, the structure of international relations fundamentally changed in the nineties. Multinational organizations like the European Union joined others either larger in scale (e.g., the World Trade Organization in 1995) or smaller in scope (e.g., NAFTA) that were all prepared to fill a vacuum. Yet, despite the apparent dilution of state sovereignty, the remaining modern, industrialized nations of the world were not without options. Transnational corporations had the potential to promote national hegemony, albeit in a more oblique fashion. Perhaps more important were the private military corporations that possessed the capability to become direct agents of state interest. However, as time would tell, particularly after the September 11 terrorist attacks on the United States, these corporate proxies contained their own unique risks.

The Rise of the Private Military Corporation

The military symbiosis between private corporate interests and the state can be traced back to the industrial revolution and the growing complexity of modern warfare. As weapons systems and logistical support evolved and became increasingly elaborate, nations came to rely on the private sector to provide the means necessary to sustain them. When the United States, for example, embarked upon the creation of blue water navy in the 1880s, it did so through a well-funded partnership with the steel industry.[20]

Subsequent mobilization efforts in both world wars significantly reinforced the relationship between national governments and corporations. The very scope and scale of twentieth-century conflict, incorporating millions of citizens in campaigns that spanned the globe, mandated cooperation between the private and public sectors. Qualitative factors played perhaps an even more important role in forging this alliance. Technological breakthroughs such as radar, synthetic materials, and atomic weapons proved to be decisive advancements, all fostered by massive, federally subsidized research.[21]

After 1945, national military institutions dedicated to prosecuting U.S. and Soviet national security interests invested enormous sums in the private sector. Whole new industries in telecommunications, transportation, and computers, among others, appeared and were developed at the bequest of a bipolar struggle for power. The Cold War took what had been a periodic relationship between the corporate world and the state, determined by war and the ensuing national emergency, and solidified it into a permanent "military-industrial complex" for the next fifty years.[22]

Ironically, the most recent impetus for private military corporations was the end of the Cold War. P. W. Singer estimates that a vast reservoir of military expertise—as many as 7 million personnel—were demobilized in the decade following the destruction of the Berlin Wall .[23] Many of these individuals found work in companies that provided intelligence collection and analysis, physical security, or military training. In terms of quality, PMCs ran the gamut, from loosely run organizations little removed from organized crime to full-scale corporate structures vested by their host governments. The relationship between these latter companies and the German government illustrates the point. Between 1999 and 2003, nearly 700 privately owned companies signed agreements with Berlin that covered a host of service support functions within the military, specifically technical support and logistics.[24] In England, the relationship between private military corporations and the defense establishment was even closer. By 2003, the British Ministry of Defense had entered into partnerships with private companies that now provide as much as 80 percent of British Army training.[25]

In the United States, the intersection of private corporations and the defense establishment grew significantly during the Reagan administration. During his first term, this was the result of massive defense spending. After 1987 the Defense Department's relationship with the private sector drew even closer, prompted by budget cuts and a new federal penchant for fiscal responsibility by privatizing government functions.[26] When the Clinton administration arrived, it championed the same concept. In the nineties, Vice President Al Gore trumpeted "reinventing government" (or REGO) as a means toward a more streamlined and efficient federal system.

Again, this policy eventually extended to the Pentagon, which adopted the logic that the U.S. military needed to mimic successful business practices in order to be more effective. The 2001 *Quadrennial Defense Review Report* noted simply that: "During the same period that the security environment shifted from a Cold War structure to one of many and varied threats, the capabilities and productivity of modern business changed fundamentally. The Department of Defense has not kept pace with the changing business environment."[27]

In practical terms, this meant outsourcing military logistics so that the armed forces could focus on the "core competency" of waging war. In 2000 various sources estimated that for every dollar the Defense Department spent, approximately 30 percent went to "tooth" (combat) while 70 percent went to "tail" (logistics). Therefore, in order to be more efficient, the military needed to eliminate its direct responsibility for maintaining bases as well as housing, pay, medical care, and food service.[28] During the Clinton administration, Dr. Jacques Gansler noted: "My top priority, as Under Secretary of Defense, is to make the Pentagon look much more like a dynamic, restructured, reengineered, world-class commercial sector business."[29]

Consequently, the period saw a rapid increase in the number of corporate personnel present in American military operations. During the First Gulf War in 1991, one out of every fifty personnel deployed was a private contractor. By the time U.S. forces deployed to Bosnia-Herzegovina in the late nineties, the ratio was one in ten.[30] In the new decade, expenditures on military contractors accelerated even more. Between 1994 and 2002, the Defense Department signed some 3,000 contracts with private firms worth an estimated $300 billion.[31]

But what value did private military contractors offer besides additional economy? One key feature was operational flexibility. PMCs were, according to one author, "more innovative, more flexible, and more pragmatic" than conventional military organizations. In practice, individual military corporations did not have to concern themselves with the labyrinthine command structure present in the Pentagon or a cumbersome reporting process mandated by civilian lawmakers.[32]

This translated into the ability to deploy to global hotspots rapidly if and when a U.S. presence was necessary. DynCorp, which provided services for American policy makers in the Balkans, noted on its website: "In Kosovo, seventy-five peacekeepers were deployed from the U.S. thirteen days after providing a quote."[33]

Military contractors also offer U.S. policy makers an attractive exception to federal statutes limiting military deployment. The War Powers Act (1973) makes no mention of this type of military force, leaving a useful loophole in existing policy. The contractor option allowed the White House to sidestep more specific proscriptions on U.S. assistance abroad. In the late nineties, when Congress imposed a 400-man limit on American military advisers serving in Columbia, it was initially undone by hiring private corporations to train local military and police units.[34]

Private corporate soldiers offer a degree of expertise that is ready on demand without the peacetime expense of maintaining it. A key requirement of successful contingency operations abroad is an understanding of relevant social, economic, and religious context. As a result, former special forces soldiers and intelligence specialists with area expertise and linguistic skills are some of the most sought after recruits for PMCs.[35] These experts apply intellectual capital often in combination with local military manpower, a potent force multiplier that mirrors counterinsurgency doctrine during the Cold War.

What these individuals lack is equally, if not more, attractive. They are employees rather than direct agents of the state.[36] Many, in fact, are not citizens of the countries that employ them.[37] Thus, in a very pragmatic sense, contractors are not the responsibility of the government hiring them. Medical care, pensions, housing, and moral support belong to the corporate domain. So too do the wounded and dead. Treatment and rehabilitation are a function of private medical insurance, not the Veterans Administration. When contractors are killed in action, they enjoy none of the official recognition granted the armed forces during wartime.[38]

Some PMCs also offer highly specialized services.[39] BDM International Inc.; Kellog, Brown & Root (KBR); and Pacific Architects and Engineering provide logistical support for their host militaries on a massive scale.[40] In 1992 KBR won the first Logistics Civil Augmentation

Program. For an initial fee of $3.9 million, KBR created contingency plans for the deployment of U.S. forces to thirteen different parts of the world. Since that time, their contract has grown to include military deployments to Bosnia, Somalia, Afghanistan, Iraq, and Uzbekistan.[41] Between 1999 and 2003, KBR served 42 million meals and cleaned 3.6 million bags of laundry in support of U.S. forces stationed in the Balkans.[42] The global war on terror significantly multiplied these opportunities. When the United States launched Operation Iraqi Freedom in 2003, KBR took responsibility for housing, dining facilities, bath and shower units, janitorial services, recreational facilities, water distribution, electrical work, carpentry, construction, and virtually every remaining noncombat effort in the country. Overall, the estimated value of contracts for operations in Iraq and Afghanistan war between 2002 and 2004 was $10.8 billion. By 2009 the total value of KBR contracts in support of operations in the region exceeded $30 billion.[43]

Other PMCs provide very specific services as well. The Vinnell Corporation specializes in training. For more than a decade, its prime responsibility has been maintaining the Saudi National Guard. AirScan provides aerial surveillance. When the U.S. Department of Defense lacked adequate platforms to support peace enforcement operations in the Balkans under Task Force Eagle, it simply purchased the capability from AirScan.[44] Private military corporations have also assumed some specific duties at home. In 2003, for example, Military Professional Resources Incorporated (MPRI) and the firm RCI shared a $171 million contract to conduct U.S. military recruiting in ten states.[45]

Operation Enduring Freedom and Operation Iraq Freedom both saw a quantum leap in private security firms contracted to provide "boots on the ground" in both countries. One of the consequences of Tommy Frank's "running start" plan for the invasion of Iraq was an absolute shortage of personnel for security duties once major combat operations were over. These involved protecting basic infrastructure—power plants, oil pipelines, and electric power lines—as well as "force protection" of coalition military units and civilians stationed in forward operating bases and larger facilities. Private military corporations quickly became responsible for checkpoints, base perimeter security, patrols, and a host of other missions. By some early estimates, civilian contractors were responsible for between 20–30 percent of essential military services in Iraq after 2003.[46] Between 15,000 and 20,000 private security personnel were on the ground by the spring of 2004.[47] These numbers increased as the war grew in intensity.

Practical utility has translated into enormous profits for the corporate military industry. Estimated earnings from the global security market were $55.6 billion in 1990. By 2010 they were as high as $200 billion.[48] In the United States, twice as much money is spent on private security as on all the police departments in the country combined. In England, approximately 250,000 people are employed as private security personnel, more than the entire British army. At present, nearly ninety major private military corporations operate in more than a hundred nations.[49] Firms such as Armor Holdings are emblematic of this trend. Originally founded in 1969 to provide body armor, Armor Holdings saw its earnings top $150 million by 2000. Flush with capital, it acquired fifteen smaller companies between 1996 and 1998. By the time it joined the global war on terror, it was named by *Fortune* magazine as one of America's fastest growing companies.[50]

Although the U.S. military as an institution recognizes the utility of contractors, they generate substantial resentment among officers and enlisted personnel. As this chapter's epigraph indicates, conventional soldiers dislike the extravagant (by military standards) pay and benefits available to contractors. Six-figure salaries, along with liberal leave policies and other benefits draw the ire of military units taking similar or greater risks. The uneven standards that govern many private military corporations, and their often-scandalous consequences, have hardened these opinions further.[51]

Private military corporations also contribute to a number of systemic problems as America fights its small wars. The simple fact is that corporate service is enormously attractive to qualified regular soldiers, particularly those serving in current special forces units. These individuals, contemplating long-term deployments and separation from family and home, see PMCs as a viable alternative to active duty. Parlaying hard-won skills into better working conditions seem a reasonable step, especially after multiple tours of duty in Iraq, Afghanistan, and other hotspots. In fact, so many personnel began leaving the regular military by 2004 that the Defense Department began raising red flags for policy makers. Testifying before Congress, Chief Master Sergeant

Table 9.1. Private military contractors, Iraq and Afghanistan, 2004–2006

Company	Contracting agency	Function	Service amount
KBR	Defense Department	Logistics	$16.0 billion
Washington Group International Inc.	Defense Department	Logistics	$1.0 billion
L-3 Communications Holdings Inc.	Defense Department	Logistics	$853.3 million
Fluor Corp.	Defense Department	Logistics	$736.8 million
Perini Corp.	Defense Department	Logistics	$720.8 million
Orasco Construction Industries	Defense Department	Logistics	$617.1 million
Blackwater USA	Defense/State Department	Security	$485.1 million
AECOM Technology Corp.	Defense Department	Logistics	$293.7 million
Triple Canopy Inc.	State Department	Security	$179.3 million
EOD Technologies	Defense Department	Logistics/Security	$133.4 million
I and S Acquisition Corp.	Defense Department	Logistics	$118.5 million
CACI International	Defense Department	Intelligence	$87.7 million
Erinys International	Defense Department	Security	$40.5 million

SOURCE: "Iraq/Afghanistan Contractors," Center for Public Integrity. http://www.publicintegrity.org..

Robert Martens, the senior enlisted adviser to Special Operations Command, stated that the loss of experienced personnel was creating "an unacceptable level of operational risk."[52] At the time, the U.S. military planned to increase the number of special operations troops from 49,000 to 52,000 between 2004–2009.[53] To alleviate this "brain drain," SOCOM and the Defense Department expanded retention efforts. Soldiers from E-4 to E-9 received an additional "special duty assignment pay" allotment of $375 a month. Senior enlisted soldiers (E-6 to E-9) and warrant officers with critical skills also received bonuses for reenlistment: $150,000 for an additional six years, $75,000 for five years, $50,000 for four years, $30,000 for three years.[54]

Despite their many virtues and consequent impact on the standing military, private military corporations also suffer from a number of severe limits. One is overspecialization. Ironically, the very feature that allows PMCs to become a viable alternative to the conventional armed forces seriously qualifies their value. Companies that provide physical security are often built to function around this mission and lack an integrated understanding of their battlefield. Bodyguards, or "shooters," subsequently have little interest in intelligence reporting and sometimes blunder into situations that quickly escalate out of their control. This was the case for Blackwater USA throughout most of its time in Iraq. Although comprised of highly qualified personnel, the firm rapidly became pariahs throughout Iraq for their aggressive, often indiscriminate use of force.[55]

Many private military corporations also stumble when they expand beyond their original specialty. This was the case of EOD Technologies (EODT) in Iraq. When the war began in 2003, EODT was a Tennessee-based company that specialized in bomb disposal. However, within two years the firm had signed contracts for force protection of forward operating bases in northern Iraq as well as the Victory Base Complex near Baghdad Airport, a mission that took it far beyond its level of expertise.[56]

More important than the individual failings of private military corporations are the systemic problems that have plagued PMCs for the last decade or more. The respective invasions of Afghanistan and Iraq have highlighted the fact that private contractors are poorly integrated into war plans as well as daily operations. Even when their missions overlap, most companies do not coordinate their activities in any comprehensive fashion. The U.S. military assigns contract officers to monitor compliance with individual agreements. The system breaks down with respect to the hundreds, if not thousands, of separate tasks performed by private firms operating in a war zone. Actual cooperation is left to local initiative.

More important, until recently the United States has failed to provide clear rules of engagement or a consistent policy governing private military corporations.[57] In the past decade or more, the absence of a coherent system has produced problems ranging from poor coordination to instances of blatant illegal activity. These problems have multiplied with the increasing use of military contractors. The reported involvement of DynCorp employees in a sex slave ring in the Balkans became part of an international scandal only a few years after the company began operations in the region.[58] Since coalition forces invaded Iraq in 2003, the country has become a magnet for private military companies and subsequent controversy. When the scandal involving the abuse of prisoners in Abu Ghraib became public a year after the invasion, contractors working for the Titan Corporation and CACI were quickly implicated for their direct involvement.[59] In May 2005 contractors employed by Zapata Engineering allegedly opened fire on U.S. Marine positions in Fallujah, an act that resulted in their brief arrest and deportation from country.[60] Blackwater, a firm that provided bodyguards for key military and civilian officials, was the cause for numerous complaints and investigations until the company's final expulsion from Iraq in 2009.[61]

The basic policy dilemma for the United States is that military contractors are neither traditional soldiers nor mercenaries. They exist in the "grey zones" of the world, to use Susan Strange's reference, where state authority has broken down or been replaced—in some cases, by transnational corporations.[62] Iraq and Afghanistan are almost textbook examples of both. Within this "zone" exist private military contractors, individuals clearly interested in personal profit but also defined by their corporate employment and the laws (or lack thereof) of the government employing them.[63]

Unfortunately, the modernized definition of a mercenary has produced little legal clarity. In 1989 the United Nations produced the

"Convention Against the Recruitment, Use, Financing and Training of Mercenaries" but failed to ratify the measure.[64] In the meantime, existing UN provisions retained the traditional definition of private contractors as individuals who fought for profit. In the new era of corporate military activity, it proved wholly inadequate. So too was U.S. policy. Until 2004 the Coalition Provisional Authority stipulated that contractors fell under U.S. and not Iraqi law. Which U.S. law was the question. The State Department Office of Defense Trade Controls was tasked with monitoring U.S. firms for compliance with law regulating the training of foreign militaries or providing military services.[65] However, according to the 2000 Military Extraterritorial Jurisdiction Act, the Secretary of Defense was responsible for prosecuting violations of law.[66]

The regulation of day-to-day operations conducted by private military corporations was even more muddled. American policy offered little guidance in instances when contractors simply refused to carry out their missions. Legal remedies were impractical on the battlefield. According to Jayson Spiegel, executive director of the Reserve Officers Association: "The great thing about a soldier is if he doesn't show up, you can shoot him. You can't shoot contractors. You can sue them, but you can't shoot them."[67] Nor was it clear who protected the contractor during combat in areas without a clear delineation between "forward" and "rear" areas of operation. According to the Department of Defense (DOD) Doctrine for Logistical Support of Joint Operations, "Force protection for DOD contractor employees is a contractor responsibility."[68] Gaps in policy have forced many private companies to create internal security subdivisions for the sake of self-preservation. Many firms that had previously applied themselves to specialized work now include well-armed cadres of veteran soldiers to protect their own employees.

Currently, private military corporations are in the process of what one historian calls "re-regulation."[69] Some of this activity is voluntary and reflective of a sense within the security industry that self-regulation is useful for the sake of market credibility as well as a useful device to preempt external sanctions. In February 2006 a consortium of firms in the United Kingdom created the British Association of Private Security Companies, which recognized "an urgent need to raise standards of operation and advocate self regulation."[70] Christopher Spearin described the trend as "self-taming of the dog of war for the sake of reputation and repeat clients."[71]

Military contractors are also under increasing state regulation. Individual countries such as Germany and South Africa have bolstered already formidable regulatory regimes that govern not only hiring processes but also training and behavior while PMCs are under contract.[72] The United States eventually caught up with these efforts in 2006 when Senator Lindsay Graham (R-SC) included an amendment to a 2007 defense spending bill that placed all civilian and military contractors working for the federal government under the jurisdiction of the Uniform Code of Military Justice (UCMJ). Previously, this type of jurisdiction applied only when the country had officially declared war. Graham's measure expanded the military's domain to include a "contingency operation" such as the deployment of American forces to Afghanistan and Iraq.[73] More recently, as part of the December 2008 Status of Forces Agreement with Iraq, the United States officially surrendered control of contractors working in Iraq. Under the agreement's provisions, contractors providing special protective services for American officials, such as Blackwater, lost the limited immunity previously granted by the U.S. government in exchange for their services.[74]

Although the United States and the international community have improved policies regulating private military corporations, significant gaps remain. Multilateral regulation remains a patchwork of inconsistent initiatives. Within the European Union, nations such as Denmark, Finland, and France have potent control mechanisms and maintain strict authority over private security companies. Italian standards, in contrast, are relatively lax.[75] Even where individual nations have a tradition of cooperative foreign policy, the consensus rapidly breaks down over PMCs.[76] The United Kingdom, along with Australia, Finland, Japan, Costa Rica, and Kenya, supported a United Nations treaty to regulate the international arms trade, a venue in which private armaments companies have made substantial profits through weapons sales and technical assistance. However, the United States was the sole country to vote against the treaty resolution in 2006.[77] In the United States, despite the Graham amendment, UCMJ standards apply only to crimes committed by PMC contractors after the fact. The actual regulation of prerequisite standards for military contractors—training, equipment, and doctrine—remains contained within individual contracts. Consequently, company practices are rarely uniform. Moreover, they are often subject to both time-sensitive deadlines and mission imperatives during actual combat operations.[78]

MPRI in the Balkans

When the United States finally embarked upon peace enforcement duties in the Balkans, it did so supported by a substantial contingent of private military contractors. One of the most notable was Military Professional Resources Inc. (MPRI). While under contract with the State Department in 1994, MPRI provided twenty of forty-five border monitors stationed to report on the efficacy of sanctions against Serbia. By the time the Dayton Accords were signed in November 1995, the company was responsible for all forty-five locations.[79]

MPRI's most lasting contribution, however, came in 1994 when the company was contracted for the "Democracy Transition Assistance Program," an international training operation undertaken in Croatia. It contributed a fifteen-man team, led by retired major general Richard Griffitts, that was responsible for retraining the Croat military. Originally, the MPRI unit taught at the Croatian Army Staff School and focused on civil-military relations and human rights. The curriculum was part of the "Partnership for Peace" program necessary for Croat entry into NATO.[80]

MPRI's role grew in January 1996, when the Croat government contracted it to be part of the Long Range Management Program. In practice, this involved MPRI staff directly in a systematic effort to transition the Croat military from old Warsaw Pact doctrine to practices comparable to the contemporary U.S. armed forces. Essentially, the company introduced the AirLand Battle concept to the Balkans. MPRI contractors furnished instruction to the Croat general staff and later assisted local commanders with small unit tactical training. The company also provided assistance during combat—Operations Flash (May 1995) and Storm (August 1995)—conducted by Croatia against Serbia.[81]

As part of the regional military reconstruction effort, MPRI received a $400 million contract from the State Department in 1996 to retrain the Bosnian Croat–Muslim Federation Army.[82] MPRI became the conduit through which some $243 million in military and economic aid flowed into the Balkans. The United States provided the bulk of this assistance, a total of $103 million. Other donors included Saudi Arabia, Kuwait, the United Arab Emirates, Malaysia, and Brunei.[83] The MPRI program focused upon management, logistics, and battalion and brigade-level tactics. To reinforce leadership and tactical skills, the company rotated commanders through its newly built Computer Simulation Center at the Pazaric School near Sarajevo.[84]

MPRI also appeared indirectly during the brief conflict between Serbia and Kosovo at the end of the nineties. When fighting broke out between the Serb government and members of the Kosovo Liberation Army (KLA), the U.S. media reported that many KLA soldiers were veterans of MPRI-led operations in Bosnia. The military commander of the KLA, Agim Ceku, had earlier served as a brigadier general during the Croat offensive against Krajina in 1995.[85]

Overall, MPRI was a remarkable success in the Balkans. Coupled with U.S. and NATO forces stationed in the region, the company proved capable of restoring a regional military balance in the former Yugoslavia. MPRI imparted the best training and tactics available in NATO to their clients, effectively offsetting Serbia's superiority in numbers with a smaller, yet potent, combined-arms scheme built around AirLand Battle Doctrine. The overall cost involved in the MPRI contracts was equally attractive. For a few hundred million dollars, the United States and other contributors purchased tentative regional stability that was far less taxing than an ongoing, massive deployment of conventional units for peace enforcement.

However, as events in Kosovo illustrated, building a regional military balance and exercising control over it were two separate issues. MPRI provided training without qualification to improve the capabilities of the Croat military. It did so without considering the potential consequences that improved military capabilities had in a region defined by its ethnic hatred. Instead, MPRI delivered the maximum utility mandated by its contract. Thus, although the corporate proxy succeeded in its short-term objectives, MPRI's contribution to a lasting Balkan stability is at best debatable.

PMCs in Colombia

The ongoing drug war in Colombia has occupied U.S policy for decades. Since the late forties, the country has suffered under various waves of violence rooted in political rivalry (La Violencia), Marxist revolutionary insurgencies, and narcotics trafficking. The latter is the most formidable challenge to Colombian stability. This is, in part, because of the geometric increase in drug profits from $1.8 million in 1970 to an estimated $7 billion by 1995.[86] With resources comparable to the state itself, the cartels have successfully undermined Colombian national sovereignty. Legal authority is subject to corruption or open attack. Judges, criminal prosecutors, and police are all targets.[87]

A military alliance between the cartels and Colombian insurgents, particularly the Fuerzas Armadas Revolucionarias de Colombia (FARC), provided the drug traffickers with the muscle necessary to challenge state authority. Backed by billions in cocaine profits, the FARC has enjoyed a new lease on life.[88] In exchange for their protection of coca fields and cartel processing facilities, guerrillas are the de facto government in many portions of Colombia. In May 1999 president Andrés Pastrana ceded 40,000 square kilometers in south central Colombia to the FARC as a peace offering, but the *narcotrafficante* alliance still controls hundreds of thousands of acres of farmland and the *campesinos* who cultivate them.[89]

Successive generations of military programs have evolved to stamp out this alliance. The most recent and important is Plan Colombia, an initiative originally sponsored by the Pastrana administration and the recipient of enormous U.S. funding.[90] Many other projects have been subsequently upgraded with new funds, including ground-based radar installations to close holes in coverage exploited by small aircraft carrying drugs north. U.S. aid also increased Colombian military mobility by providing UH-60 and UH-1H helicopters.[91] Millions of dollars were also dedicated to training programs. U.S. advisers assisted in the creation of specialized units such as the Fuerza de Despliegue Rápido in 1998 (Rapid Deployment Force).[92] Thousands of Colombian military personnel attended courses in U.S. facilities that addressed basic tactics, logistics, and individual combat skills.[93]

If there was one weak point in the contemporary drug war, it was with respect to the number of U.S. military personnel authorized to serve in Colombia. While U.S. policy makers were willing to contribute billions to halt the flow of narcotics into the United States, they remained consistently reticent when it came to contributing flesh and blood to the cause. In July 2000, the Congress placed an official limit (500) on temporary and permanent military personnel allowed in Colombia.[94]

Private military corporations developed into an alternative to congressional restrictions. Contractors acting as civilian employees of the U.S. government allowed the Clinton and Bush administrations to supplement official military programs without violating existing law. Security firms assisted in ongoing training programs. Defence Systems Columbia (DSC), a subsidiary of Armor Holdings, instructed Columbian police as well as the 14th and 15th Brigades of the national army. Other contracts involved physical security. In addition to its training duties, DSC was charged with security for British Petroleum's facilities in the Casanare region of central Colombia.[95] DynCorp was one of the most active private military corporations in Colombia. By 2001, the company had received a $600 million contract for training, aerial surveillance, and intelligence gathering.[96]

As Plan Colombia unfolded, aerial operations conducted by private contractors played an important part in the counternarcotics program. The Aviation Development Corporation assisted the U.S. military and Colombian authorities to control the ground-based radar surveillance network. Contractors were actively involved in the crop eradication program adopted by the Colombian military. Utilizing Vietnam-era OV-10 Broncos for "crop dusting" coca fields, Eagle Aviation Services and Technology, along with DynCorp, assisted the government in spraying thousands of acres with herbicides.[97]

As noted in chapter 6, the overall effectiveness of Plan Colombia is difficult to measure. When evaluating the portions of it conducted by private military corporations, additional qualifications emerge. In 2001 the American media reported that U.S. contractors involved in social development programs such as road building and alternative agriculture were paying the FARC a "war tax" for the right to operate in their territory.[98] In other words, as they pursued projects dedicated to separate guerrillas and narcotics traffickers from the general population, contractors were being co-opted by these very forces. The decision made sense in business terms. Payment of the "war tax" allowed the private firms to complete their projects without bloodshed. However, when viewed using the lens of state authority, their mission was an utter failure.

At the core of the problem was the difference in priorities between the host government and the private military corporation. When the Colombian Defense Ministry published *Democratic Security and Defence Policy* in 2003, the introductory passage from president Álvaro Uribe struck a hard note: "There can be only one response to terrorism: its defeat."[99] It was clear the government was prepared to endure great sacrifices in what was, and continues to be, a ruthless campaign against drugs, insurgency, and terrorism. The same could not be said of the private contractor. Rather than embrace or institutionally internalize the degree of dedication apparent in the policy document, private military corporations focused instead on their economic viability or, as was the case with the British Petroleum pipelines in Casenare, their direct investments in Colombia. Tellingly, private contractors are never mentioned in *Democratic Security and Defence Policy*.

While PMCs were almost certainly useful to Plan Colombia with respect to personnel and costs, they failed to embody its spirit or its final objectives. Contractors lent their expertise to the practical tasks of finding, fixing, and eliminating guerillas and drug traffickers. They did so in a relatively cost effective manner for the United States. However, cost effectiveness translated poorly when it came to reconstructing the legitimacy of the Colombian government. Restoring links between the people and national leadership involves bridging a complex array of social, economic, and political gaps, all of which require a degree of subtlety and, more important, a sustained commitment that foreign corporate actors cannot provide.

Conclusions

The private military corporation appeared at a time when outsourcing was firmly established in both the private and public sectors. Postindustrial America has embraced the service economy. This is apparent today throughout the civilian sector. For the U.S. military, the advantages of a similar course became increasingly obvious once the Cold War with the Soviet Union was over. For much of the current generation of conflict, the premium has shifted from overly expensive weapons systems, difficult to justify in an era were social welfare is a prime concern for aging polities, to armed intervention augmented by intellectual capital, some of which is available for purchase.[100] The wealth of experience available as a result of the Cold War and current war against terror allows policy makers an enormous array of options to address almost any conceivable logistical, intelligence, or security contingency.

The private contractor also offers the very attractive prospect of distance. Low-intensity war is an ugly, indecisive exercise in hegemony. Although popular in their early stages, the respective invasions of Afghanistan and Iraq have since invited controversy and divisiveness, and they have changed the American political landscape since 2006.[101] The inclusion of contractors into combat missions allows policy makers room to shift the burden of conflict to a less visible constituency. Combat deaths and injuries suffered by contractors are afterthoughts at best in the public discourse. Conversely, when a PMC commits bad acts, as was the case with Blackwater or ArmorGroup, public retribution is a simple matter. Contractors do not enjoy the benefit of the doubt in cases of alleged atrocities. The anticorporate climate of the present day makes condemnation a popular option.

While useful, this system has finite limits. A major problem within the private security industry is a function of time. Age has begun to diminish the available pool of current and potential contractors. Men in their prime at the end of the Cold War are now in their forties and fifties.[102] Simple tasks that were once routine are now subject to the unpredictable physical infirmity that is a reality of middle age. A new stream of combat veterans is replenishing the vast reservoir of talent, but it will never return to its past glory.

A second limiting factor is the law. Private military corporations today face mushrooming constraints on the use of force.[103] A successively increasing array of national and international laws have caught up with the private security industry in the past decade. Contractors no longer enjoy the discretion that the early stages of the Afghanistan and Iraq wars created and tolerated. Thus, while the potential for profit remains formidable, the overall scrutiny PMCs now must endure is equally significant and a necessary price for doing the business of war.

Conclusions

The very nature of war makes certainty impossible.

—USMC Doctrinal Publication, *Warfighting*

Vietnam Analogies

The Vietnam War is alive and well in America's many contemporary conflicts. As a country, we have chosen to listen to the famous dictum and learn from the past in order to avoid its mistakes. Critics of our current wars reflexively apply Vietnam's failures to explain our own. Whether applied to public opinion, the battle for indigenous "hearts and minds," or matters of law and presidential authority, the Vietnam template can be made overly simplistic. More important to the story is understanding the depth and degree to which the past war actually shapes our military affairs.

In terms of grand strategy, Vietnam, Iraq, and Afghanistan share the same tunnel vision that warps U.S. policy and creates dangerous diplomatic blind spots. The two eras suffer from what is the strategic opportunity cost of too much time, effort, and talent too narrowly applied to a specific set of objectives. Richard Nixon warned of the risks of this approach in 1970 when he argued for a foreign policy more carefully calibrated to pragmatic interests than unreachable principles: "We are not involved in the world because we have com mitments, we have commitments because we are involved. Our interests must shape our commitments, rather than the other way around."[1] In his June 2009 Cairo speech, Barack Obama adopted this same pragmatism in an appeal to the Arab world based on its common interests with the United States.[2]

Politically, Vietnam and our current wars are essentially presidential litmus tests. In the early stages of both conflicts, decisive action—illustrated after Tonkin Gulf and Operation Enduring Freedom—proved to be a boon for the White House. However, as the wars unspooled, public discontent regarding cost and candor soon mired the respective administrations in a war of public perception. The failure to effectively answer domestic concerns, a trait shared by Lyndon Johnson and George W. Bush, ultimately affected not only support for the war effort, but also handicapped the domestic policy agendas of each era.

Latter-day public support for war has proven to be consistently fickle yet critical to the effective use of force abroad.[3] It is shaped by a variety of factors: the length of the conflict, its imminence in daily life, and popular tolerance for its brutality. Modern developments in communications technology, from satellite transmissions in the sixties to the World Wide Web today, invite war into homes and offices in real time and unquestionably complicate contemporary diplomacy and military affairs.[4]

In *How Democracies Lose Small Wars,* Gil Merom argues that modern societies allow their revulsion of war to dictate the collective will to fight. Modern polities, particularly their educated and affluent elements, cannot endure the horror produced by combat. In fact, as technology improves war's lethality, it becomes increasingly easy to reach this threshold of pain. Merom further explains that it is not necessary for a majority of society to reach this point; an articulate, dedicated minority is sufficient to disrupt domestic support for war. In the sixties, the loosely organized student antiwar movement was adequate for this purpose. After the September 11 attacks, many of these same baby boomers, now mature members of the American establishment, were even more formidable opponents to military action.[5]

Drawing military analogies between Vietnam and the present is a more problematic exercise. In *Beating Goliath: Why Insurgencies Win,* Jeffrey Record illustrates the clear distinctions separating military operations in South Vietnam and Iraq. One of the more obvious departures regards the size of opposing forces. Record estimates that in 1968 the Viet Cong and North Vietnamese Army were able to field between

250,000 and 300,000 personnel. In contrast, U.S. military and coalition forces overwhelmingly outnumbered Iraqi insurgents from 2003 onward. Moreover, the Iraq and Afghan insurgencies are divided by religious, ethnic, and local rivalries that bear little comparison to communist operations in South Vietnam.[6]

Some military analogies do apply, however. Both periods began with conventional force structures and doctrines that took years to recognize and incorporate the complexities of asymmetrical conflict. The initial show of force made by regular American units between 1965 and 1968 eventually gave way to a coordinated effort to win both the "big war" and popular support for the Saigon government. During Operation Iraqi Freedom, the rapidly diminishing relevance of "shock and awe" after 2003 led the American military on a similar search for more relevant methodologies. Thus, Creighton Abrams, William Colby, David Petraeus, and H. R McMaster share credit for understanding the need to move beyond what comprised the conventional wisdom of the day. More important, the military institutions of both periods proved adaptable to their proposals. What separates the contemporary military from its Vietnam era predecessor, however, is the degree to which the former has evolved to meet the contingencies of present warfare.

Vietnam Legacies and the Evolution of American Small Wars

Vietnam produced a crisis of faith regarding American military power. For much of this book's purview, public distrust and impatience shaped American military options by establishing broad limits for military action. In practice, this post-Vietnam consensus provided the political foundation for Weinberger (and Powell) Doctrine. It is what truncated military efforts in Grenada and Panama. It established the parameters of the Gulf War in 1990 and later the operating conditions for humanitarian assistance missions in the nineties. Although the September 11 attacks momentarily reversed these restrictions, they did not vanish and, indeed, returned back to the forefront of political debate after a few short years when Barrack Obama won the presidency in 2008.

Conversely, restored public faith in the military's legitimacy has also prompted many of America's small wars. Ronald Reagan tested this faith successfully in Grenada but failed miserably in Central America. More broadly, the period after Vietnam was also punctuated by fears of new, nontraditional threats to U.S. security at home. The drug war is perhaps the best example of a domestic problem that has been progressively militarized by a combination of reasonable concern, overheated rhetoric, and misapplied faith in military utility. The same conflation of domestic paranoia and national security mechanisms has dominated the last ten years of the discourse regarding terrorism. The past taboo of being "soft" on communism is currently superseded by new domestic litmus tests of strength. The ongoing lifespan of the Patriot Act is one case in point.

Within the American military, Vietnam created the impetus for reform across a broad spectrum of strategy, doctrine, and basic operations. Civilian and military leaders understood that change was necessary to maintain the military's relevance in the hostile policy environment of the seventies. More important, change was a necessity to ensure national survival at a time when the Soviet Union was moving past strategic parity with the United States. Consequently, the post-Vietnam debate within the armed forces produced concessions (the all-volunteer military), but also an understanding that old military standards were no longer adequate to national defense. The 1973 Yom Kippur War drove home the point that modern conflict was too rapid and lethal for existing systems of mobilization. The subsequent evolution of the "forward defense" concept into the AirLand Battle Doctrine reflected the desire (albeit flawed) to prevail in the main military arena of the Cold War.

Soviet collapse initiated a new round of debate regarding military effectiveness. Celebrations over American victory against Iraq in 1991 gave way to the realization that nontraditional environments would largely define U.S. military deployments around the world. For much of the decade, policy makers grappled with the fact that absolute definitions of "victory" and "defeat" no longer applied to fighting wars. Peacekeeping, peace enforcement, and a multitude of new missions required a combination of military and nonmilitary measures designed to prevail over nonstate actors while simultaneously incorporating them into the end product of nation building. To paraphrase a famous quotation from the Vietnam War, the military had "to save the village in order to save it." The military as an institution clearly struggled with the subtleties necessary for effective small wars doctrine. This effort produced the nebulous concept of "military operations other than war." On the other end of the spectrum, the Pentagon presumed the ability to micromanage nontraditional conflict by including a graduated response matrix in training for units bound for global hotspots like the Balkans.[7]

Contemporary U.S. doctrine represents the continuing search for the proper balance of military and civilian methods. As Petraeus "doctrine" during the Iraqi surge made evident, the United States now actively incorporates nonmilitary factors into its war plans. The newest generation of manuals, such as *Field Manual 3-24: Counterinsurgency,* with their emphasis on nonkinetic operations and human terrain, reflect an institution that has finally internalized functions necessary to succeed on a postmodern battlefield.[8]

Unfortunately, effective reforms arrived very late and are the exception to most of the military history addressed in this book. By tradition, the United States armed forces have avoided doctrine that combines military and political functions.[9] When the military did include political considerations after 1973, it did so more with the domestic polity in mind than any foreign enemy. Weinberger Doctrine was perhaps the best illustration of this intent. Some of its preconditions—"if we decide it is necessary to put combat troops into a given situation, we should do so wholeheartedly, and with the clear intention of winning"—represent simple common sense. However, the assertion that "there must be some reasonable assurance we will have the support of the American people and their elected representatives in Congress" more appropriately expresses a schism in U.S. civil-military relations than operating principles for war.[10]

For most of the last forty years, the U.S. military has deliberately resisted the pitfalls presented by small wars. This intent appears throughout the historical evolution of Powell Doctrine.[11] As a staff officer under Caspar Weinberger, Colin Powell supported starkly delineated guidelines for U.S. military deployments abroad. Once he rose to prominence within the defense establishment, Powell revised Weinberger Doctrine to avoid the incrementalism that had plagued the military during Vietnam. Consequently, he became an advocate of overwhelming military force applied to limited military objectives. Operation Desert Storm was the best-known expression of Powell Doctrine and enjoyed a significant cachet long after his retirement in 1993. Its immediate successor, rapid decisive operations, or "shock and awe," carried this approach into the next century. Emphasizing the United States' significant technological advantages over any conceivable enemy, new doctrine built around the precise application of firepower seemed a natural next step. A 1996 study of shock and awe proclaimed that "there is no external adversary in the world that can successfully challenge the extraordinary power of the American military . . . in regional or conventional war."[12]

At the close of the twentieth century, rapid decisive operations were a tempting palliative, which offered apparently easy alternatives to rapidly shrinking military budgets and capabilities. The replacement for Powell Doctrine reassured policy makers and military officers alike that U.S. technology, coupled with the destructiveness of contemporary weapons systems and the high level of training maintained in a peacetime military, would be adequate "force multipliers" for defense. More important, shock and awe did not require a major mobilization of government resources or public will. It seemed, at least before the events of September 11, the best means to square the circle of declining capabilities and growing demands on American power.[13]

When the American military embraced shock and awe, it repeated the same basic mistakes of the Vietnam War with a more modern gloss. As Sarah Sewall observed as late as 2006, core American military concepts remained fixed in an old framework regarding war: "Large massed formations, heavier weapons employed at increasing distances, and overwhelming force at the strategic and tactical level were the hallmarks of U.S. planning. Unconventional war, if it reared its head, was relegated to the subculture of U.S. special operations. But wishing away messy, multidimensional, and lengthy conflicts has not been an adequate solution."[14] During the invasion of Afghanistan and throughout much of the first two years of Operation Iraqi Freedom, the updated offshoot of Powell Doctrine held sway. It was not until the occupation of Iraq began to unravel that the American defense establishment was forced to confront the fact that it could not prevail with existing forces and methods.

What accounts for the longevity of the conventional model? It may be that Caspar Weinberger and Colin Powell are but two examples of well-meaning reformers who failed to anticipate either their own bias or the long-term consequences of their decisions. In this respect, they share many historical similarities with previous military and civilian policy makers.[15] More likely is the fact that Powell, Weinberger, and a generation of American leaders came of age in an era that provided the epistemology for a process that Melvyn Leffler succinctly described as "the assessment of threat, the calculation of interest, the enunciation of values, and the mobilization of power."[16] That era was the Cold War.

Continuity and the Cold War

The basic decisions made during the Cold War gave voice and form to American military policy for more than half a century and continue to exert enormous influence today. The National Security Act of 1947 created the basic framework of institutions—the National Security Council, the Department of Defense, and the Central Intelligence Agency—that still shape U.S. military policy. The Cold War also established critical precedents for military action. Collective security (NATO), multilateral responses to aggression (Korea), and unilateral, preemptive intervention (Cuba, the Dominican Republic, etc.) were all products of the period.[17] So too were the multitude of unconventional responses to communism from the coup against Arbenz in 1954 to American sponsorship of Nicaraguan contras thirty years later.

As a result, the Cold War created immense institutional and conceptual inertia in the U.S. military establishment. Noticeable throughout the narrative on U.S. small wars in the modern era is the absence of a dramatic or revolutionary approach. Organizationally, U.S. military planners were satisfied to merely tinker with existing structures and policies. Whether the threat involved insurgency, narcotics trafficking, or terrorism, the Pentagon and its civilian overseers were content to add additional substrata of departments, committees, or bureaus. Consequently, new threats and responses became simple adjuncts of firmly established institutions and their existing prerogatives. This type of thinking relegated special forces to a supporting role for the conventional military in the seventies. The same inertia was readily apparent in the nineties—a period of global flux in need of drastically new thinking—when the JCS published *Joint Vision 2010,* a document that was a warmed-over version of systems management from the sixties.

In this vein, it is clear that the Cold War produced a type of conceptual hubris that is still evident in the military today. A common intellectual thread that draws the past and present together is the basic assumption that knowledge applied to the art of war follows a linear path and is perfectible. This belief existed when Robert McNamara unleashed American firepower against North Vietnam with the expectation that an appropriate application of force could produce a predictable political result.[18] In the past, math and science were critical factors in measuring missile trajectories and nuclear throw weight. In its contemporary form, military perfectibility exists in the social sciences (e.g., anthropology, linguistics, and political science) and computer software such as the Reactive Information Propagation Planning for Lifelike Exercises (RIPPLE) program that govern the actions of 1,600 Iraqi role players at the National Training Center.[19] The concept of perfectibility persists because Americans assume that victory in war is simply a matter of better data manipulation.[20]

Ongoing Reform and the Construction of New Blinders

One consequence of apparent success is the temptation to err too far on the side of change. The short-term effectiveness of the Iraqi surge and new counterinsurgency doctrine has bred a sense that victory is currently possible on the postmodern battlefield. David Petraeus's scholar-warrior archetype is now the standard by which aspiring senior officers are judged within their respective services branches. Although this is clearly the trajectory of the current U.S. military institution, is it necessarily good?

Using this template, American policy can be prosecuted by what Robert Kaplan described in 2003 as "groups of quiet professionals" operating in the shadows of international relations.[21] These same individuals also have the option of overt relationships, through military training, which similarly can produce diplomatic leverage and international influence.[22] Kaplan's paradigm recalls the heyday of the CIA during the Cold War when covert action against Arbenz and Mossadeq redefined U.S. foreign policy.[23]

Today, Kaplan's model is problematic for almost too many reasons to count. Despite the fact that the war on terror heavily influences U.S. national security policy, it is not a global threat on par with communism. Maintaining a hard line against Soviet expansion was much easier than subsequent crusades—human rights, democratization, counternarcotics, or weapons of mass destruction—that represented an increasingly diverse and sometimes contradictory set of interests.[24] Presently, the United States and its allies regularly diverge on decisions pertaining to both security objectives and the means to obtain them. Differences are clear in countries where the United States has a longstanding security relationship, such as Pakistan, or the more recent partnership with the al-Maliki government in Baghdad.[25]

The new emphasis on counterinsurgency has also sparked considerable friction within the U.S. military. Central to this discussion is the fact that the small wars approach marginalizes whole service branches. When *FM 24-3* was published in 2006, it devoted a five-page annex to airpower.[26] Where do the Air Force strategic bomber and missile fleets fit in the new conventional wisdom? The Navy faces a similar dilemma with respect to its carrier battle groups. In what now appears to be a complete reversal of roles, special operations and small war doctrine are now driving much of the conventional military.[27]

This dynamic has created more than a small degree of stress inside the military establishment. Outwardly, the respective wars in Iraq, Afghanistan, and Libya, as well as elsewhere in the war on terror, are driving America's twenty-first-century military mission. However, the lion's share of the defense budget, promotions, and institutional recognition remains with the conventional and nuclear force structure.[28] Consequently, although small wars enjoy greater public notoriety, the military as a whole is guided and directed by older, better-established mechanisms within the Pentagon and national security community.

Operationally, the result of this tension is a compromise: the application of systems management to modern counterinsurgency. Human-terrain mapping and effects-based operations reflect continuity with the past and are an outgrowth of the impulse to organize combat space. The modern battlefield is now a catchall that includes the traditional kinetic elements of war with new variables such as culture, economics, ethnicity, and media.[29]

While institutional compromise possesses a certain superficial logic, it has produced increasing confusion for units deployed to fight. The accumulating complexity of doctrines has reached the point where they now overwhelm commanders in the field.[30] A 2009 study by the U.S. Joint Forces Command indicates that decision times noticeably slow as increasingly complex factors compete for leadership attention.[31] This is particularly the case as decision making travels down the chain of command. Company-grade officers and their noncommissioned counterparts—Charles C. Krulak's "strategic corporal"—individuals most important to success on the battlefield, commonly find themselves inundated with information at moments that require simplicity and decisiveness.[32] Ironically, a methodology designed to augment U.S. fighting capacity too many times blunts the sharp edge of the spear.

On the opposite end of the scale, modernized counterinsurgency lacks clarity when applied either to strategic ends or means. The war on terror is by definition unlike previous conflicts fought by the United States. It does not possess a unifying protagonist or ideology that is global in nature, in the manner of German militarism, Nazism, or Soviet communism in the previous century. Instead, although the product of economic, social, and political factors is synonymous with instability, the small wars of the present are situational, the product of local particularity at their source.

The most effective U.S. responses to these small wars have been those that incorporate this very particularity of time, place, and circumstance. Each is unique. What proved effective in Tal Afar cannot be repeated again in the eastern reaches of Afghanistan or the Horn of Africa. There is an inherent danger in this practice, what one senior Army officer defined as a "provisional theory of reality" that is critical to individual projects but is dangerous and unworkable in the larger policy arena.[33] Small wars require flexibility and subjectivity, qualities that do not possess the consistency necessary to guide U.S. national security strategy or its military as an institution. It is for these reasons that the current emphasis on small wars will likely recede as the global war on terror winds down.[34]

This would be an unfortunate outcome. It would represent the potential loss of knowledge gained since September 11—a scenario not unlike what was lost from the Vietnam War in the seventies replayed in a future context. Future wars, as history has taught, will not fall neatly into the expectations of any power. In fact, it is possible that America's next conflict may be an asymmetrical war conducted between modern nation-states.

Evidence of this is present in the 1999 publication of *Unrestricted Warfare.* A product of the Chinese People's Liberation Army, the work is premised on the simple principle that the "first rule is there are no rules."[35] Its authors maintain that China's goal is to deliberately avoid U.S. strengths in the event of a war and to find a means to manipulate these strengths to their advantage. In practice, this would mean an attack on the fragile technological infrastructure that holds together so much of the world's telecommunications, commercial systems, and social institutions.[36] This form of war would have less to do with damage to military personnel or facilities than to political legitimacy or public opinion. In the contemporary, affluent, information-driven United States, perception governs much of what is possible or probable. Understanding this, the September 11 terrorists built their plan around the goal of inflicting psychological trauma. A future enemy possessing far more formidable resources will likely return to this same place to attack what is difficult to shield yet essential to protect.

Notes

Introduction

1. Address by George W. Bush, president of the United States delivered to a joint session of Congress and the American people," *Vital Speeches of the Day* 67 (1 Oct. 2001): 760–763.
2. By 2009 the Department of Homeland Security was comprised of more than 225,000 employees. See http://www.dhs.gov/index.shtm.
3. Donald H. Rumsfeld, "Transforming the Military," *Foreign Affairs* 81 (May/June 2002): 20–32.
4. Rupert Smith, *The Utility of Force: The Art of War in the Modern World* (New York: Alfred A. Knopf, 2007), 3–28.
5. "Troops Committed War Crimes, Say Americans," *Angus Reid Global Monitor,* 18 June 2006. http://www.angus-reid.com.
6. "Most Americans Still Upset About Iraq Invasion," *Angus Reid Global Monitor,* 8 Mar. 2008. http://www.angus-reid.com.
7. Leslie H. Gelb, with Richard K. Betts, *The Irony of Vietnam: The System Worked* (Washington, DC: Brookings Institution, 1979), 332.
8. Lydia Saad, "Republicans and Democrats Disagree on War, but Support Troops," *Gallup News Service* (Sept. 2006). http://www.gallup.com.
9. For an excellent comparative examination, see Michael J. Englehart, "America Can Win, Sometimes: U.S. Success and Failure in Small Wars," *Conflict Quarterly* 9 (Winter 1989): 20–35.
10. Tarak Barkawi, "On the Pedagogy of 'Small Wars,'" *International Affairs* 80 (Jan. 2004): 20–21, 26–27.
11. "Transcript of President Bush's Address to a Joint Session of Congress," 20 Sept. 2001. http://archives.cnn.com/2001/US/09/20/gen.bush.transcript. See also Melvyn P. Leffler, "9/11 and American Foreign Policy," *Diplomatic History* 29 (June 2005): 395–413.
12. Michael J. Engelhardt, "America Can Win Sometimes: U.S. Success and Failure in Small Wars." *Conflict Quarterly* 9 (Winter 1989): 20–35;

Harry G. Summers Jr., *On Strategy: A Critical Analysis of the Vietnam War* (New York: Dell, 1982).

13. Robert M. Cassidy, "Back to the Street without Joy: Counterinsurgency Lessons from Vietnam and Other Small Wars," *Parameters* 34 (Summer 2004): 73–83.
14. Robert M. Cassidy, "The Long Small War: Indigenous Forces for Counterinsurgency," *Parameters* 36 (Summer 2006): 47–62; James S. Corum and Wray R. Johnson, *Airpower in Small Wars: Fighting Insurgents and Terrorists* (Lawrence: Univ. Press of Kansas, 2003).
15. Roger Spiller, "Military History and Its Fictions," *Journal of Military History* 70 (Oct. 2006): 1081–1097; Mark Moyar, "The Current State of Military History," *Historical Journal* 50 (Mar. 2007): 225–240.
16. Beatrice Heuser, "Small Wars in the Age of Clausewitz: The Watershed Between Partisan War and People's War," *Journal of Strategic Studies* 33 (Feb. 2010): 141–143; Roger Beaumont, "Small Wars: Definitions and Dimensions," *Annals of the American Academy of Political and Social Science* 541 (Sept. 1995): 21–23.
17. Russell F. Weigley, *The American Way of War: A History of United States Military Strategy and Policy* (Bloomington: Indiana Univ. Press, 1973), xxii. A classic study of this tendency and its persistence may be found in Donald Higginbotham, *The War of American Independence: Military Attitudes, Policies, and Practice, 1763–1789* (New York: Macmillan, 1971).
18. Warren W. Hassler, *With Shield and Sword: American Military Affairs, Colonial Times to the Present* (Ames: Iowa State Univ. Press, 1982), 208–212, 240–258.
19. Cassidy, "The Long Small War," 49–50.
20. For an example of the process of nation building in Cuba, see Jack McCallum, *Leonard Wood: Rough Rider, Surgeon, Architect of American Imperialism* (New York: New York Univ. Press, 2006), 111–196.
21. U.S. Marine Corps, *Small Wars Manual* (Washington, DC: Government Printing Office, 1940). For an excellent history of these conflicts see Max Boot, *The Savage Wars of Peace: Small Wars and the Rise of American Power* (New York: Basic Books, 2002). For an overview of the manual itself, see Keith B. Bickel, *Mars Learning: The Marine Corps Development of Small War Doctrine, 1915–1940* (Boulder, CO: Westview Press, 2001).
22. See Michael D. Gambone, *Capturing the Revolution: The United States, Central America, and Nicaragua, 1961–1972* (Westport, CT: Praeger, 2001).
23. Steven Palmer, "Carlos Fonseca and the Construction of Sandinismo in Nicaragua," *Latin American Research Review* 23 (1988): 91–109.
24. Frank G. Hoffman, "Small Wars Revisited: The United States and Nontraditional Wars," *Journal of Strategic Studies* 28 (Dec. 2005): 922–927. The Zapatista in Mexico drew early attention for its use of the Internet to spread its message. See Naomi Klein, *Fences and Windows: Dispatches*

from the Front Lines of the Globalization Debate (New York: Picador USA, 2002), 208–223.

25. Hoffman, "Small Wars Revisited," 916.
26. Michael R. Melillo, "Outfitting a Big-War Military with Small War Capabilities," *Parameters* 36 (Autumn 2006): 27–33.
27. U.S. Dept. of the Army, *FM 3-24: Counterinsurgency* (Washington, DC: U.S. Dept. of the Army, 2006).
28. John Lewis Gaddis, *Strategies of Containment: A Critical Appraisal of Postwar American national Security Policy* (New York: Oxford Univ. Press, 1982), vii. The original terms comes from Jack H. Hexter, *On Historians* (Cambridge, MA: Harvard Univ. Press, 1979), 241–243.
29. See T. Christopher Jespers, "Analogies at War: Vietnam, the Bush Administration's War in Iraq, and the Search for a Usable Past," *Pacific Historical Review* 74 (Aug. 2005): 411–426; "Interchange: Legacies of the Vietnam War," *Journal of American History* 93 (Sept. 2006): 452–490.

1. The Cold War and Limited Conflict

1. Books on Vietnam are legion in number. For two classic works that remain excellent studies of the war see Stanley Karnow, *Vietnam: A History* (New York: The Viking Press, 1983) or Neil Sheehan, *A Bright Shining Lie: John Paul Vann and America in Vietnam* (New York: Vintage Books, 1988).
2. Roger Beaumont, "Small Wars: Definitions and Dimensions," *Annals of the American Academy of Political and Social Science* 541 (Sept. 1995): 20–35. See also Patrick Brogan, *The Fighting Never Stopped: A Comprehensive Guide to World Conflict Since 1945* (New York: Vintage Books, 1990); Robert B. Asprey, *War in the Shadows: The Guerrilla in History* (New York: William Morrow & Co., 1994).
3. For a recent examination of Cold War–era American policy, see John Lewis Gaddis, *The Cold War: A New History* (New York: Penguin Books, 2005), 83–118.
4. Most general histories focus on this development. See, for example, Arthur T. Hadley, *The Straw Giant: America's Forces: Triumphs and Failures* (New York: Avon Books, 1987), 74–99.
5. For an excellent overview of the immediate postwar in America see James T. Patterson, *Grand Expectations: The United States, 1945–1974* (New York: Oxford Univ. Press, 1996), 3–81.
6. Warren W. Hassler, *With Shield and Sword: American Military Affairs, Colonial Times to the Present* (Ames, IA: Iowa State Univ. Press, 1982), 356; Maurice Matloff, ed., *American Military History* (Washington, DC: Government Printing Office, 1973), 530–531.
7. Dean Acheson, *Present at the Creation: My Years in the State Department* (New York: W.W. Norton & Co., 1987), 217–225.

8. Michael D. Gambone, *Eisenhower, Somoza, and the Cold War in Nicaragua, 1954–1961* (Westport, CT: Praeger, 1997), 78–84. For a discussion of the formation of the Truman Doctrine see Denise M. Bostdorff, *Proclaiming the Truman Doctrine: The Cold War Call to Arms* (College Station, TX: Texas A&M Univ. Press, 2008), 91–133.
9. George Friedman and Meredith Friedman, *The Future of War: Power, Technology and American World Dominance in the 21st Century* (New York: Crown, 1996), 69–89; Allan R. Millett and Peter Maslowski, *For the Common Defense: A Military History of the United States of America* (New York: The Free Press, 1994), 498–507. For a broader study on American attitudes see Paul Boyer, *By the Bombs Early Light: American Thought and Culture at the Dawn of the Nuclear Age*. New York: Pantheon Books, 1985). See also Paul Dickson, *The Electronic Battlefield* (London: Marion Boyars, 1976), 32–54.
10. For a contemporary argument on the limited use of nuclear weapons, see Henry A. Kissinger, *Nuclear Weapons and Foreign Policy* (New York: Harper & Brothers, 1957). An argument for the productive use of ground forces may be found in Maxwell D. Taylor, *The Uncertain Trumpet* (New York: Harper & Brothers, 1959).
11. John Weeks, *The Airborne Soldier* (New York: Blandford Press, 1986), 20–29, 43–47.
12. Sarah-Jane Corke, *U.S. Covert Operations and Cold War Strategy: Truman, Secret Warfare, and the CIA, 1945–1953* (New York: Routledge, 2008), 10–44. See also Michael Maclear, *The Ten Thousand Day War: Vietnam: 1945–1975* (New York: St. Martin's Press, 1981), 10–12 for the exploits of the "Deer Team" in French Indochina. In Roger Hilsman, *American Guerrilla: My War Behind Japanese Lines* (New York: Brassey's, Inc., 1990), the author recounts his experiences in Burma.
13. Aaron Bank, *From OSS to Green Beret: The Birth of Special Forces* (Novato, CA: Presidio Press, 1986), 157; David Tucker and Christopher J. Lamb, *United States Special Operations Forces* (New York: Columbia Univ. Press, 2007), 79–80; Michael McClintock, *Instruments of Statecraft: U.S. Guerrilla Warfare, Counter-Insurgency, Counter-Terrorism, 1940–1990* (New York: Pantheon Books, 1992), 59–60.
14. Bank, *From OSS to Green Beret,* 160–164, 172–189. Bank mentions the Lodge Bill on page 153, which allowed aliens to attain citizenship after two years of honorable military service. See also McClintock, *Instruments of Statecraft,* 77–82.
15. Chester J. Pach, *Arming the Free World: The Origins of the United States Military Assistance Program, 1945–1950* (Chapel Hill, NC: Univ. of North Carolina Press, 1991), 7–14.
16. Ibid., 29–62. See also Gambone, *Eisenhower, Somoza, and the Cold War in Nicaragua,* 84–88.

17. For study of Latin American inclusion into U.S. strategic planning see Robert Holden, *Armies Without Nations: Public Violence and State Formation in Central America, 1821–1960* (New York: Oxford Univ. Press, 2004). A more dated, but still excellent examination may also be found in David Green, *The Containment of Latin America* (Chicago: Quadrangle Books, 1971).
18. *Public Papers of the Presidents, Harry Truman, 1947* (Washington, DC: Government Printing Office, 1963), 176–180.
19. Arnold A. Offner, *Another Such Victory: President Truman and the Cold War, 1945–1953* (Stanford, CA: Stanford Univ. Press, 2002), 185–212; Pach, *Arming the Free World,* 89–129.
20. Pach, *Arming the Free World,* 134; Elizabeth Edwards Spalding, *The First Cold Warrior: Harry Truman, Containment, and the Remaking of Liberal Internationalism* (Lexington: Univ. Press of Kentucky, 2006), 61–102.
21. Spalding, *The First Cold Warrior,* 106; Judith S. Jeffrey, *Ambiguous Commitments and Uncertain Policies: Truman Doctrine in Greece, 1947–1952* (Lanham, MD: Lexington Books, 2000), 133–136, 142–144.
22. Jeffrey, *Ambiguous Commitments and Uncertain Policies,* 182; Zachary Karabell, *Architects of Intervention: The United States, the Third World, and the Cold War, 1945–1962* (Baton Rouge, LA: Louisiana State Univ. Press, 1999), 17–36.
23. Pach, *Arming the Free World,* 198.
24. U.S. Dept. of State, Division of Publications, Office of Public Affairs, *The Military Assistance Program* (Washington, DC: Government Printing Office, 1949), 3.
25. Senator Gravel Edition, *The Pentagon Papers: The Defense Department History of U.S. Decisionmaking on Vietnam,* I (Boston: Beacon Press, 1971), 36; Robert Blum, *Drawing the Line: The Origin of the American Containment Policy in East Asia* (New York: W.W. Norton & Co., 1982), 125.
26. Bank, *From OSS to Green Beret,* 156, 158. See also David H. Hackworth, *About Face: The Odyssey of an American Warrior* (New York: Simon & Schuster, 1991), 59–60.
27. Rod Paschall, *Witness to War: Korea* (New York: Perigee Books, 1995), 87–90, 110–116; Tucker and Lamb, *United States Special Operations Forces,* 85.
28. Rod Paschall, *A Study in Command and Control: Special Operations in Korea, 1951–1953* (Carlisle, PA: U.S. Army Military History Institute, June 1988), 30.
29. Gambone, Eisenhower, *Somoza, and the Cold War in Nicaragua,* 81.
30. Maurice Matloff, ed., *American Military History* (Washington, DC: Government Printing Office, 1973), 573.
31. U.S. Dept. of Defense, *Semiannual Report of the Secretary of Defense, 1 January–30 June 1953* (Washington, DC: Government Printing Office, 1954),

7; U.S. Dept. of Defense, *Semiannual Report of the Secretary of Defense, 1 January–30 June 1957* (Washington, DC: Government Printing Office, 1957), 4.

32. U.S. Senate, Committee on Foreign Relations, *The Senate Foreign Relation Committee's Historical Series: Military Assistance Program, 1949* (New York: Garland, 1979), 73, 94–95, 147–148.
33. U.S. Dept. of State, *The Military Assistance Program,* 3.
34. U.S., Office of the President, *First Report to the Congress on the Mutual Security Program* (Washington, DC: Government Printing Office, 1951), 44; Robert A. Packenham, *Liberal America and the Third World: Political Development Ideas in Foreign Aid and Social Science* (Princeton: Princeton Univ. Press, 1973), 49–50.
35. U.S. Dept. of Defense, *Semiannual Report of the Secretary of Defense, 1 January–30 June 1957* (Washington, DC: Government Printing Office, 1958), 2, 51, 86–94. Between 1950 and 1958, U.S. allies participating in the MSP contributed $138 billion of their own money for defense. See U.S. Dept. of Defense, *Semiannual Report of the Secretary of Defense, 1 January–30 June 1958* (Washington, DC: Government Printing Office, 1959), 67.
36. Defense, *Semiannual Report of the Secretary of Defense, 1 January–30 June 1958,* 69; U.S. Dept. of Defense, *Annual Report for Fiscal Year 1961* (Washington, DC: Government Printing Office, 1962), 1, 39, 94–95.
37. Taylor, *The Uncertain Trumpet,* 4, 17; A. J. Bacevich, *The Pentomic Era: The U.S. Army between Korea and Vietnam* (Washington, DC: National Defense Univ. Press, 1986), 9.
38. For contemporary criticism of the New Look, see Bernard Brodie, "Strategy Hits Dead End," *Harper's Magazine* 211 (Oct. 1955): 33–37; Robert E. Osgood, *Limited War: The Challenge to American Security* (Chicago: Univ. of Chicago Press, 1957).
39. Ronald H. Spector, *Advice and Support: The Early Years, 1941–1960* (Washington, DC: Center for Military History, 1986), 190–200.
40. Regarding the contemporary Army, see James M. Gavin, *War and Peace in the Space Age* (New York: Harper & Brothers, 1958); Bacevich, *The Pentomic Era,* 71–100.
41. NIE-99, "Estimate of the World Situation through 1955," 23 Oct. 1953, in *Foreign Relations of the United States, 1952–1954, National Security Affairs* (Washington, DC: Government Printing Office, 1984), 2:554.
42. Gambone, *Eisenhower, Somoza, and the Cold War in Nicaragua,* 197. In Nicaragua, the U.S. country team discovered that the Somoza regime was actively re-exporting surplus military assistance to other countries.
43. Kevin Shillington, *History of Africa* (New York: St. Martin's Press, 1995), 374–394; Ronald Oliver and J. D. Fage, *A Short History of Africa* (New York: Penguin Books, 1995), 221.
44. See George C. Herring, *America's Longest War: The United States and Vietnam, 1950–1975* (New York: McGraw Hill, 1996), 72–79; Joseph Buttinger,

Vietnam: A Political History (New York: Praeger, 1968), 454–459; Denis Warner, *The Last Confucian* (New York: Macmillan, 1963), 194–223; John H. Coatsworth, *Central American and the United States: The Clients and the Colossus* (New York: Twayne, 1993), 90–121; Cole Blasier, *The Giant's Rival: The USSR and Latin America* (Pittsburgh: Univ. of Pittsburgh Press, 1987), 75–92.

45. Blaufarb, *The Counterinsurgency Era,* 53.
46. Michael R. Beschloss, *The Crisis Years: Kennedy and Khrushchev, 1960–1963* (New York: Edward Burlingame, 1991), 41.
47. David Halberstam, *The Best and Brightest* (New York: Random House, 1969), 55–56, 77.
48. Ibid., 90–91.
49. Hassler, *With Shield and Sword,* 375–376; NSAM 2, "Development of Counter-Guerrilla Forces," 3 Feb. 1961. National Archives and Records Administration (hereafter NARA), RG 59, General Records of the Dept. of State, National Security Action Memoranda Files, 1961–1968, Box 1.
50. U.S. Dept. of the Army, Office of the Chief of Staff, "A United States Military Program," 27 June 1961, John F. Kennedy Library (JFK), National Security Files, Departments and Agencies, Box 265.
51. Special National Intelligence Estimate (SNIE) 80–62, 17 Jan. 1961, in U.S. Dept. of State, Foreign Relations of the United States, 1961–1963, *The American Republics* (Washington, DC: Government Printing Office, 1996), 12:211.
52. SNIE 80–62, 17 Jan. 1961.
53. Che Guevara, *Guerrilla Warfare* (New York: Vintage Groups, 1969), 1, 4–5.
54. Tad Szulc, *Fidel: A Critical Portrait* (New York: Avon Books, 1968), 568, 574.
55. See Don Bohning, *The Castro Obsession: U.S. Covert Operations Against Cuba, 1959–1965* (Washington, DC: Potomac Books, 2005) for a recent study of the issue.
56. Halberstam, *The Best and the Brightest,* 91.
57. NSAM 2, 3 Feb. 1961; Edward A. Jamison (Director, Office of Inter-American Regional Political Affairs) to Robert F. Woodward (Assistant Secretary of State for Inter-American Affairs), 17 July 1961. NARA, RG 59, State Dept. Lot Files, 643D310, 66D131, Box 3; George S. Newman (State) to Jeffrey C. Kitchen (Deputy Assistant Secretary of State for Politico-Military Affairs), 25 July 1961, NARA, RG 59, National Security Action Memoranda Files, 1961–1968, Box 1.
58. NSAM 124, "Establishment of the Special Group (Counter-Insurgency)," 18 Jan. 1962, JFK, NSF, Meetings and Memoranda, Box 319; Memorandum to the Members of the Special Group, "Establishment of the Special Group," 2 Jan. 1962, JFK, NSF, Meetings and Memoranda, Box

319; McClintock, *Instruments of Statecraft,* 168 (emphasis added). See also Charles D. Ameringer, *U.S. Foreign Intelligence: The Secret Side of American History* (Lexington, MA: Lexington Books, 1990), 293.

59. John O. Bell (Deputy Coordinator for Foreign Assistance) to Roy R. Rubottom (Ambassador to Argentina), 27 May 1961, NARA, RG 59, State Dept. Lot Files, 63D127, Box 2; Edward A Jamison (Director, Office of Inter-American Regional Political Affairs) to Richard N. Goodwin (Special Council to the President), 26 Feb. 1962, memorandum, NARA, RG 59, State Dept. Lot Files, 65D159, 66D131, Box 5.
60. NSAM 206, "Military Assistance for Internal Security in Latin America," 4 Dec. 1962, NARA, RG 59, NSAM Files, 1961–1968, Box 5.
61. "Jungle Faculty," *Newsweek,* 6 Mar. 1961, 33.
62. McClintock, *Instruments of Statecraft,* 187–222; Charles M. Simpson, *Inside the Green Berets: The First Thirty Years, A History of the U.S. Army Special Forces* (Novato, CA: Presidio Press, 1983), 82–83.
63. James Dunkerley, *Power in the Isthmus: A Political History of Modern Central America* (New York: Verso, 1988), 446–447.
64. McClintock, *Instruments of Statecraft,* 216, 230–257; U.S. Dept. of the Army, *FM 33-1: Psychological Operations, U.S. Army Doctrine* (Washington, DC: U.S. Dept. of the Army, May 1965), 44.
65. U.S. Dept. of State, Bureau of Intelligence and Research, "The New Militarism in South America: Agent for Modernization?" 28 Aug. 1969, NARA, RG 59, Subject-Numeric File, 1967–1969, Box 2109.
66. For an excellent example of this scholarship, see Robert H. Holden, "Constructing the Limits of State Violence in Central America: Towards a New Research Agenda," *Journal of Latin American Studies* 28 (May 1996): 435–460.
67. Memorandum of Conversation, Roy R. Rubottom and Pedro Beltran, 23 Oct. 1957, NARA, RG 59, State Dept. Lot Files, Lot 59D573, Box 3.
68. Embajada de Chile to the Dept. of State, "Chile and the 'Armaments Race,' in Latin America," 1 Nov. 1966, NARA, RG 59, Subject-Numeric File, 1964–1966, Box 1655.
69. U.S. Defense Attaché (Santiago) to Dept. of the Air Force, 16 Sept. 1966, NARA, RG 59, Deputy Assistant Secretary of State for Politico-Military Affairs, Office of Operations, Subject Files, 1962–1966, Box 6; "The Latin American Arms Race," *Economist,* 2 Nov. 1967, 1–4.
70. U.S. Dept. of State, Bureau on Intelligence and Research, "Third-Country Arms Sales to Latin America," 9 Feb. 1971, NARA, RG 59, Subject-Numeric File, 1970–1973, Box 1763; U.S. Dept. of State, Bureau on Intelligence and Research, "Latin America: The Outlook for Arms Spending," 5 Mar. 1973, NARA, RG 59, Subject-Numeric File, 1970–1973, Box 1763.

71. Coatsworth, *Central America and the United States,* 122–137.
72. Senate, *Military Assistance Program, 1949,* 711. For an excellent study of the U.S. effort in Vietnam, see Shelby L. Stanton, *Green Berets at War: U.S. Army Special Forces in Southeast Asia, 1956–1975* (New York: Ivy Books, 1985).
73. Guenther Lewy, *America in Vietnam* (New York: Oxford Univ. Press, 1978), 4–5. See also *The Pentagon Papers,* 66.
74. Regarding early political support of the Diem regime, see Edward Landsdale, *In the Midst of Wars: An American's Mission to Southeast Asia* (New York: Harper & Row, 1964).
75. Spector, *Advice and Support,* 270.
76. Ibid., 225, 282–286, 295–302.
77. Ibid., 340; William S. Turley, *The Second Indochina War,* 2nd ed. (New York: Rowman & Littlefield, 2009), 43–48.
78. Lewy, *America in Vietnam,* 22; Turley, *The Second Indochina War,* 57–85.
79. Sheehan, *A Bright Shining Lie,* 379.
80. Blaufarb, *The Counterinsurgency Era,* 245–248.
81. For a perspective on both of these programs, see the classic study by Jeffrey Race, *War Comes to Long An: Revolutionary Conflict in a Vietnamese Province* (Berkeley: Univ. of California Press, 1972), 53–59, 132–134.
82. Blaufarb, *The Counterinsurgency Era,* 214–221.
83. Robert M. Cassidy, "Back to the Street without Joy: Counterinsurgency Lessons from Vietnam and Other Small Wars," *Parameters* 34 (Summer 2004): 75–79.
84. Anthony Zinni and Tony Kolz, *The Battle for Peace: A Frontline Vision of America's Power and Purpose* (New York: Palgrave Macmillan, 2006), 16–21; Blaufarb, *The Counterinsurgency Era,* 256–258.
85. Sheehan, *A Bright Shining Lie,* 652–657; Lewy, *America in Vietnam,* 123–125; Blaufarb, *The Counterinsurgency Era,* 239–242.
86. George Donelson Moss, *Vietnam: An American Ordeal,* 5th ed. (Upper Saddle River, NJ: Pearson Prentice Hall, 2006), 242–244, 310–312, 341–344; Sheehan, *A Bright Shining Lie,* 731–733; Lewy, *America in Vietnam,* 191–192. While the South Vietnamese Army had rapidly increased its operational tempo by 1970, severe deficiencies remained in terms of morale, discipline, and desertion. Additionally, South Vietnamese combat forces were very poorly integrated with pacification efforts. For a detailed explanation, see Lewy, *America in Vietnam,* 162–189.
87. See Jeffrey J. Clarke, *Advice and Support: The Final Years, 1965–1973* (Washington, DC: Center of Military History, 1988).
88. Karnow, *Vietnam,* 436.
89. James F. Dunnigan, *How to Make War: A Comprehensive Guide to Modern Warfare* (New York: Quill, 1983), 308–322.

90. Turley, *The Second Indochina War,* 93–100; Blaufarb, *The Counterinsurgency Era,* 80–81.
91. Sheehan, *A Bright Shining Lie,* 540–541.
92. Gaddis, *The Cold War,* 129–134.
93. Memorandum, Robert Komer to K. R. Hansen (Bureau of Budget), "Guerrilla Warfare Problem," 18 Sept. 1961, JFK, NSF, Meetings and Memoranda, Box 326.
94. "Truman Doctrine," 12 Mar. 1947, in *Documents of American Diplomacy: From the American Revolution to the Present,* ed., Michael D. Gambone (Westport, CT: Greenwood Press, 2002), 307.
95. Robert Warren Stevens, Vain Hopes, *Grim Realities: The Economic Consequences of the Vietnam War* (New York: New Viewpoints, 1976), 82–102. For a broader examination of American defense spending during the Cold War, see Diane Kunz, *Guns and Butter: America's Cold War Economic Diplomacy* (New York: Free Press, 1997).
96. Henry Kissinger, *Diplomacy* (New York: Simon & Schuster, 1994), 696–702; Frank G. Hoffman, "Small Wars Revisited: The United States and Nontraditional Wars," *Journal of Strategic Studies* 28 (Dec. 2005): 920–922; Tarak Barkawi, "On the Pedagogy of 'Small Wars,'" *International Affairs* 80 (Jan. 2004): 20–22; John Lewis Gaddis, *We Now Know: Rethinking Cold War History* (New York: Oxford Univ. Press, 1997), 189–220; Frank Ninkovich, *The Wilsonian Century: U.S. Foreign Policy since 1900* (Chicago: Univ. of Chicago Press, 1999), 215–245. For a postwar examination of American public opinion, see Leslie Gelb, *The Irony of Vietnam: The System Worked* (Washington, DC: Brookings Institution, 1979).

2. The Seventies Nadir and Recovery

1. James T. Patterson, *Restless Giant: The United States from Watergate to Bush v. Gore* (New York: Oxford Univ. Press, 2005), 13.
2. George Herring, *America's Longest War: The United States and Vietnam, 1950–1975,* 3rd ed. (New York: McGraw-Hill, 1996), 265. For a complete breakdown of troop withdrawals between January 1968 and July 1972, see Guenter Lewy, *America in Vietnam* (New York: Oxford Univ. Press, 1978), 147.
3. Richard M. Nixon, "First Annual Report to the Congress on United States Foreign Policy for the Seventies," 18 Feb. 1970, http://www.presidency.ucsb.edu.
4. George Donelson Moss, *Vietnam: An American Ordeal,* 5th ed. (Upper Saddle River, NJ: Pearson Prentice Hall, 2006), 344–348.
5. Neil Sheehan, *A Bright Shining Lie: John Paul Vann and America in Vietnam* (New York: Vintage Books, 1988), 745–788; Stanley Karnow, *Vietnam: A History* (New York: Viking Press, 1983), 640–650.

6. George H. Gallup, *The Gallup Poll: Public Opinion, 1972–1977* (Wilmington, DE: Scholarly Resources, 1978), 306, 325.
7. Gerald R. Ford, *A Time to Heal* (New York: Harper & Row, 1979), 22.
8. For a more recent examination of this particular topic, see John Lewis Gaddis, *The Cold War: A New History* (New York: Penguin Books, 2005), 172–173.
9. For an in-depth study of one of these covert actions at the height of the Cold War, see Nick Cullather, *Secret History: The CIA's Classified Account of Its Operations in Guatemala, 1952–1954* (Stanford, CA: Stanford Univ. Press, 1999).
10. James Cannon, *Time and Chance: Gerald Ford's Appointment with History* (Ann Arbor: Univ. of Michigan Press, 1998), 397.
11. Pat Towell and David M. Maxfield, "94th Congress Backed Ford's Defense Policy," *Congressional Quarterly* (2 Oct. 1976): 2701. For an important work on the context of the period, see T. Christopher Jespersen, "Kissinger, Ford and Congress: The Very Bitter End in Vietnam," *Pacific Historical Review* 71 (Aug. 2002): 439–473.
12. Gallup, *The Gallup Poll,* 391.
13. J. Edward Lee and H. C. Haynsworth, *Nixon, Ford, and the Abandonment of South Vietnam* (Jefferson, NC: McFarland & Co., 2002), 75–77.
14. Ford, *A Time to Heal,* 128–129.
15. Douglas Brinkley, *Gerald R. Ford* (New York: Henry Holt & Co., 2007), 106–108. For an important study of Ford's divergence from Kissinger on this topic, see Jeremi Suri, *Henry Kissinger and the American Century* (Cambridge: Belknap Press, 2007), 242–246.
16. Brinkley, *Gerald R. Ford,* 100–104.
17. Susan L. Marquis, *Unconventional Warfare: Rebuilding U.S. Special Operations Forces* (Washington, DC: Brookings Institution Press, 1997), 38–39.
18. A detailed description of the incident and rescue operation may be found in Daniel P. Bolger, *Americans at War: An Era of Violent Peace, 1975–1986* (Novato, CA: Presidio Press, 1988), 19–98.
19. Ford, *A Time to Heal,* 284.
20. Cannon, *Time and Chance,* 399.
21. Ford, *A Time to Heal,* 283.
22. Lloyd C. Gardner, "Foreign Policy in IV Acts," *Nation* 221 (19 July 75): 41–45; Roger Morris, "What to Make of Mayaguez," *New Republic* 172 (14 June 75): 9–12.
23. NSDM 348, "U.S. Defense and Military Posture," 20 Jan. 1977, 1, Ford Library, National Security Advisor, NSSM's and NSDM's, 1974–1977, Box 1.
24. Ibid., 4.
25. News Release, "Address by the Honorable James R. Schlesinger, Secretary of Defense, before National Security Industrial Association Dinner,"

Sheraton Park Hotel, Washington, DC, 24 Sept. 1974, Ford Library, Martin R. Hoffman Papers, Subject File, Box 27.

26. "Statement by General George S. Brown, USAF, Chairman, Joint Chiefs of Staff, before the Senate Armed Services Committee," n.d., Ford Library, Edward W. Savage Files, Box 4.
27. "Statement of the Secretary of Defense, James R. Schlesinger, to the Congress on the FY 1976 and Transition Budgets, FY 1977 Authorization Request and FY 1976–1980 Defense Programs," 5 Feb. 1975, 7, Ford Library, Martin R. Hoffman Papers, Subject File, 27.
28. Ibid., 8.
29. Ibid., 44.
30. Ibid., 5; Office of the Assistant Secretary of Defense (Public Affairs), "Address by the Honorable James R. Schlesinger, Secretary of Defense, before the Economic Club of New York, Waldorf-Astoria," New York, 22 Jan. 1975, press release, Ford Library, Edward R. Hoffman Papers, Subject File, Box 27.
31. "Opening Remarks by Secretary of Defense James R. Schlesinger," Pentagon News Conference, 20 Oct. 1975, Martin R. Hoffman Papers, Subject File, Box 27.
32. Towell and Maxfield, "94th Congress Backed Ford's Defense Policy," 2702.
33. Secretary of Defense Donald Rumsfeld, "FY77 U.S. Defense Budget Perspectives," 8 Mar. 1976, Ford Library, Office of the Editorial Staff, Charles McCall Files, Box 57.
34. Towell and Maxfield, "94th Congress Backed Ford's Defense Policy," 2701–2704.
35. Richard Lock-Pullan, *U.S. Intervention Policy and Army Innovation: From Vietnam to Iraq* (New York: Routledge, 2006), 55; Terry Terriff, *The Nixon Administration and the Making of U.S. Nuclear Strategy* (Ithaca, NY: Cornell Univ. Press, 1995), 1–17.
36. See Office of the Assistant Secretary of Defense (Public Affairs), "Remarks by Secretary of Defense James R. Schlesinger at Farewell Ceremony, Pentagon," 10 Nov. 1975, Ford Library, Martin R. Hoffman Papers, Subject File, Box 27.
37. U.S. Arms Control and Disarmament Agency, *World Military Expenditures and Arms Trade, 1963–1973* (Washington: U.S. Arms Control and Disarmament Agency, 1974), 69, Ford Library, Edward W. Savage Files, Box 4.
38. NSDM 293, "US Approach toward Enhancing the Allied Contribution to the Defense of NATO," 3 May 1975, 1, Ford Library, National Security Advisor, NSSM's and NSDM's, 1974–1977, Box 1. See also Diane B. Kunz, *Guns and Butter: America's Cold War Economic Diplomacy* (New York: Free Press, 1997).
39. Gaddis, *The Cold War,* 154–155.

40. Memorandum for Lieutenant General Brent Scowcroft, "Issues Paper on CSCE," 14 Jan. 1975, Ford Library, National Security Advisor, NSC Europe, Canada, and Oceanic Affairs, Staff Files, General Subject Files, Box 44.
41. Thomas J. McCormick, *America's Half-Century: United States Foreign Policy in the Cold War and After,* 2nd ed. (Baltimore: Johns Hopkins Univ. Press, 1995), 238–241.
42. "War Powers Act," 7 Nov. 1973, in *Documents of American Diplomacy: From the Revolution to the Present,* ed. Michael D. Gambone (Westport, CT: Greenwood Press, 2002), 396–401.
43. Memorandum, Henry A. Kissinger to the President, "Foreign Assistance Legislation," n.d., Ford Library, NSA, Presidential Subject File, Box 6.
44. Richard T. Kennedy and Susan B. Schiffer (NSC) to Secretary Kissinger, "Foreign Assistance Legislation," 16 Sept. 1974, memorandum, Ford Library, NSA, Presidential Subject File, Box 6.
45. Henry Kissinger to the President, "Foreign Assistance Requests for FY 1976," 9 Dec. 1974, memorandum, Ford Library, NSA, Presidential Subject File, Box 6.
46. Clinton E. Granger (NSC) to Brent Scowcroft, "FY 76 and 77 Security Assistance," 22 July 1976, memorandum, Ford Library, NSA, Presidential Subject File, 1974–1977, Box 7. For specific details on Israeli security assistance, circa 1974, see NSDM 270, "Military Assistance for Israel," 24 Sept. 1974, Ford Library, National Security Advisor, NSSM's and NSDM's, 1974–1976, Box 1.
47. One well-known study of Central America may be found in Walter LaFeber, *Inevitable Revolutions: The United States in Central America* (New York: W. W. Norton & Co., 1984). For an excellent examination of the Nicaraguan Revolution, see Matilde Zimmermann, *Sandinista: Carlos Fonseca and the Nicaraguan Revolution* (Durham, NC: Duke Univ. Press, 2000).
48. Central Intelligence Agency, Memorandum for the Honorable Zbigniew Brzezinski, Assistant to the President for National Security Affairs, "Communist Intervention Comparison," 15 Aug. 1979, Carter Library, Staff Office Files, National Security Advisor, Staff Materials, Box 3.
49. Hamilton Jordon to President Carter, memorandum, n.d., Carter Library, Staff Offices, Chief of Staff (Jordan), Confidential File, Box 33.
50. Cyrus Vance, *Hard Choices: Critical Years in America's Foreign Policy* (New York: Simon & Schuster, 1983), 27–29. See also Burton I. Kaufman, *The Presidency of James Earl Carter, Jr.* (Lawrence: Univ. Press of Kansas, 1993), 37–50.
51. Kaufman, *The Presidency of James Earl Carter, Jr.*, 38.
52. Jimmy Carter, *Keeping Faith: Memoirs of a President* (New York: Bantam Books, 1982), 144.

53. Zbigniew Brzezinski to the President, "Your 8:15 A.M. Meeting with Key Congressmen Responsible for Foreign Assistance Legislation," 8 Mar. 1977, memorandum, Carter Library, White House Central File, Subject File, Box 25.
54. Zbigniew Brzezinski, *Power and Principle: Memoirs of the National Security Advisor, 1977–1981* (New York: Farrar, Strauss & Giroux, 1985), 53–55.
55. Vance, *Hard Choices,* 45, 71–75.
56. Zbigniew Brzezinski to Mondale and Muskie (State), "The Carter Transformation of Our Strategic Doctrine," 2 Sept. 1980, memorandum, Carter Library, Mondale Papers, Box 1.
57. Carter, *Keeping Faith,* 222–223.
58. Ibid., 80–83.
59. Ibid., 212.
60. In a memo to the NSC, one White House official claimed that the Navy "suffers from schizophrenia induced by the SSBN/SLBM fleet, the surface fleet, the carrier-based air fleet, and the amphibian appendage of ground forces, the Marine Corps." See William E. Odom (White House) to Zbigniew Brzezinski, "Talking Points for Your Meeting with Ex-Secretaries of the Navy," 19 May 1980, memorandum, Carter Library, Staff Office Files, National Security Advisor, General Odom File, Box 2.
61. Office of the White House Press Secretary, "Statement by the President," 1 Feb. 1978, Carter Library, Staff Office Files, National Security Advisor, Subject File, Box 5.
62. George C. Wilson, "Joint Chiefs of Staff Break with Carter on Budget Planning for Defense Needs," *Washington Post,* 30 May 1980, A1.
63. Ibid.; George C. Wilson, "Arms Readiness: Glass Half Empty, Half Full," *Washington Post,* 1 Nov. 1980, A2.
64. Beth Bailey, *America's Army: Making the All-Volunteer Force* (Cambridge, MA: Belknap Press of Harvard Univ. Press, 2009), 88–129.
65. Central Intelligence Agency, Memorandum of the Special Coordination Committee, "Secretary of Defense's Memorandum, 17 November 1980," 3 Dec. 1980, Carter Library, Staff Office Files, National Security Advisor, Odom File, Box 33.
66. George C. Wilson, "Outlook Grim in a War for Mideast Oil," *Washington Post,* 28 Oct. 1980, A1.
67. Jeffrey Record, *The Rapid Deployment Force and U.S. Military Intervention in the Persian Gulf: Special Report* (Cambridge, MA: Institute for Foreign Policy Analysis, Feb. 1981), 25.
68. Ibid., 2.

69. William E. Odom to Zbigniew Brzezinski, "Enhancement of Our Intervention Capability," 11 Jan. 1980, memorandum, Carter Library, Staff Office Files, National Security Advisor, Subject File, Box 51.
70. "Carter Doctrine," 23 Jan. 1980, in *Documents of American Diplomacy,* ed. Michael D. Gambone (Westport, CT: Greenwood, 2002), 419–421.
71. Secretary of Defense (Brown) to the Secretary of State (Muskie), "FY 82 Security Assistance Program," 22 July 1980, memorandum, Carter Library, Brzezinski Collection, Box 23.
72. Zbigniew Brzezinski to the President, "A Long-Term Strategy for Coping with the Consequences of the Soviet Action in Afghanistan," 9 Jan. 1980, memorandum, Carter Library, National Security Affairs, Country File, Box 1.
73. Zbigniew Brzezinski to the President, "Reflections on Soviet Intervention in Afghanistan," 26 Dec. 1979, 3, memorandum, Carter Library, Brzezinski Collection, Geographic File, Box 17. See also Michael Oksenberg (NSC) to Zbigniew Brzezinski, "Afghanistan," 28 Dec. 1979, memorandum, Carter Library, National Security Affairs, Country File, Box 1.
74. Zbigniew Brzezinski to the President, "Unity and the New Foreign Policy Team," 1 May 1980, memorandum, Carter Library, Brzezinski Collection, Box 23.
75. Richard Lock-Pullen, "'An Inward Looking Time': The United States Army, 1973–1976," *Journal of Military History* 67 (Apr. 2003): 486.
76. Roger J. Spiller, "In the Shadow of the Dragon: Doctrine and the U.S. Army after Vietnam," *RUSI Journal* 142 (Dec. 1997): 43.
77. Maurice Matloff, ed., *American Military History* (Washington, DC: Center of Military History, 1973), 616.
78. Frederick W. Kagan, *Finding the Target: The Transformation of American Military Policy* (New York: Encounter Books, 2006), 20–21.
79. Harry G. Summers Jr., *On Strategy: A Critical Analysis of the Vietnam War* (New York: Dell, 1982), 26–27.
80. For an interesting counterpoint to this particular theory, see John A. Nagl, *Learning to Eat Soup with a Knife: Counterinsurgency Lessons from Malaya and Vietnam,* 2nd ed. (Chicago: Univ. of Chicago Press, 2005), 27–28, 205–208. See also Max Boot, *The Savage Wars of Peace: Small Wars and the Rise of American Power* (New York: Basic Books, 2002).
81. Summers, *On Strategy,* 21.
82. Sheehan, *A Bright Shining Lie,* 285; Marquis, *Unconventional Warfare,* 34.
83. Brian McAllister Linn, *The Echo of Battle: The Army's Way of War* (Cambridge, MA: Harvard Univ. Press, 2007), 193–195.
84. George Herring, *America's Longest War,* 2nd ed. (New York: Alfred A. Knopf, 1986), 273.

85. Gaddis, *The Cold War,* 149–155.
86. Linn, *The Echo of Battle,* 197.
87. Lock-Pullen, "'An Inward Looking Time,'" 490; A. J. Bacevich, "Old Myths, New Myths: Renewing American Military Thought," *Parameters* 18 (1988): 15–25.
88. Lock-Pullan, *U.S. Intervention Policy and Army Innovation,* 48–49.
89. William C. Westmoreland, *A Soldier Reports* (New York: Dell, 1980), 565.
90. Kagan, *Finding the Target,* 14; William H. Chafe, *The Unfinished Journey: America Since World War II,* 4th ed. (New York: Oxford Univ. Press, 1999), 445–450; James T. Patterson, *Grand Expectations: The United States, 1945–1974* (New York: Oxford Univ. Press, 1996), 783–786.
91. Dunnigan and Macedonia, *Getting It Right,* 146.
92. Ibid., 106–107.
93. James Kitfield, *Prodigal Soldiers: How a Generation of Officers Born of Vietnam Revolutionized the American Style of War* (New York: Simon & Schuster, 1995), 125–131; Powell, *My American Journey,* 182–204.
94. Lock-Pullan, *U.S. Intervention Policy and Army Innovation,* 53–54.
95. Dunnigan and Macedonia, *Getting It Right,* 97–98.
96. McAllister Linn, *The Echo of Battle,* 197.
97. Colin Powell, *A Soldier's Way,* 155–156. Lock-Pullan, *U.S. Intervention Policy and Army Innovation,* 57.
98. William L. Hauser, "Armies and Society," *Military Review* 52 (July 1974): 4; John H. Moellering, "Future Civil-Military Relations: The Army Turns Inward?" *Military Review* 53 (July 1973): 72–80. See also Zeb B. Bradford and Frederic J. Brown, *The United States Army in Transition* (Beverley Hills, CA: Sage Publications, 1973), 169–213. For a more recent study, see Orrin Schwab, *A Clash of Cultures: Civil-Military Relations during the Vietnam War* (Westport, CT: Praeger Security Studies, 2006), 143–160.
99. David H. Petraeus, "Lessons of History and Lessons of Vietnam," *Parameters* 16 (Autumn 1986): 43–53. See also David H. Petraeus, "Light Infantry in Europe: Strategic Flexibility and Conventional Deterrence," *Military Review* 64 (Dec. 1984): 33–55.
100. Lock-Pullan, *U.S. Intervention Policy and Army Innovation,* 61–64.
101. Linn, *The Echo of Battle,* 201.
102. Ibid., 203.
103. Ibid., 208–209.
104. Gen. George S. Brown, "U.S. General Purpose Forces: A Need for Modernization," *Commanders Digest* 19 (27 May 1976), 2–3, Ford Library, Office of the Editorial Staff, Charles McCall Files, Box 57.
105. Rick Atkinson, *Crusade: The Untold Story of the Persian Gulf* (New York: Houghton Mifflin Co., 1993), 254–255.
106. Samuel C. Sarkesian, *The New Battlefield* (Westport, CT: Greenwood Publications, 1987), 87. See also Dunnigan and Macedonia, *Getting It Right,* 93.

107. William E. Colby and Peter Forbath, *Honorable Men: My Life in the CIA* (New York: Simon & Schuster, 1978), 340–346, 389–452; Rhodri Jeffreys-Jones, *The CIA and American Democracy* (New Haven, CT: Yale Univ. Press, 1989), 191–193; Frank J. Smist, *Congress Oversees the United States Intelligence Community, 1947–1989* (Knoxville: Univ. of Tennessee Press, 1990), 25–81.

108. William E. Colby (CIA) to Melvin Price (Chairman, House Committee on Armed Services), n.d., Ford Library, White House Central File, Box 5.

109. Jack Marsh (White House) to Henry A. Kissinger, "Revised Executive Order Establishing Restrictions on Intelligence Agencies," 16 Oct. 1975, memorandum, Ford Library, White House Central File, Box 5.

110. Michael McClintock, *Instruments of Statecraft: U.S. Guerrilla Warfare, Counter-Insurgency, Counter-Terrorism, 1940–1990* (New York: Pantheon Books, 1992), 314.

111. Lock-Pullan, *US Intervention Policy and Army Innovation,* 104–105. See also Richard Duncan Downie, *Learning from Conflict: The U.S. Military in Vietnam, El Salvador, and the Drug War* (Westport, CT: Praeger, 1998).

112. Thomas K. Adams, *U.S. Special Operations Forces in Action: The Challenge of Unconventional War* (Portland, OR: Frank Cass, 1998), 157.

113. Ibid., 156.

114. Marquis, *Unconventional Warfare,* 42.

115. David Tucker and Christopher J. Lamb, *United States Special Operations Forces* (New York: Columbia Univ. Press, 2007), 94.

116. Adams, *U.S. Special Forces in Action,* 160.

117. Charlie Beckwith, *Delta Force* (New York: Harcourt Brace Jovanovich, 1983), 94–104.

118. Arthur T. Hadley, *The Straw Giant: America's Armed Forces: Triumphs and Failures* (New York: Avon Books, 1987), 3–28.

119. Charles G. Cogan, "Desert One and Its Disorders," *Journal of Military History* 67 (Jan. 2003): 201–216.

120. Beckwith, *Delta Force,* 276–280. A relation of the operation also appears in Richard Marcinko, *Rogue Warrior* (New York: Pocket Books, 1992), 195–199.

121. Richard Halloran, "Mission End: Blazing Aircraft and Brave Men," *New York Times,* 27 Apr. 1980, A1.

122. Douglas E. Kneeland, "Reagan Says Carter Acted Too Late with Iran Mission," *New York Times,* 1 May 1980, B10; Bernard Nossiter, "Waldheim Proposes Reviving Inquiry Panel on Iran," *New York Times,* 26 Apr. 1980, 10.

123. A specific breach of operational security had occurred when Marine pilots training with the rescue force broke security in early 1980. The Pentagon was actively considering canceling the mission because of this lapse. See Hadley, *Straw Giant,* 10–13.

124. "Pentagon Reports on Rescue Effort, But Senate Is Denied Some Details," *New York Times,* 8 May 1980, A14.

125. Bernard Gwertzman, "U.S. Attempt to Rescue Iran Hostages Fails," *New York Times,* 25 Apr. 1980, A1.

126. U.S. Joint Chiefs of Staff, Special Operations Review Group, *Rescue Mission Report* (Washington, DC: Joint Chiefs of Staff, Aug. 1980), 57.

127. Ibid., 58.

128. John M. Collins, *Special Operations Forces: An Assessment* (Washington: National Defense Univ. Press, 1994).

129. There is a large body of scholarship addressing women in modern military service. See David J. Armor, "Race and Gender in the U.S. Military," *Armed Forces and Society* 23 (Fall 1996): 7–27; Cynthia Nantais and Martha F. Lee, "Women in the United States Military: Protectors or Protected? The Case of Prisoner of War Melissa Rathburn-Nealy," *Journal of Gender Studies* 8 (July 1999): 181–191; Anna Simmons, "Women in Combat: It's Still a Bad Idea," *Parameters* 31 (Summer 2001): 89–100; Elizabeth G. Book, "Military Women: 200,000 and Counting," *National Defense* 86 (Oct. 2001): 14–15; Holly Yeager, "Soldiering Ahead," *Wilson Quarterly* 31 (Summer 2007): 54–62.

130. James R. Schlesinger, "A Testing Time for America," *Fortune* (Feb. 1976): 77.

131. Peter G. Boyle, *Eisenhower* (New York: Pearson Longman, 2005), 36–46. The term is attributed to Eisenhower's defense secretary, Charlie Wilson.

3. Low-Intensity War in the Eighties

1. Ronald Reagan, "Foreign Affairs: The Need for Leadership," *Vital Speeches of the Day* 44 (1 May 1978): 422.
2. See Condoleezza Rice, "U.S.-Soviet Relations," in *Looking Back on the Reagan Presidency,* ed., Larry Berman (Baltimore: Johns Hopkins Univ. Press, 1990), 71–89.
3. Frank Ninkovich, *The Wilsonian Century: U.S. Foreign Policy since 1900* (Chicago: Univ. of Chicago Press, 1999), 258–264.
4. Alexander L. George and Eric K. Stern, "Harnessing Conflict in Foreign Policy Making: From Devil's to Multiple Advocacy," *Presidential Studies Quarterly* 32 (Sept. 2002): 484–508.
5. Richard Lock-Pullan, "How to Rethink War: Conceptual Innovation and AirLand Battle Doctrine," *Journal of Strategic Studies* 28 (Aug. 2005): 696.
6. See T. Christopher Jespers, "Analogies at War: Vietnam, the Bush Administration's War in Iraq, and the Search for a Usable Past," *Pacific Historical Review* 74 (Aug. 2005): 411–426; "Interchange: Legacies of the Vietnam War," *Journal of American History* 93 (Sept. 2006): 452–490.

7. Robert Timberg, *The Nightingale's Song* (New York: Simon & Schuster, 1995), 14–19.
8. *Public Papers of the Presidents of the United States, Ronald Reagan, 1983* (Washington, DC: Government Printing Office, 1984), 362–364.
9. Edmund Morris, *Dutch* (New York: Random House, 1999), 434–438.
10. Bernard Gwertzman, "First Principles: There May Be More to Foreign Policy Than Stopping the Soviet," *New York Times*, 26 Apr. 1981, E1.
11. George Schultz, *Turmoil and Triumph: My Years as Secretary of State* (New York: Charles Scribner's Sons, 1993), 649–651.
12. Dale R. Herspring, *The Pentagon and the Presidency: Civil-Military Relations From FDR to George Bush* (Lawrence: Univ. Press of Kansas, 2005), 269–270. See also Caspar W. Weinberger, *Into the Arena: A Memoir of the 20th Century* (Washington, DC: Regnery, 2001), 267–286. Schultz's accord with Weinberger was short-lived. See Schultz, *Turmoil and Triumph*, 84, 103.
13. John Lewis Gaddis, *The United States and the End of the Cold War: Implications, Reconsiderations, Provocations* (New York: Oxford Univ. Press, 1992), 121–122.
14. Jeane Kirkpatrick, "Dictatorships and Double Standards," *Commentary* 68 (Nov. 1979): 34–45.
15. *Public Papers of the Presidents of the United States, Ronald Reagan, 1985* (Washington, DC: Government Printing Office, 1988), 135.
16. Thomas K. Adams, *U.S. Special Operations Forces in Action: The Challenge of Unconventional Warfare* (Portland, OR: Frank Cass, 1998), 175.
17. Jeane J. Kirkpatrick, "Anti-Communist Insurgency and American Policy," *National Interest* 1 (Fall 1985): 555.
18. NSDD-32, "U.S. National Security Strategy," 20 May 1982, 1, Ronald Reagan Library, NSDD File.
19. See, for example, "Report by the Comptroller General of the United States: U.S. Military Aid to El Salvador and Honduras," 22 Aug. 1985, Ronald Reagan Library, White House Staff & Office, Oliver L. North Files, Box 2.
20. NSDD-277, "National Policy and Strategy for Low Intensity Conflict," 4. Ronald Reagan Library, NSDD File.
21. Paul Kennedy, *The Rise and Fall of Great Powers: Economic Change and Military Conflict from 1500 to 2000* (New York: Vintage Books, 1987), xv–xxv. For more recent examples, see Paul Kennedy, "Empire without 'Overstretch,'" *Wilson Quarterly* 26 (Summer 2002): 62–63; Paul Kennedy, "The Next American Century?" *World Policy Journal* 16 (Spring 1999): 52–58.
22. NSDD-32, "U.S. National Security Strategy," 3, Ronald Reagan Library, NSDD File.
23. Central Intelligence Agency, National Foreign Assessment Center, "Cuba-Nicaragua: Support for Central American Revolutionaries, Nicaragua:

Export of the Revolution—The First Six Months," 15 Jan. 1980, Jimmy Carter Library (hereafter JCL), NSA, Country File, Box 57.

24. White House, Office of the Press Secretary, "Address by the President to the Nation," 16 Mar. 1986, Ronald Reagan Library, WHORM, Subject File, Foreign Operations, Mutual Security, #582444.
25. Central Intelligence Agency, "Analysis of Major Roger Miranda's Documents and Debriefings," n.d., Ronald Reagan Library, White House Staff and Office Files, Robert S. Pastorino Files, Box 92376. The State Department contested these estimates during the Carter administration. See Warren Christopher to the President, "Determination Necessary to Permit Immediate Assistance to Nicaragua, in Particular Certification That the Government of Nicaragua Is Not Supporting Terrorist Activities," 25 Aug. 1980, memorandum, JCL, Staff Office Files, National Security Affairs, Subject File, Box 50.
26. Alfonso Sapia-Bosch to William P. Clark, "Nicaraguan Subversion in Central America, an Update since May 1982," memorandum, Ronald Reagan Library White Staff and Office Files, Executive Secretariat, NSC, Country File, Latin America, Box 32.
27. Marvin E. Gettleman, Patrick Lacefield, Louis Menashe, et al., eds., *El Salvador: Central America in the Cold War* (New York: Grove Press, 1981), 6–54; John H. Coatsworth, *Central America and the United States: The Clients and the Colossus* (New York: Twayne, 1994), 163–206; John Lindsay-Poland, *Emperors in the Jungle: The Hidden History of the U.S. in Panama* (Durham, NC: Duke Univ. Press, 2003), 1–9, 195–201. For a recent defense of Reagan-era policy, see Timothy C. Brown, *The Real Contra War: Highlander Peasant Resistance in Nicaragua* (Norman: Univ. of Oklahoma Press, 2001).
28. White House to George P. Schultz (State), Caspar W. Weinberger (Defense), William J. Casey (CIA), and Gen. John W. Vessey (JCS), "Central America," memorandum, n.d., Ronald Reagan Library, White House Staff and Office, 1981–1989, William P. Clark Files, Box 1.
29. NSDD-17, "National Security Decision Directive on Cuba and Central America," 4 Jan. 1982, Ronald Reagan Library, NSDD File.
30. U.S. General Accounting Office, *U.S. Military Aid to El Salvador and Honduras,* GAO/C-NSIAD-85–7 (Washington, DC: GAO, 22 Aug. 1985), ii, Ronald Reagan Library, White House Staff and Office Files, Oliver L. North File, Box 2.
31. U.S. Dept. of the Army, Army Intelligence and Security Command, Army Intelligence and Threat Analysis Center, *Army Intelligence Survey: El Salvador* 3 (Sept. 1983): 1-6, 1-7, Ronald Reagan Library, White House Staff Offices, Oliver North File, Box 78.
32. William L. Stearman (NSC) to William P. Clark, "Reinventing the

Wheel in El Salvador," 23 July 1982, memorandum, Ronald Reagan Library, White Staff Offices, Oliver L. North Files, Box 128.

33. Ibid.

34. Evidence of this resistance is abundant. See, for example, Chauncey A. Alexander (chairman, Council on Hemispheric Affairs) to Ronald Reagan, 6 May 1981, memorandum; Rep. Richard L. Ottinger (D-NY) to Ronald Reagan, 2 Dec. 1981; Sen. Robert C. Byrd (D-WV) and Rep. Thomas P. O'Neill Jr. (D-MA) to Ronald Reagan, 28 July 1983, Ronald Reagan Library, WHORM Subject File, Foreign Operations, Mutual Security, #051204, #024720, #157590.

35. "The Speaker Speaks on Nicaragua," n.d., Ronald Reagan Library, WHORM Subject File, Foreign Operations, Mutual Security, #582444.

36. GAO, *U.S. Military Aid to El Salvador and Honduras,* 37–38.

37. For a recent critique, see Clara Nieto, *Masters of War: Latin America and U.S. Aggression from the Cuban Revolution through the Clinton Years* (New York: Seven Stories Press, 2003), 312–398. For a contemporary study of the Reagan years, see Walter LaFeber, *Inevitable Revolutions: The United States in Central America* (New York: W. W. Norton & Co., 1984), 271–293.

38. Edward S. Herman and Frank Brodhead, *Demonstration Elections: U.S. Staged Elections in the Dominican Republic, Vietnam, and El Salvador* (Boston: South End Press, 1984), 104–112.

39. James Dunkerely, *Power in the Isthmus: A Political History of Modern Central America* (New York: Verso, 1988), 376–377.

40. Coatsworth, *Central America and the United States,* 169–176; Christopher J. Bailey, "President Reagan, the U.S. Senate, and American Policy, 1981–1986," *Journal of American Studies* 21 (Aug. 1987): 167–181.

41. William P. Clark from Roger Fontaine (NSC), "Sec. Weinberger Recommends US Trainers Carry M-16s in El Salvador," 13 Mar. 1982, memorandum, Ronald Reagan Library, White House Staff and Office File, Executive Secretariat, NSC, Country File, Latin America, Box 29. See also Neil C. Livingstone, "Fighting Terrorism and 'Dirty Little Wars,'" *Air University Review* 35 (Mar./Apr. 1984): 4–16.

42. GAO, *U.S. Military Aid to El Salvador and Honduras,* 37.

43. NSDD-17 notes the decision to "provide military training for indigenous units and leaders both in and out of country."

44. Public Law 97–377, 21 Dec. 1982, Digital National Security Archives (hereafter DNSA).

45. Timberg, *Nightingale's Song,* 411–452.

46. See President's Special Review Board, *Report of the President's Special Review Board* (Washington, DC: Government Printing Office, 1987); *Report of the Congressional Committees Investigating the Iran-Contra Affair* (Washington, DC: Government Printing Office, 1987).

47. Peter Kornbluh, "The Iran-Contra Scandal: A Postmortem," *World Policy Journal* 5 (Winter 1987/1988): 129–150. See also John P. Burke, "The Neutral/Honest Broker Role in Foreign Policy Decision Making: A Reassessment," *Presidential Studies Quarterly* 35 (June 2005): 229–258; Scott R. Meinke and William D. Anderson, "Influencing from Impaired Administrations: Presidents, White House Scandals, and Legislative Leadership," *Legislative Studies Quarterly* 26 (Nov. 2001): 639–659.
48. Robert M. Kimmitt (Executive Secretary, NSC), "Lebanon Report to Congress," 14 Dec. 1983, George Bush Library, National Security Affairs, Donald P. Gregg Files, Country File, Box 1.
49. Colin L. Powell, *My American Journey* (New York: Ballantine Books, 1995), 291–292.
50. "The Uses of Military Power," remarks prepared for delivery by the Honorable Caspar W. Weinberger, Secretary of Defense, to the National Press Club, Washington, DC, 28 Nov. 1984, http://www.pbs.org. See also Weinberger, *Into the Arena,* 308–313.
51. Ninkovitch, *The Wilsonian Century,* 196–203; Stanley Karnow, *Vietnam: A History* (New York: Viking Press, 1983), 196–197.
52. John Lewis Gaddis, *Strategies of Containment: A Critical Appraisal of Postwar American National Security Policy* (New York: Oxford Univ. Press, 1982), 225–227. For a more specific study of the "McNamara Line" and Vietnam, see Paul Dickson, *The Electronic Battlefield* (London: Marion Boyars, 1976), 55–83.
53. Brian McAllister Linn, *The Echo of Battle: The Army's Way of War* (Cambridge, MA: Harvard Univ. Press, 2007), 199.
54. Adams, *U.S. Special Operations Forces in Action,* 173.
55. *Report by the Comptroller General of the United States,* 41.
56. NSDD-100, "Enhanced U.S. Military Activity and Assistance for the Central American Region," 28 July 1983, Ronald Reagan Library, NSDD Files.
57. Stockholm International Peace Research Institute, *SIPRI Yearbook, 1990: World Armaments and Disarmament* (New York: Oxford Univ. Press, 1990), 147. Figures are in 1990 dollars.
58. Ibid., 149.
59. Herspring, *The Pentagon and the Presidency,* 277.
60. Wayne A. Downing, "Firepower, Attrition, Maneuver—US Army Operations Doctrine: A Challenge for the 1980s and Beyond," *Military Review* 77 (1997): 144–145.
61. Ibid., 146. For a recent excellent study, see Lock-Pullan, "How to Rethink War," 683. See also John L. Romjue, *American Army Doctrine for the Post-Cold War* (Washington, DC: Center of Military History, 1997), 16–21.
62. McAllister Linn, *The Echo of Battle,* 215–216; James F. Dunnigan and Raymond M. Macedonia, *Getting It Right: American Military Reforms after*

Vietnam to the Persian Gulf and Beyond (New York: William Morrow & Co., 1993), 178–185. The author trained at the JRTC in November 1987 as part of the 3/504 Parachute Infantry Regiment.

63. M. A. Hadley, "Special Operations and the AirLand Battle," *Military Review* (Sept. 1985): 73–83.
64. Dunnigan and Macedonia, *Getting It Right,* 94.
65. Robert H. Kupperman, Debra van Opstal, and David Williamson, "Terror, the Strategic Tool: Response and Control," *Annals of the American Academy of Political and Social Science* 463 (Sept. 1982): 24–38; See also Sam C. Sarkesian, *The New Battlefield: The United States and Unconventional Conflicts* (New York: Greenwood Press, 1986).
66. Sarkesian, *The New Battlefield,* 217.
67. The extent of this influence was and is open to debate. See Cole Blasier, *The Hovering Giant: U.S. Responses to Revolutionary Change in Latin America* (Pittsburgh: Univ. of Pittsburgh Press, 1985).
68. Sam C. Sarkesian, *America's Forgotten Wars: The Counterrevolutionary Past and Lessons for the Future* (Westport, CT: Greenwood Press, 1984), 233–244.
69. Sarkesian, *The New Battlefield,* 233.
70. Peter Kornbluh, "Nicaragua: U.S. Proinsurgency Warfare Against the Sandinistas," in *Low-Intensity Warfare: Counterinsurgency, Proinsurgency, and Antiterrorism in the Eighties,* eds., Michaeld T. Klare and Peter Kornbluh (New York: Pantheon Books, 1988), 136–157.
71. NSC, *Report to the Congress on U.S. Capabilities to Engage in Low Intensity Conflict and Conduct Special Operations* (19 Oct. 1987), iii, DNSA.
72. Michael McClintock, *Instruments of Statecraft: U.S. Guerrilla Warfare, Counter-Insurgency, Counter-Terrorism, 1940–1990* (New York: Pantheon Books, 1992), 351.
73. Charles M. Simpson, *Inside the Green Berets: The First Thirty Years* (San Francisco: Presidio Press, 1983), 219.
74. Ronald H. Cole, *Operation Urgent Fury: The Planning and Execution of Joint Operations in Grenada, 12 October—2 November 1983* (Washington, DC: Joint History Office, Office of the Chairman of the Joint Chiefs of Staff, 1997), 4.
75. Ibid., 43–44; Ronald H. Cole, *Operation Just Cause: The Planning and Execution of Joint Operations in Panama, February 1988—January 1990* (Washington, DC: Joint History Office, Office of the Chairman of the Joint Chiefs of Staff, 1995), 38.
76. Cole, *Operation Just Cause,* 71.
77. P. J. Budahn, " Senate Passes Plan for Reorganizing Special Operations," *Army Times* (19 Aug. 1986): 4.
78. Evan Thomas, "A Warrior Elite for the Dirty Jobs," *Time* (13 Jan. 1986): 16.

79. Ibid.

80. Adams, *U.S. Special Operations Forces in Action,* 196–197.

81. James A. Russell, "SOF: They Can't Get There from Here," *Military Logistics Forum* 2 (Apr. 1986): 41.

82. Adams, *U.S. Special Operations Forces in Action,* 211–212.

83. Ibid., 214–217; USSOCOM, *Special Operations in Operation Earnest Will* (MacDill Air Force Base, FL: USSOCM History Office, 1995); William J. Crowe, *The Line of Fire: From Washington to the Gulf, the Politics and Battles of the New Military* (New York: Simon & Schuster, 1993), 187–211.

84. For a detailed study of the entire operation, see John W. Partin, *Special Operations Forces in Operation Earnest Will / Prime Chance I* (MacDill Air Force Base, FL: USSOCOM, 1998).

85. Sarkesian, *The New Battlefield,* 200–202.

86. NSDD-99, "United States Security Strategy for the Near East and South Asia," 12 July 1983; NSDD-114, *U.S. Policy toward the Iran-Iraq War,* 26 Nov. 1983, Ronald Reagan Library, NSDD Files.

87. Ibid., 2.

88. Stephen Coll, *Ghost Wars: The Secret History of the CIA Afghanistan, and Bin Laden, from the Soviet Invasion to September 10, 2001* (New York: Penguin Books, 2004), 42–43, 46. See also Robert Gates, *From the Shadows: The Ultimate Insider's Story of Five Presidents and How They Won the Cold War* (New York: Simon & Schuster, 2007), 143–149.

89. John Prados, "Notes on the CIA's Secret War in Afghanistan," *Journal of American History* 89 (Sept. 2002): 467.

90. Zbigniew Brzezinski to the President, "A Long-Term Strategy for Coping with the Consequences of the Soviet Action in Afghanistan," 2 Jan. 1980, memorandum; Michael Oksenberg (NSC) to Brzezinski, "Afghanistan," 28 Dec. 1979, memorandum, JCL, National Security Advisor Country File, Box 1; Zbigniew Brzezinski to the President, "Reflections on Soviet Intervention in Afghanistan," 26 Dec. 1979, memorandum, JCL, Brzezinski Papers, Box 17.

91. Larry P. Goodson, *Afghanistan's Endless War: State Failure, Regional Politics, and the Rise of the Taliban* (Seattle: Univ. of Washington Press, 2001), 54–58. Specific American plans are available through the Cold War International History Project and the Digital National Security Archive.

92. Coll, *Ghost Wars,* 58; Mohammad Yousaf and Mark Adkin, *The Bear Trap: Afghanistan's Untold Story* (London: Leo Cooper, 1992), 78–96.

93. Jose Desloge, "Reagan Meets with Freedom Fighters," *Free Afghanistan Report* no. 5 (May 1983): 1, Ronald Reagan Library, WHORM Alpha File, Box 9. See also George Crile, *Charlie Wilson's War: The Extraordinary Story of the Largest Covert Operation in History* (New York: Atlantic Monthly Press, 2003), 509–510.

94. Coll, *Ghost Wars,* 65–66.

95. NSC, "Foreign Intelligence and National Security Policy Developments, October–December 1983," 24, Ronald Reagan Library, White House Staff and Office Files, Box 91129. See also Goodson, *Afghanistan's Endless War,* 58–61.
96. Prados, "Notes on the CIA's Secret War in Afghanistan," 468; Yousaf and Adkin, *The Bear Trap,* 105; Goodson, *Afghanistan's Endless War,* 61.
97. Central Intelligence Agency, Foreign Assessment Center, "The Afghan Insurgents and Pakistan: Problems for Islamabad and Moscow," Jan. 1980, JCL, Staff Office Files, National Security Advisor, General Odom File, Box 1.
98. Crile, *Charlie Wilson's War,* 307–323.
99. Charles G. Cogan, "Partners in Time: The CIA and Afghanistan since 1979," *World Policy Journal* 10 (Summer 1993): 76–77; Gates, *From the Shadows,* 348–350.
100. Cogan, "Partners in Time," 81.
101. Robert G. Wirsing, "In India's Lengthening Shadow: The U.S.-Pakistan Strategic Alliance and the War in Afghanistan," *Asian Affairs* 34 (Fall 2007): 151–172; Brahma Chellaney, "Lessons from Fighting Terrorism in Southern Asia," in *The Use of Force: Military Power and International Politics,* 6th ed., ed. Robert J. Art and Kenneth N. Waltz (New York: Rowman & Littlefield, 2004), 459; Shakyi Bhatt, "State Terrorism vs. Jihad in Kashmir," *Journal of Contemporary Asia* 33 (2003): 220–223; Jaideep Saikia, "The ISI Reaches East: Anatomy of a Conspiracy," *Studies in Conflict and Terrorism* 25 (2002): 185–197.
102. Prados, "Notes on the CIA's Secret War in Afghanistan," 471.
103. Michael Klare, "The Kalashnikov Age," *Bulletin of the Atomic Scientists* 55 (Jan./Feb. 1999): 18–23.
104. Gaddis, *The United States and the End of the Cold War,* 119, 126–130.
105. Richard L. Millett, "The Aftermath of Intervention: Panama, 1990," *Journal of Interamerican Studies and World Affairs* 32 (Spring 1990): 4.
106. Jorge I. Dominguez, "Insurgency in Latin America and the Common Defense," *Political Science Quarterly* 101 (1986): 807–823.
107. Brown, *The Real Contra War,* 199–208.
108. William M. Leogrande, "From Reagan to Bush: The Transition in US Policy towards Central America," *Journal of Latin American Studies* 22 (Oct. 1990): 595–621.

4. The First Gulf War and the New World Order

1. John Lewis Gaddis, *The Cold War: A New History* (New York: Penguin Books, 2005), 238.
2. Rupert Smith, *The Utility of Force: The Art of War in the Modern World* (New York: Alfred A. Knopf, 2007), 5–8.

3. Brent Scowcroft, "Why We Didn't Remove Saddam," *Time*, 2 Mar. 1998, 31.
4. Howard Jones, *Crucible of Power: A History of American Foreign Relations From 1897*, 2nd ed. (New York: Rowman & Littlefield, 2008), 525–532.
5. Gaddis, *The Cold War*, 255. The president repeated this theme throughout his trip. See George H. W. Bush, "Future United States and Soviet Relations: Overcome Distrust to Build Lasting Peace," *Vital Speeches of the Day* 57 (1 Sept. 1991): 674–676.
6. Gaddis, *The Cold War*, 255–256.
7. William Safire, "Bush at the U.N.," *New York Times*, 16 Sept. 1991, 19.
8. William J. Clinton, *My Life* (New York: Alfred A. Knopf, 2004), 425.
9. For examples of the contemporary theoretical debate, see Alexander Wendt, "Constructing International Politics," *International Security* 20 (Summer 1995): 71–81, and John J. Mearsheimer, "Back to the Future: Instability in Europe after the Cold War," *International Security* 15 (Summer 1990): 5–56.
10. Paul N. Stockton, "The New Game on the Hill: The Politics of Arms Control and Strategic Force Modernization," *International Security* 16 (Autumn 1991): 146–170; Alex Mintz and Chi Huang, "Defense Expenditures, Economic Growth, and the 'Peace Dividend,'" *American Political Science Review* 84 (Dec. 1990): 1283–1293; J. Davidson Alexander, "Military Conversion Policies in the USA: 1940s and 1990s," *Journal of Peace Research* 31 (Feb. 1994): 19–33; James H. Lebovic, "Riding Waves or Making Waves? The Services and the U.S. Defense Budget, 1981–1993," *American Political Science Review* 88 (Dec. 1994): 839–852; Alex Mintz and Randolph T. Stevenson, "Defense Expenditures, Economic Growth, and the 'Peace Dividend': A Longitudinal Analysis of 103 Countries," *Journal of Conflict Resolution* 39 (June 1995): 283–305.
11. P. Fessler, "Armed Services Panels Begin to Ponder Spending Plans," *Congressional Quarterly Weekly Report* 50 (22 Feb. 1992): 417; R. Theodore Roth, "The Impact of Decreased Defense Spending on Employment in the United States," *Armed Forces and Society* 18 (Spring 1992): 383–405; Michael D. Ward and David R. Davis, "Sizing up the Peace Dividend: Economic Growth and Military Spending in the United States, 1948–1996," *American Political Science Review* 86 (Sept. 1992): 748–755.
12. G. Hager, "What to Do with Defense Savings?" *Congressional Quarterly Weekly Report* 50 (7 Mar. 1992): 524. See also Eugene R. Wittkopf and James M. McCormick, "Congress, the President, and the End of the Cold War: Has Anything Changed?" *Journal of Conflict Resolution* 42 (Aug. 1998): 440–466.
13. Stockholm International Peace Research Institute, *SIPRI Yearbook, 1996: Armaments, Disarmament and International Security* (New York: Oxford Univ. Press, 1996), 359. Figures are in 1996 dollars.

14. Samantha Power, *"A Problem from Hell": America and the Age of Genocide* (New York: Basic Books, 2002), 454–458. Similar limits appeared during the Kosovo intervention in 1999. See also Bruce W. Jentleson and Rebecca L. Britton, "Still Pretty Prudent: Post-Cold War American Public Opinion on the Use of Military Force," *Journal of Conflict Resolution* 42 (Aug. 1998): 395–417. See also Serge Schemann, "Not Taking Losses Is One Thing: Winning Is Another," *New York Times,* 3 Jan. 1999, 1, 5; Larry M. Bartels, "The American Public's Defense Spending Preferences in the Post-Cold War," *Public Opinion Quarterly* 58 (Winter 1994): 479–508; Bruce Russett, Thomas Hartley, and Shoon Murray, "The End of the Cold War, Attitude Change, and the Politics of Defense Spending," *Political Science and Politics* 27 (Mar. 1994): 17–21.
15. Dale R. Herspring, *The Pentagon and the Presidency: Civil-Military Relations from FDR to George W. Bush* (Lawrence: Univ. Press of Kansas, 2005), 313–318. For a study of prewar preparations, see Bob Woodward, *The Commanders* (New York: Simon & Schuster, 1991).
16. The most authoritative assessment of air power in the First Gulf War is U.S. Air Force, *Gulf War Air Power Survey,* 5 vols. (Washington, DC: Government Printing Office, 1993). See also U.S. House of Representatives, Committee on Armed Services, *Defense for a New Era: Lessons of the Persian Gulf War* (Washington, DC: Brassey's, 1992), 7–11, 16–21; Thomas A. Keaney and Eliot A. Cohen, *Revolution in Warfare? Air Power in the Persian Gulf* (Annapolis, MD: Naval Institute Press, 1995), 45–104.
17. George Friedman and Meredith Friedman, *The Future of War: Power, Technology & American World Dominance in the 21st Century* (New York: Crown, 1996), 253–281; Keaney and Cohen, *Revolution in Warfare?,* 45–104.
18. Thomas K. Adams, *U.S. Special Operations Forces in Action: The Challenge of Unconventional Warfare* (Portland, OR: Frank Cass, 1998), 233–234; See also Michael R. Gordon and Bernard E. Trainor, *The General's War: The Inside Story of the Conflict in the Gulf* (New York: Little, Brown & Co., 1995), 241–248.
19. For an overview of SOF missions during Operation Desert Storm, see U.S. Dept. of Defense, *Conduct of the Persian Gulf War: Final Report to Congress* (Washington, DC: U.S. Dept. of Defense, Apr. 1992), 523–541.
20. *Fifth Special Forces Group (Airborne) in Desert Shield and Desert Storm* (Chapter 38 Special Forces Association, Ft. Campbell, KY, 1991), 110–117; Adams, *U.S. Special Operations Forces in Action,* 238. See also Susan L. Marquis, *Unconventional Warfare: Rebuilding U.S. Special Operations Forces* (Washington, DC: Brookings Institution Press, 1997), 228–229, 232.
21. *Special Forces, The First Fifty Years: The United States Army Special Forces, 1952–2002* (Tampa, FL: Faircount, 2002), 239; U.S. Dept. of Defense, *Conduct of the Persian Gulf War,* 527.

22. U.S. Dept. of the Army, *Certain Victory: The United States Army in the Gulf War* (Washington, DC: Government Publishing Office, 1993), 198; *Fifth Special Forces Group (Airborne) in Desert Shield and Desert Storm,* 120–148; Adams, *U.S. Special Operations Forces in Action,* 239–240.
23. U.S. Special Operations Command, History and Research Office, *United States Special Operations Command History* (MacDill Air Force Base, FL: USSOCOM, 1999), 34–44.
24. Marquis, *Unconventional Warfare,* 239–244.
25. Grace Halsell, "Iraq: Military Victory, Moral Defeat," *Washington Report on Middle East Affairs* 10 (30 Nov. 1991): 64; "No Desert Quagmire," *National Review* 43 (13 May 1991): 14–17.
26. George H. W. Bush and Brent Scowcroft, *A World Transformed* (New York: Vintage Books, 1998), 491.
27. Stephen J. Kobrin, "Back to the Future: Neomedievalism and the Postmodern Digital World Economy," *Journal of International Affairs* 51 (Spring 1998): 361–386.
28. Jessica T. Matthews, "Power Shift: The Rise of Global Civil Society," *Foreign Affairs* 76 (Jan./Feb. 1997): 50–67.
29. Samuel P. Huntington, "The Clash of Civilizations?" *Foreign Affairs* 72 (Summer 1993): 22–49; J. E. Spence, "Ethnicity and International Relations," *International Affairs* 72 (July 1996): 439–443.
30. Daniel P. Moynihan, *Pandaemonium: Ethnicity in International Politics* (New York: Oxford Univ. Press, 1993), 63–106; Michael Barone, "Ethnic Tribes and Pandemonium," *U.S. News and World Report,* 15 Feb. 1993, 55–56.
31. Moynihan, *Pandaemonium,* 15.
32. Martin van Creveld, *The Transformation of War* (New York: Free Press, 1991), 214.
33. Huntington, "The Clash of Civilizations?" 26–27, 29–35; Abigail McCarthy, "Religious Wars . . . and Religious Peace," *Commonweal* (12 Mar. 1993): 6–7; Jonathan Fox, "Two Civilizations and Ethnic Conflict: Islam and the West," *Journal of Peace Research* 38 (July 2001): 459–472. Fox argues that the overall level of religious conflict did not change after the collapse of Soviet Communism. His study, however, did not take into account the scale of ethnic and religious conflict following the Cold War.
34. Susan Strange, *The Retreat of the State: The Diffusion of Power in the World Economy* (New York: Cambridge Univ. Press, 1996), 3–4, 7, 73.
35. A key example was Mexico after the passage of NAFTA in 1993. See Naomi Klein, *Fences and Windows: Dispatches from the Front Lines of the Globalization Debate* (New York: Picador USA, 2002), 208–223.
36. Kobrin, "Back to the Future," 361–386.
37. Huntington, "The Clash of Civilizations?" 22.

38. See, for example, Bruce Wallace, "A Nation in Search of a Modern Braveheart," *Maclean's* 109 (28 Oct. 1996): 28–31; Keith B. Richburg, "McDonald's Attacker Convicted in France: Farmer Vows Fight Against U.S. Inroads," *Washington Post,* 14 Sept. 2000, A28.
39. Francis Fukuyama, "The End of History?" *National Interest* 16 (Summer 1989): 4.
40. Francis Fukuyama, *The End of History and the Last Man* (New York: Free Press, 1992), 3–12, 99–108, 236–253, 261, 334.
41. Robert Kaplan, "The Coming Anarchy," *Atlantic Monthly* 273 (Feb. 1994): 59.
42. National Commission on Terrorist Attacks upon the United States, *The 9/11 Commission Report: Final Report of the National Commission on Terrorist Attacks upon the United States* (New York: W. W. Norton & Co., 2004), 334–338.
43. Roger W. Barnett, *Asymmetrical Warfare: Today's Challenge to U.S. Military Power* (Washington, DC: Brassey's, 2003), 21.
44. Jeffrey Boutwell and Michael T. Klare, eds., *Light Weapons and Civil Conflict: Controlling the Tools of Violence* (Lanham, MD: Rowan & Littlefield, 1999), 1–2.
45. Michael T. Klare, "The Kalashnikov Age," *Bulletin of the Atomic Scientists* 55 (Jan./Feb. 1999): 18.
46. Klare, "The Kalashnikov Age," 21; See also Michael T. Klare, "The International Trade in Light Weapons: What Have We Learned?" in *Light Weapons and Civil Conflict,* 9–28.
47. Boutwell and Klare, eds., *Light Weapons and Civil Conflict,* 10.
48. Ralph Peters, "Our New Old Enemies," *Parameters* 29 (Summer 1999): 22–38. See also Ralph Peters, "The Plague of Ideas," *Parameters* 30 (Winter 2000/2001): 4–21.
49. Ralph Peters, "The Culture of Future Conflict," *Parameters* 25 (Winter 1995–96): 18–27.
50. Metz, "A Strategic Context for Third Tier Conflict," 4–15. Susan Strange refers to these areas as "grey zones." See Strange, *The Retreat of the State,* 189.
51. Matthews, "Power Shift," 50–67.
52. Samuel R. Berger, "Challenges Approaching the 21st Century," in *At the End of the American Century: America's Role in the Post-Cold War World,* ed. Robert L. Hutchins (Baltimore: Johns Hopkins Univ. Press, 1998), 184–188. The bulk of Berger's postmortem on Clinton-era policies focuses on economic trade agreements.
53. "Risky Returns: Doing Business in Chaotic and Violent Countries," *Economist* 355 (20 May 2000): 85–88.

54. Louis I. Shelley, "Transnational Organized Crime: An Imminent Threat to the Nation State?" in *Classic Readings in International Relations*, ed. Phil Williams, Donald Goldstein, and Jay Shafritz (New York: Harcourt Brace & Co., 1999), 601–622.
55. Paul Kennedy, "Maintaining American Power: From Injury to Recovery," in *The Age of Terror: America and the World After September 11,* ed., Strobe Talbot and Nayan Chanda (New York: Basic Books, 2001), 58–59.
56. Bush, "The Possibility of a New World Order," 450–452.
57. Francis Fukuyama, "Reflections on the End of History Five Years Later," *History and Theory* 34 (1995): 27–43.
58. Scowcroft, "Why We Didn't Remove Saddam," 31.
59. National Security Review 12, "Review of National Defense Strategy," 3 Mar. 1989, http://bushlibrary.tamu.edu.
60. National Security Directive 47, "Counterintelligence and Security Countermeasures," 5 Oct. 1990; National Security Review 29, "Intelligence Capabilities: 1992–2005," 15 Nov. 1991, http://bushlibrary.tamu.edu.
61. Roberto Belloni, "Rethinking 'Nation-Building': The Contradictions of the Neo-Wilsonian Approach to Democracy Promotion," *Whitehead Journal of Diplomacy and International Relation* 8 (Winter/Spring 2007): 97–109.
62. U.S. Agency for International Development, Office of Foreign Disaster Assistance, "Situation Report No. 6: IRAQ—Displaced Persons/Refugees," 16 Apr. 1991, 1, George Bush Library (hereafter GBL), Staff Files, NSC, Nancy Bearg Dyke Files, Box 32. USAID reported 800,000 refugees had massed near the Turkish border and approximately 1 million displaced persons had entered Iran. See also Anthony Zinni and Tony Kolz, *The Battle for Peace: A Frontline Vision of America's Power and Purpose* (New York: Palgrave Macmillan, 2006), 50–52.
63. Nancy Bearg Dyke (NSC) to Robert M. Gates, "Deteriorating Kurdish Refugee Situation and Response," 17 Apr. 1991, memorandum, GBL, Staff Files, NSC, Nancy Bearg Dyke Files, Box 34.
64. Montgomery (NSC) to Dyke (NSC), 19 Apr. 1991, memorandum, GBL, Staff Files, NSC, Nancy Bearg Dyke Files, Box 34. The memo makes specific mention of the intention that "any Iraqi interference with humanitarian operations by the military, paramilitary or other security forces will not be tolerated."
65. Harry Rowan (International Security Affairs) to Nancy Dyke (NSC), "Humanitarian Assistance to the People of Iraq," 3 Mar. 1991, memorandum, GBL, Staff Files, Nancy Bearg Dyke Files, Box 31.
66. Ibid; Nicholas Rostow (NSC) to Brent Scowcroft, "Draw Down of Defense Department Stocks for Disaster Assistance in the Persian Gulf

Region," 5 Apr. 1991, GBL, Staff Files, NSC, Nancy Bearg Dyke Files, Box 33.

67. USAID, "Situation Report No. 6: IRAQ—Displaced Persons/Refugees," 1–2.
68. "Iraq Displaced Persons Humanitarian Assistance—Encouraging International Military Support," 18 Apr. 1991, cable, GBL, Staff Files, NSC, Nancy Bearg Dyke Files, Box 32.
69. White House Situation Room, "U.S. Statement on Redeployment from Iraq," 12 July 1991, 3, memorandum, GBL, Staff Files, NSC, Nancy Bearg Dyke Files, Box 35.
70. Ibid.
71. Situation Report, CTF Provide Comfort to USCINCEUR, 17 Apr. 1991. GBL, Staff Files, NSC, Nancy Bearg Dyke Files, Box 32.
72. Zinni and Kolz, *The Battle for Peace,* 73, 75–82.
73. Central Intelligence Agency, "Iraq-Kuwait: Situation Report #746," 30 May 1991, spot commentary, GBL, Staff Files, NSC, Nancy Bearg Dyke Files, Box 33.
74. Rick Atkinson, *Crusade: The Untold Story of the Persian Gulf War* (New York: Houghton Mifflin Co., 1993), 227–228.
75. Brian McAllister Linn, *The Echo of Battle: The Army's Way of War* (Cambridge, MA: Harvard Univ. Press, 2007), 221.
76. Robert R. Leonard, *The Art of Maneuver: Warfare Theory and Airland Battle* (Novato, CA: Presidio Press, 1994), 261.
77. James F. Dunnigan and Raymond M. Macedonia, *Getting It Right: American Military Reforms after Vietnam to the Persian Gulf and Beyond* (New York: William Morrow & Co., 1993), 208–209.
78. See Richard M. Swain, *"Lucky War": Third Army in Desert Storm* (Fort Leavenworth, KS: Command and General Staff College, 1994); Timothy M. Karcher, "The Victory Disease," *Military Review* 83 (July/Aug. 2002): 9–17. See also Timothy M. Karcher, *Understanding the "Victory Disease": From Little Bighorn to Mogadishu* (Fort Leavenworth, KS: Combat Studies Institute Press, 2004).
79. John L. Romjue, *American Army Doctrine for the Post–Cold War* (Washington, DC: Center of Military History, 1997), 35.
80. Ibid., 48.
81. Ibid., 98.
82. U.S. Dept. of the Army, Headquarters, *FM 100-5: Operations* (Fort Monroe, VA: U.S. Army Training and Doctrine Command, June 1993), 6-12.
83. Ibid., 13-0.
84. David Tucker and Christopher J. Lamb, *United States Special Operations Forces* (New York: Columbia Univ. Press, 2007), 100–106, 167, 171.

85. U.S. Dept. of the Army, Headquarters, *FM 100-5: Operations,* 13-2.
86. Ibid., 13-4.
87. See chapter 2. For a specific contemporary source on Soviet military interests in eastern Africa, see Central Intelligence Agency, Memorandum for the Honorable Zbigniew Brzezinski, Assistant to the President for National Security Affairs, "Communist Intervention Comparison," 15 Aug. 1979, Carter Library, Staff Office Files, National Security Advisor, Staff Materials, Box 3.
88. John W. Harbeson, "The Horn of Africa: From Chaos, Political Renewal," *Current History* 90 (May 1991): 223–224.
89. Michael Maren, "Video Warriors: Clinton, Somalia, and the Politics of Pictures," *Village Voice* 38 (19 Oct. 1993): 31–32; Stephen Hess, "Crisis, TV, and Public Pressure," *Brookings Review* 12 (Winter 1992): 48.
90. "Fact Sheet: Somalia-Operation Restore Hope," *U.S. Department of State Dispatch* (21 Dec. 1992): 899; Jeffrey Clark, "Debacle in Somalia," *Foreign Affairs* 72 (1993/1994): 113.
91. Dr. Omar Mohallim (Vice President, Interim Government) to Brent Scowcrost [*sic*] (National Security Advisor), 18 Nov. 1992, GBL, WHORM Subject File, 98–0101-F, Box 2.
92. Clark, "Debacle in Somalia," 115, 120.
93. Boutros Boutros-Gali to George Bush, 24 Nov. 1992, GBL, WHORM Subject File, 98–0101-F, Box 2.
94. Ibid.
95. Rev. Harold S. Weiss (Bishop, Northeastern Pennsylvania Synod) to George Bush, 10 Sept. 1992; Carl Dickerson (President Black Business Association of Los Angeles) to George Bush, 6 Oct. 1992; Alfred H. Moses (President, American Jewish Committee), 3 Dec. 1992. GBL, WHORM Subject File, 98–0101-F, Box 2.
96. Senator Carl Levin to George Bush, 23 Oct. 1992; U.S. House of Representatives, House Select Committee on Hunger to George Bush, 12 Dec. 1992, GBL, WHORM Subject File, 98–0101-F, Box 1.
97. Letter, Newt Gingrich to George Bush, 3 Dec. 1992, GBL, WHORM Subject File, 98–0101-F, Box 1.
98. John R. Bolton, "Wrong Turn in Somalia," *Foreign Affairs* 73 (Jan./Feb. 1994): 57–58.
99. Ramesh Thakur, "From Peacekeeping to Peace Enforcement: The UN Operation in Somalia," *Journal of Modern African Studies* 32 (Sept. 1994): 390–391, 402.
100. NSD-74, "Peacekeeping and Emergency Humanitarian Relief Policy," 24 Nov. 1992, Digital National Security Archive (hereafter DNSA).
101. Thakur, "From Peacekeeping to Peace Enforcement," 395.
102. George Bush to Boutros Boutros-Gali, 4 Dec. 1994; John M. Orday to Brent Scowcroft, "President's Meeting with Congressional Members on

Somalia, December 4, 1992, 11:00 A.M., cabinet Room," 3 Dec. 1992, memorandum, GBL, WHORM Subject File, 98–0101-F, Box 2.

103. "Fact Sheet: Somalia-Operation Restore Hope," 898.
104. "The Gift of Hope," *Time,* 28 Dec. 1992, 20.
105. Marquis, *Unconventional Warfare,* 252.
106. *Special Forces, The First Fifty Years,* 256; Brent Scowcroft to Richard A. Clark, "Situation Update Somalia," 10 Dec. 1992, memorandum, GBL, WHORM Subject File, 98–0101-F, Box 2.
107. Brent Scowcroft to Richard A. Clark, "Situation Update Somalia," 17 Dec. 1992, memorandum, GBL, WHORM Subject File, 98–0101-F, Box 2.
108. Col. Daniel G. Brown, Chief, Combined Arms Assessment Team (CAAT) Somalia, 27–28 Jan., memorandum, AHEC, Somalia Crisis Papers, Box 1.
109. Stanton, "After Action Report: Wanwaylan Incident, 30 December 1992," 2 Jan. 1993.
110. Walter Clarke and Jeffrey Herbst, "Somalia and the Future of Humanitarian Intervention," *Foreign Affairs* 75 (Mar./Apr. 1996): 75–79.
111. "Assertive Multilateralism," *Economist* 328 (25 Sept. 1993): 20; John Gerard Ruggie, "Third Try at World Order? America and Multilateralism after the Cold War," *Political Science Quarterly* 109 (Autumn 1994): 554; Francis Kofi Abiew and Tom Keating, "Outside Agents and the Polities of Peacebuilding and Reconciliation," *International Journa*l (Winter 1999/2000): 100.
112. Thakur, "From Peacekeeping to Peace Enforcement," 396; Curtis, "The Inevitable Slide into Coercive Peacemaking," 310–319.
113. Eric Schmitt, "U.S. Forces to Stay in Somalia to End Warlord Violence," *New York Times,* 28 Aug. 1993, 1.
114. See Mark F. Duffield, *Into the Beehive: The Somali Habr Gidr Clan as an Adaptive Enemy* (Fort Leavenworth, KS: U.S. Army Command and General Staff College, Dec. 1999).
115. Tucker and Lamb, *United States Special Operations Forces,* 115.
116. Clarke and Herbst, "Somalia and the Future of Humanitarian Intervention," 82.
117. Thakur, "From Peacekeeping to Peace Enforcement," 399.
118. U.S. Dept. of State, Bureau of International Organizational Affairs, "Clinton Administration Policy on Reforming Multilateral Peace Operations (PDD 25)," 22 Feb. 1996; Clarke and Herbst, "Somalia and the Future of Humanitarian Intervention," 70–71.
119. Robert C. Shaw, "Integrating Conventional and Special Operations Forces," *Military Review* 77 (July/Aug. 1997): 37.
120. Ibid., 38–41; Ian Martin, "Haiti: Mangled Multilateralism," *Foreign Policy* No. 95 (Summer 1994): 85. See also Henry F. Carey, "U.S. Domestic

Politics and the Emerging Humanitarian Intervention Policy: Haiti, Bosnia, and Kosovo," *World Affairs* 164 (Fall 2001): 77.

121. USMHI, Combat Training Center, "Lessons Learned: Project 1995-B, 1995," AHEC, Lawson W. Magruder Papers, 1995, Box 1. For an interesting postscript on the nature of the Somali conflict by 2003, see Hailes Janney, "Conflict Turns to Chaos in Somalia," *Jane's Intelligence Review* 15 (Jan. 2003): 18–21.
122. U.S. Dept. of the Army, Headquarters, *FM 100-5: Operations,* 13-0 to 13-5. See also TRADOC Pamphlet 525–56, *Planners Guide to Military Operations Other Than War* (Washington, DC: U.S. Dept. of the Army, Headquarters, Training and Doctrine Command, 1 Sept. 1993).
123. Rose, "Peace Operations and Change in the U.S. Military," 142–148
124. Wray Ross Johnson, "From Counterinsurgency to Stability and Support Operations: The Evolution of United States Military Doctrine for Foreign Internal Conflict, 1961–1996" (Ph.D. diss., Florida State Univ., 1997), 314–398.
125. John Lewis Gaddis, "And Now This: Lessons from the Old Era for the New One," in *The Age of Terror: America and the World After September 11,* ed. Strobe Talbot and Nayan Chanda (New York: Basic Books, 2001), 3–6.
126. Ian Roxborough, *The Hart-Rudman Commission and Homeland Defense* (Carlisle, PA: Strategic Studies Institute, Sept. 2001), 5.
127. Richard S. Williamson, "Nation-Building: The Dangers of Weak, Failing, and Failed States," *Whitehead Journal of Diplomacy and International Relations* 8 (Winter/Spring 2007): 11.
128. Ibid.

5. "Peace," Nation Building, and the New World Disorder

1. William J. Clinton, "A Strategy for Foreign Policy: Assistance to Russia," *Vital Speeches* 58 (1 May 1992): 421–425.
2. U.S. Senate, Committee on Armed Services, *Nominations before the Senate Armed Services Committee, First Session, 103rd Congress* (Washington: Government Printing Office, 1994), 12.
3. David Halberstam, *War in a Time of Peace: Bush, Clinton, and the Generals* (New York: Scribner, 2001), 241–243.
4. Ibid., 173–176.
5. Warren Christopher, "Ceasefire between the Branches," *Foreign Affairs* 60 (Summer 1982): 998.
6. I. M. Destler, Leslie H. Gelb, and Anthony Lake, *Our Own Worst Enemy: The Unmaking of American Foreign Policy* (New York: Simon & Schuster, 1984), 261–288.

7. For a critique of Clinton foreign policy in his second term, see Zbigniew Brzezinski, Brent Scowcroft, and Richard Murphy, "Differentiated Containment," *Foreign Affairs* 76 (May/June 1997): 20–29.
8. Willie Curtis, "The Inevitable Slide into Coercive Peacemaking: The U.S. Role in the New World Order," *Defense Analysis* 10 (Dec. 1994): 305–321.
9. Committee on Armed Services, *Nominations before the Senate Armed Services Committee, First Session, 103rd Congress,* 11–12. See also Anthony Zinni and Tony Kolz, *The Battle for Peace: A Frontline Vision of America's Power and Purpose* (New York: Palgrave Macmillan, 2006), 35–50.
10. Anthony Lake, "The Need for Engagement," *U.S. Department of State Dispatch* 5 (5 Dec. 1994): 804–808. For a discussion of the transition from the Bush to Clinton administrations, see Gearoid O. Tuathail and Timothy W. Luke, "Present at the (Dis)integration: Deterritorialization and Reterritorialization in the New Wor(l)d Order," *Annals of the Association of American Geographers* 84 (Sept. 1994): 381–398.
11. Steven Metz, "A Strategic Context for Third Tier Conflict," *Military Review* 75 (Dec. 1994–Feb. 1995): 4–15. See also "From Containment to Enlargement: Remarks of Anthony Lake, Assistant to the President for National Security Affairs" (Washington, DC: School of Advanced International Studies, 21 Sept. 1993); Anthony Lake, "Confronting Backlash States," *Foreign Affairs* 73 (Mar./Apr. 1994): 45; Lake, "The Need for Engagement," 804–808.
12. Warren Christopher, "American Foreign Policy: The Strategic Priorities," *Vital Speeches of the Day* 60 (1 Jan. 1994): 163.
13. Lake, "Confronting Backlash States," 45–48; David Pion-Berlin, "Will Soldiers Follow? Economic Integration and Regional Security in the Southern Cone," *Journal of Interamerican Studies and World Affairs* 42 (Spring 2000): 43–69.
14. Anthony Lake, "Laying the Foundations for a New American Century," *U.S. Department of State Dispatch* 7 (29 Apr. 1996): 2208–2212; Madeleine K. Albright, "A Call for American Consensus," *Time,* 22 Nov. 1999, 55–57.
15. Pion-Berlin, "Will Soldiers Follow?" 43–69.
16. Madeline K. Albright, "Enlarging NATO: Why Bigger Is Better," *Economist* 342 (15 Feb. 1997): 21–23.
17. Anthony Lake, "After the Wars—What *Kind* of Peace?" in *After the Wars: Reconstruction in Afghanistan, Indochina, Central America, Southern Africa, and the Horn of Africa,* ed. Anthony Lake (New Brunswick, NJ: Transaction, 1990), 16.
18. Albright, "The Testing of American Foreign Policy," 52.
19. Lake, "Laying the Foundations for a New American Century," 208–212.

20. Ibid., 10–17.
21. Lake, "Confronting Backlash States," 45–55. See also Akan Malici, "Thinking About Rogue Leaders: Really Hostile or Just Frustrated?" *Whitehead Journal of Diplomacy and International Relations* 8 (Summer/Fall 2007): 103–111.
22. See Robert D. Kaplan, "The Coming Anarchy," *Atlantic Monthly* 273 (Feb. 1994): 44–76.
23. Warren Christopher, "America's Leadership, America's Opportunity," *Foreign Policy,* no. 98 (Spring 1995): 6–28.
24. David Tucker and Christopher J. Lamb, "Peacetime Engagements," in *America's Armed Forces: A Handbook of Current and Future Capabilities,* ed. Sam C. Sarkesian and Robert E. Connor (Westport, CT: Greenwood Press, 1996), 300–316.
25. Anthony Lake, "Entering the 21st Century: Challenges Confronting America's Military," *U.S. Department of State Dispatch* 7 (17 June 1996): 318–321.
26. Ibid.
27. William S. Cohen, "The Empire Strikes Back," *Problems of Post-Communism* 42 (Jan./Feb. 1995): 13–19.
28. Madeleine K. Albright, "Foreign Policy: Strategic Goals," *U.S. Department of State Dispatch* 9 (May 1998): 10–14; Albright, "The Testing of American Foreign Policy," 59–62.
29. Albright, "The Testing of American Foreign Policy," 59.
30. Anthony Lake, "The U.S. Faces Key Foreign Policy Challenges," *U.S. Department of State Dispatch* 7 (3 June 1996): 279–284.
31. Madeleine Albright with Bill Woodward, *Madame Secretary* (New York: Miramax Books, 2003), 382. The 1998–1999 crisis in Kosovo receives three chapters in her autobiography.
32. John Barry and Evan Thomas, "The Kosovo Cover-Up," *Newsweek* 135 (15 May 2000): 22–26.
33. John Lewis Gaddis, *We Now Know: Rethinking Cold War History* (New York: Oxford Univ. Press, 1998), 43, 50, 117, 191–194.
34. James T. Patterson, *Restless Giant: The United States from Watergate to Bush v. Gore* (New York: Oxford Univ. Press, 2005), 350.
35. See, for example, Andrew Sullivan, "Lies That Matter," *New Republic* (14–21 Sept. 1998): 22.
36. "Iraq and Impeachment," *Christian Science Monitor* (18 Dec. 1998): 10; Greg Hitt, "Democrats Back Clinton on Iraq Attack, Rebuke Lott for Questioning Operation," *Wall Street Journal,* 18 Dec. 1998, A16. See also Paul Mann, "White House Pummeled on Mass Terror Threat, *Aviation Week and Space Technology* 151 (26 July 1999): 30; "Apologize," *New Republic* 221 (22 Nov. 1999): 9; "Bill Clinton's Favorite Bombers," *Weekly Standard* 5 (20 Sept. 1999): 2.

37. Edward N. Luttwak, "A Post-Heroic Military Policy," *Foreign Affairs* 75 (July/Aug. 1996): 33.
38. The actual end of modern industrial war is open to debate. Rupert Smith cites the First Gulf War, but also carries this concept back to the 1973 Yom Kippur War. See Rupert Smith, *The Utility of Force: The Art of War in the Modern World* (New York: Alfred A. Knopf, 2007), 3–28.
39. See Andrew Rathmell, "Towards Postmodern Intelligence," *Intelligence and National Security* 17 (Autumn 2002): 87–104; Martin van Creveld, *The Transformation of War* (New York: Free Press, 1991), 35–36, 59. See also Ulric Shannon, "Human Security and the Rise of Private Armies," *New Political Science* 22 (Mar. 2000): 103–115. For a good discussion of the Clausewitzian form of war, see Barry R. Posen, "Nationalism, the Mass Army, and Military Power," *International Security* 18 (Fall 1993): 80–124.
40. Luttwak, "A Post-Heroic Military Policy," 33–45.
41. Archie Clemins, "Where Is the Peace Dividend Now?" *U.S. Naval Institute Proceedings* 125 (Sept. 1999): 42–45.
42. Deborah Avant, "U.S. Military Attitudes toward Post-Cold War Missions," *Armed Forces and Society* 27 (Fall 2000): 37–57.
43. Ralph Peters, "Hucksters in Uniform," *Washington Monthly* 31 (May 1999): 9.
44. Robert Timberg, "The Tailhook Legacy," *U.S. Naval Institute Proceedings* 133 (Sept. 2007): 4.
45. James Warren, "Small Wars and Military Culture," *Society* 36 (Sept./Oct. 1999): 56–61.
46. Writing on this subject is voluminous. For a contemporary example, see "Conduct Unbecoming: Lesbians and Gays in the U.S. Military," *Armed Forces and Society* 20 (Summer 1994): 633–637. For additional scholarship on the issue of women in the military, see Molly Yeager, "Soldiering Ahead," *Wilson Quarterly* 31 (Summer 2007): 54–62; Anna Simons, "Women in Combat Units: It's Still a Bad Idea," *Parameters* 31 (Summer 2001): 89–100; David J. Armor, "Race and Gender in the U.S. Military," *Armed Forces and Society* 23 (Fall 1996): 7–27.
47. Donald G. Rose, "Peace Operations and Change in the U.S. Military," *Defense Analysis* 17 (Aug. 2001): 139–157.
48. Luttwak, "Post-Heroic Military Policy," 41.
49. U.S., Joint Chiefs of Staff, *National Security Strategy of the United States* (Washington, DC: U.S. Dept. of Defense, Jan. 1992), 1.
50. Ibid., 4–5.
51. Ibid., 4.
52. Les Aspin, *The Bottom-Up Review: Forces for a New Era* (Washington, DC: U.S. Dept. of Defense, 1993), 1.
53. Ibid., 2.
54. Ibid., 5.

55. Ibid., 9.
56. Ibid., 13.
57. Jeffrey Record, *Ready for What and Modernized Against Whom? A Strategic Perspective on Readiness and Modernization* (Carlisle, PA: Strategic Studies Institute, 1995), 3. Daniel J. Kaufman, "The Army," in *America's Armed Forces: A Handbook of Current and Future Capabilities,* ed. Sam C. Sarkesian and Robert E. Connor. (Westport, CT: Greenwood Press, 1996), 26, 34–35.
58. J. Isaacs, "Defense Spending—Workfare for the '90s?" *Bulletin of the Atomic Scientists* 48 (Apr. 1992): 3–5.
59. Tom Donnelly, "One War Too Many," *Jane's Defence Weekly* 32 (8 Dec. 1999): 28–34.
60. General Carl W. Stiner, "United States Special Operations Forces: A Strategic Perspective," draft, Dec. 1992, Army Heritage and Education Center (hereafter AHEC), Carl W. Stiner Papers, Box 25.
61. U.S. Special Operations Command, Directorate of Intelligence, "Africa: A Study in Chaos," Oct. 1992, AHEC, Stiner Papers, Box 25.
62. Stiner (USCINCSOC) to Adm. Larson (USCINCPAC), Subject: "Forward Basing of Special Operations Forces in the Pacific," 7 Dec. 1992; Stiner (USCINCSOC) to Gen. Riscassi (USCINCUNC), Subject: "Forward Basing of Special Operations Forces in the Pacific," 7 Dec. 1992, AHEC, Stiner Papers, Box 24.
63. George J. Church, "A Chronic Case of Impotence," *Time* 139, 8 June 1992, 39.
64. Harry F. Carey, "U.S. Domestic Politics and the Emerging Humanitarian Intervention Policy: Haiti, Bosnia, and Kosovo," *World Affairs* 164 (Fall 2001): 72.
65. Carey, "U.S. Domestic Politics and the Emerging Humanitarian Intervention Policy," 75–76.
66. Lenard J. Cohen, "Bosnia and Herzegovina: Fragile Peace in a Segmented State," *Current History* 95 (Mar. 1996): 104–105.
67. Ibid., 107.
68. Ibid., 107–108.
69. Howard Jones, *Crucible of Power: A History of American Foreign Relations From 1897,* 2nd ed. (New York: Rowman & Littlefield, 2008), 556.
70. Headquarters, Task Force Eagle, "Operational Guidance D+60 thru D+180," 27 Feb. 1996, AHEC, Task Force Eagle Papers, 1995–1996, Box 1.
71. Lieutenant Colonel Jeffrey W. Hammond, "Commanding a Field Artillery Battalion in a Peace Enforcement Environment—Operation Joint Endeavor," USAWC Personal Experience Monograph, 1998, AHEC, Army War College Personal Experience Monographs.

72. Carey, "U.S. Domestic Politics and the Emerging Humanitarian Intervention Policy," 77.
73. "Beyond D+120: Tasks We Don't Want, May Get," n.d., AHEC, Melissa E. Patrick Papers, 1995–1996, Box 1.
74. Headquarters, U.S. Army Europe, Office of the Chief of Public Affairs, *A Soldier's Guide to Bosnia-Herzegovina,* 12, n.d., AHEC, Task Force Eagle Papers, 1995–1996, Box 1.
75. Headquarters, 1st Brigade, 1st Armored Division, "RFCT 52 Lessons Learned," 19 Apr. 1996, AHEC, Melissa E. Patrick Papers, 1995–1996, Box 1.
76. Colonel Gregory Fontenot (HQ, 1st Brigade, 1st Armored Division) to Commander 1st Armored Division, "Lessons Learned," 21 Feb. 1997, AHEC, Task Force Eagle Papers, 1995–1996, Box 1.
77. Major General William L. Nash (Task Force Eagle) to Lieutenant General Thomas D. Burnette (Deputy Chief of Staff for Operations and Plans), "After Action Report," 1 June 1997, II-14-II-15, II-25-II-26, AHEC, Task Force Eagle Papers, 1995–1996, Box 1.
78. Cohen, "Bosnia and Herzegovina," 110.
79. John Schindler, "Bosnia: Five Years after Dayton," *Jane's Intelligence Review* 12 (May 2000): 18–21.
80. Deborah Avant, "Mercenaries," *Foreign Policy,* no. 143 (July/Aug. 2004): 21.
81. Ernest Evans, "The Clinton Administration and Peacekeeping in Civilian Conflicts," *World Affairs* 159 (Summer 1996): 24.
82. Russell W. Glenn, "No More Principles of War?" *Parameters* 28 (Spring 1998): 48–67. See also Robert S. Frost, *The Growing Imperative to Adopt "Flexibility" as an American Principle of War* (Carlisle, PA: Strategic Studies Institute, 1999). For a later example of this argument on a broader strategic level, see Ralph Peters, "Stability, America's Enemy," *Parameters* 31 (Winter 2001/2002): 5–20.
83. Rathmell, "Towards Postmodern Intelligence," 87–104.
84. Faye Bowers, "Security Tips Hinge on Winning Trust," *Christian Science Monitor* (30 Oct. 2003): 2.
85. U.S. Joint Chiefs of Staff, *National Military Strategy of the United States of America, 1995: A Strategy of Flexible and Selective Engagement* (Washington, DC: U.S. Dept. of Defense, 1995), i–ii, 4.
86. U.S. Joint Chiefs of Staff, *National Military Strategy of the United States of America: Shape, Respond, Prepare Now: A Military Strategy for a New Era, 1997* (Washington, DC: U.S. Dept. of Defense, 1997), 4–5, 8–10.
87. Ibid., 17.
88. U.S. Joint Chiefs of Staff, *Joint Vision 2010* (Washington, DC: JCS, 1996), 1–2.

89. Ibid., 4.

90. Ibid., 16–20. See also Barbara Starr, "CIA Looks to Web to Solve Data Overload," *Jane's Defence Weekly* 28 (23 July 1997): 29–30.

91. U.S. Joint Chiefs of Staff, *Joint Vision 2010,* 1–2, 10–16.

92. Tom Regan, "Wars of the Future . . . Today," *Christian Science Monitor* (24 June 1999): 13. See also William S. Cohen, "The Atlantic Alliance: A View from the Pentagon," *Joint Force Quarterly* Issue 21 (Spring 1999): 31–35.

93. Thomas K. Adams, "Future Warfare and the Decline of Human Decisionmaking," *Parameters* 31 (Winter 2001/2002): 57–71. See also Scott Gourley, "U.S. Army's Warriors for the New Century," *Jane's Defence Weekly* 27 (8 Jan. 1997): 23–24.

94. Michael O'Hanlon, "Clinton's Strong Defense Legacy," *Foreign Affairs* 82 (Nov./Dec. 2003): 126–134.

95. Steven Metz, "Racing toward the Future: The Revolution in Military Affairs," *Current History* 96 (Apr. 1997): 186. See also William S. Cohen, "Cohen Responds to National Defense Panel Report," *Program Manager* 27 (Jan./Feb. 1998): 27–38.

96. Metz, "Racing Towards the Future," 187–188; George Friedman and Meredith Friedman, *The Future of War: Power, Technology and American World Dominance in the 21st Century* (New York: Crown, 1996), 253–281.

97. Norman Friedman, *Terrorism: Afghanistan, and America's New Way of War* (Annapolis, MD: Naval Institute Press, 2003), 108–120. See also Madeleine K. Albright, "The William Cohen Lecture: Combining Force and Diplomacy to Secure America's Future," *U.S. Department of State Dispatch* 10 (Nov. 1999): 15–19; Serge Schemann, "Not Taking Losses Is One Thing: Winning Is Another," *New York Times,* 3 Jan. 1999, 1, 5.

98. Joint Pub 3-07.3, *Joint Tactics, Techniques, and Procedures for Peacekeeping Operations* (Washington, DC: JCS, 29 Apr. 1994); *FM 100-23: Peace Operations* (Washington, DC: U.S. Dept. of the Army, Dec. 1994); Joint Pub 3-07, *Joint Doctrine for Military Operations Other Than War* (Washington, DC: JCS, 16 June 1995).

99. Quoted in Wray Ross Johnson, "From Counterinsurgency to Stability and Support Operations: The Evolution of United States Military Doctrine for Foreign Internal Conflict, 1961–1996" (Ph.D. diss., Florida State Univ., 1997), 312. See also, U.S. Dept. of the Army, Headquarters, *FM 100-20: Stability and Support Operations* (Washington, DC: U.S. Dept. of the Army, Apr. 1996).

100. U.S. Dept. of Defense, Assistant Secretary of Defense for Special Operations and Low Intensity Conflict, *SOF Vision 2020* (MacDill Air Force Base, FL: USSOCOM, 1996), 6.

101. Ibid., 15.

102. Thomas R. Searle, *"Clearing the Way": U.S. Special Operations Forces in the Humanitarian Demining of Afghanistan, Eritrea, and Ethiopia, 1988–1996* (MacDill Air Force Base, FL: USSOCOM, 1996), 35–39.
103. U.S. Army Training and Doctrine Command, Center for Army Lessons Learned, *Stability and Support Operations (SASO): Tactics, Techniques, and Procedures for SASO* (Fort Leavenworth, KS: TRADOC, 1998), 1.
104. For recounts of this process, see Lieutenant Colonel Jeffrey W. Hammond, "Commanding a Field Artillery Battalion in a Peace Enforcement Environment—Operation Joint Endeavor," USAWC Personal Experience Monograph, 1998; Lieutenant Colonel Christopher Tucker, "Warfighting to Peacekeeping: Challenges in Command," USAWC Personal Experience Monograph, 1999, AHEC, Army War College Personal Experience Monographs.
105. Colonel Alan W. Thrasher (HQ, 1st Armored Division Artillery) to Commander, 1st Armored Division, "Bosnia Lessons Learned," 10 Mar. 1997, memorandum, AHEC, Task Force Eagle Papers, 1995–1996, Box 1.
106. U.S. Army, Training and Doctrine Command, Center for Army Lessons Learned, *Stability Operations and Support Operations (SOSO): Tactics, Techniques, and Procedures for SOSO* (Fort Leavenworth, KS: TRADOC, 2003), 11–29.
107. Ibid., 13.
108. Charles C. Krulak, "The Strategic Corporal: Leadership in the Three Block War," *Marine Corps Gazette* 83 (Jan. 1999): 18–22.
109. White House, Office of the Press Secretary, "A National Security Strategy for a New Century," 5 Jan. 2000, 5, http://www.clintonpresidentialcenter.org.
110. Ibid., 11, 18.
111. William S. Cohen, "Principles for a National Security Consensus," *Washington Quarterly* 24 (Spring 2001): 76.
112. Steven Metz, "The Air Force Role in United Nations Peacekeeping," *Airpower Journal* 7 (Winter 1993): 68–72.
113. Tom Donnelly, "One War Too Many," *Jane's Defence Weekly* 32 (8 Dec. 1999): 28–34.
114. Richard Haass, "Paradigm Lost," *Foreign Affairs* 74 (Jan./Feb. 1995): 49–50.

6. The Drug War

1. "Escobar's Dead End," *Time,* 13 Dec. 1993, 46.
2. Ibid.
3. John Morton Blum, *Years of Discord: American Politics and Society, 1961–1974* (New York: W. W. Norton & Co., 1991), 310–311, 319–320.

4. J. Samuel Fitch, "The Decline of US Military Influence in Latin America," *Journal of Interamerican Studies and World Affairs* 35 (Summer 1993): 1–49. See also Russell Crandall, "Explicit Narcotization: U.S. Policy toward Colombia during the Samper Administration," *Latin American Politics and Society* 43 (Autumn 2001): 95–120. This is essentially the argument made in John Lindsay-Poland, *Emperors in the Jungle: The Hidden History of the U.S. in Panama* (Durham, NC: Duke Univ. Press, 2003), 103–137. See also John H. Coatsworth, *Central America and the United States: The Clients and the Colossus* (New York: Twayne, 1994); William Avilés, "Institutions, Military Policy, and Human Rights in Colombia," *Latin American Perspectives* 28 (Jan. 2001): 31–55.
5. Francisco Gutierrez, "Institutionalizing Global Wars: State Transformation in Colombia, 1978–2002," *Journal of International Affairs* 57 (Fall 2003): 136.
6. Peter N. Carroll, *It Seemed Like Nothing Happened: America in the 1970s,* 3rd ed. (New Brunswick, NJ: Rutgers Univ. Press, 2000), 264–267.
7. Jeremy Kuzmarov, "From Counter-Insurgency to Narco-Insurgency: Vietnam and the International War on Drugs," *Journal of Public Policy* 20 (2008): 348.
8. For a brief history of the Colombian cartels, see Robert Filippone, "The Medellín Cartel: Why We Can't Win the Drug War," *Studies in Conflict and Terrorism* 17 (Oct. 1994): 323–326.
9. See Michael D. Gambone, *Capturing the Revolution: The United States, Central America, and Nicaragua, 1961–1972* (Westport, CT: Praeger, 2001), 21–44.
10. Stephen Ambrose, *Nixon: The Triumph of a Politician, 1962–1972* (New York: Simon & Schuster, 1989), 125–126, 144–145, 260–265.
11. Ibid., 263.
12. Blum, *Years of Discord,* 333.
13. Kuzmarov, "From Counter-Insurgency to Narco-Insurgency," 345.
14. Ibid., 351–352, 354.
15. "The Pragmatic President," *Congressional Quarterly Researcher* 16 (2 June 2006): 492.
16. "Nixon's Shift," *Congressional Quarterly Researcher* 10 (28 July 2000): 607.
17. See David F. Musto and Pamela Korsmeyer, *The Quest for Drug Control: Politics and Federal Policy in a Period of Increasing Substance Abuse, 1963–1981* (New Haven: Yale Univ. Press, 2002).
18. Kuzmarov, "From Counter-Insurgency to Narco-Insurgency," 351–352.
19. Jefferson Morley and Malcolm Byrne, "The Drug War and 'National Security': The Making of a Quagmire, 1969–1973," *Dissent* 36 (Winter 1989): 42–45; William Walker, *Drug Control in the Americas* (Albuquerque: Univ. of New Mexico Press, 1989), 191–192.

20. Musto and Korsmeyer, *The Quest for Drug Control,* 192–196. See also Elaine B. Sharp, "Agenda Setting and Policy Results: Lessons from Three Drug Policy Episodes," *Policy Studies Journal* 20 (Dec. 1992): 545–546.
21. Musto and Korsmeyer, *The Quest for Drug Control,* 206.
22. Ibid., 211.
23. "The Pragmatic President," 491, 493.
24. Richard B. Craig, "Colombian Narcotics and United States–Colombian Relations," *Journal of Interamerican Studies and World Affairs* 23 (Aug. 1981): 259–262.
25. Peter Reuter, "Foreign Demand for Latin American Drugs: The USA and Europe," in *Latin America and the Multinational Drug Trade,* ed. Elizabeth Joyce and Carlos Malamud (London: Macmillan Press, 1998), 25–26, 27–28; U.S. Dept. of Justice, Drug Enforcement Administration, *Narcotics Situation Report* (Washington, DC: U.S. Dept. of Justice, 1981), 16. U.S. Dept. of Justice, Drug Enforcement Administration, *Annual Report, Fiscal Year 1986* (Washington, DC: U.S. Dept. of Justice, 1987), 3.
26. Bruce Michael Bagley, "The New Hundred Years War? U.S. National Security Policy and the War on Drugs in Latin America," *Journal of Interamerican Studies and World Affairs* 30 (Spring 1988): 161–162; P. Andreas and E. C. Bertram, "Dead-End Drug Wars," *Foreign Policy,* no. 85 (Winter 1991): 106–129.
27. Donald Mabry, "The U.S. Military and the War on Drugs in Latin America," *Journal of Interamerican Studies and World Affairs* 30 (Summer/Autumn 1988): 53; Tom Clancy, *Clear and Present Danger* (New York: G. P. Putnam, 1989).
28. Bagley, "The New Hundred Years War?" 165.
29. Cynthia McClintock, "The War on Drugs: The Peruvian Case," *Journal of Interamerican Studies and World Affairs* 30 (Summer/Autumn 1988): 130.
30. NSDD 221, "Narcotics and National Security" 8 Apr. 1986, 1, Ronald Reagan Library, NSDD File.
31. Ibid., 2–3. See also Gen. John R. Galvin (Southern Command) to Edwin Meese, 27 Mar. 1987, Ronald Reagan Library, White House Staff and Offices, 1981–1989, Colin Powell Files, Box 92476.
32. Ibid., 3. See also U.S. Air Force, "Slides on International Narcotics Trafficking and U.S. Counter-Drug Initiatives," 1986, Digital National Security Archives (hereafter DNSA), http://www.nsarchives.chadwyck.com.
33. U.S. Air Force, "Slides on International Narcotics Trafficking and U.S. Counter-Drug Initiatives," 1986, DNSA.
34. Bagley, "The New Hundred Years War?" 163.
35. Mabry, "The U.S. Military and the War on Drugs in Latin America," 55.
36. U.S. Air Force, "Slides on International Narcotics Trafficking and U.S. Counter-Drug Initiatives," 1986.

37. Bagley, "The New Hundred Years War?" 168.

38. Filippone, "The Medellin Cartel," 333; Charles Lane, "Just Say No," *New Republic* 215 (25 Nov. 1996): 4. See also Lee Hamilton (Chair, House Select Committee to Investigate Covert Arms Transactions with Iran) to Robert A. Bermingham, "Allegations Re: Contra Involvement with Drug Smuggling," 23 July 1987, Ronald Reagan Library, Robert Pastorino Files, Box 1.

39. Mabry, "The U.S. Military and the War on Drugs in Latin America," 57–58, 61.

40. Andreas and Bertram, "Dead-End Drug Wars," 108.

41. William J. Bennett (Director, Office of National Drug Control Policy) to John Sununu (White House Chief of Staff), 4 Apr. 1989, memorandum, George Bush Library (hereafter GBL), "P" File.

42. National Security Directive 13, "Cocaine Trafficking," 7 June 1989; National Security Directive 18, "International Counternarcotics Strategy," 21 Aug. 1989, http://bushlibrary.tamu.edu.

43. Peter Zirnite, "The Militarization of the Drug War in Latin America," *Current History* 97 (Apr. 1998): 167.

44. John Schall to David Bates, "Working Group on Anti-Drug Policy," 26 July 1989, memorandum, GBL, "P" File.

45. Robert S. Ross (Executive Assistant to the Attorney General) to John H. Sununu (White House Chief of Staff), "Concerns Over the Pending National Drug Strategy," 27 July 1989; Gary M. Chase (Acting Director of Congressional Affairs, CIA) to Bernard H. Martin (Acting Director, Office of Management and Budget), 10 May 1991; Paul J. McNulty (Principle Deputy Director, Dept. of Justice) to Richard Darman (Director, Office of Management and Budget), 19 Sept. 1991, GBL, "P" File, Box 10.

46. Mark A. Sherman, "An Inquiry Regarding the International and Domestic Legal Problems Presented in the United States v. Noriega," *University of Miami Inter-American Law Review* 20 (Spring 1989): 393–428.

47. Richard F. Riccardelli, "Waging Limited War on Drugs: New Strategies for the Nineties," *Military Review* (Oct. 1994): 25–31.

48. General Accounting Office, Report to the Chairman, Subcommittee on Legislation and National Security, Committee on Government Operations, House of Representatives, *Drug Control: Status Report on DOD Support to Counternarcotics Activities,* GAO/NSIAD-91–117 (Washington, DC: GAO, June 1991), 3, 32–33.

49. Ibid., 15–19.

50. General Accounting Office, Report to Congressional Requesters, *Drug Control: Heavy Investment in Military Surveillance Is Not Paying Off,* GAO/NSIAD-93–220 (Washington, DC: GAO, Sept. 1993), 18.

51. Ibid., 17.

52. Bob Martinez (Office of National Drug Control Policy) to George Bush, 4 Sept. 1992, GBL, "P" File.
53. Raphael F. Perl, "Clinton's Foreign Drug Policy," *Journal of Interamerican Studies and World Affairs* 35 (Winter 1993–1994): 143–144; Rafael Pardo, "Colombia's Two-Front War," *Foreign Affairs* 79 (July/Aug. 2000): 64–73.
54. GAO, *Drug Control: Heavy Investment in Military Surveillance Is Not Paying Off*, 29.
55. For the policy debate with the Republican Congress after 1994, see Perl, "Clinton's Foreign Drug Policy," 149.
56. Coletta Youngers, "Cocaine Madness: Counternarcotics and Militarization in the Andes," *NACLA Report on the Americas* 34 (Nov./Dec. 2000): 16–25.
57. U.S. House of Representatives, Committee on Government Reform and Oversight, *National Drug Policy: A Review of the Status of the Drug War, Seventh Report*, 19 Mar. 1996. http://www.fas.org/irp/offdocs/pdd14_house.htm.
58. Stephen P. Howard, "The Military War on Drugs: Too Many Assets, Too Few Results," Research Report, National Defense Fellows Program, Air Univ., Apr. 2001, 30.
59. "Grant U.S. Aid Listed by Country, Counter-Narcotics Programs, Entire Region, 1996–2000," http://justf.org.
60. The specific parameters were established under Section 1000 of the 1989 Defense Authorization Act and were subsequently modified over time to redefine U.S. assistance.
61. Youngers, "Cocaine Madness," 19.
62. Madeleine K. Albright, "Enlarging NATO: Why Bigger Is Better," *Economist* 342 (15 Feb. 1997): 21–23.
63. U.S. Senate, Foreign Relations Committee, "Trip Report: Minority Staff Delegation to Colombia, 27–31 May 2002" (Washington, DC: June 2002), http://ciponline.org/Colombia/02053101.pdf. See also Volker C. Franke and Justin Reed, "Squeezing a Balloon: Plan Colombia and America's War on Drugs," in *Terrorism and Peacekeeping: New Security Challenges*, ed., Volker C. Franke (Westport, CT: Praeger, 2005), 186.
64. Adam Isacson, "Washington's 'New War' in Colombia: The War on Drugs Meets the War on Terror," *NACLA Report on the Americas* 36 (Mar./Apr. 2003): 13–15.
65. Adam Isacson, "The U.S. Military in the War on Drugs," in *Drugs and Democracy in Latin America: The Impact of U.S. Policy*, ed. Coletta A. Youngers and Eileen Rosin (Boulder, CO: Lynne Rienner, 2005), 49.
66. Isacson, "Washington's 'New War' in Colombia," 13.
67. According to Gallup, Bush's job approval rating peaked at 90 percent in September 2001 and declined to 69 percent by July 2002. See Frank

Newport, "Bush Job Approval Update," *Gallup News Service*, 29 July 2002, http://www.gallop.com.

68. Emma Björnehed, "Narco-Terrorism: The Merger of the War on Drugs and the War on Terror," *Global Crime* 6 (Aug.–Nov. 2004): 313.
69. *Just the Facts, A Civilian's Guide to U.S. Defense and Security Assistance to Latin America and the Caribbean.* http://justf.org.
70. Juan Gabriel Tokatlian, "A New Doctrine of Insecurity? U.S. Military Deployment in South America," *NACLA Report on the Americas* 41 (Sept./Oct. 2008): 6–11.
71. Winifred Tate, "Repeating Past Mistakes: Aiding Counterinsurgency in Colombia," *NACLA Report on the Americas* 34 (Sept./Oct. 2000): 16–20.
72. William R. Daly, "Counterdrug OPS Offer a Chance to Excel," *U.S. Naval Institute Proceedings* 130 (Mar. 2004): 67–72.
73. U.S. Southern Command, *Command Strategy 2016: Partnership for the Americas* (Miami: U.S. SOUTHCOM, Mar. 2007), 11.
74. Ibid., 12.
75. See U.S. Dept. of the Army, *FM 3-0: Operations* (Washington, DC: U.S. Dept. of the Army, Feb. 2008).
76. Ibid., 13.
77. George Withers, Adam Isacson, Lisa Haugaard, et. al, *Ready, Aim, Foreign Policy: How the Pentagon's Role in Foreign Policy Is Growing, and Why Congress—and the American Public—Should Be Worried* (Washington, DC: CIP/LAWGEF/WOLA, Mar. 2008), 11–13.
78. See U.S. Dept. of Health and Human Services, Substance Abuse and Mental Health Services Administration, Office of Applied Studies, *Results from the 2007 National Survey on Drug Use and Health: National Findings* (Rockville, MD: SAMHSA, Sept. 2008).
79. GAO, *Drug Control: Heavy Investment in Military Surveillance Is Not Paying Off*, 3–4, 10, 21.
80. Ibid., 16–18.
81. Ana Arana, "The New Battle for Central America," *Foreign Affairs* 80 (Nov./Dec. 2001): 88–89.
82. Kenneth Sharpe, "Realpolitik or Imperial Hubris: The Latin American Drug War and U.S. Foreign Policy in Iraq," *Orbis* 50 (June 2006): 481–499.
83. Andreas and Bertram, "Dead-End Drug Wars," 106–129.
84. Richard F. Riccardelli, "Waging Limited War on Drugs: New Strategies for the Nineties," *Military Review* (Oct. 1994): 25–31.
85. Arana, "The New Battle for Central America," 88–89.
86. David Passage, *The United States and Colombia: Untying the Gordian Knot* (Carlisle, PA: Strategic Studies Institute, Mar. 2000), 4.
87. Julia E. Sweig, "What Kind of War for Colombia? History Repeating Itself?" *Foreign Affairs* 81 (Sept./Oct. 2002): 122–141.

88. Brian Loveman, *For la Patria: Politics and the Armed Forces in Latin America* (Wilmington, DE: Scholarly Resources, 1999), 236–239. See also John H. Coatsworth, "Beyond Armed Actors: A Look at Civil Society," *Revista: Harvard Review of Latin America* 3 (Spring 2003): 3–7; Robin Kirk, *More Terrible Than Death: Massacres, Drugs, and America's War in Colombia* (New York: Public Affairs, 2003).
89. Alex McDougall, "State Power and Its Implications for Civil War in Colombia," *Studies in Conflict and Terrorism* 32 (Apr. 2009): 322–345; Aleida Ferreyra and Renata Segura, "Examining the Military in the Local Sphere: Colombia and Mexico," *Latin American Perspectives* 27 (Mar. 2000): 23–26. See also James L. Zackrison and Eileen Bradley, "Colombian Sovereignty Under Siege," *Strategic Forum,* no. 112 (May 1997): 1–6.
90. Ernani Dearaujo, "In Need of a Fix: Reforming Plan Colombia," *Harvard International Review* 23 (Winter 2002): 9.
91. Geoff Simons, *Colombia: A Brutal History* (London: SAQI, 2004), 56–57, 65, 96–97; Maria Clemencia Ramírez Lemus, Kimberley Stanton, and John Walsh, "Colombia: A Vicious Circle of Drugs and War," in *Drugs and Democracy in Latin America: The Impact of U.S. Policy,* ed. Coletta A. Youngers and Eileen Rosin (Boulder, CO: Lynne Rienner, 2005), 124–127. For more recent data, see the United Nations Office of the High Commissioner for Human Rights at http://www.ohchr.org.
92. Avilés, "Institutions, Military Policy, and Human Rights in Colombia," 33–37, 41–42; Jorge Orlando Melo, "The Drug Trade, Politics and the Economy: The Colombian Experience," in *Latin America and the Multinational Drug Trade,* ed. Elizabeth Joyce and Carlos Malamud (London: Macmillan, 1998), 71; Timothy P. Wickham-Crowley, "Elites, Elite Settlements, and Revolutionary Movements in Latin America, 1950–1980," *Social Science History* 18 (Winter 1994): 543–574.
93. William E. Leogrande and Kenneth E. Sharpe, "Two Wars or One? Drugs, Guerrillas, and Colombia's New Violencia," *World Policy Journal* 17 (Fall 2000): 2.
94. Nazih Richani, "The Political Economy of Violence: The War-System in Colombia," *Journal of Interamerican Studies and World Affairs* 39 (Summer 1997): 40–41.
95. Michael G. Roskin, "Crime and Politics in Colombia: Considerations for US Involvement," *Parameters* 31 (Winter 2001–2002): 129; Craig, "Colombian Narcotics and United States-Colombian Relations," 244.
96. Francisco E. Thoumi, "Why the Illegal Psychoactive Drugs Industry Grew in Colombia," *Journal of Interamerican Studies and World Affairs* 34 (Autumn 1992): 40.
97. Ramírez Lemus, Stanton, and Walsh, "Colombia: A Vicious Circle of Drugs and War," 99–100; for a more recent survey, see Eliza Griswold, "Medellín's Mean Streets," *National Geographic* 207 (Mar. 2005): 73–92.

98. Contemporary media accounts often commented on Pablo Escobar's popularity. See "Colombia: Robin the Hood," *Economist* 326 (30 Jan. 1993): 44.

99. Orlando Melo, "The Drug Trade, Politics and the Economy," 64–67.

100. Ferreyra and Segura, "Examining the Military in the Local Sphere," 28.

101. United Nations, Office on Drugs and Crime, *World Drug Report, 2009* (Vienna: UNODC, 2009), 197, 199.

102. Mark Peceny and Michael Durnan, "The FARC's Best Friend: U.S. Antidrug Policies and the Deepening of Colombia's Civil War in the 1990s," *Latin American Politics and Society* 48 (Summer 2006): 111.

103. Ibid.

104. Zackrison and Bradley, "Colombian Sovereignty Under Siege," 1–6. See also U.S. Office of the Vice President, "White Paper on Insurgent/Terrorist Involvement in International Drug Trade," 31 Dec. 1985, DNSA.

105. George H. Franco, "Their Darkest Hour: Colombia's Government and the Narco-Insurgency," *Parameters* 30 (Summer 2000): 83–94.

106. Björnehed, "Narco-Terrorism," 310–311.

107. Peceny and Durnan, "The FARC's Best Friend," 107, 109.

108. Filippone, "The Medellin Cartel," 326.

109. Peceny and Durnan, "The FARC's Best Friend," 103; Filippone, "The Medellin Cartel," 325, 335.

110. Simons, *Colombia: A Brutal History,* 54–59. See also Peter Dale Scott, *Drugs, Oil, and War: The United States in Afghanistan, Colombia, and Indochina* (Lanham, MA: Rowman & Littlefield, 2003), 71–83.

111. Marc W. Chernick, "The Paramilitarization of the War in Colombia," *NACLA Report on the Americas* 31 (Mar./Apr. 1998): 28–33; Michael McClintock, *Instruments of Statecraft: U.S. Guerrilla Warfare, Counter-Insurgency, Counter-Terrorism, 1940–1990* (New York: Pantheon Books, 1992), 222–223; Scott, *Drugs, Oil, and War,* 76–80.

112. Passage, *The United States and Colombia,* 12.

113. Jim Bain, "Pressure Mounts on Colombian Government to Tackle Rebels," *Jane's Defence Weekly* 27 (19 Feb. 1997): 18–19.

114. Roskin, "Crime and Politics in Colombia," 129.

115. Kim Cragin and Bruce Hoffman, *Arms Trafficking in Colombia* (Santa Monica, CA: RAND, 2003), xv, xvii–xxi, 4–6, 9–14, 20.

116. Hal Klepak, "Colombia: Why Doesn't the War End?" *Jane's Intelligence Review* 12 (June 2000): 41–45.

117. James W. Wilkie, ed., *Statistical Abstract of Latin America* (Los Angeles: UCLA Latin American Center Publications, 1996), 32:340. West Germany provided the remaining balance.

118. Ibid., 344.

119. Ibid., 346. A total of 20,753 of Latin American military personnel were trained during this time period.
120. Franke and Reed, "Squeezing a Balloon," 184.
121. Ingrid Vaicius and Adam Isacson, "The 'War on Drugs' Meets the 'War on Terror': The United States' Military Involvement in Colombia Climbs to the Next Level," *Center for International Policy: Colombia Program: International Policy Report* (Feb. 2003), 3. http://www.ciponline.org.
122. Klepak, "Colombia: Why Doesn't the War End?" 43–44.
123. Jeremy McDermott, "War Resumes after Collapse of Colombian Peace Process," *Jane's Intelligence Review* 14 (Apr. 2002): 9–10.
124. Peter Chalk, "The 'War on Drugs': Is the USA's Colombia Policy Working?" *Jane's Intelligence Review* 12 (Dec. 2000): 41–42; Vaicius and Isacson, "The 'War on Drugs' Meets the 'War on Terror,'" 5.
125. Martin Dayani, "Terror Focuses on Colombia," *Jane's Defence Weekly* 37 (23 Jan. 2002): 21.
126. Klepak, "Colombia: Why Doesn't the War End?" 43–44.
127. Passage, *The United States and Colombia,* 19.
128. Sweig, "What Kind of War for Colombia?" 122–141.
129. Republic of Colombia, Presidency of the Republic, Ministry of Defence, *Democratic Security and Defence Policy* (Bogota: Ministry of Defence, 2003), 5.
130. Ibid. See also Thomas A. Marks, *Sustainability of Colombian Military/Strategic Support for "Democratic Security"* (Carlisle, PA: Strategic Studies Institute, July 2005), 7.
131. Ministry of Defence, *Democratic Security and Defence Policy,* 14.
132. Marks, *Sustainability of Colombian Military/Strategic Support for "Democratic Security,"* 1, 4–8.
133. "Grant Military and Police Aid to Colombia, 1996–2009," *Just the Facts: A Civilian's Guide to U.S. Defense and Security Assistance to Latin America and the Caribbean* (http://justf.org). These programs include NADR Anti-Terrorism Assistance and the Counter-Terrorism Fellowship Program.
134. Ibid.
135. Thomas Marks, *Colombian Army Adaptation to FARC Insurgency* (Carlisle, PA: Strategic Studies Institute, Jan. 2002), 9.
136. Sharpe, "Realpolitik or Imperial Hubris," 490–499.
137. Stockholm International Peace Research Institute, "The SIPRI Military Expenditure Database," http://milexdata.sipri.org. See also Raúl Zibechi, "Military Crisis in South America: The Results of Plan Colombia," *Americas Program Special Report* (26 Mar. 2008): 2, http://americas.irc-online.org.
138. Sweig, What Kind of War for Colombia?" 122–141.
139. Cragin and Hoffman, *Arms Trafficking in Colombia,* 41.

140. Vaicius and Isacson, "The 'War on Drugs' Meets the 'War on Terror,'" 7.

141. Fernando Garcia Arganaras, "The Drug War at the Supply End: The Case of Bolivia," *Latin American Perspectives* 24 (Sept. 1997): 62.

142. Money laundering through the national banking system was quasi-official state policy in Bolivia and Peru as well. See Peter R. Andreas and Kenneth E. Sharpe, "Cocaine Politics in the Andes," *Current History* 91 (Feb. 1992): 74–79; David Scott Palmer, "Peru, the Drug Business and Shining Path: Between Scylla and Charybdis?" *Journal of Interamerican Studies and World Affairs* 34 (Autumn 1992): 65–88; McClintock, "The War on Drugs: The Peruvian Case," 129.

143. E. M. Frost, "Success at What Price?" *Jane's Defence Weekly* 31 (1 Nov. 2000): 19. See also Andrew Webb-Vidal, "Officers Challenge Chávez as Violence Spills across Border," *Jane's Intelligence Review* 14 (Apr. 2002): 14–15.

144. *Below the Radar: U.S. Military Programs with Latin America, 1997–2007* (Washington, DC: Center for International Policy, Mar. 2007), 1, 3.

145. Fitch, "The Decline of U.S. Military Influence in Latin America," 15.

146. U.S. Dept. of State, Bureau for International Narcotics and Law Enforcement Affairs, *International Narcotics Controlled Strategy Report, 2005* (Washington, DC: Government Printing Office, 2005), 7, 20, 26–27.

147. Crandall, "Explicit Narcotization," 111.

148. United Nations, Office on Drugs and Crime, *Coca Cultivation in the Andean Region: A Survey of Bolivia, Colombia, and Peru* (New York: United Nations, June 2008), 7.

149. Ibid., 17, 90.

150. Andreas and Bertram, "Dead-End Drug Wars," 106–129.

151. Youngers, "Cocaine Madness," 17.

152. Tokatlian, "A New Doctrine of Insecurity?" 6–11.

153. Youngers, "Cocaine Madness," 23.

154. Lesley Gill, "Colombia: What Next?" *NACLA Report on the Americas* 42 (Jan./Feb. 2009): 30–32.

155. Cornelius Friesendorf, "Squeezing the Balloon? United States Air Interdiction and the Restructuring of the South American Drug Industry in the 1990s," *Crime, Law and Social Change* 44 (2005): 43.

7. The War on Terror

1. Charles Knight, Melissa Murphy, and Michael Mousseau, "The Sources of Terrorism," *International Security* 28 (Autumn 2003): 192–198; Jonathan Fox, "Two Civilizations and Ethnic Conflict: Islam and the West," *Journal of Peace Research* 38 (July 2001): 459–472; Stephen J. Kobrin, "Back to the Future: Neomedievalism and the Postmodern Digital World Economy," *Journal of International Affairs* 51 (Spring 1998): 361–386.

2. Thomas Homer-Dixon, "The Rise of Complex Terrorism," *Foreign Policy*, no. 128 (Jan./Feb. 2002): 52–62; N. D. Jayaprakash, "Terrorism: Hiroshima to New York," *Economic and Political Weekly* 36 (20–26 Oct. 2001): 3988–3992. See also Jeffrey Boutwell and Michael T. Klare, eds., *Light Weapons and Civil Conflict: Controlling the Tools of Violence* (Lanham, MD: Rowan & Littlefield, 1999); Michael T. Klare, "The Kalashnikov Age," *Bulletin of the Atomic Scientists* 55 (Jan./Feb. 1999): 18–23.
3. David Kilcullen, *The Accidental Guerrilla: Fighting Small Wars in the Midst of a Big One* (New York: Oxford Univ. Press, 2009), 6, 28–38.
4. See, for example, instances of attacks on U.S. civilian personnel in the early stages of the war in Neil Sheehan, *A Bright Shining Lie: John Paul Vann and America in Vietnam* (New York: Vintage Books, 1988), 499–585.
5. Nick Cullather, *Secret History: The CIA's Classified Account of Its Operations in Guatemala, 1952–1954* (Stanford, CA: Stanford Univ. Press, 1999), 40–46, 64–71; Stephen Schlesinger and Stephen Kinzer, *Bitter Fruit: The Untold Story of the American Coup in Guatemala* (New York: Anchor Books, 1990), 165–172; Michael McClintock, *Instruments of Statecraft: U.S. Guerrilla Warfare, Counter-Insurgency, Counter-Terrorism, 1940–1990* (New York: Pantheon Books, 1992), 230–257. See also Ralph Peters, "The New Warrior Class Revisited," *Small Wars and Insurgencies* 13 (Summer 2002): 16–25.
6. Bonnie Cordes, Bruce Hoffman, Brian M. Jenkins, et. al, *Trends in International Terrorism, 1982 and 1983* (Santa Monica, CA: RAND, 1984), 5.
7. Embassy (Tripoli) to State, "Campaign Against Terrorism: A Longer Term Perspective," 9 Apr. 1973, cable, Digital National Security Archive, http://www.narchive.chadwyck.com (hereafter DNSA).
8. Central Intelligence Agency, "Terrorism and the Fedayeen," Sept. 1972, DNSA.
9. Ibid.
10. Embassy (Tel Aviv) to State, "Campaign Against Terror," 23 Mar. 1973, DNSA.
11. Richard M. Nixon to William P. Rogers (State), "Actions to Combat Terrorism," 25 Sept. 1972, memorandum, 2, DNSA.
12. William P. Rogers (State) to Richard M. Nixon, "Measures to Combat Terrorism," 21 Sept. 1972, memorandum, DNSA. See also Brian M. Jenkins, *Combating Terrorism Becomes a War* (Santa Monica, CA: RAND, May 1984), 1, Army Heritage and Education Center (hereafter AHEC), Brian M. Jenkins Papers, Box 1.
13. Secretary of State (Rogers), "Combating of Terrorism," 9 Sept. 1972, DNSA.
14. John R. Stevenson (State) to William P. Rogers, "Draft Convention for the Prevention and Punishment of Certain Acts of International Terrorism," 22 Sept. 1972, memorandum, DNSA.

15. Ibid.
16. Office of the Attorney General to Melvin R. Laird (Defense), 10 Nov. 1972, DNSA.
17. Thomas C. Tompkins, *Military Countermeasures to Terrorism in the 1980s* (Santa Monica, CA: RAND, Aug. 1984), 26–28.
18. See, for example, Planning and Coordination Staff, Bureau of Intelligence and Research, U.S. Dept. of State, "State Department Conference on Terrorism," 29 Dec. 1972, DNSA; Konrad Kellen, *Terrorists—What Are They Like? How Some Terrorists Describe Their Words and Actions* (Santa Monica, CA: RAND, Nov. 1979), 1–11.
19. Robert S. Ingersoll (State) to Gerald R. Ford, "Combating Terrorism," 18 Feb. 1975, memorandum, 2–3, Ford Library, National Security Advisor, NSC Latin American Affairs, Staff Files, 1974–1977, Box 10.
20. Ibid., 8.
21. Ibid., 9–10.
22. U.S. Central Intelligence Agency, National Foreign Assessment Center, *International Terrorism in 1977,* RP 78–10255U, Aug. 1978, ii, 4. See also Brian M. Jenkins, *Terrorism in the 1980s* (Santa Monica, CA: RAND, Dec. 1980), 3–5, DNSA.
23. CIA, *International Terrorism, 1977,* 10. Between 1968 and 1977, these two methods comprised 63.5 percent of all terrorist attacks.
24. Ibid., 4.
25. Brian M. Jenkins to David Aaron (Special Assistant to the President for National Security Affairs), "An Independent Review of U.S. Capabilities for Combatting Terrorism," Sept. 1979, memorandum, Jimmy Carter Library, Staff Office Files, National Security Advisor, Odom File, Box 52.
26. Ibid., 7.
27. Specific acts constituting terrorism were considered to be assassination, hijacking, kidnapping, hostage holding, bombing, arson, armed attack, and extortion. See National Security Council, Special Coordination Committee, Executive Committee on Terrorism, *The United States Government Antiterrorism Program: An Unclassified Summary Report* (Washington, DC: National Security Council, June 1979), 11.
28. Ibid., 7–8.
29. Ibid., 11.
30. See, for example, Executive Order 12170, "Blocking Iranian Government Property," 14 Nov. 1979, DNSA.
31. U.S. Central Intelligence Agency, National Foreign Assessment Center, *International Terrorism in 1979,* PA 80–10072U, Apr. 1980, 1, 6, DNSA.
32. National Security Decision Directive 277, "National Policy and Strategy for Low Intensity Conflict," 15 June 1987, DNSA.

33. Central Intelligence Agency, National Foreign Assessment Center, "Grow ing Terrorist Danger for Americans," 23 Dec. 1981, DNSA; James W. Nance (White House) to Ronald Reagan, "U.S. General Kidnapped in Italy," 17 Dec. 1981, DNSA.
34. National Security Council, "Orchestrating a Relevant Response," June 1985, DNSA.
35. George Schultz, "Terrorism and the Modern World," *Current Policy,* no. 629 (25 Oct. 1985): 2. See also NSDD-176, "Combating Terrorism in Central America,"9 July 1985.
36. John Tagliabue, "Car Bomb Kills 2 on U.S. Airbase in West Germany," *New York Times,* 9 Aug. 1985, 1; James P. Markham, "Bombing at PX in Frankfurt Wounds 34," *New York Times,* 24 Nov. 1985, 2.
37. James M. Markham, "Discovery in West Berlin: Arab Suspect Visited Libya," *New York Times,* 26 Apr. 1986, A6.
38. For an overview of terrorist incidents, see U.S. Dept. of State, Bureau of Intelligence and Research, *Thirteen Months of Anti-U.S. Terrorism,* Report 1025-AR, 13 Mar. 1985, DNSA.
39. Robert Oakley, "International Terrorism," *Foreign Affairs* 65 (1986): 613.
40. Robert B. Oakley, "International Terrorism: Current Trends and U.S. Response," *Current Policy,* no. 706 (15 May 1985): 1–7.
41. Don Gregg and David Menarchik (Office of the Vice President) to George Bush, "U.S. Policy on Combatting Terrorism and Terrorism Task Force," 10 Jan. 1986, memorandum, DNSA.
42. Nancy Bearg Dyke (National Security Advisor to the Vice President) to George Bush, "Meeting on Terrorism with National Security Council Advisors," 26 Jan. 1981, memorandum, DNSA.
43. NSDD 30, "Managing Terrorist Incidents," 10 Apr. 1982, 1–2, DNSA.
44. U.S. State Dept., *Report to Congress: The Anti-Terrorism Assistance Program* (Washington, DC: GPO, Mar. 1985), 1–4. See also Raphael F. Perl, "Terrorism, the Future, and U.S. Foreign Policy," *Congressional Research Service,* IB95112 (13 Sept. 2001): 11.
45. NSDD 207, "The National Program for Combatting Terrorism," 20 Jan. 1986, 1–2, DNSA.
46. Oliver L. North (NSC) to John M. Poindexter (NSC), "Protection of U.S. Personnel," 6 Dec. 1984, Ronald Reagan Library, White House Staff and Office Files, 1981–1989, Oliver L. North Files, Box 92.
47. NSDD 179, "Task Force on Combatting Terrorism," 20 July 1985, DNSA.
48. Jenkins, *Combating Terrorism,* 1; C. Boyden Gray to the Vice President, "Secretary Shultz's Remarks to the President and Cabinet on Terrorism," 2 July 1985, memorandum, George Bush Library, Office of the Vice President, Subject Files, Box 1.

49. Vice Admiral J. A. Lyons, Deputy Chief of Naval Operations to the Chief of Naval Operations, "Counter-Terrorism Support Actions," 13 Jan. 1984, memorandum, DNSA. See also Richard Marcinko with John Weisman, *Rogue Warrior* (New York: Pocket Books, 1992), 281–293.
50. U.S. Dept. of the Army, Headquarters, *FM 100-37: Terrorism Counter-action* (Washington, DC: U.S. Dept. of the Army, July 1987).
51. Edward F. Bruner, Christopher Bolkcom, and Ronald O'Rourke, "Special Operations Forces in Operation Enduring Freedom: Background and Issues for Congress," *CRS Report for Congress,* RS21048 (15 Oct. 2001): 1. See also Alan W. Dowd, "Special Forces and the Campaign Against Terror," *World & I* 19 (Mar. 2004): 249–253.
52. NSDD 277, "National Policy and Strategy for Low Intensity Conflict," 15 June 1987, 3.
53. John M. Poindexter (NSC), "Meeting with the National Security Planning Group," 18 Jan. 1985, memorandum, DNSA.
54. NSDD-205, "Acting Against Libyan Support of International Terrorism," 8 Jan. 1986, 1.
55. Christopher Greenwood, "International Law and the War Against Terrorism," *International Affairs* 78 (Apr. 2002): 301–317. See also David Owen, "State Terrorism, Internationalism and Collective Action," *Review of International Studies* 13 (Apr. 1987): 82–87. Owen's particular objection is to the lack of proportionality that would justify a unilateral military response.
56. CIA manuals discovered by the U.S. media were regularly published in the eighties. See *The Freedom Fighter's Manual: Practical Guide to Liberating Nicaragua from Oppression and Misery by Paralyzing the Military-Industrial Complex of the Traitorous Marxist State without Having to Use Special Tools and with Minimal Risk for the Combatant* (New York: Grove Press, 1985).
57. George Bush to Ronald Reagan, 2 June 1987, DNSA.
58. Walter Laqueur, "Postmodern Terrorism," *Foreign Affairs* 75 (Sept.–Oct. 1996): 25–27.
59. U.S. Dept. of State, *Secretary of State's Advisory Panel Report on Overseas Security* (Washington, DC: U.S. Dept. of State, June 1985), 7–8, DNSA.
60. Directorate of Intelligence, Central Intelligence Agency, *Terrorism Review,* 21 Feb. 1991, DNSA.
61. Counterterrorist Center, Central Intelligence Agency, "International Terrorism in 1997: A Statistical View," 1, DNSA.
62. Thomas Homer-Dixon, "The Rise of Complex Terrorism," *Foreign Policy* No. 128 (Jan./Feb. 2002): 52–62. See also Klare, "The Kalashnikov Age," 18–23. Another key area of concern was the spread of shoulder-

launched missiles. See Thomas B. Hunter, "The Proliferation of MANPADS," *Jane's Intelligence Review* 13 (Sept. 2001): 42–45.

63. "U.S. Policy on Counterterrorism," 21 June 1995, Presidential Decision Directive (PDD) 39, 1, DNSA.
64. Madeleine K. Albright, "The William Cohen Lecture: Combining Force and Diplomacy to Secure America's Future," *U.S. Department of State Dispatch* 10 (Nov. 1999): 18.
65. John Deutch, "Terrorism," *Foreign Policy,* no. 108 (Autumn 1997): 14.
66. Ibid., 17.
67. Raphael F. Perl, "Terrorism: U.S. Response to Bombings in Kenya and Tanzania: A New Policy Direction?" *Congressional Research Service* 98–733F (1 Sept. 1998), 2.
68. U.S. Dept. of Justice, Federal Bureau of Investigation, Counterterrorism Threat Assessment and Warning Unit, National Security Division, *Terrorism in the United States, 1998* (Washington, DC: U.S. Dept. of Justice, 1998), 3–10.
69. Executive Order 12947, "Prohibiting Transactions with Terrorists Who Threaten to Disrupt the Middle East Peace Process," *Federal Register* 60 (25 Jan. 1995).
70. Executive Order 13129, "Blocking Property and Prohibiting Transactions with the Taliban," *Federal Register* 64 (7 July 1999).
71. Perl, "Terrorism," 2.
72. U.S. Dept. of Justice, *Terrorism in the United States, 1998,* 11, 15–16. Three specific federal laws are cited that gave the FBI "extraterritorial jurisdiction" in instances of terrorism: the Comprehensive Crime Control Act (1984), the Omnibus Diplomatic Security and Antiterrorist Act (1986), and the Antiterrorism and Effective Death Penalty Act (1996).
73. Susan B. Epstein, "Embassy Security: Background, Funding, and the Budget," *Congressional Research Service,* RL30662 (4 Oct. 2001): 7, 10. In 1998 it stood at $280.1 million. Total 1999 requests for appropriations were $1.7 billion.
74. Perl, "Terrorism," 2–3.
75. U.S. General Accounting Office, *Combating Terrorism: Issues to Be Resolved to Improve Counterterrorism Operations,* GAO/NSIAD-99-135 (Washington, DC: GAO, May 1999), 5.
76. Perl, "Terrorism," 6 (emphasis added).
77. Office of the Press Secretary, The White House, "Fact Sheet: Combating Terrorism: Presidential Decision Directive 62," 22 May 1998, DNSA.
78. Jeffrey D. Brake, "Terrorism and the Military's Role in Domestic Crisis Management: Background and Issues for Congress, *Congressional Research Service* RL30938 (19 Apr. 2001): 2–4.

79. *The 9/11 Commission Report: Final Report of the National Commission on Terrorist Attacks upon the United States* (New York: W. W. Norton & Co., 2004), 254–277.
80. Raphael F. Perl, "National Commission on Terrorism Report: Background and Issues for Congress," *Congressional Research Service* RS20598 (6 Feb. 2001), 3–4.
81. Richard B. Cheney, "Meeting the Challenge of the War on Terrorism," (Washington, DC: Heritage Foundation, 17 Oct. 2003), 2.
82. Melani McAlister, "A Cultural History of the War without End," *Journal of American History* 89 (Sept. 2002): 455.
83. Tom Donnelly, "Strategic Strife," *Jane's Defence Weekly* 34 (29 Nov. 2000): 24–28.
84. *The National Security Strategy of the United States of America,* 17 Sept. 2002, http://www.whitehouse.gov/nsc/nssall.html.
85. Melanie Bright, "Armed Forces and the Environment: Part Two—The U.S. Army," *Jane's Defence Weekly* 40 (1 Oct. 2003): 29–33. See also Michael Sirak, "U.S. Looks to Build on Non-Lethal Weapon Support," *Jane's Defence Weekly* 40 (12 Nov. 2003): 9.
86. Kim Burger, "New Direction for U.S. Army," *Jane's Defence Weekly* 46 (27 Aug. 2003): 23.
87. Andrew Koch, Michael Sirak, and Kim Burger, "QDR 2001: The Battle Begins," *Jane's Defence Weekly* 35 (16 May 2001): 24–27.
88. U.S. Dept. of Defense, *Quadrennial Defense Review Report* (Washington, DC: U.S. Dept. of Defense, 30 Sept. 2001), 5, 42.
89. Ibid., 29.
90. Ibid., 40–42, 47–48.
91. U.S. Joint Chiefs of Staff, *Joint Vision 2010* (Washington, DC: JCS, 1996).
92. Norman Friedman, *Terrorism: Afghanistan, and America's New Way of War* (Annapolis, MD: Naval Institute Press, 2003), 157, 171–174; U.S. Special Operations Command, History and Research Office, *United States Special Operations Command History* (MacDill Air Force Base, FL: USSOCOM, 2002), 81.
93. "Special Forces and Counter-Terrorism," *Military Technology* 30 (Dec. 2006): 76–77.
94. Michael Fitzsimmons, "The Importance of Being Special: Planning for the Future of U.S. Special Operations Forces," *Defense and Security Analysis* 19 (Sept. 2003): 204.
95. "Special Forces and Counter-Terrorism," 77. The reported budget for FY 2007 was $6.2 billion. See U.S. Special Operations Command, *Posture Statement, 2007* (Washington, DC: USSOCOM, 2007), 10.
96. Ibid.
97. Joshua Kucera, "U.S. Boosts Special Forces to Meet Iraqi Challenge," *Jane's Defence Weekly* 41 (18 Feb. 2004): 10. See also U.S. Special Opera-

tions Command, *2005 Annual Report* (MacDill Air Force Base, FL: USSOCOM, 2005), 15–17.

98. Harold Kennedy, "Special Operations Command Plans for Expanded Role in U.S. War on Terrorism," *National Defense* 89 (Apr. 2005): 40.

99. Grace V. Jean, "'Lawrences of the World'," *National Defense* 93 (Apr. 2009): 26.

100. Linda Robinson, "Men on a Mission: U.S. Special Forces Are Retooling for the War on Terror. Here's the Plan," *U.S. News and World Report* 141 (11 Sept. 2006): 37.

101. "Special Forces and Counter-Terrorism," 76.

102. David S. Maxwell, "Operation Enduring Freedom—Philippines: What Would Sun Tzu Say?" *Military Review* 84 (May/June 2004): 20.

103. C. H. Briscoe, "Why the Philippines? ARSOF's Expanded Mission in the War on Terror," *Special Warfare* 17 (Sept. 2004): 2–3.

104. "Special Forces and Counter-Terrorism," 78. See also U.S. Dept. of State, *Pattern of Global Terrorism, 2000* (Washington, DC: U.S. Dept. of State, Apr. 2001), 56.

105. C. H. Briscoe, "Reflections and Observations on ARSOF Operations during Balikatan 02–1," *Special Warfare* 17 (Sept. 2004): 55; U.S. Special Operations Command, *Posture Statement, 2007,* 17.

106. Max Boot and Richard Bennet, "Treading Softly in the Philippines," *Weekly Standard* 14 (5–12 Jan. 2009): 28.

107. Briscoe, "Reflections and Observations on ARSOF Operations during Balikatan 02–1," 56–57; Maxwell, "Operation Enduring Freedom—Philippines," 21, 23.

108. Boot and Bennet, "Treading Softly in the Philippines," 23.

109. Ibid., 28.

110. Pat Paterson, "Into Africa: A New Frontier in the War on Terror," *United States Naval Institute Proceedings* 132 (May 2006): 32–36.

111. Ibid.

112. "Special Forces and Counter-Terrorism," 78.

113. Paterson, "Into Africa," 34–35; U.S. Special Operations Command, *Posture Statement, 2007,* 9.

114. Ibid; Cameron Duodu, "Somalia: Why the New American 'Blueprint' Is Dangerous for Africa," *New African,* no. 459 (Feb. 2007): 48.

115. Moussa Diop Mboup, Michael Mihalka, and Douglas Lathrop, "Misguided Intentions: Resisting AFRICOM," *Military Review* 89 (July/Aug. 2009): 89.

116. Scott Johnson, "Africa Turns Away Troops," *Newsweek* 154 (16 Nov. 2009), http://www.proquest.com. See also Carlton W. Fulford, "Thinking through U.S. Strategic Options for Africa," *Naval War College Review* 62 (Winter 2009): 30–43.

117. Luz Estella Nagle, *Plan Colombia: Reality of the Colombian Crisis and Implications for Hemispheric Security* (Carlisle, PA: Strategic Studies Institute, 2002), 39.
118. Martin Dayani, "Terror Focuses on Colombia," *Jane's Defence Weekly* 37 (23 Jan. 2002): 21.
119. Jeremy McDermott, "War Resumes after Collapse of Colombian Peace Process," *Jane's Intelligence Review* 14 (Apr. 2002): 11.
120. Kim Burger, "USA Turns Up Heat on Colombia Insurgents," *Jane's Defence Weekly* 39 (8 Jan. 2003): 6.
121. Jeremy McDermott, "Uribe Gains the Upper Hand in Colombia's Guerrilla War," *Jane's Intelligence Review* 15 (Dec. 2003): 16–17.
122. Jeremy McDermott, "Washington Increases Assistance to Colombia," *Jane's Defence Weekly* 41 (4 Feb. 2004): 10.
123. McDermott, "War Resumes after Collapse of Colombian Peace Process," 9–10; Jeremy McDermott, "FARC Gives Notice of a Urban Campaign," *Jane's Intelligence Review* 14 (Sept. 2002): 24–25.
124. Jeremy McDermott, "Rebels Bide Their Time," *Jane's Defence Weekly* (7 Jan. 2004): 23.
125. "Special Forces and Counter-Terrorism," 77–78.
126. See John Gidduck, *Terror at Beslan: A Russian Tragedy with Lessons for America's Schools* (Golden, CO: Archangel Group, 2005), 47–107.
127. Roxana Tiron, "Counterinsurgency in Iraq Provides Template for Fighting Terrorism," *National Defense* 89 (Apr. 2005): 40; Kilcullen, *The Accidental Guerrilla,* 263–289.
128. Raphael F. Perl, " International Terrorism: Threat, Policy, and Response," *Military Technology* (Dec. 2006): 67.
129. See David Vine, "Enabling the Kill Chain," *Chronicle of Higher Education* 54 (30 Nov. 2007): B9.
130. Fitzsimmons, "The Importance of Being Special," 212.
131. Daniel L. Byman, "Friends Like These: Counterinsurgency and the War on Terrorism," *International Security* 31 (Fall 2006): 79–115.

8. Iraq and Afghanistan

1. Rashid Khalidi, "Iraq and American Empire," *New Political Science* 28 (Mar. 2008): 125–134. Khalidi was also a critic of the first war against Iraq.
2. *The 9/11 Commission Report: Final Report of the National Commission on Terrorist Attacks upon the United States* (New York: W. W. Norton & Co., 2004), 330–338.
3. Dale R. Herspring, *Rumsfeld's Wars: The Arrogance of American Power* (Lawrence: Univ. Press of Kansas, 2008), 81–83.

4. See earlier references in chapter 2. Richard Lock-Pullan, *U.S. Intervention Policy and Army Innovation: From Vietnam to Iraq* (New York: Routledge, 2006), 64–66. See also Joshua A. Kutner, "U.S. Forces Fall Short on 'Rapid, Decisive Operations,' Says Admiral," *National Defense* 84 (June 2000): 13; David Tucker and Christopher J. Lamb, *United States Special Operations Forces* (New York: Columbia Univ. Press, 2007), 179–204.
5. U.S. Dept. of the Army, Headquarters, *FM 100-5: Operations* (Fort Monroe, VA: U.S. Army Training and Doctrine Command, June 1993).
6. Jay D. Pellerin, "Tanks and 'Shock and Awe'," *Armor* 112 (Sept./Oct. 2003): 32–40; Sean Griffin, "Time to Reevaluate Rapid Decisive Operations," *U.S. Naval Institute Proceedings* 135 (Jan. 2009): 77.
7. Christopher Ankersen, "Rapid Decisive Ops are Risky Business," *U.S. Naval Institute Proceedings* 129 (Oct. 2003): 52.
8. Tucker and Lamb, *United States Special Operations Forces,* 104–106; Tommy Franks, *American Soldier* (New York: Regan Books, 2004), 260–261.
9. Michael DeLong, *Inside CENTCOM: The Unvarnished Truth about the Wars in Afghanistan and Iraq* (Washington, DC: Regnery, 2004), 40–42, 45–49; John A. Nagl, *Learning to Eat Soup with a Knife: Counterinsurgency Lessons from Malaya and Vietnam,* 2nd ed. (Chicago: Univ. of Chicago Press, 2005), xxi–xxii.
10. Stephen Biddle, "Special Forces and the Future of Warfare," *Military Technology* 30 (Mar. 2006): 14.
11. James A. Schroder, "Observations: ARSOF in Afghanistan," *Special Warfare* 15 (Sept. 2002): 50–52.
12. Michael O'Hanlon, "A Flawed Masterpiece," *Foreign Affairs* 81 (May/June 2002): 47.
13. Herspring, *Rumsfeld's Wars,* 78–88, 114–125, 129–131.
14. Literature on this topic in 2002 alone is voluminous. See Jason Vest, "Pentagon Hawks Take Wing," *Nation* 275 (16 Dec. 2002): 16–17, and Perry M. Smith, "The Rumsfeld Way: Leadership Wisdom of a Battle-Hardened Maverick," *U.S. Naval Institute Proceedings* 128 (Oct. 2002): 110.
15. One postinvasion study may be found in U.S. Senate, Committee on Foreign Relations, *Tora Bora Revisited: How We Failed to Get Bin Laden and Why It Matters Today* (Washington, DC: Government Printing Office).
16. DeLong, *Inside CENTCOM,* 55; Senate Foreign Relations Committee, *Tora Bora Revisited,* 7, 10–12.
17. Anthony H. Cordesman, *The Lessons of Afghanistan: War Fighting, Intelligence, and Force Transformation* (Washington, DC: CSIS Press, 2002), 64.
18. Adam Geibel, "Operation Anaconda, Shah-i-Khot Valley, Afghanistan, 2–10 Mar. 2002," *Military Review* 82 (May/June 2002): 72–77; Gregory J. Ford, "Lessons Learned from Afghanistan: A Battalion S2's Perspective," *Military Intelligence Professional Bulletin* 30 (Jan.–Mar. 2004): 21.

19. Cordesman, *Lessons of Afghanistan,* 67.
20. David W. Barno, "Fighting 'The Other War': Counterinsurgency Strategy in Afghanistan, 2003–2005," *Military Review* 87 (Sept./Oct. 2007): 32–44. For an excellent memoir on the war in Afghanistan, see Benjamin Tupper, *Welcome to Afghanistan, Send More Ammo* (Rhinebeck, NY: Epigraph, 2009).
21. David Kilcullen argues that local alienation became an important recruiting tool for the insurgency in Afghanistan. See David Kilcullen, *The Accidental Guerrilla: Fighting Small Wars in the Midst of a Big One* (New York: Oxford Univ. Press, 2009), 39–114.
22. Patrick Donahue and Michael Fenzel, "Combating a Modern Insurgency: Combined Task Force Devil in Afghanistan," *Military Review* 88 (June 2008): 76, 81.
23. Barno, "Fighting 'The Other War,'" 35.
24. Ibid., 34; Donahue and Fenzel, "Combating a Modern Insurgency," 85–86. See also Mark Jones and Wes Rehorn, "Special Operations Forces: Integrating SOF into Joint Warfighting," *Military Review* 83 (May/June 2003): 2–7. For USAID doctrine, see U.S. Agency for International Development, *Fragile States Strategy,* PD-ACA-999 (Washington, DC: USAID, Jan. 2005), 2.
25. Barno, "Fighting 'The Other War,'" 42–43.
26. Emma Björnehed, "Narco-Terrorism: The Merger of the War on Drugs and the War on Terror," *Global Crime* 6 (Aug.–Nov. 2004): 309.
27. Dennis Steele, "President's Afghan Timetable Twists Afghan Arms to Shoulder the Load," *Army* 60 (Jan. 2010): 21, 25; John Barry and Michael Hirsh, "Mission Impossible?" *Newsweek* 154 (14 Dec. 2009): 12
28. Fred W. Baker, "McChystal Notes Progress in Afghanistan," *U.S. Department of Defense Information* (5 Feb. 2010), http://www.proquest.com.
29. Barry and Hirsh, "Mission Impossible?" 12.
30. H. R. McMaster, "The Human Element: When Gadgetry Becomes Strategy," *World Affairs* 171 (Winter 2009): 33–36, 39–41. See also Richard D. Hooker, H. R. McMaster, and Dave Grey, "Getting Transformation Right," *Joint Forces Quarterly* 38 (Third Quarter 2005): 20–27.
31. Herspring, *Rumsfeld's Wars,* 68–88.
32. Franks, *American Soldier,* 361–363.
33. Charles H. Briscoe, Kenneth Finlayson, Robert W. Jones, et al., *All Roads Lead to Baghdad: Army Special Operations Forces in Iraq* (Fort Bragg, NC: USASOC History Office, 2006), 22–25.
34. Ibid., 24–25. In his memoir, Bush played down criticism of deficiencies in postwar planning. See George W. Bush, *Decision Points* (New York: Crown, 2010), 247–250.
35. Les Aspin, *The Bottom-Up Review: Forces for a New Era* (Washington, DC: U.S. Dept. of Defense, 1993), 9.

36. Briscoe, Finlayson, Jones, et al., *All Roads Lead to Baghdad,* 77.
37. *Peshmerga* means "those who face death." See *All Roads Lead to Baghdad,* 193–198, 372–376; Kerim Yildiz, *The Kurds of Iraq: The Past, Present, and Future* (Ann Arbor, MI: Pluto Press, 2004), 16–20.
38. Briscoe, Finlayson, Jones, et al., *All Roads Lead to Baghdad,* 190.
39. See, for example, William R. Hawkins, "Iraq: Heavy Forces and Decisive Warfare," *Parameters* 33 (Autumn 2003): 61–67.
40. Briscoe, Finlayson, Jones, et al., *All Roads Lead to Baghdad,* 353.
41. Ibid., 350–351. See also Evan Wright, *Generation Kill: Devil Dogs, Iceman, Captain America, and the New Face of American War* (New York: Berkley Caliber, 2005), 315–321.
42. Nora Bensahel, Olga Oliker, Keith Crane, et al., *After Saddam: Prewar Planning and the Occupation of Iraq* (Santa Monica, CA: RAND, 2008), xx.
43. Central Command created Task Force IV in January 2003 to address postwar planning. The Defense Department had both the Office of Special Plans, a prewar planning agency, and the Office of Reconstruction and Humanitarian Assistance, established on 20 Jan. 2003 by NSPD-24.
44. Bensahel, Oliker, Crane, et. al, *After Saddam,* xxvi. See also John M. Collins, "You Can't Assume Nothin,'" *U.S. Naval Institute Proceedings* 129 (May 2003): 50.
45. Michael Peck, "Marines Share Hard-Earned Knowledge," *National Defense* 90 (July 2005): 30–32; Dexter Filkins, "The Fall of the Warrior King," *New York Times Magazine,* 23 Oct. 2005, 52–66. See also Dick Camp, *Operation Phantom Fury: The Assault and Capture of Fallujah, Iraq* (Osceola, WI: Zenith Press, 2009).
46. Matt Carr, "The Barbarians of Fallujah," *Race and Class* 50 (July–Sept. 2008): 21–36.
47. Michael Ware, "Chasing Ghosts," *Time* 166 (26 Sept. 2005): 32–38. See also Nagl, *Learning to Eat Soup with a Knife,* xiii.
48. Eric Schmitt, "Effort to Train New Iraqi Army Is Facing Delays," *New York Times,* 20 Sept. 2004, 1; William McDonough, "Time for a New Strategy," *Parameters* 38 (Autumn 2008): 109–110.
49. William B. Caldwell, and Steven M. Leonard, "Field Manual 3–07, Stability Operations: Upshifting the Engine of Change," *Military Review* 88 (July/Aug. 2008): 8.
50. See Laura Geldhof, Maureen Green, Remi Hajjar, et al., "Intelligent Design: COIN Operations and Intelligence Collection and Analysis," *Military Review* 86 (Sept./Oct. 2006): 30–37.
51. Travis Patriquin and Rajiv Chandrassekaran, "Using Occam's Razor to Connect the Dots: The Ba'ath Party and the Insurgency in Tal Afar," *Military Review* 87 (Jan./Feb. 2007): 16–25.
52. Chris Gibson, "Battlefield Victories and Strategic Success: The Path Forward in Iraq," *Military Review* 86 (Sept./Oct. 2006): 49. Gibson uses

the acronym SWET to describe "sewage, water, electricity, and trash removal" under basic services. For an additional example, see Stanley T. Grip, "The Afghani Model," *Army* 58 (May 2008): 47–54.

53. Niel Smith, "Retaking Sa'ad: Successful Counterinsurgency in Tal Afar," *Armor* 116 (July/Aug. 2007): 26–35.
54. Patriquin and Chandrassekaran, "Using Occam's Razor to Connect the Dots," 23.
55. John S. Brown, "Mogadishu 1993, Tal Afar 2004 and Army Transformation," *Army* 57 (Feb. 2007): 78–80.
56. U.S. Dept. of the Army, *FM-3-24: Counterinsurgency* (Washington, DC: U.S. Dept. of the Army, 15 Dec. 2006). Appendix D contains the section on counterinsurgency and legality.
57. U.S. Dept. of the Army, *FM 3-0: Operations* (Washington, DC: U.S. Dept. of the Army, Feb. 2008), 1–1.
58. Ibid., see chap. 3, "Full Spectrum Operations."
59. Petraeus, "Multinational Force-Iraq Commander's Counterinsurgency Guidance," *Military Review* 88 (Sept–Oct 2008): 2.
60. Ibid.
61. See, for example, U.S. Dept. of the Army, Headquarters, *FM 100-5: Operations* (Washington, DC: U.S. Dept. of the Army, June 1993).
62. Jonathan Rauch, "A Bad Idea That Deserves a Try," *National Journal* 39 (20 Jan. 2007): 15–16.
63. Peter R. Mansoor and Mark S. Ulrich, "Linking Doctrine to Action: A New COIN Center-of-Gravity Analysis," *Military Review* 87 (Sept./Oct. 2007): 45.
64. Frederick Kagan and Kimberly Kagan, "The Patton of Counterinsurgency," *Weekly Standard* 13 (10 Mar. 2008): 27–33.
65. Operation Phantom Thunder (June–July 2007), Operation Phantom Strike (Aug. 2007), and Operation Phantom Phoenix (Jan. 2008) followed the initial surge in quick succession. See Kagan and Kagan, "The Patton of Counterinsurgency," 30.
66. Max Boot, "We Are Winning. We Haven't Won," *Weekly Standard* 13 (4 Feb. 2008): 31.
67. Dennis Steele, "After Action Report: The Surge from Gen. Petraeus' Perspective," *Army* 58 (Dec. 2008): 29; McDonough, "Time for a New Strategy," 111. Petraeus put the number of Sons of Iraq at over 100,000. See David H. Petraeus, "Gen. Petraeus' Second Iraq Report," *Army* 58 (June 2008): 41, 44.
68. "Counterterror Coordinator," *Special Warfare* 21 (July/Aug. 2008): 12; Robert W. Wagner, "USASOC: Resolute and Ready," *Army* 58 (Oct. 2008): 172; U.S. Special Operations Command, *Posture Statement, 2007* (Washington, DC: USSOCOM, 2007), 8.

69. Petraeus, "Gen. Petraeus' Second Iraq Report," 40.
70. Boot, "We Are Winning. We Haven't Won," 32.
71. Andrew J. Bacevich, "Surge to Nowhere," *Current* Issue 500 (Feb. 2008): 15.
72. Mitchell M. Zais, "Iraq: The Way Ahead," *Military Review* 88 (Jan./Feb. 2008): 113.
73. "Most Americans Still Upset About Iraq Invasion," *Angus Reid Global Monitor,* 8 Mar. 2008. http://www.angus-reid.com.
74. Cordesman, *The Lessons of Afghanistan,* 19.
75. Edward B. Atkeson, "Shock and Awe?" *Army* 53 (May 2003): 8–12.
76. Huba Wass de Czege, "Systemic Operational Design: Learning and Adapting in Complex Missions," *Military Review* 89 (Jan./Feb. 2009): 2–12.
77. Robert W. Cone, "The Changing National Training Center," *Military Review* 86 (May/June 2006): 70–79.
78. See Nathaniel C. Fick and John A. Nagl, "Counterinsurgency Field Manual: Afghanistan Edition," *Foreign Policy* 170 (Jan./Feb. 2009): 42–47.
79. T. Christian Miller, Mark Hosenball and Ron Moreau, "The Gang That Couldn't Shoot Straight: Six Billion Dollars Later, The Afghan National Police Can't Begin to Do Their Jobs Right—Never Mind Relieve American Forces," *Newsweek* 155 (29 Mar. 2010), http://www.proquest.com.

9. Private Military Corporations in the New Century

1. Lawrence W. Serewicz, "Globalization, Sovereignty and Military Revolution: From Mercenaries to Private International Security Companies," *International Politics* 39 (Mar. 2002): 75–89.
2. Ibid., 75.
3. David Shearer, *Private Armies and Military Intervention* (New York: Oxford Univ. Press, 1998), 27–29.
4. For a representative portion of this debate, see Alex Mintz and Chi Huang, "Defense Expenditures, Economic Growth, and the 'Peace Dividend,'" *American Political Science Review* 84 (Dec. 1990): 1283–1293.
5. Dave Whyte, "Lethal Regulation: State-Corporate Crime and the United Kingdom Government's New Mercenaries," *Journal of Law and Society* 30 (Dec. 2003): 583.
6. Martin van Creveld, *The Transformation of War* (New York: Free Press, 1991), 187. See also Serge Schemann, "Not Taking Losses Is One Thing: Winning Is Another," *New York Times,* 3 Jan. 1999, 1, 5.
7. For an examination of the historical conditions that created an emphasis on volunteerism, see Deborah Avant, "From Mercenary to Citizen Armies: Explaining Change in the Practice of War," *International Organization* 54 (Winter 2000): 41–72.

8. For a more pessimistic outlook, see Robert D. Kaplan, "The Coming Anarchy," *Atlantic Monthly* 273 (Feb. 1994): 44–76.
9. Paul Kennedy, "Maintaining American Power: From Injury to Recovery," in *The Age of Terror: America and the World after September 11,* ed. Strobe Talbot and Nayan Chanda (New York: Basic Books, 2001), 58–59.
10. Susan Strange, "The Erosion of the State," *Current History* 96 (Nov. 1997): 367–368.
11. Ibid., 365. Strange specifically cites the influence on financial structures as well as the "material life" of affected nations.
12. P. W. Singer, "Peacekeepers, Inc.," *Policy Review* 119 (June/July 2003): 62–63.
13. Samuel R. Berger, "Challenges Approaching the 21st Century," in *At the End of the American Century: America's Role in the Post-Cold War World,* ed. Robert L. Hutchins (Baltimore: Johns Hopkins Univ. Press, 1998), 184–188. The bulk of Berger's postmortem on Clinton-era policies focuses on economic trade agreements.
14. Kevin A. O'Brien, "Military-Advisory Groups and African Security: Privatised Peacekeeping?" *International Peacekeeping* 5 (Autumn 1998): 78–105; David J. Francis, "Mercenary Intervention in Sierra Leone: Providing National Security or International Exploitation?" *Third World Quarterly* 20 (1999): 319–338; Robert Mandel, *Armies without States: The Privatization of Security* (Boulder, CO: Lynne Rienner, 2002), 20–23.
15. "Risky Returns: Doing Business in Chaotic and Violent Countries," *Economist* 355 (20 May 2000): 85–88. Control Risks Group has responded to more than 1,100 cases kidnapping and extortion since 1975. See Jack Kelly, "Safety at a Price: Security Business Is Booming, Sophisticated, Global Business," *Pittsburgh Post Gazette* (13 Feb. 2000), http://www.post-gazette.com.
16. Mandel, *Armies without States,* 9–13.
17. Singer, "Peacekeepers, Inc.," 63; Deborah Avant, "The Privatization of Security and Change in the Control of Force," *International Studies Perspectives* 5 (2004): 153.
18. Overall, the number of forces committed to UN peacekeeping deployments declined during the 1990s from 76,000 in 1994 to approximately 15,000 in 1998. Singer, "Peacekeepers, Inc.," 59–70; Davis B. Bobrow and Mark A. Boyer, "Maintaining System Stability: Contributions to Peacekeeping Operations," *Journal of Conflict Resolution* 41 (Dec. 1997): 723–748; David Shearer, "Outsourcing War," *Foreign Policy* Issue 112 (Fall 1998): 70.
19. Whyte, "Lethal Regulation," 587. See also Madelaine Drohan, *Making a Killing: How and Why Corporations Use Armed Force to Do Business* (Guilford, CT: Lyons Press, 2003), 216–242; Sean Creehan, "Soldiers of Fortune 500," *Harvard International Review* 23 (Winter 2002): 6–7.

20. The Army-Navy Gun Foundry Board was created by the Naval Appropriations Act of 1883. See Allan R. Millett and Peter Maslowski, *For the Common Defense: A Military History of the United States of America* (New York: Free Press, 1994), 265–270; Michael A. Bernstein, "American Economic Expertise from the Great War to the Cold War: Some Initial Observations," *Journal of Economic History* 50 (June 1990): 407, 416.
21. Walter E. Grunden, Yutaka Kawamura, Edward Kolchinsky, et. al, "Laying the Foundation for Wartime Research: A Comparative Overview of Science Mobilization in National Socialist Germany, Japan, and the Soviet Union," *Osiris* 20 (2005): 79–106; David M. Kennedy, *Freedom from Fear: The American People in Depression and War, 1929–1945* (New York: Oxford Univ. Press, 2001), 615–668.
22. Atsushi Akera, "IBM's Early Adaptation to Cold War Markets: Cuthbert Hurd and His Applied Science Field Men," *Business History Review* 76 (Winter 2002): 767–802; Jonathan Soffer, "The National Association of Manufacturers and the Militarization of American Conservatism," *Business History Review* 75 (Winter 2001): 775–805; James T. Patterson, *Grand Expectations: The United States, 1945–1973* (New York: Oxford Univ. Press, 1996), 313–315; Ben Baack and Edward Ray, "The Political Economy of the Origins of the Military-Industrial Complex in the United States," *Journal of Economic History* 45 (June 1985): 369–375.
23. P. W. Singer, *Corporate Warriors: The Rise of the Privatized Military Industry* (Ithaca, NY: Cornell Univ. Press, 2003), 53.
24. Elke Krahmann, "Private Military Services in the UK and Germany: Between Partnership and Regulation," *European Security* 14 (June 2005): 283.
25. Ibid., 280–81; Whyte, "Lethal Regulation," 586. For a good examination of this trend, see also Kevin A. O'Brien, "PMCs, Myths and Mercenaries: The Debate on Private Military Companies," *Defence and International Security* 145 (Feb. 2000): 59–64.
26. Ann Markusen, "The Case Against Privatizing National Security," *Dollars and Sense* 253 (May/June 2004): 26–27.
27. U.S. Dept. of Defense, *Quadrennial Defense Review Report* (Washington, DC: U.S. Dept. of Defense, 30 Sept. 2001), 49.
28. Bryan Bender, "Moving with the Times," *Jane's Defence Weekly* 34 (15 Nov. 2000): 20–23; Nelson D. Schwartz and Noshua Watson, "The Pentagon's Private Army," *Fortune* 147 (17 Mar. 2003): 100–107. For an earlier piece on this trend, see Kirsten Sellars, "Old Dogs of War Learn New Tricks," *New Statesman* 126 (25 Mar. 1997): 24–26; Stephen Newbold, "Competitive Sourcing and Privatization: An Essential USAF Strategy," *Air Force Journal of Logistics* 23 (Spring 1999): 28–34.
29. Markusen, "The Case Against Privatising National Security," 28.
30. Deborah Avant, "Mercenaries," *Foreign Policy* (July/Aug. 2004): 21.

31. Shawn Macomber, "You're Not in the Army Now," *American Spectator* 37 (Nov. 2004): 26–30. By fiscal year 2003–2004, approximately 8 percent, or $30 billion, of the U.S. defense budget was spent on private military corporations. See Whyte, "Lethal Regulation," 577.
32. Doug Brooks, "Messiahs or Mercenaries? The Future of International Private Military Services," *International Peacekeeping* 7 (Winter 2000): 131; Ulric Shannon, "Human Security and the Rise of Private Armies," *New Political Science* 22 (Mar. 2000): 103–105.
33. Wayne Madsen, "Mercenaries in Kosovo: The U.S. Connection to the KLA," *Progressive* 63 (Aug. 1999): 30.
34. Macomber, "You're Not in the Army Now," 27.
35. Faye Bowers, "Security Tips Hinge on Winning Trust," *Christian Science Monitor* (30 Oct. 2003): 2; Kevin Whitelaw, Julian E. Barnes, and David E. Kaplan, "The Devil Really Is in the Details," *U.S. News and World Report* (16 Aug. 2004): 24.
36. Steven Brayton, "Outsourcing War: Mercenaries and the Privatization of Peacekeeping," *Journal of International Affairs* 55 (Spring 2002): 303–329; Michael D. Gambone, *Eisenhower, Somoza, and the Cold War in Nicaragua* (Westport, CT: Praeger, 1997), 78–84.
37. South Africans are commonly employed by American and British companies by virtue of their previous military experience and relatively cheaper cost.
38. Francis, "Mercenary Intervention in Sierra Leone," 333–335.
39. Singer organizes PMC service into three categories: implementation/command, advisory and training, and nonlethal aid and assistance. See Singer, *Corporate Warriors,* 93.
40. David Isenberg, "Combat for Sale: The New, Post-Cold War Mercenaries," *USA Today Magazine* (Mar. 2000): 13. For a good breakdown of specific specialization fields, see James Larry Taulbee, "The Privatization of Security: Modern Conflict, Globalization and Weak State," *Civil Wars* 5 (Summer 2002): 4.
41. Stan Crock, Thomas F. Armistead, Anthony Bianco, and Stephanie Anderson Forest, "Outsourcing War," *Business Week,* 15 Sept. 2003, 68–76.
42. Schwartz and Watson, "The Pentagon's Private Army," 100–107.
43. Pratap Chatterjee, *Haliburton's Army: How a Well-Connected Texas Oil Co. Revolutionized the Way America Makes War* (New York: Nation Books, 2009), 214; "Top 100 Defense Contractors," *Government Executive* 34 (Aug. 2002): 34–35; John Helyar, "Fortunes of War," *Fortune* 150 (26 July 2004): 80–81. See also Center for Public Integrity at http://www.publicintegrity.com.
44. Robert Wall, "Army Leases 'Eyes' to Watch Balkans," *Aviation Week and Space Technology* 153 (30 Oct. 2000): 68.

45. Schwartz and Watson, "The Pentagon's Private Army," 100–107.
46. Crock et al., "Outsourcing War," 68–76. See also Jeremy Kahn and Nelson D. Schwartz, "Private Sector Soldiers," *Fortune* 149 (3 May 2004): 33–36.
47. "United States: Dangerous Work: Private Security Firms in Iraq," *Economist* (10 Apr. 2004): 22–23.
48. Christopher Spearin, "Private Security Companies and Humanitarians: A Corporate Solution to Securing Humanitarian Spaces?" *International Peacekeeping* 8 (Spring 2001): 20–43; Avant, "The Privatization of Security and Change in the Control of Force," 154.
49. Kelly, "Safety at a Price." See also Filiz Zabci, "Private Military Companies: 'Shadow Soldiers' of Neocolonialism," *Capital and Class* 92 (Summer 2007): 3.
51. Brooks, "Messiahs or Mercenaries?" 133. DynCorp was listed as the thirteenth largest U.S. defense contractor in 2002. Booz Allen & Hamilton was listed as thirty-firth the same year. See "Top 100 Defense Contractors," *Government Executive* 34 (Aug. 2002): 38–41.
51. A more recent example involved ArmorGroup employees providing security in Afghanistan. See Ken Stier, "Afghan Embassy Scandal's Link to Cost-Cutting Security," *Time* (11 Sept. 2009), http://www.time.com.
52. Macomber, "You're Not in the Army Now," 30.
53. Michael D. McPherson, "Dollars and Sense: Private Sector Lures Special Operations Troops," *Armed Forces Journal International* 141 (June 2004): 26.
54. U.S. Special Operations Command, Public Affairs Office, "DOD Approves Retention Initiatives for Special Forces," 3 Feb. 2005, http://www.news.soc.mil.
55. Michael Duffy, "When Private Armies Take to the Front Lines," *Time* 163 (12 Apr. 2004): 32–33.
56. Bill Brewer, "EODT Suing Former Workers," *Knoxville News Sentinel* (6 May 2009), http://www.knoxnews.com.
57. For an interesting discussion of this ambiguity on the ground in Iraq, see Tucker Carlson, "Hired Guns," *Esquire* 141 (Mar. 2004): 130–139.
58. Cam Simpson, "U.S. Stalls in Human Trafficking," *Chicago Tribune* (27 Dec. 2005), http://www.chicagotribune.com; Russell Mokhiber and Robert Weissman, "Bad Apples in a Rotten System: The 10 Worst Corporations of 2002," *Multinational Monitor* 23 (Dec. 2002): 14.
59. James Kwok, "Armed Entrepreneurs: Private Military Companies in Iraq," *Harvard International Review* 28 (Spring 2006): 36. See also Naomi Klein, "Shameless in Iraq," *Nation* (12 July 2004): 14.
60. Griff Witte, "Contractors Deny They Shot at Marines, Allege Mistreatment," *Washington Post,* 10 June 2005, A18.

61. "Private Security Companies," *Military Technology* 31 (Feb. 2007): 41–45; Daniel Bergner, "The Other Army," *New York Times Magazine,* 14 Aug. 2005, 28–35.
62. Susan Strange, *The Retreat of the State: The Diffusion of Power in the World Economy* (New York: Cambridge Univ. Press, 1996), 189. See also Stephen J. Kobrin, "Back to the Future: Neomedievalism and the Postmodern Digital World Economy," *Journal of International Affairs* 51 (Spring 1998): 361–386.
63. Tony Lynch and A. J. Walsh, "The Good Mercenary?" *Journal of Political Philosophy* 8 (June 2000): 133–153; Gerry Cleaver, "Subcontracting Military Power: The Privatization of Security in Contemporary Sub-Saharan Africa," *Crime, Law and Social Change* 33 (Mar. 2000): 133, 144–146. Cleaver provides examples of South African and British law pertaining to mercenaries.
64. Isenberg, "Combat for Sale," 15. See also Singer, "Peacekeepers, Inc.," 65–69.
65. Eugene B. Smith, "The New Condottieri and U.S. Policy: The Privatization of Conflict and Its Implications," *Parameters* 32 (Winter 2002/2003): 104–119.
66. Avant, "Mercenaries," 24.
67. Linda Robinson and Douglas Pasternak, "America's Secret Armies," *U.S. News and World Report* (4 Nov. 2002): 38–44.
68. Daniel Burton-Rose and Wayne Madsen, "Corporate Soldiers: The U.S. Government Privatizes the Use of Force," *Multinational Monitor* 20 (Mar. 1999): 17–19.
69. Whyte, "Lethal Regulation," 580.
70. BAPSC website at http://www.bapsc.org.uk/about_us.asp.
71. Spearin, "Private Security Companies and Humanitarians," 30. See also Sabelo Gumedze, "Regulating the Private Security Sector in South Africa," *Social Justice* 34 (2007): 198.
72. See Krahmann, "Private Military Services in the UK and Germany," 277–295; Gumedze, "Regulating the Private Security Sector in South Africa," 195–207.
73. Marc Lindemann, "Civilian Contractors Under Military Law," *Parameters* 37 (Autumn 2007): 83, 88.
74. James Risen and Timothy Williams, "U.S. Looks for Blackwater Replacement in Iraq," *New York Times,* 30 Jan. 2009. See also *Agreement between the United States and the Republic of Iraq on the Withdrawal of United States Forces from Iraq and the Organization of Their Activities during Their Temporary Presence in Iraq,* art. 12, http://graphics8.nytimes.com/packages/pdf/world/200811.

75. See the Confederation of European Security Services at http://www.coess.org/studies.htm.
76. The Montreux Document is one recent attempt to rectify this situation. See James Cockayne, "Regulating Private Military and Security Companies: The Content, Negotiation, Weaknesses and Promise of the Montreux Document," *Journal of Conflict and Security Law* 13 (Winter 2008): 401–428.
77. Grace Jean, "United States and Britain at Odds Over Weapons Sales Regulations," *National Defence* 92 (Dec. 2007): 26.
78. Andrew Gray and Randall Mikkelson, "U.S. to Tighten Rules for Iraq Contractors," *Reuters,* Oct. 30, 2007, http://www.reuters.com.
79. Smith, "The New Condottieri and U.S. Policy," 104–119.
80. Yves Goulet, "MPRI: Washington's Freelance Advisors," *Jane's Intelligence Review* 10 (July 1998): 38–41.
81. Ibid; Shearer, *Private Armies,* 56–63.
82. Colum Lynch, "For U.S. Firms War Becomes a Business," *Boston Globe,* 1 Feb. 1997, 1. See also Ken Silverstein, *Private Warriors* (New York: Verso, 2000), 171–174.
83. Goulet, "MPRI," 40; Silverstein, "Privatizing War," 11–17.
84. Goulet, "MPRI," 40.
85. Wayne Madsen, "Mercenaries in Kosovo: The U.S. Connection to the KLA," *Progressive* 63 (Aug. 1999): 29.
86. Shannon, "Human Security and the Rise of Private Armies," 111–115.
87. Julia E. Sweig, "What Kind of War for Colombia? History Repeating Itself?" *Foreign Affairs* 81 (Sept./Oct. 2002): 122–141.
88. George H. Franco, "Their Darkest Hour: Colombia's Government and the Narco-Insurgency," *Parameters* 30 (Summer 2000): 83–94. FARC strength increased to approximately 15,000 by 2000.
89. According to official estimates, 244,530 acres were under coca cultivation in 2007. UN Office on Drugs and Crime, *Coca Cultivation in the Andean Region: A Survey of Bolivia, Colombia, and Peru* (New York: United Nations, June 2008), 7.
90. Volker C. Franke and Justin Reed, "Squeezing a Balloon: Plan Colombia and America's War on Drugs," in *Terrorism and Peacekeeping: New Security Challenges,* ed. Volker C. Franke (Westport, CT: Praeger, 2005), 184.
91. Ingrid Vaicius and Adam Isacson, "The 'War on Drugs' Meets the 'War on Terror': The United States' Military Involvement in Colombia Climbs to the Next Level," *Center for International Policy: Colombia Program. International Policy Report,* Feb. 2003, 3. http://www.ciponline.org.
92. Jeremy McDermott, "War Resumes after Collapse of Colombian Peace Process," *Jane's Intelligence Review* 14 (Apr. 2002): 9–10.

93. Peter Chalk, "The 'War on Drugs': Is the USA's Colombia Policy Working?" *Jane's Intelligence Review* 12 (Dec. 2000): 41–42; Vaicius and Isacson, "The 'War on Drugs' Meets the 'War on Terror'," 5. Between 1999 and 2007, the United States trained 70,928 Colombian military and policy personnel. See "Grant Military and Police Aid to Colombia, 1996–2011," *Just the Facts: A Civilian's Guide to U.S. Defense and Security Assistance to Latin America and the Caribbean,* http://justf.org. These programs include NADR Anti-Terrorism Assistance and the Counter-Terrorism Fellowship Program.
94. U.S. Dept. of State, "State Department Fact Sheet: Civilian Contractors and U.S. Military Personnel Supporting Plan Colombia," 22 May 2001, http://ciponline.org.
95. Whyte, "Lethal Regulation," 595.
96. Wayne Madsen, "Peruvian No-Fly Zone," *Progressive* 65 (June 2001): 35. A member of the board of directors is retired Air Force General Michael Carns, who had been designated to replace James Woolsey in 1995 as CIA director.
97. Ibid. See also Ignacio Gomez, "U.S. Mercenaries in Colombia," *Colombia Journal Online* (16 July 2000), http://www.colombiajournal.org.
98. Tod Robberson, "Guerrillas Profiting from U.S. Aid to Colombia, Officials Say," *Dallas Morning News,* 25 Apr. 2001, http://web.lexis-nexis.com.
99. Republic of Colombia, Presidency of the Republic, Ministry of Defence, *Democratic Security and Defence Policy* (Bogota: Ministry of Defence, 2003), 5.
100. Crock et al., "Outsourcing War," 68–76.
101. By June 2006, a majority of Americans (57 percent) asked by the Opinion Research Corporation believed that American troops had committed atrocities in Iraq. "Troops Committed War Crimes, Say Americans," *Angus Reid Global Monitor* (18 June 2006), http://www.angus-reid.com.
102. Taulbee, "The Privatization of Security," 16.
103. Roger W. Barnett, *Asymmetrical Warfare: Today's Challenge to U.S. Military Power* (Washington, DC: Brassey's, 2003), 14.

Conclusions

1. Henry Kissinger, *Diplomacy* (New York: Simon & Schuster, 1994), 711–712. For a good history of this topic, see Joan Hoff, *Nixon Reconsidered* (New York: Basic Books, 1994).
2. The White House, Office of the Press Secretary, "Remarks by the President on a New Beginning," Cairo Univ., 4 June 2009, http://www.whitehouse.gov/the-press-office/remarks-president-cairo-university-6-04-09.

3. Jeremy Black, "Determinisms and Other Issues," *Journal of Military History* 68 (Oct. 2004): 1224–1225.
4. James J. Wirtz, "The 'Unlessons' of Vietnam," *Defense Analysis* 17 (Apr. 2001): 41–57.
5. Gil Merom, *How Democracies Lose Small Wars: State Society, and the Failures of France in Algeria, Israel in Lebanon, and the United States in Vietnam* (New York: Cambridge Univ. Press, 2003), 15, 60–63; Rachel Riedner and Kevin Mahoney, *Democracies to Come: Rhetorical Action, Neoliberalism, and Communities of Resistance* (Lanham, MA: Lexington Books, 2008), 1–37.
6. Jeffrey Record, *Beating Goliath: Why Insurgencies Win* (Washington, DC: Potomac Books, 2007), 67–69, 75. See also Guenther Lewy, *America in Vietnam* (New York: Oxford Univ. Press, 1978), 129–131, 147, 455.
7. U.S. Army, Training and Doctrine Command, Center for Army Lessons Learned, *Stability Operations and Support Operations (SOSO): Tactics, Techniques, and Procedures for SOSO (*Fort Leavenworth, KS: TRADOC, 2003), 11–29.
8. Barry R. Posen, "The Sources of Military Doctrine," in *The Use of Force: Military Power and International Politics,* 6th ed., ed. Robert J. Art and Kenneth N. Waltz (New York: Rowman & Littlefield, 2004), 23–24. See also David H. Petraeus, "Multinational Force-Iraq Commander's Counterinsurgency Guidance," *Military Review* 88 (Sept./Oct. 2008): 2; Jonathan Rauch, "A Bad Idea That Deserves a Try," *National Journal* 39 (20 Jan. 2007): 15–16.
9. See Colin S. Gray, "The American Way of War: Critique and Implications," in *Rethinking the Principles of War,* ed. Anthony D. McIvor (Annapolis, MD: Naval Institute Press, 2005), 13–40.
10. "The Uses of Military Power," remarks prepared for delivery by the Honorable Caspar W. Weinberger, Secretary of Defense, to the National Press Club, Washington, DC, 28 Nov. 1984, http://www.pbs.org. See also Weinberger, *Into the Arena,* 308–313.
11. Walter LaFeber, "The Rise and Fall of Colin Powell and the Powell Doctrine," *Political Science Quarterly* 124 (Spring 2009): 71–90.
12. Harlan K. Oilman and James P. Wade, *Shock and Awe: Achieving Rapid Dominance* (Washington, DC: National Defense Univ., 1996), 1.
13. Robert Mandel, "The Wartime Utility of Precision versus Brute Force in Weaponry," *Armed Forces and Society* 30 (Winter 2004): 171–201.
14. Sarah Sewell, "Modernizing U.S. Counterinsurgency Practice: Rethinking Risk and Developing a National Strategy," *Military Review* 86 (Sept./Oct. 2006): 103.
15. See, for example, Bruce Kuklick, *Blind Oracles: Intellectuals and War from Kennan to Kissinger* (Princeton, NJ: Princeton Univ. Press, 2006).
16. Melvyn Leffler, "9/11 and American Foreign Policy," *Diplomatic History* 29 (June 2005): 395.

17. Ibid., 396–402.
18. David Milne, "'Our Equivalent of Guerrilla Warfare': Walt Rostow and the Bombing of North Vietnam, 1961–1968," *Journal of Military History* 71 (Jan. 2007): 169–203.
19. Robert W. Cone, "NTC: The Changing National Training Center," *Military Review* 86 (May/June 2006): 75.
20. H. R. McMaster, "The Human Element: When Gadgetry Becomes Strategy," *World Affairs* 171 (Winter 2009): 31–43; Michael G. Dana, "Shock and Awe Has Failed," *U.S. Naval Institute Proceedings* 130 (May 2004): 66–69.
21. Robert D. Kaplan, "Supremacy by Stealth," *Atlantic Monthly* 292 (July/Aug. 2003): 67–68.
22. Ibid., 76–77.
23. Kenneth Sharpe, "Realpolitik or Imperial Hubris: The Latin American Drug War and U.S. Foreign Policy in Iraq," *Orbis* 50 (June 2006): 481–499. For some recent studies on U.S. Cold War intervention, see Stephen G. Rabe, *U.S. Intervention in British Guiana: A Cold War Story* (Chapel Hill, NC: Univ. of North Carolina Press, 2005); Don Bohning, *The Castro Obsession: U.S. Covert Operations Against Cuba, 1959–1965* (Washington, DC: Potomac Books, 2005); Nick Cullather, *Secret History: The CIA's Classified Account of Its Operations in Guatemala, 1952–1954* (Stanford, CA: Stanford Univ. Press, 1999).
24. J. Samuel. Fitch, "The Decline of US Military Influence in Latin America," *Journal of Interamerican Studies and World Affairs* 35 (Summer 1993): 1–49.
25. A. J. Bacevich, "The Petraeus Doctrine," *Atlantic Monthly* 302 (Oct. 2008): 17–20.
26. Charles J. Dunlap, "Nobody Asked Me but . . . We have a Serious COIN Shortage," *United States Naval Institute Proceedings* 133 (May 2007): 162.
27. William Fleser, "Operational Net Assessment: Implications and Opportunities for SOF," *Special Warfare* 15 (Dec. 2002): 12–17.
28. John A. Nagl, *Learning to Eat Soup with a Knife: Counterinsurgency Lessons from Malaya and Vietnam,* 2nd ed. (Chicago: Univ. of Chicago Press, 2005), 5.
29. Huba Wass de Czege, "Systemic Operational Design: Learning and Adapting in Complex Missions," *Military Review* 89 (Jan./Feb. 2009): 2–12.
30. The lack of institutional consistency between the separate service branches has actually increased the proliferation of new doctrines. See Richard M. Cavagnol, "Lessons from Vietnam," *Marine Corps Gazette* 91 (May 2007): 17.

31. Sean Griffin, “Time to Reevaluate Rapid Decisive Operations,” *U.S. Naval Institute Proceedings* 135 (Jan. 2009): 77–79.
32. Charles C. Krulak, “The Strategic Corporal: Leadership in the Three Block War,” *Marine Corps Gazette* 83 (Jan. 1999): 18–22.
33. Wass de Czege, “Systemic Operational Design,” 5.
34. Richard H. Kohn, “Coming Soon: A Crisis in Civil-Military Relations,” *World Affairs* 170 (Winter 2008): 73.
35. Qiao Liang and Wang Xiangsui, *Unrestricted Warfare* (Beijing: PLA Literature and Arts Publishing House, 1999), 2.
36. See Vincent Wei-cheng Wang, and Gwendolyn Stamper, “Asymmetrical War? Implications for China's Information Warfare Strategies,” *American Asian Review* 20 (Winter 2002): 167–202; James Fallows, “Cyber Warriors,” *Atlantic Monthly* 305 (Mar. 2010): 58–63.

Selected Bibliography

Archives

Army Heritage and Education Center, U.S. Military History Institute, Carlisle, PA

Army War College Personal Experience Monographs

Kevin M. Born Papers, 1984–1997

William W. Crouch Papers, 1996–1997

Brian M. Jenkins Papers, 1979–1984

Lawson W. Magruder Papers, 1995

Jim Roddy Paschall Papers, 1959–1999

Melissa E. Patrick Papers, 1995–1996

Somalia Crisis Papers, 1992–1993

Carl W. Stiner Papers, 1988–1992

Task Force Eagle Papers, 1995–1996

George H. W. Bush Library, Texas A&M Univ., College Station

Bush Presidential Records, P-2/P-5 Files

Bush Presidential Records, White House Office of Records Management (WHORM) Files, Subject Files

Bush Presidential Records, White House Staff and Office Files, National Security Council

Office of Vice President George Bush, Subject Files

Jimmy Carter Presidential Center, Atlanta, GA

Donated Historical Materials

Zbigniew Brzezinski Collection

Walter F. Mondale Papers

Staff Office Files

National Security Advisor Files

White House Central File

Digital National Security Archives, George Washington Univ., Washington, DC
http://nsarchive.chadwyck.com
Dwight D. Eisenhower Presidential Library, Abilene, KS
Joseph M. Dodge Papers
Gerald R. Ford Presidential Library, Ann Arbor, MI
Martin R. Hoffman Papers
National Security Advisor's Files
Edward W. Savage Files
White House Central Files
White House Editorial/Speechwriting Staff Files
White House Operations Office Files
John F. Kennedy Presidential Library, Boston
National Security Files
National Archives and Records Administration, College Park, MD
Records Group 59 NARA, General Records of the Dept. of State
Records Group 263 Records of the Central Intelligence Agency
Records Group 306 Records of the U.S. Agency for International Development
Records Group 333 Records of International Military Agencies
Ronald W. Reagan Presidential Library, Simi Valley, CA
WHORM Alphabetical File, 1981–1989
WHORM Subject File, 1981–1989
White House State and Office Files, 1981–1989
William P. Clark Files
Counterterrorism and Narcotics, NSC
Crisis Management Center (CMC), NSC
Michael K. Deaver Files
Executive Secretariat, NSC
Latin American Directorate, NSC
Robert C. McFarland Files
Oliver L. North Files
Robert A. Pastorino Files
John Poindexter Files
Colin L. Powell Files

Primary Sources

"From Containment to Enlargement: Remarks of Anthony Lake, Assistant to the President for National Security Affairs." Washington, DC: School of Advanced International Studies, 21 Sept. 1993.

National Commission on Terrorist Attacks upon the United States. *The 9/11 Commission Report: Final Report of the National Commission on Terrorist Attacks upon the United States.* New York: W.W. Norton & Co., 2004.

Republic of Colombia. Presidency of the Republic. Ministry of Defence. *Democratic Security and Defence Policy.* Bogota: Ministry of Defence, 2003.

Stockholm International Peace Research Institute. *SIPRI Yearbook, 1990: World Armaments and Disarmament.* New York: Oxford Univ. Press, 1990.

UK Secretary of State for Foreign and Commonwealth Affairs. *Ninth Report of the Foreign Affairs Committee: Private Military Companies, Session 2001–2002.* Oct. 2002.

UN Commission on Human Rights. "Report on the Question of the Use of Mercenaries as a Means of Violating Human Rights and Impeding the Exercise of the Eight of Peoples to Self-Determination." Special Rapporteur, 50th sess., item 9, 12. New York: United Nations, Jan. 1994.

———. "Report on the Question of the Use of Mercenaries as a Means of Violating Human Rights and Impeding the Exercise of the Right of Peoples to Self-Determination." Special Rapporteur, 53d sess., item 7, 20. New York: United Nations, Feb. 1997.

UN Office on Drugs and Crime. *Coca Cultivation in the Andean Region: A Survey of Bolivia, Colombia, and Peru.* New York: United Nations, June 2006.

———. *World Drug Report, 2009.* Vienna: UN Office on Drugs and Crime, 2009.

U.S. Air Force. *Gulf War Air Power Survey.* 5 vols. Washington, DC: Government Printing Office, 1993.

U.S. Army, John F. Kennedy Special Warfare Center and School. *Army Special Operations Forces Reference Data.* Washington, DC: Government Publication Office, 1991.

U.S. Army, Training and Doctrine Command, Center for Army Lessons Learned. *CMTC Trends Compendium: Stability and Support Operations.* Fort Leavenworth, KS: TRADOC, 1998.

———. *Stability Operations and Support Operations (SASO): Tactics, Techniques, and Procedures for SASO.* Fort Leavenworth, KS: TRADOC, 1998.

———. *Stability Operations and Support Operations (SOSO): Tactics, Techniques, and Procedures.* Fort Leavenworth, KS: TRADOC, 2003.

U.S. Army Europe, Headquarters, Office of the Chief of Public Affairs. *Operation Joint Forge after Action Report.* Heidelberg, Germany: Logicon Technical Services, 2000.

———. *A Soldier's Guide to Bosnia-Herzegovina,* n.d.

U.S. Dept. of the Army, Headquarters. ARTEP 31-807-30-MTP. *Mission Training Plan for the Special Forces Company: Unconventional Warfare.* Washington, DC: U.S. Dept. of the Army, Sept. 1988.

———. *FM 31-73: Advisor Operations for Stability Operations.* Washington, DC: U.S. Dept. of the Army, Oct. 1967.

———. *FM 100-5: Operations.* Washington, DC: U.S. Dept. of the Army, June 1993.

———. TC 31-20-1. *The Role of US Army Special Forces.* Washington, DC: U.S. Dept. of the Army, Oct. 1976.

U.S. Dept. of Defense. *Conduct of the Persian Gulf War: Final Report to Congress.* Washington, DC: GPO, Apr. 1992.

———. *Terrorist Group Profiles.* Washington, DC: Government Publication Office, 1988.

U.S. Dept. of Defense, Assistant Secretary of Defense for Special Operations and Low Intensity Conflict. *SOF Vision 2020.* MacDill Air Force Base, FL: USSOCOM, 1996.

U.S. Dept. of Defense, Joint Forces Command. *Stability Operations: Joint Operating Concept.* Suffolk, VA: U.S. Joint Forces Command, Sept. 2004.

U.S. Dept. of Health and Human Services, Substance Abuse and Mental Health Services Administration, Office of Applied Studies. *Results from the 2007 National Survey on Drug Use and Health: National Findings.* Rockville, MD: SAMHSA, Sept. 2008.

U.S. Dept. of Justice, Drug Enforcement Administration. *The Drug Enforcement Administration: Annual Report, Fiscal Year 1986.* Washington, DC: U.S. Dept. of Justice, 1987.

———. *Narcotics Situation Report.* Washington, DC: U.S. Dept. of Justice, Aug. 1979.

U.S. Dept. of Justice, Drug Enforcement Administration, National Narcotics Intelligence Consumers Committee. *Annual Report, Fiscal Year 1986.* Washington, DC: U.S. Dept. of Justice, 1987.

———. *Narcotics Situation Report.* Washington, DC: U.S. Dept. of Justice, 1981.

———. *The NNICC Report, 1985–1986: The Supply of Illicit Drugs to the United States from Foreign and Domestic Sources in 1985 and 1986 (with Near Term Projections).* Washington, DC: U.S. Dept. of Justice, June 1987.

U.S. Dept. of State, Division of Publications, Office of Public Affairs. *The Military Assistance Program.* Washington, DC: Government Printing Office, 1949.

U.S. General Accounting Office. *International Terrorism: FBI Investigates Domestic Activity to Identify Terrorists: Report to the Chairman, Subcommittee on Civil and Constitutional Rights, Committee on the Judiciary, House of Representatives.* Washington, DC: GAO, 1990.

———. Report to the Chairman, Subcommittee on Legislation and National Security. Committee on Government Operations. House of Representatives. *Drug Control: Status Report on DOD Support to Counternarcotics Activities.* Washington, DC: GAO, June 1991.

———. Report to Congressional Requesters. *Drug Control: Heavy Investment in Military Surveillance Is Not Paying Off.* Washington, DC: GAO, 1993.

U.S. Government Accountability Office. *Military Personnel: Reporting Additional Servicemember Demographics Could Enhance Congressional Oversight,* GAO-05–952. Washington, DC: GAO, Sept. 2005.

U.S. House of Representatives, Committee on Armed Services. Committee on International Relations, Subcommittee on the Western Hemisphere. *Overview of U.S. Policy toward the Western Hemisphere, February 27, 2003.* Washington, DC: Government Printing Office, 2003.

———. *Counternarcotics Strategies in Latin America, March 30, 2006.* Washington, DC: Government Printing Office, 2006.

———. *Defense for a New Era: Lessons of the Persian Gulf War.* Washington, DC: Brassey's, 1992.

U.S. Joint Chiefs of Staff. *Joint Vision 2010.* Washington, DC: Joint Chiefs of Staff, 1996.

———. *National Military Strategy of the United States of America: Shape, Respond, Prepare Now: A Military Strategy for a New Era, 1997.* Washington, DC: JCS, 1997.

———. *National Military Strategy of the United States of America, 1995: A Strategy of Flexible and Selective Engagement.* Washington, DC: JCS, 1995.

U.S. Joint Chiefs of Staff, Special Operations Review Group. *Rescue Mission Report.* Washington, DC: Joint Chiefs of Staff, Aug. 1980.

U.S. National Security Council. *Report to Congress on U.S. Capabilities to Engage in Low Intensity Conflict and Conduct Special Operations.* Washington, DC: NSC, 1987.

U.S. National Security Council, Special Coordination Committee, Executive Committee on Terrorism. *The United States Government Antiterrorism Program: An Unclassified Summary Report.* Washington, DC: National Security Council, June 1979.

U.S. Office of the Vice President. *White Paper on Insurgent/Terrorist Involvement in International Drug Trade.* Washington, DC: Office of the Vice President, 31 Dec. 1985.

U.S. Senate, Committee on Armed Services. *Nominations before the Senate Armed Services Committee, First Session, 103rd Congress.* Washington: Government Printing Office, 1994.

U.S. Senate, Committee on Foreign Relations. *The Senate Foreign Relation Committee's Historical Series: Military Assistance Program, 1949.* New York: Garland, 1979.

———. *Tora Bora Revisited: How We Failed to Get Bin Laden and Why It Matters Today.* Washington, DC: Government Printing Office.

U.S. Special Operations Command. *2005 Annual Report.* MacDill Air Force Base, FL: USSOCOM, 2005.

———. *United States Special Forces Posture Statement, 2003–2004*. Washington, DC: Assistant Secretary of Defense for Special Operations and Low-Intensity Conflict, 2004.

U.S. Special Operations Command, History and Research Office. *United States Special Operations Command History*. MacDill Air Force Base, FL: USSOCOM, 1999.

———. *United States Special Operations Command History*. MacDill Air Force Base, FL: USSOCOM, 2002.

———. *Special Operations in Peace and War*. MacDill Air Force Base, FL: USSOCOM, 1996

Secondary Sources

Acheson, Dean. *Present at the Creation: My Years in the State Department*. New York: W. W. Norton & Co., 1969.

Adams, Thomas K. "Future Warfare and the Decline of Human Decisionmaking." *Parameters* 31 (Winter 2001/2002): 57–71.

———. "The New Mercenaries and the Privatization of Conflict." *Parameters* 29 (Summer 1999): 103–117.

———. "Private Military Companies: Mercenaries for the 21st Century." *Small Wars and Insurgencies* 13 (Summer 2002): 54–67.

———. *U.S. Special Operations Forces in Action: The Challenge of Unconventional War*. Portland, OR: Frank Cass, 1998.

Akera, Atsushi. "IBM's Early Adaptation to Cold War Markets: Cuthbert Hurd and His Applied Science Field Men." *Business History Review* 76 (Winter 2002): 767–802.

Albright, Madeleine K. "A Call for American Consensus." *Time* (22 Nov. 1999): 55–57.

———. "Foreign Policy: Strategic Goals." *U.S. Department of State Dispatch* 9 (May 1998): 10–14.

———. "A New NATO for a New Century." *U.S. Department of State Dispatch* 10 (Apr. 1999): 6–10.

———. "The Testing of American Foreign Policy." *Foreign Affairs* 77 (Nov./Dec. 1998): 50–64.

———. "The William Cohen Lecture: Combining Force and Diplomacy to Secure America's Future." *U.S. Department of State Dispatch* 10 (Nov. 1999): 15–19.

Albright, Madeleine, with Bill Woodward. *Madame Secretary*. New York: Miramax Books, 2003.

Alexander, J. Davidson. "Military Conversion Policies in the USA: 1940s and 1990s." *Journal of Peace Research* 31 (Feb. 1994): 19–33.

Ameringer, Charles D. *U.S. Foreign Intelligence: The Secret Side of American History*. Lexington, MA: Lexington Books, 1990.

Andreas, Peter R., and E. C. Bertram. "Dead-End Drug Wars." *Foreign Policy,* no. 85 (Winter 1991): 106–129.

Andreas, Peter R., and Kenneth E. Sharpe. "Cocaine Politics in the Andes." *Current History* 91 (Feb. 1992): 74–79.

"Army Leases 'Eyes' to Watch Balkans." *Aviation Week and Space Technology* 153 (30 Oct. 2000): 68.

Art, Robert J., and Kenneth N. Waltz. *The Use of Force: Military Power and International Politics.* 6th ed. New York: Rowman & Littlefield, 2004.

Aspin, Les. *The Aspin Papers: Sanctions, Diplomacy, and War in the Persian Gulf.* Washington, DC: Center for Strategic Studies, 1991.

Asprey, Robert B. *War in the Shadows: The Guerrilla in History.* New York: William Morrow and Co., 1994.

Association of the U.S. Army. *Special Operations Forces: An Overview.* Arlington, VA: AUSA, Institute of Land Warfare, 1998.

Atkinson, Rick. *An Army at Dawn: The War in North Africa, 1942–1943.* New York: Henry Holt and Co., 2002.

———. *Crusade: The Untold Story of the Persian Gulf War.* New York: Houghton Mifflin Co., 1993.

Avant, Deborah. "From Mercenary to Citizen Armies: Explaining Change in the Practice of War." *International Organization* 54 (Winter 2000): 41–72.

———. "Mercenaries." *Foreign Policy,* no. 143 (July/Aug. 2004): 20–28.

———. "The Privatization of Security and Change in the Control of Force." *International Studies Perspectives* 5 (2004): 153–157.

———. "U.S. Military Attitudes toward Post-Cold War Missions." *Armed Forces and Society* 27 (Fall 2000): 37–57.

Avilés, William. "Institutions, Military Policy, and Human Rights in Colombia." *Latin American Perspectives* 28 (Jan. 2001): 31–55.

Baack, Ben, and Edward Ray. "The Political Economy of the Origins of the Military-Industrial Complex in the United States." *Journal of Economic History* 45 (June 1985): 369–375.

Bacevich, A. J. *The New American Militarism: How Americans Are Seduced by War.* New York: Oxford Univ. Press, 2005.

———. *The Pentomic Era: The U.S. Army between Korea and Vietnam.* Washington, DC: National Defense Univ. Press, 1986.

———. "The Petraeus Doctrine." *Atlantic Monthly* 302 (Oct. 2008): 17–20.

Baer, Robert. "Iraq's Mercenary King." *Vanity Fair* (Apr. 2006): 136–142.

Bagley, Bruce Michael. "The New Hundred Years War? U.S. National Security and the War on Drugs in Latin America." *Journal of Interamerican Studies and World Affairs* 30 (Spring 1988): 161–182.

Bailey, Beth. *America's Army: Making the All-Volunteer Force.* Cambridge, MA: Belknap Press of Harvard Univ. Press, 2009.

Baker, Pauline H. "Fixing Failing States: The New Security Agenda." *Whitehead Journal of Diplomacy and International Relations* 8 (Winter/Spring 2007): 85–96.

Bank, Aaron. *From OSS to Green Berets: The Birth of Special Forces.* Novato, CA: Presidio Press, 1986.

Barkawi, Tarak. "On the Pedagogy of 'Small Wars,'" *International Affairs* 80 (Jan. 2004): 19–37.

Barnett, Roger W. *Asymmetrical Warfare: Today's Challenge to U.S. Military Power.* Washington, DC: Brassey's, 2003.

Barone, Michael. "Ethnic Tribes and Pandemonium." *U.S. News and World Report* (15 Feb. 1993): 55–56.

Bartels, Larry M. "The American Public's Defense Spending Preferences in the Post-Cold War." *Public Opinion Quarterly* 58 (Winter 1994): 479–508.

Beaumont, Roger. "Small Wars: Definitions and Dimensions." *Annals of the American Academy of Political and Social Science* 541 (Sept. 1995): 20–35.

Beckwith, Charlie A. *Delta Force.* New York: Harcourt Brace Jovanovich, 1983.

Beelman, Maud S. "Business of War." *IRE Journal* 26 (Mar./Apr. 2003): 24–25.

Belloni, Roberto. "Rethinking 'Nation-Building': The Contradictions of the Neo-Wilsonian Approach to Democracy Promotion." *Whitehead Journal of Diplomacy and International Relation* 8 (Winter/Spring 2007): 97–109.

Bensahel, Nora, Olga Oliker, Keith Crane, et. al. *After Saddam: Prewar Planning and the Occupation of Iraq.* Santa Monica, CA: RAND, 2008.

Bergner, Daniel. "The Other Army." *New York Times Magazine,* 14 Aug. 2005, 28–35.

Berkowitz, Bruce. *The New Face of War: How War Will Be Fought in the 21st Century.* New York: Free Press, 2003.

Bernstein, Michael A. "American Economic Expertise from the Great War to the Cold War: Some Initial Observations." *Journal of Economic History* 50 (June 1990): 407–416.

Beschloss, Michael R. *The Crisis Years: Kennedy and Khrushchev, 1960–1963.* New York: Edward Burlingame, 1991.

Betts, Richard K. *Soldiers, Statesmen, and Cold War Crises.* Cambridge, MA: Harvard Univ. Press, 1977.

Bhatt, Shakti. "State Terrorism vs. Jihad in Kashmir." *Journal of Contemporary Asia* 33 (2003): 215–224.

Bickel, Keith B. *Mars Learning: The Marine Corps Development of Small Wars Doctrine, 1915–1940.* Boulder, CO: Westview Press, 2001.

Björnehed, Emma. "Narco-Terrorism: The Merger of the War on Drugs and the War on Terror." *Global Crime* 6 (Aug.–Nov. 2004): 305–324.

Blank, Jonah. "Want Peacekeepers with Spine? Hire the World's Fiercest Mercenaries." *U.S. News and World Report* (30 Dec. 1996): 42–44.

Blaufarb, Douglas S. *The Counterinsurgency Era: U.S. Doctrine and Performance, 1950 to the Present.* New York: Free Press, 1977.

Blight James G., and Janet M. Lang. *The Fog of War: Lessons from the Life of Robert S. McNamara.* New York: Rowman & Littlefield, 2005.

Bobrow, Davis B., and Mark A. Boyer. "Maintaining System Stability: Contributions to Peacekeeping Operations." *Journal of Conflict Resolution* 41 (Dec. 1997): 723–748.

Bohning, Don. *The Castro Obsession: U.S. Covert Operations Against Cuba, 1959–1965.* Washington, DC: Potomac Books, 2005.

Bolger, Daniel P. *Americans at War: An Era of Violent Peace, 1975–1986.* Novato, CA: Presidio Press, 1988.

———. "Special Operations and the Grenada Campaign." *Parameters* (Dec. 1988): 49–61.

Bolton, John R. "Wrong Turn in Somalia." *Foreign Affairs* 73 (Jan./Feb. 1994): 56–66.

Boot, Max. *The Savage Wars of Peace: Small Wars and the Rise of American Power.* New York: Basic Books, 2002.

———. "We Are Winning. We Haven't Won." *Weekly Standard* 13 (4 Feb. 2008): 28–36.

Bostdorff, Denise M. *Proclaiming the Truman Doctrine: The Cold War Call to Arms.* College Station: Texas A&M Univ. Press, 2008.

Boutwell, Jeffrey, and Michael T. Klare, eds. *Light Weapons and Civil Conflict: Controlling the Tools of Violence.* Lanham, MD: Rowan & Littlefield, 1999.

Boyer, Paul. *By the Bombs Early Light: American Thought and Culture at the Dawn of the Nuclear Age.* New York: Pantheon Books, 1985.

Braudy, Leo. *From Chivalry to Terrorism: War and the Changing Nature of Masculinity.* New York: Alfred A. Knopf, 2003.

Brayton, Steven. "Outsourcing War: Mercenaries and the Privatization of Peacekeeping." *Journal of International Affairs* 55 (Spring 2002): 303–329.

Brinkley, Douglas. *Gerald R. Ford.* New York: Henry Holt & Co., 2007.

Briscoe, Charles H., Kenneth Finlayson, Robert W. Jones, et al. *All Roads Lead to Baghdad: Army Special Operations Forces in Iraq.* Fort Bragg, NC: USASOC History Office, 2006.

Brogan, Patrick. *The Fighting Never Stopped: A Comprehensive Guide to World Conflict since 1945.* New York: Vintage Books, 1990.

Brooks, Doug. "Messiahs or Mercenaries? The Future of International Private Military Services." *International Peacekeeping* 7 (Winter 2000): 129–144.

Brown, Timothy C. *The Real Contra War: Highlander Peasant Resistance in Nicaragua.* Norman: Univ. of Oklahoma Press, 2001.

Brunn, Stanley D. ed. *11 September and Its Aftermath: The Geopolitics of Terror.* Portland, OR: Frank Cass, 2004.

Brzezinski, Zbigniew. *Power and Principle: Memoirs of the National Security Advisor, 1977–1981.* New York: Farrar, Strauss & Giroux, 1985.

Burk, James. "The Decline of Mass Armed Forces and Compulsory Military Service." *Defense Analysis* 8 (Apr. 1992): 45–59.

Burton-Rose, Daniel, and Wayne Madsen. "Corporate Soldiers: The U.S. Government Privatizes the Use of Force." *Multinational Monitor* 20 (Mar. 1999): 17–19.

Bush, George H. W., and Brent Scowcroft. *A World Transformed.* New York: Vintage Books, 1998.

Bush, George W. *Decision Points.* New York: Crown, 2010.

Byman, Daniel L. "Friends Like These: Counterinsurgency and the War on Terrorism." *International Security* 31 (Fall 2006): 79–115.

Caldwell, William B., and Steven M. Leonard. "Field Manual 3–07, Stability Operations: Upshifting the Engine of Change." *Military Review* 88 (July/Aug. 2008): 6–13.

Campbell, Kenneth J. *A Tale of Two Quagmires: Iraq, Vietnam, and the Hard Lessons of War.* Boulder, CO: Paradigm, 2007.

Cannon, James. *Time and Chance: Gerald Ford's Appointment with History.* Ann Arbor: Univ. of Michigan Press, 1998.

Carlson, Tucker. "Hired Guns." *Esquire* 141 (Mar. 2004): 130–139.

Carr, Barry, and Steven Ellner, eds. *The Latin American Left: From the Fall of Allende to Perestroika.* Boulder, CO: Westview Press, 1993.

Carter, Jimmy. *Keeping Faith: Memoirs of a President.* New York: Bantam Books, 1982.

Cassidy, Robert M. "Back to the Street without Joy: Counterinsurgency Lessons from Vietnam and Other Small Wars." *Parameters* 34 (Summer 2004): 73–83.

———. "The Long Small War: Indigenous Forces for Counterinsurgency." *Parameters* 36 (Summer 2006): 47–62.

Chaliand, Gérard, ed. *Guerrilla Strategies: An Historical Anthology from the Long March to Afghanistan.* Berkeley: Univ. of California Press, 1982.

Cheney, Richard B. "Meeting the Challenge of the War on Terrorism." Washington, DC: Heritage Foundation, 17 Oct. 2003, 1–6.

———. "Rising to the Challenge: The Right Choices for America's Defense." *Harvard International Review* 14 (Summer 1992): 8–11.

Chernick, Marc W. "The Paramilitarization of the War in Colombia." *NACLA Report on the Americas* 31 (Mar./Apr. 1998): 28–33.

Christopher, Warren. "American Foreign Policy: The Strategic Priorities." *Vital Speeches of the Day* 60 (1 Jan. 1994): 162–167.

———. "America's Leadership, America's Opportunity." *Foreign Policy,* no. 98 (Spring 1995): 6–28.

Christopher, Warren, and Nicholas Burns. "Carrying Forward America's Diplomatic Tradition." *U.S. Department of State Dispatch* 7 (23 Dec. 1997): 617–621.

Clark, Jeffrey. "Debacle in Somalia." *Foreign Affairs* 72 (1993/1994): 109–123.

Clarke, Jeffrey J. *Advice and Support: The Final Years, 1965–1973.* Washington, DC: Center of Military History, 1988.

Clarke, Walter, and Jeffrey Herbst. "Somalia and the Future of Humanitarian Intervention." *Foreign Affairs* 75 (Mar./Apr. 1996): 70–85.

Cleaver, Gerry. "Subcontracting Military Power: The Privatization of Security in Contemporary Sub-Saharan Africa." *Crime, Law and Social Change* 33 (Mar. 2000): 131–149.

Clemins, Archie. "Where Is the Peace Dividend Now?" *U.S. Naval Institute Proceedings* 125 (Sept. 1999): 42–45.

Clinton, William J. *My Life.* New York: Alfred A. Knopf, 2004.

Coatsworth, John H. "Beyond Armed Actors: A Look at Civil Society." *Revista: Harvard Review of Latin America* 3 (Spring 2003): 3–7.

———. *Central America and the United States: The Clients and the Colossus.* New York: Twayne, 1994.

Cogan, Charles G. "Partners in Time: The CIA and Afghanistan since 1979." *World Policy Journal* 10 (Summer 1993): 73–82.

Cohen, William S. "The Atlantic Alliance: A View from the Pentagon." *Joint Force Quarterly,* no. 21 (Spring 1999): 31–35.

———. "Cohen Responds to National Defense Panel Report." *Program Manager* 27 (Jan./Feb. 1998): 27–38.

———. "The Empire Strikes Back." *Problems of Post-Communism* 42 (Jan./Feb. 1995): 13–19.

———. "Principles for a National Security Consensus." *Washington Quarterly* 24 (Spring 2001): 75–81.

Colby, William, and Peter Forbath. *Honorable Men: My Life in the CIA.* New York: Simon & Schuster, 1978.

Cole, Ronald H. *Operation Just Cause: The Planning and Execution of Joint Operations in Panama, February 1988—Jan. 1990.* Washington, DC: Joint History Office, Office of the Chairman of the Joint Chiefs of Staff, 1995.

———. *Operation Urgent Fury: The Planning and Execution of Joint Operations in Grenada, 12 Oct.—2 November 1983.* Washington, DC: Joint History Office, Office of the Chairman of the Joint Chiefs of Staff, 1997.

Coleman, James R. "Constraining Modern Mercenaries." *Hastings Law Journal* 55 (June 2004): 1493–1538.

Coll, Stephen. *Ghost Wars: The Secret History of the CIA Afghanistan, and Bin Laden, from the Soviet Invasion to September 10, 2001.* New York: Penguin Books, 2004.

Collins, John M. *Special Operations Forces: An Assessment.* Washington, DC: National Defense Univ. Press, 1994.

Cordesman, Anthony H. *The Lessons of Afghanistan: War Fighting, Intelligence, and Force Transformation.* Washington, DC: CSIS Press, 2002.

Corera, Gordon. "Special Operations Forces Take Care of War on Terror." *Jane's Intelligence Review* 15 (Jan. 2003): 42–47.

Corke, Sarah-Jane. *U.S. Covert Operations and Cold War Strategy: Truman, Secret Warfare, and the CIA 1945–1953.* New York: Routledge, 2008.

Corum, James S., and Wray R. Johnson. *Airpower in Small Wars: Fighting Insurgents and Terrorists.* Lawrence: Univ. Press of Kansas, 2003.

Cragin, Kim, and Bruce Hoffman. *Arms Trafficking in Colombia.* Santa Monica, CA: RAND, 2003.

Craig, Richard B. "Colombian Narcotics and United States–Colombian Relations." *Journal of Interamerican Studies and World Affairs* 23 (Aug. 1981): 243–270.

Crandall, Russell. "Explicit Narcotization: U.S. Policy toward Colombia during the Samper Administration." *Latin American Politics and Society* 43 (Autumn 2001): 95–120.

Creehan, Sean. "Soldiers of Fortune 500." *Harvard International Review* 23 (Winter 2002): 6–7.

Crile, George. *Charlie Wilson's War: The Extraordinary Story of the Largest Covert Operation in History.* New York: Atlantic Monthly Press, 2003.

Crock, Stan, Thomas F. Armistead, Anthony Bianco, and Stephanie Anderson Forest. "Outsourcing War." *Business Week,* 15 Sept. 2003, 68–76.

Crowe, William J. *The Line of Fire: From Washington to the Gulf, the Politics and Battles of the New Military.* New York: Simon & Schuster, 1993.

Cullather, Nick. *Secret History: The CIA's Classified Account of Its Operations in Guatemala, 1952–1954.* Stanford, CA: Stanford Univ. Press, 1999.

Curtis, Willie. "The Inevitable Slide into Coercive Peacemaking: The U.S. Role in the New World Order." *Defense Analysis* 10 (Dec. 1994): 305–321.

Daly, William R. "Counterdrug OPS Offer a Chance to Excel." *U.S. Naval Institute Proceedings* 130 (Mar. 2004): 67–72.

Dana, Michael G. "Shock and Awe Has Failed." *U.S. Naval Institute Proceedings* 130 (May 2004): 66–69.

de B. Tallion, J. Paul. *The Evolution of Special Forces in Counter-Terrorism: The British and American Experiences.* Westport, CT: Praeger, 2001.

DeLong, Michael. *Inside CENTCOM: The Unvarnished Truth about the Wars in Afghanistan and Iraq.* Washington, DC: Regnery, 2004.

Del Rosso, Stephen J. "The Insecure State: Reflections on 'The State' and 'Security' in a Changing World." *Daedalus* 124 (Spring 1995): 175–207.

Destler, I. M., Leslie H. Gelb, and Anthony Lake. *Our Own Worst Enemy: The Unmaking of American Foreign Policy.* New York: Simon & Schuster, 1984.

Dominguez, Jorge I. "Insurgency in Latin America and the Common Defense." *Political Science Quarterly* 101 (1986): 807–823.

Donahue, Patrick, and Michael Fenzel. "Combating a Modern Insurgency: Combined Task Force Devil in Afghanistan." *Military Review* 20 (June 2008): 74–89.

Downie, Richard Duncan. *Learning from Conflict: The U.S. Military in Vietnam, El Salvador, and the Drug War.* Westport, CT: Praeger, 1998.

Downing, Wayne A. "Firepower, Attrition, Maneuver—U.S. Army Operations Doctrine: A Challenge for the 1980s and Beyond." *Military Review* 77 (Jan./Feb. 1997): 144–150.

Drohan, Madelaine. *Making a Killing: How and Why Corporations Use Armed Force to Do Business.* Guilford, CT: Lyons Press, 2003.

Duffy, Michael. "When Private Armies Take to the Front Lines." *Time* 163 (12 Apr. 2004): 32–33.

Dunkerley, James. *Power in the Isthmus: A Political History of Modern Central America.* New York: Verso, 1988.

Dunn, Brian J. *The First Gulf War and the Army's Future.* Arlington, VA: AUSA, Institute of Land Warfare, 1997.

Dunnigan, James F. *How to Make War: A Comprehensive Guide to Modern Warfare.* New York: Quill, 1983.

Dunnigan, James F., and Raymond M. Macedonia. *Getting It Right: American Military Reforms after Vietnam to the Persian Gulf and Beyond.* New York: William Morrow & Co., 1993.

Engelhardt, Michael J. "America Can Win Sometimes: U.S. Success and Failure in Small Wars." *Conflict Quarterly* 9 (Winter 1989): 20–35.

Eversmann, Matt, and Dan Schilling. *The Battle of Mogadishu: Firsthand Accounts of the Men of Task Force Ranger.* New York: Ballantine Books, 2004.

Fallows, James. "Cyber Warriors." *Atlantic Monthly* 305 (Mar. 2010): 58–63.

Farer, Tom, ed. *Transnational Crime in the Americas: An Inter-American Dialogue Book.* New York: Routledge, 1999.

Ferreyra, Aleida, and Renata Segura. "Examining the Military in the Local Sphere: Colombia and Mexico." *Latin American Perspectives* 27 (Mar. 2000): 18–35.

Fick, Nathaniel C., and John A. Nagl. "Counterinsurgency Field Manual: Afghanistan Edition." *Foreign Policy* 170 (Jan./Feb. 2009): 42–47.

Fifth Special Forces Group (Airborne) in Desert Shield and Desert Storm. Chapter 38 Special Forces Association, Ft. Campbell, KY, 1991.

Filippone, Robert. "The Medellin Cartel: Why We Can't Win the Drug War." *Studies in Conflict and Terrorism* 17 (Oct. 1994): 323–344.

Fitch, J. Samuel. "The Decline of US Military Influence in Latin America." *Journal of Interamerican Studies and World Affairs* 35 (Summer 1993): 1–49.

Fitzsimmons, Michael. "The Importance of Being Special: Planning for the Future of U.S. Special Operations Forces." *Defense and Security Analysis* 19 (Sept. 2003): 203–218.

Ford, Gerald R. *A Time to Heal.* New York: Harper & Row, 1979.

"*Fortune's* 100 Fastest-Growing Companies in America." *Fortune* 142 (4 Sept. 2000): 118–120.

Fox, Jonathan. "Nationalism versus Civilizations: An Assessment of Alternate Theories on the Future of Ethnic Identity and Conflict." *National Identities* 5 (2003): 283–307.

———. "Two Civilizations and Ethnic Conflict: Islam and the West." *Journal of Peace Research* 38 (July 2001): 459–472.

Francis, David J. "Mercenary Intervention in Sierra Leone: Providing National Security or International Exploitation?" *Third World Quarterly* 20 (1999): 319–338.

Franco, George H. "Their Darkest Hour: Colombia's Government and the Narco-Insurgency." *Parameters* 30 (Summer 2000): 83–94.

Franke, Volker C., ed. *Terrorism and Peacekeeping: New Security Challenges.* Westport, CT: Praeger, 2005.

Franks, Tommy. *American Soldier.* New York: Regan Books, 2004.

Friedman, George, and Meredith Friedman. *The Future of War: Power, Technology and American World Dominance in the 21st Century.* New York: Crown, 1996.

Friedman, Norman. *Terrorism, Afghanistan, and America's New Way of War.* Annapolis, MD: Naval Institute Press, 2003.

Friedman, Thomas L. *The Lexus and the Olive Tree: Understanding Globalization.* New York: Farrar, Strauss & Giroux, 1999.

Friesendorf, Cornelius. "Squeezing the Balloon? United States Air Interdiction and the Restructuring of the South American Drug Industry in the 1990s." *Crime, Law and Social Change* 44 (2005): 35–78.

Frost, Robert S. *The Growing Imperative to Adopt "Flexibility" as an American Principle of War.* Carlisle, PA: Strategic Studies Institute, 1999.

Fukuyama, Francis. *The End of History and the Last Man.* New York: Free Press, 1992.

———. "Reflections on the End of History Five Years Later." *History and Theory* 34 (1995): 27–43.

Gaddis, John Lewis. *The Cold War: A New History.* New York: Penguin Books, 2005.

———. *The Long Peace: Inquiries into the History of the Cold War.* New York: Oxford Univ. Press, 1987.

———. *The United States and the End of the Cold War: Implications, Reconsiderations, Provocations.* New York: Oxford Univ. Press, 1992.

———. *We Now Know: Rethinking Cold War History.* New York: Oxford Univ. Press, 1998.

———. *Strategies of Containment: A Critical Appraisal of Postwar American National Security Policy.* New York: Oxford Univ. Press, 1982.

Gallup, George H. *The Gallup Poll: Public Opinion, 1972–1977.* Wilmington, DE: Scholarly Resources, 1978.

Gambone, Michael D. *Capturing the Revolution: The United States, Central America, and Nicaragua, 1961–1972.* Westport, CT: Praeger, 2001.

———. *Eisenhower, Somoza, and the Cold War in Nicaragua.* Westport, CT: Praeger, 1997.

Gandy, Bruce A. "The Bolivarian Revolution." *U.S. Naval Institute Proceedings* 132 (May 2006): 26–30.

Garcia Arganaras, Fernando. "The Drug War at the Supply End: The Case of Bolivia." *Latin American Perspectives* 24 (Sept. 1997): 59–80.

Gaston, E. L. "Mercenarism 2.0? The Rise of the Modern Private Security Industry and Its Implications for International Humanitarian Law Enforcement." *Harvard International Law Journal* (Winter 2008): 221–248.

Gates, Robert M. *From the Shadows: The Ultimate Insider's Story of Five President's and How They Won the Cold War.* New York: Simon & Schuster, 1996.

Gavin, James M. *War and Peace in the Space Age.* New York: Harper & Brothers, 1958.

Gelb, Leslie H., with Richard K. Betts. *The Irony of Vietnam: The System Worked.* Washington, DC: Brookings Institution, 1979.

Gibson, Chris. "Battlefield Victories and Strategic Success: The Path Forward in Iraq." *Military Review* 86 (Sept./Oct. 2006): 47–59.

Gonzalez, Roberto J. "Towards Mercenary Anthropology?" *Anthropology Today* 23 (June 2007): 14–19.

Goodson, Larry P. *Afghanistan's Endless War: State Failure, Regional Politics, and the Rise of the Taliban.* Seattle, WA: Univ. of Washington Press, 2001.

Gordon, Michael R., and Bernard E. Trainor. *The General's War: The Inside Story of the Conflict in the Gulf.* New York: Little, Brown & Co., 1995.

Goulet, Yves. "MPRI: Washington's Freelance Advisors." *Jane's Intelligence Review* 10 (July 1998): 38–41.

Green, David. *The Containment of Latin America.* Chicago: Quadrangle Books, 1971.

Grunden, Walter E., Yutaka Kawamura, Edward Kolchinsky, et. al. "Laying the Foundation for Wartime Research: A Comparative Overview of Science Mobilization in National Socialist Germany, Japan, and the Soviet Union." *Osiris* 20 (2005): 79–106.

Haass, Richard N. "Paradigm Lost." *Foreign Affairs* 74 (Jan.–Feb. 1993): 43–58.

Hackworth, David H. *About Face: The Odyssey of an American Warrior.* New York: Simon & Schuster, 1991.

Hadley, Arthur T. *The Straw Giant: America's Armed Forces: Triumphs and Failures.* New York: Avon Books, 1987.

Halberstam, David. *The Best and Brightest.* New York: Random House, 1969.

———. *War in a Time of Peace: Bush, Clinton and the Generals.* New York: Scribner, 2001.

Hallion, Richard P. *Storm over Iraq: Air Power and the Gulf War.* Washington: Smithsonian Institution Press, 1992.

Hammer, Joshua. "Cowboy Up." *New Republic* 230 (24 May 2004): 18–19.

Harris, Geoff. "Civilianizing Military Functions in Sub-Saharan Africa." *African Security Review* 12 (Nov. 2003): 83–89.

Hawkins, William R. "Iraq: Heavy Forces and Decisive Warfare." *Parameters* 33 (Autumn 2003): 61–67.

Hazen, William E., and Barbara Anne Wilson. *The Purposes and Practices of Guerrilla Warfare: A Structured Anthology.* Washington, DC: Center for Research in Social Systems, June 1969.

Heiss, Mary Ann. *Empire and Nationhood: The United States, Great Britain, and Iranian Oil, 1950–1954.* New York: Columbia Univ. Press, 1997.

Herman, Edward S., and Frank Brodhead. *Demonstration Elections: U.S.-Staged Elections in the Dominican Republic, Vietnam, and El Salvador.* Boston: South End Press, 1984.

Herring, George C. *America's Longest War: The United States and Vietnam, 1950–1975.* 3rd ed. New York: McGraw-Hill, 1996.

Herspring, Dale R. *The Pentagon and the Presidency: Civil-Military Relations from FDR to George Bush.* Lawrence: Univ. Press of Kansas, 2005.

———. *Rumsfeld's Wars: The Arrogance of American Power.* Lawrence: Univ. Press of Kansas, 2008.

Heuser, Beatrice. "Small Wars in the Age of Clausewitz: The Watershed between Partisan War and People's War." *Journal of Strategic Studies* 33 (Feb. 2010): 139–162.

Hilsman, Roger. *An American Guerrilla: My War behind Japanese Lines.* Washington, DC: Brassey's, 1990.

Hirrel, Leo P. *Response to Terrorism: U.S. Joint Forces Command and the Attacks of 11 September 2001.* Norfolk, VA: U.S. Joint Forces Command, 2003.

Hoffman, Frank G. "Small Wars Revisited: The United States and Nontraditional Wars." *Journal of Strategic Studies* 28 (Dec. 2005): 913–940.

Holden, Robert H. *Armies without Nations: Public Violence and State Formation in Central America, 1821–1960.* New York: Oxford Univ. Press, 2004.

Hooker, Richard D., and H. R. McMaster. "Getting Transformation Right." *Joint Forces Quarterly* 38 (2005): 20–27.

Hunter, Thomas B. "The Proliferation of MANPADS." *Jane's Intelligence Review* 13 (Sept. 2001): 42–45.

Huntington, Samuel P. "The Clash of Civilizations?" *Foreign Affairs* 72 (Summer 1993): 22–49.

Hutchins, Robert L., ed. *At the End of the American Century: America's Role in the Post-Cold War World.* Baltimore: Johns Hopkins Univ. Press, 1998.

Isacson, Adam, Joy Olson, and Lisa Haugaard. *Below the Radar: U.S. Military Programs with Latin America, 1997–2007.* Washington, DC: CIP/LAWGEF/WOLA, Mar. 2007.

Isenberg, David. "Combat for Sale: The New, Post-Cold War Mercenaries." *USA Today Magazine* (Mar. 2000): 12–16.

———. "The New Mercenaries." *Christian Science Monitor* 90 (13 Oct. 1998): 19.

Jeffrey, Judith S. *Ambiguous Commitments and Uncertain Policies: Truman Doctrine in Greece, 1947–1952.* Lanham, MD: Lexington Books, 2000.

Jeffreys-Jones, Rhodri. *The CIA and American Democracy.* New Haven: Yale Univ. Press, 1989.

Jentleson, Bruce W., and Rebecca L. Britton. "Still Pretty Prudent: Post-Cold War American Public Opinion on the Use of Military Force." *Journal of Conflict Resolution* 42 (Aug. 1998): 395–417.

Jespersen, T. Christopher. "Kissinger, Ford and Congress: The Very Bitter End in Vietnam." *Pacific Historical Review* 71 (Aug. 2002): 439–473.

Johnson, Wray Ross. "From Counterinsurgency to Stability and Support Operations: The Evolution of United States Military Doctrine for Foreign Internal Conflict, 1961–1996." Ph.D. diss., Florida State Univ., 1997.

Jones, Mark, and Wes Rehorn. "Special Operations Forces: Integrating SOF into Joint Warfighting." *Military Review* 83 (May/June 2003): 2–7.

Joyce, Elizabeth, and Carlos Malamud, eds. *Latin America and the Multinational Drug Trade.* London: Macmillan Press, 1998.

Kagan, Frederick W. *Finding the Target: The Transformation of American Military Policy.* New York: Encounter Books, 2006.

Kagan, Frederick, and Kimberly Kagan. "The Patton of Counterinsurgency." *Weekly Standard* 13 (10 Mar. 2008): 27–33.

Kahn, Jeremy, and Nelson D. Schwartz. "Private Sector Soldiers." *Fortune* 149 (3 May 2004): 33–36.

Kaplan, Robert D. "The Coming Anarchy." *Atlantic Monthly* 273 (Feb. 1994): 44–76.

———. "Supremacy by Stealth." *Atlantic Monthly* 292 (July/Aug. 2003): 66–83.

Karabell, Zachary. *Architects of Intervention: The United States, the Third World, and the Cold War, 1945–1962.* Baton Rouge: Louisiana State Univ. Press, 1999.

Karnow, Stanley. *Vietnam: A History.* New York: Viking Press, 1983.

Kaufman, Burton I. *The Presidency of James Earl Carter, Jr.* Lawrence: Univ. Press of Kansas, 1993.

Keaney, Thomas A., and Eliot A. Cohen. *Revolution in Warfare? Air Power in the Persian Gulf.* Annapolis, MD: Naval Institute Press, 1995.

Keegan, John. *The Face of Battle.* London: Penguin Books, 1976.

Kelly, Jack. "Safety at a Price: Security Is a Booming, Sophisticated, Global Business." *Pittsburgh Post-Gazette* (13 Feb. 2000), accessed at http://www.post-gazette.com.

Kibbe, Jennifer D. "The Rise of the Shadow Warriors." *Foreign Affairs* 83 (Mar./Apr. 2004): 102–115.

Kilcullen, David. *The Accidental Guerrilla: Fighting Small Wars in the Midst of a Big One.* New York: Oxford Univ. Press, 2009.

Kinnard, Douglas. *The War Managers.* Wayne, NJ: Avery, 1985.

Kissinger, Henry A. *Diplomacy.* New York: Simon & Schuster, 1994.

———. *White House Years.* Boston: Little, Brown & Co., 1979.

Kitfield, James. *Prodigal Soldiers: How the Generation of Officers Born of Vietnam Revolutionized the American Style of War.* New York: Simon & Schuster, 1995.

Klare, Michael T. "The Kalashnikov Age." *Bulletin of the Atomic Scientists* 55 (Jan./Feb. 1999): 18–23.

Klare, Michael T., and Peter Kornbluh, eds. *Low-Intensity Warfare: Counterinsurgency, Proinsurgency, and Antiterrorism in the Eighties.* New York: Pantheon Books, 1988.

Kobrin, Stephen J. "Back to the Future: Neomedievalism and the Postmodern Digital World Economy." *Journal of International Affairs* 51 (Spring 1998): 361–386.

Koch, Andrew. "Covert Warriors." *Jane's Defence Weekly* 39 (19 Mar. 2003): 22–27.

Kohn, Richard H. "Coming Soon: A Crisis in Civil-Military Relations." *World Affairs* 170 (Winter 2008): 69–80.

Krahman, Elke. "Private Military Services in the UK and Germany: Between Partnership and Regulation." *European Security* 14 (June 2005): 277–295.

Kunz, Diane B. *Guns and Butter: America's Cold War Economic Diplomacy.* New York: Free Press, 1997.

Kuzmarov, Jeremy. "From Counter-Insurgency to Narco-Insurgency: Vietnam and the International War on Drugs." *Journal of Public Policy* 20 (2008): 344–378.

Kwok, James. "Armed Entrepreneurs." *Harvard International Review* 28 (Spring 2006): 34–37.

LaFeber, Walter. *Inevitable Revolutions: The United States in Central America.* New York: W. W. Norton & Co., 1984.

Lake, Anthony. "Confronting Backlash States." *Foreign Affairs* 73 (Mar./Apr. 1994): 45–55.

———. Entering the 21st Century: Challenges Confronting America's Military." *U.S. Department of State Dispatch* 7 (17 June 1996): 318–321.

———. Laying the Foundations for a New American Century." *U.S. Department of State Dispatch* 7 (29 Apr. 1996): 208–212.

———. "The Need for Engagement." *U.S. Department of State Dispatch* 5 (5 Dec. 1994): 804–808.

———. "The U.S. Faces Key Foreign Policy Challenges." *U.S. Department of State Dispatch* 7 (3 June 1996): 279–284.

———, ed. *After the Wars: Reconstruction in Afghanistan, Indochina, Central America, Southern Africa, and the Horn of Africa.* New Brunswick, NJ: Transaction, 1990.

Landsdale, Edward. *In the Midst of Wars: An American's Mission to Southeast Asia.* New York: Harper & Row, 1964.

Lebovic, James H. "Riding Waves or Making Waves? The Services and the U.S. Defense Budget, 1981–1993." *American Political Science Review* 88 (Dec. 1994): 839–852.

Lee, J. Edward, and H. C. Haynsworth. *Nixon, Ford and the Abandonment of South Vietnam.* Jefferson, NC: McFarland & Co., 2002.

Leibstone, Marvin. "The U.S. Military and 'the Peace & Stability Industry.'" *Military Technology* 30 (June 2006): 8.

Leogrande, William M. "From Reagan to Bush: The Transition in US Policy toward Central America." *Journal of Latin American Studies* 22 (Oct. 1990): 595–621.

Lewy, Guenther. *America in Vietnam.* New York: Oxford Univ. Press, 1978.

Liang, Qiao, and Wang Xiangsui. *Unrestricted Warfare: China's Master Plan to Destroy America.* Panama City: Pan American, 2002.

Lindsay-Poland, John. *Emperors in the Jungle: The Hidden History of the U.S. in Panama.* Durham, NC: Duke Univ. Press, 2003.

Lock-Pullan, Richard. "'An Inward Looking Time': The United States Army, 1973–1976." *Journal of Military History* 67 (Apr. 2003): 483–511.

———. "How to Rethink War: Conceptual Innovation and AirLand Battle Doctrine." *Journal of Strategic Studies* 28 (Aug. 2005): 679–702.

———. *U.S. Intervention Policy and Army Innovation: From Vietnam to Iraq.* New York: Routledge, 2006.

Lord, Carnes. "The Role of the United States in Small Wars." *Annals of the American Academy of Political and Social Science* 541 (Sept. 1995): 89–100.

Loveman, Brian. *For la Patria: Politics and the Armed Forces in Latin America.* Wilmington, DE: Scholarly Resources, 1999.

Lumpe, Lora. "U.S. Foreign Military Training: Global Reach, Global Power, and Oversight Issues." *Foreign Policy in Focus* (May 2002): 1–54.

Lynch, Tony and A.J. Walsh. "The Good Mercenary?" *Journal of Political Philosophy* 8 (June 2000): 133–153.

Lynn, John A. *Battle: A History of Combat and Culture*. Boulder, CO: Westview Press, 2003.

Luttwak, Edward N. "A Post-Heroic Military Policy." *Foreign Affairs* 75 (July/Aug. 1996): 33–45.

Mabry, Donald. "The U.S. Military and the War on Drugs in Latin America." *Journal of Interamerican Studies and World Affairs* 30 (Summer/Autumn 1988): 53–76.

Macomber, Shawn. "You're Not in the Army Now." *American Spectator* 37 (Nov. 2004): 26–30.

MacKay, Malcolm L. "What's Wrong with Mercenaries?" *U.S. Naval Institute Proceedings* 131 (June 2005): 80.

Maclear, Michael. *The Ten Thousand Day War: Vietnam, 1945–1975*. New York: St. Martin's Press, 1981.

Madsen, Wayne. "Mercenaries in Kosovo: The U.S. Connection to the KLA." *Progressive* 63 (Aug. 1999): 29–31.

———. "Peruvian No-Fly Zone." *Progressive* 65 (June 2001): 35.

Mandel, Robert. *Armies without States: The Privatization of Security*. Boulder, CO: Lynne Rienner, 2002.

———. "The Wartime Utility of Precision versus Brute Force in Weaponry." *Armed Forces and Society* 30 (Winter 2004): 171–201.

Mansoor, Peter R., and Mark S. Ulrich, "Linking Doctrine to Action: A New COIN Center-of-Gravity Analysis." *Military Review* 87 (Sept./Oct. 2007): 45–51.

Manwaring, Max G. *Strategic Effects of the Conflict with Iraq: Latin America*. Carlisle, PA: Strategic Studies Institute, 2003.

Marcinko, Richard, with John Weisman. *Rogue Warrior*. New York: Pocket Books, 1992.

Marks, Thomas A. *Colombian Army Adaptation to FARC Insurgency*. Carlisle, PA: Strategic Studies Institute, Jan. 2002.

———. *Sustainability of Colombian Military/Strategic Support for "Democratic Security."* Carlisle, PA: Strategic Studies Institute, July 2005.

Markusen, Ann. "The Case Against Privatising National Security." *Dollars and Sense* 253 (May/June 2004): 24–29.

Marquis, Susan L. *Unconventional Warfare: Rebuilding U.S. Special Operations Forces*. Washington, DC: Brookings Institution Press, 1997.

Martin, Ian. "Haiti: Mangled Multilateralism." *Foreign Policy* No. 95 (Summer 1994): 72–89.

Matloff, Maurice ed. *American Military History*. Washington, DC: Center of Military History, 1973.

Matthews, Jessica T. "Power Shift: The Rise of Global Civil Society." *Foreign Affairs* 76 (Jan./Feb. 1997): 50–67.

McAlister, Melani. "A Cultural History of the War without End." *Journal of American History* 89 (Sept. 2002): 439–455.

McAllister Linn, Brian. *The Echo of Battle: The Army's Way of War.* Cambridge, MA: Harvard Univ. Press, 2007.

McCarthy, Abigail. "Religious Wars . . . and Religious Peace." *Commonweal* (12 Mar. 1993): 6–7.

McClintock, Cynthia. "The War on Drugs: The Peruvian Case." *Journal of Interamerican Studies and World Affairs* 30 (Summer/Autumn 1988): 127–142.

McClintock, Michael. *Instruments of Statecraft: U.S. Guerrilla Warfare, Counter-Insurgency, Counter-Terrorism, 1940–1990.* New York: Pantheon Books, 1992.

McDonough, William. "Time for a New Strategy." *Parameters* 38 (Autumn 2008): 109–119.

McGhie, Stuart. "Soldiers, Inc." *Jane's Defence Weekly* 37 (22 May 2002): 22–26.

McMaster, H. R. "The Human Element: When Gadgetry Becomes Strategy." *World Affairs* 171 (Winter 2009): 31–43.

McPherson, Michael D. "Dollars and Sense: Private Sector Lures Special Operations Troops." *Armed Forces Journal International* 141 (June 2004): 26.

McRaven, William H. *Spec Ops: Case Studies in Special Operations Warfare: Theory and Practice.* Novato, CA: Presidio Press, 1995.

Meara, William R. *Contra Cross: Insurgency and Tyranny in Central America, 1979–1989.* Annapolis, MD: Naval Institute Press, 2006.

Mearsheimer, John J. "Back to the Future: Instability in Europe after the Cold War." *International Security* 15 (Summer 1990): 5–56.

Melillo, Michael R. "Outfitting a Big-War Military with Small-War Capabilities." *Parameters* 36 (Autumn 2006): 22–35.

Merom, Gil. *How Democracies Lose Small Wars: State Society, and the Failures of France in Algeria, Israel in Lebanon, and the United States in Vietnam.* New York: Cambridge Univ. Press, 2003.

Metz, Steven. "The Air Force Role in United Nations Peacekeeping." *Airpower Journal* 7 (Winter 1993): 68–72.

———. *American Strategy: Issues and Alternatives for the Quadrennial Defense Review.* Carlisle, PA: Strategic Studies Institute, 2000.

———. "Racing Toward the Future: The Revolution in Military Affairs." *Current History* 96 (Apr. 1997): 184–188.

———. "Strategic Asymmetry." *Military Review* 81 (July/Aug. 2001): 23–31.

———. "A Strategic Context for Third Tier Conflict." *Military Review* 75 (Dec. 1994/Feb. 1995): 4–15.

Millett, Richard L. "The Aftermath of Intervention: Panama 1990." *Journal of Interamerican Studies and World Affairs* 32 (Spring 1990): 1–15.

Mintz, Alex, and Chi Huang. "Defense Expenditures, Economic Growth, and the 'Peace Dividend.'" *American Political Science Review* 84 (Dec. 1990): 1283–1293.

Mintz, Alex, and Randolph T. Stevenson. "Defense Expenditures, Economic Growth, and the 'Peace Dividend': A Longitudinal Analysis of 103 Countries." *Journal of Conflict Resolution* 39 (June 1995): 283–305.

Mokhiber, Russell, and Robert Weissman. "Bad Apples in a Rotten System: The 10 Worst Corporations of 2002." *Multinational Monitor* 23 (Dec. 2002): 8–19.

Moore, Harold G., and Joseph L. Galloway. *We Were Soldiers Once . . . and Young.* New York: Random House, 1992.

Morris, Edmund. *Dutch: A Memoir of Ronald Reagan.* New York: Random House, 1999.

Moss, George Donelson. *Vietnam: An American Ordeal.* 5th ed. Upper Saddle River, NJ: Pearson Prentice Hall, 2006.

Moyar, Mark. "The Current State of Military History." *Historical Journal* 50 (Mar. 2007): 225–240.

Moynihan, Daniel P. *Pandaemonium: Ethnicity in International Politics.* New York: Oxford Univ. Press, 1993.

Mueller, John. "Is There Still a Terrorist Threat?" *Foreign Affairs* 85 (Sept./Oct. 2006): 2–8.

Musto, David F., and Pamela Korsmeyer. *The Quest for Drug Control: Politics and Federal Policy in a Period of Increasing Substance Abuse, 1963–1981.* New Haven: Yale Univ. Press, 2002.

Nagl, John A. *Learning to Eat Soup with a Knife: Counterinsurgency Lessons from Malaya and Vietnam.* 2nd ed. Chicago: Univ. of Chicago Press, 2005.

Nagle, Luz Estella. *Plan Colombia: Reality of the Colombian Crisis and Implications for Hemispheric Security.* Carlisle, PA: Strategic Studies Institute, 2002.

Newbold, Stephen. "Competitive Sourcing and Privatization: An Essential USAF Strategy." *Air Force Journal of Logistics* 23 (Spring 1999): 28–34.

Nieto, Clara. *Masters of War: Latin America and U.S. Aggression from the Cuban Revolution through the Clinton Years.* New York: Seven Stories Press, 2003.

O'Brien, Kevin A. "Military-Advisory Groups and African Security: Privatized Peacekeeping?" *International Peacekeeping* 5 (Autumn 1998): 78–105.

———. "PMCs, Myths and Mercenaries: The Debate on Private Military Companies." *Defence and International Security* 145 (Feb. 2000): 59–64.

Oborne, Peter. "Making a Killing." *Spectator* 296 (11 Dec. 2004): 22–23.

Offner, Arnold A. *Another Such Victory: President Truman and the Cold War, 1945–1953.* Stanford, CA: Stanford Univ. Press, 2002.

Operation Enduring Freedom: October 2001–March 2002. Washington, DC: U.S. Army Center of Military History, 2004.

Pach, Chester J. *Arming the Free World: The Origins of the United States Military Assistance Program, 1945–1950.* Chapel Hill: Univ. of North Carolina Press, 1991.

Packenham, Robert A. *Liberal America and the Third World: Political Development Ideas in Foreign Aid and Social Science.* Princeton: Princeton Univ. Press, 1973.

Palmer, David Scott. "Peru, the Drug Business and Shining Path: Between Scylla and Charybdis?" *Journal of Interamerican Studies and World Affairs* 34 (Autumn 1992): 65–88.

Partin, John W. *Special Operations Forces in Operation Earnest Will / Prime Chance I.* MacDill Air Force Base, FL: USSOCOM, 1998.

Paschall, Rod. *A Study in Command and Control: Special Operations in Korea, 1951–1953.* Carlisle, PA: U.S. Army Military History Institute, June 1988.

———. *Witness to War: Korea.* New York: Perigee Books, 1995.

Passage, David. *The United States and Colombia: Untying the Gordian Knot.* Carlisle, PA: Strategic Studies Institute, Mar. 2000.

Patriquin, Travis, and Rajiv Chandrassekaran. "Using Occam's Razor to Connect the Dots: The Ba'ath Party and the Insurgency in Tal Afar." *Military Review* 87 (Jan./Feb. 2007): 16–25.

Patterson, James T. *Restless Giant: The United States from Watergate to Bush v. Gore.* New York: Oxford Univ. Press, 2005.

Peceny, Mark, and Michael Durnan. "The FARC's Best Friend: U.S. Antidrug Policies and the Deepening of Colombia's Civil War in the 1990s." *Latin American Politics and Society* 48 (Summer 2006): 95–116.

Pelletiere, Stephen C. *Humanitarian Operations and the Middle East: The Hostility Factor.* Carlisle, PA: Strategic Studies Institute, 1993.

Perl, Raphael F. "International Terrorism: Threat, Policy, and Response." *Military Technology* 30 (Dec. 2006): 66–75.

———. "Clinton's Foreign Drug Policy." *Journal of Interamerican Studies and World Affairs* 35 (Winter 1993–1994): 143–152.

Peters, Ralph. "The American Mission." *Parameters* 29 (Autumn 1999): 2–9.

———. "The Atlantic Century." *Parameters* 33 (Autumn 2003): 4–16.

———. "The Culture of Future Conflict." *Parameters* 25 (Winter 1995–1996): 18–27.

———. "Hucksters in Uniform." *Washington Monthly* 31 (May 1999): 9–12.

———. "The New Warrior Class Revisited." *Small Wars and Insurgencies* 13 (Summer 2002): 16–25.

———. "Our New Old Enemies." *Parameters* 29 (Summer 1999): 22–38.

———. "The Plague of Ideas." *Parameters* 30 (Winter 2000/2001): 4–21.

———. "Stability, America's Enemy." *Parameters* 31 (Winter 2001/2002): 5–20.

Peters, William C. "On Law, Wars, and Mercenaries: The Case for Courts-Martial Jurisdiction over Civilian Contractor Misconduct in Iraq." *Brigham Young University Law Review* 2 (2006): 367–414.

Petraeus, David H. "Multinational Force-Iraq Commander's Counterinsurgency Guidance." *Military Review* 88 (Sept./Oct. 2008): 2–4.

Pion-Berlin, David. "Will Soldiers Follow? Economic Integration and Regional Security in the Southern Cone." *Journal of Interamerican Studies and World Affairs* 42 (Spring 2000): 43–69.

Posen, Barry R. "Nationalism, the Mass Army, and Military Power." *International Security* 18 (Fall 1993): 80–124.

Powell, Colin L. *My American Journey*. New York: Ballantine Books, 1996.

Power, Samantha. *"A Problem from Hell": America and the Age of Genocide*. New York: Basic Books, 2002.

Prados, John. ed. *America Confronts Terrorism: Understanding the Danger and How to Think About It*. Chicago: Ivan R. Dee, 2002.

———. "Notes on the CIA's Secret War in Afghanistan." *Journal of American History* 89 (Sept. 2002): 466–471.

Press, Eyal. "Clinton Pushes Military Aid." *Progressive* 61 (Feb. 1997): 20–23.

Priest, Dana. *The Mission: Waging War and Keeping Peace with America's Military*. New York: W. W. Norton & Co., 2003.

"Private Security Companies." *Military Technology* 31 (Feb. 2007): 41–45.

Rabe, Stephen G. *U.S. Intervention in British Guiana: A Cold War Story*. Chapel Hill: Univ. of North Carolina Press, 2005.

Race, Jeffrey. *War Comes to Long An: Revolutionary Conflict in a Vietnamese Province*. Berkeley, CA: Univ. of California Press, 1972.

Rathmell, Andrew. "Towards Postmodern Intelligence." *Intelligence and National Security* 17 (Autumn 2002): 87–104.

Record, Jeffrey. *Beating Goliath: Why Insurgencies Win*. Washington, DC: Potomac Books, 2007.

———. *The Rapid Deployment Force and U.S. Military Intervention in the Persian Gulf: Special Report*. Cambridge, MA: Institute for Foreign Policy Analysis, Feb. 1981.

———. *Ready for What and Modernized Against Whom? A Strategic Perspective on Readiness and Modernization*. Carlisle, PA: Strategic Studies Institute, 1995.

Regan, Tom. "Wars of the Future . . . Today." *Christian Science Monitor* (24 June 1999): 13.

Riccardelli, Richard F. "Waging Limited War on Drugs: New Strategies for the Nineties." *Military Review* 74 (Oct. 1994): 25–31.

Richani, Nazih. "The Political Economy of Violence: The War-System in Colombia." *Journal of Interamerican Studies and World Affairs* 39 (Summer 1997): 37–81.

"Risky Returns: Doing Business in Chaotic and Violent Countries." *Economist* 355 (20 May 2000): 85–88.

Robinson, Linda, and Douglas Pasternak. "America's Secret Armies." *U.S. News and World Report* (4 Nov. 2002): 38–44.

Romjue, John L. *American Army Doctrine for the Post-Cold War.* Washington, DC: Center of Military History, 1997.

Rose, Donald G. "Peace Operations and Change in the U.S. Military." *Defense Analysis* 17 (Aug. 2001): 139–157.

Roskin, Michael G. "Crime and Politics in Colombia: Considerations for US Involvement." *Parameters* 31 (Winter 2001–2002): 126–134.

Roth, R. Theodore. "The Impact of Decreased Defense Spending on Employment in the United States." *Armed Forces and Society* 18 (Spring 1992): 383–405.

Roxborough, Ian. *The Hart-Rudman Commission and Homeland Defense.* Carlisle, PA: Strategic Studies Institute, Sept. 2001.

Ruben, Elizabeth. "An Army of One's Own." *Harper's Magazine* 294 (Feb. 1997): 44–56.

Russett, Bruce, Thomas Hartley, and Shoon Murray. "The End of the Cold War, Attitude Change, and the Politics of Defense Spending." *Political Science and Politics* 27 (Mar. 1994): 17–21.

Saikia, Jaideep. "The ISI Reaches East: Anatomy of a Conspiracy." *Studies in Conflict and Terrorism* 25 (2002): 185–197.

Sarkesian, Sam C. America's Forgotten Wars: The Counterrevolutionary Past and Lessons for the Future. Westport, CT: Greenwood Press, 1984.

———. *The New Battlefield: The United States and Unconventional Conflicts.* Westport, CT: Greenwood Press, 1986.

Sarkesian, Sam C., and Robert E. Connor, eds. *America's Armed Forces: A Handbook of Current and Future Capabilities.* Westport, CT: Greenwood Press, 1996.

Sarkesian, Sam C., John Allen Williams, and Stephen J. Cimbala. *U.S. National Security: Policymakers, Processes, and Politics.* Boulder, CO: Lynne Rienner, 2002.

Schemann, Serge. "Not Taking Losses Is One Thing: Winning Is Another." *New York Times* (3 Jan. 1999), 1, 5.

Schultz, George. *Turmoil and Triumph: My Years as Secretary of State.* New York: Charles Scribner's Sons, 1993.

Schwartz, Nelson D., and Noshua Watson. "The Pentagon's Private Army." *Fortune* 147 (17 Mar. 2003): 100–107.

Scott, Peter Dale. *Drugs, Oil, and War: The United States in Afghanistan, Colombia, and Indochina.* Lanham, MA: Rowman & Littlefield, 2003.

Scowcroft, Brent. *Foreign Policy, Military Strategy, and Defense Management.* Colorado Springs: USAF Academy, 1984.

Searle, Thomas R. *"Clearing the Way": U.S. Special Operations Forces in the Humanitarian Demining of Afghanistan, Eritrea, and Ethiopia, 1988–1996.* MacDill Air Force Base, FL: USSOCOM, 1996.

Sellars, Kirsten. "Old Dogs of War Learn New Tricks." *New Statesman* 126 (25 Mar. 1997): 24–26.

Serewicz, Lawrence W. "Globalization, Sovereignty and Military Revolution: From Mercenaries to Private International Security Companies." *International Politics* 39 (Mar. 2002): 75–89.

Sewall, Sarah. "Modernizing U.S. Counterinsurgency Practice: Rethinking Risk and Developing a National Strategy." *Military Review* 86 (Sept./Oct. 2006): 103–109.

Shafer, D. Michael. *Deadly Paradigms: The Failure of U.S. Counterinsurgency Policy.* Princeton, NJ: Princeton Univ. Press, 1988.

Shannon, Ulric. "Human Security and the Rise of Private Armies." *New Political Science* 22 (Mar. 2000): 103–115.

Sharpe, Kenneth. "Realpolitik or Imperial Hubris: The Latin American Drug War and U.S. Foreign Policy in Iraq." *Orbis* 50 (June 2006): 481–499.

Shaw, Robert C. "Integrating Conventional and Special Operations Forces." *Military Review* 77 (July/Aug. 1997): 37–41.

Shearer, David. "Outsourcing War." *Foreign Policy,* no. 112 (Fall 1998): 68–82.

———. *Private Armies and Military Intervention.* New York: Oxford Univ. Press, 1998.

———. "Privatising Protection." *World Today* 57 (Aug./Sept. 2001): 29–31.

Sheehan, Neil. *A Bright Shining Lie: John Paul Vann and America in Vietnam.* New York: Vintage Books, 1988.

Sherwin, Martin. *A World Destroyed.* New York: Vintage Books, 1987.

Silverstein, Ken. *Private Warriors.* New York: Verso, 2000.

———. "Privatizing War." *Nation* 265 (28 July 1997): 11–17.

Simons, Geoff. *Colombia: A Brutal History.* London: SAQI, 2004.

Singer, P. W. *Corporate Warriors: The Rise of the Privatized Military Industry.* Ithaca, NY: Cornell Univ. Press, 2003.

———. "Peacekeepers, Inc." *Policy Review* 119 (June/July 2003): 59–70.

Smist, Frank J. *Congress Oversees the United States Intelligence Community, 1947–1989.* Knoxville: Univ. of Tennessee Press, 1990.

Smith, Eugene B. "The New Condottieri and U.S. Policy: The Privatization of Conflict and Its Implications." *Parameters* 32 (Winter 2002/2003): 104–119.

Smith, Niel. "Retaking Sa'ad: Successful Counterinsurgency in Tal Afar." *Armor* 116 (July/Aug. 2007): 26–35.

Smith, Rupert. *The Utility of Force: The Art of War in the Modern World.* New York: Alfred A. Knopf, 2007.

Soffer, Jonathan. "The National Association of Manufacturers and the Militarization of American Conservatism." *Business History Review* 75 (Winter 2001): 775–805.

Spalding, Elizabeth Edwards. *The First Cold Warrior: Harry Truman, Containment, and the Remaking of Liberal Internationalism.* Lexington: Univ. Press of Kentucky, 2006.

Spalding, Rose J. *Capitalists and Revolution in Nicaragua: Opposition and Accommodation, 1979–1993.* Chapel Hill: Univ. of North Carolina Press, 1994.

Spearin, Christopher. "Contracting a Counterinsurgency? Implications for US Policy in Iraq and Beyond." *Small Wars and Insurgencies* 18 (Dec. 2007): 541–558.

———. "Private Security Companies and Humanitarians: A Corporate Solution to Securing Humanitarian Spaces?" *International Peacekeeping* 8 (Spring 2001): 20–43.

Special Forces, The First Fifty Years: The United States Army Special Forces, 1952–2002. Tampa, FL: Faircount LLC for SEA, 2002.

Spector, Ronald H. *Advice and Support: The Early Years, 1941–1960.* Washington, DC: Center for Military History, 1986.

Spence, J. E. "Ethnicity and International Relations." *International Affairs* 72 (July 1996): 439–443.

Spiller, Roger J. "In the Shadow of the Dragon: Doctrine and the U.S. Army after Vietnam." *RUSI Journal* 142 (Dec. 1997): 41–54.

———. "Military History and Its Fictions." *Journal of Military History* 70 (Oct. 2006): 1081–1097.

Stanton, Shelby L. *Green Berets at War: U.S. Army Special Forces in Southeast Asia, 1956–1975.* New York: Ivy Books, 1985.

Stockton, Paul N. "Beyond Micromanagement: Congressional Budgeting for a Post-Cold War Military." *Political Science Quarterly* 110 (Summer 1995): 233–259.

———. "The New Game on the Hill: The Politics of Arms Control and Strategic Force Modernization." *International Security* 16 (Autumn 1991): 146–170.

Stohl, Rachel. Questionable Reward: Arms Sales and the War on Terrorism. *Arms Control Today* 38 (Jan./Feb. 2008): 17–38.

Strachan, Hew, ed. *Big Wars and Small Wars: The British Army and the Lessons of War in the Twentieth Century.* New York: Routledge, 2006.

Strange, Susan. "The Erosion of the State." *Current History* 96 (Nov. 1997): 365–369.

———. *The Retreat of the State: The Diffusion of Power in the World Economy.* New York: Cambridge Univ. Press, 1996.

Summers, Harry G., Jr. *On Strategy: A Critical Analysis of the Vietnam War.* New York: Dell, 1982.

Suri, Jeremi. *Henry Kissinger and the American Century.* Cambridge: Belknap Press, 2007.

Sweig, Julia E. "What Kind of War for Colombia? History Repeating Itself?" *Foreign Affairs* 81 (Sept./Oct. 2002): 122–141.

Szulc, Tad. *Fidel: A Critical Portrait.* New York: Avon Books, 1968.

Talbot, Strobe, and Nayan Chanda, eds. *The Age of Terror: America and the World After September 11.* New York: Basic Books, 2001.

Taulbee, James Larry. "Mercenary Mischief and the Maldives." *Defense Analysis* 5 (June 1989): 153–155.

———. "The Privatization of Security: Modern Conflict, Globalization and Weak State." *Civil Wars* 5 (Summer 2002): 1–24.

Taylor, Maxwell D. *The Uncertain Trumpet.* New York: Harper & Brothers, 1959.

Terriff, Terry. *The Nixon Administration and the Making of U.S. Nuclear Strategy.* Ithaca, NY: Cornell Univ. Press, 1995.

Terriff, Terry, Aaron Karp, and Regina Karp, eds. *Global Insurgency and the Future of Armed Conflict: Debating Fourth-Generation Warfare.* New York: Routledge, 2008.

Thakur, Ramesh. "From Peacekeeping to Peace Enforcement: The UN Operation in Somalia." *Journal of Modern African Studies* 32 (Sept. 1994): 387–410.

Thayer, Charles W. *Guerrilla.* New York: Signet Book, 1965.

Thoumi, Francisco E. "Why the Illegal Psychoactive Drugs Industry Grew in Colombia." *Journal of Interamerican Studies and World Affairs* 34 (Autumn 1992): 37–63.

Timberg, Robert. *The Nightingale's Song.* New York: Simon & Schuster, 1995.

Tokatlian, Juan Gabriel. "La polemica sobre la legalacion de drogas en Colombia, el Presidente Samper y los Estados Unidos." *Latin American Research Review* 35 (2000): 37–83.

Tomajczyk, Stephen E. *U.S. Elite Counter-Terrorist Forces.* Osceola, WI: Motorbooks International, 1997.

Toyne Sewell, Patrick. "Private Security Companies: The Reasons Why." *Military Technology* 31 (Mar. 2007): 60–61.

Traynor, Ian. "The Privatisation of War." *Guardian* (10 Dec. 2003): 1.

Tuathail, Gearoid O., and Timothy W. Luke. "Present at the (Dis)integration: Deterritorialization and Reterritorialization in the New Wor(l)d Order." *Annals of the Association of American Geographers* 84 (Sept. 1994): 381–398.

Tucker, David, and Christopher J. Lamb. *United States Special Operations Forces.* New York: Columbia Univ. Press, 2007.

Tucker, Robert W., Michael Howard, Gary Schmitt, et. al. "One Year On: Power, Purpose and Strategy in American Foreign Policy." *National Interest,* no. 69 (Fall 2002): 5–34.

Turley, William S. *The Second Indochina War.* 2nd ed. New York: Rowman & Littlefield, 2009.

Vance, Cyrus. *Hard Choices: Critical Years in America's Foreign Policy.* New York: Simon & Schuster, 1983.

van Creveld, Martin. *The Rise and Decline of the State.* New York: Cambridge Univ. Press, 1999.

———. *The Transformation of War.* New York: Free Press, 1991.

van Niekerk, Phillip. "Making a Killing: The Business of War." *Center for Public Integrity* (21 Apr. 2002). http://www.publicintegrity.org.

Vitas, Robert A., and John Allen Williams, eds. *U.S. National Security Policy and Strategy, 1987–1994: Documents and Policy Proposals.* Westport, CT: Greenwood Press, 1996.

Walker, Thomas W., ed. *Nicaragua without Illusions: Regime Transition and Structural Adjustment in the 1990s.* Wilmington, DE: Scholarly Resources, 1997.

Walker, William. *Drug Control in the Americas.* Albuquerque: Univ. of New Mexico Press, 1989.

Wall, Robert. "Army Leases 'Eyes' to Watch Balkans." *Aviation Week and Space Technology* 153 (30 Oct. 2000): 68.

Walter, Knut. *The Regime of Anastasio Somoza Garcia, 1936–1956.* Chapel Hill: Univ. of North Carolina Press, 1993.

Ward, Michael D., and David R. Davis. "Sizing up the Peace Dividend: Economic Growth and Military Spending in the United States, 1948–1996." *American Political Science Review* 86 (Sept. 1992): 748–755.

Warf, Barney, and Amy Glasmeier. "Introduction: Military Spending, the American Economy, and the End of the Cold War." *Economic Geography* 69 (Apr. 1993): 103–106.

Warner, Denis. *The Last Confucian.* New York: Macmillan, 1963.

Warren, James. "Small Wars and Military Culture." *Society* 36 (Sept./Oct. 1999): 56–61.

Wass de Czege, Huba. "Systemic Operational Design: Learning and Adapting in Complex Missions." *Military Review* 89 (Jan./Feb. 2009): 2–12.

Watson, Alexander. "Culture and Combat in the Western World, 1900–1945." *Historical Journal* 51 (2008): 529–546.

Wei-cheng Wang, Vincent, and Gwendolyn Stamper. "Asymmetrical War? Implications for China's Information Warfare Strategies." *American Asian Review* 20 (Winter 2002): 167–202.

Weinberger, Caspar W. *In the Arena: A Memoir of the 20th Century.* Washington, DC: Regnery, 2001.

Wendt, Alexander. "Collective Identity Formation and the International State." *American Political Science Review* 88 (June 1994): 384–396.

———. "Constructing International Politics." *International Security* 20 (Summer 1995): 71–81.

———. "Why a World State Is Inevitable." *European Journal of International Relations* 9 (Dec. 2003): 491–542.

Whyte, Dave. "Lethal Regulation: State-Corporate Crime and the United Kingdom Government's New Mercenaries." *Journal of Law and Society* 30 (Dec. 2003): 575–600.

Wickham-Crowley, Timothy P. "Elites, Elite Settlements, and Revolutionary Movements in Latin America, 1950–1980." *Social Science History* 18 (Winter 1994): 543–574.

Wirsing, Robert G. "In India's Lengthening Shadow: The U.S.-Pakistan Strategic Alliance and the War in Afghanistan." *Asian Affairs* 34 (Fall 2007): 151–172.

Wirtz, James J. "The 'Unlessons' of Vietnam." *Defense Analysis* 17 (Apr. 2001): 41–57.

Wishnick, Elizabeth. *Strategic Consequences of the Iraq War: U.S. Security Interests in Central Asia Reassessed.* Carlisle, PA: Strategic Studies Institute, May 2004.

Wittkopf, Eugene R., and James M. McCormick. "Congress, the President, and the End of the Cold War: Has Anything Changed?" *Journal of Conflict Resolution* 42 (Aug. 1998): 440–466.

Woodward, Bob. *The Commanders.* New York: Simon & Schuster, 1991.

Young, Marilyn B. *The Vietnam Wars, 1945–1990.* New York: HarperPerennial, 1991.

Youngers, Coletta A. "Cocaine Madness: Counternarcotics and Militarization in the Andes." *NACLA Report on the Americas* 34 (Nov./Dec. 2000): 16–23, 55–57.

Youngers, Coletta A., and Eileen Rosin. *Drugs and Democracy in Latin America: The Impact of U.S. Policy.* Boulder, CO: Lynne Rienner, 2005.

Yousaf, Mohammad, and Mark Adkin. *The Bear Trap: Afghanistan's Untold Story.* London: Leo Cooper, 1992.

Zabci, Filiz. "Private Military Companies: 'Shadow Soldiers' of Neo-Colonialism." *Capital and Class* 92 (Summer 2007): 1–10.

Zackrison, James L., and Eileen Bradley. "Colombian Sovereignty Under Siege." *Strategic Forum,* no. 112 (May 1997): 1–6.

Zais, Mitchell M. "Iraq: The Way Ahead." *Military Review* 88 (Jan./Feb. 2008): 112–116.

Zarate, Juan Carlos. "The Emergence of a New Dog of War: Private International Security Companies, International Law, and the New World Disorder." *Stanford Journal of International Law* 34 (1998): 75–156.

Zimmerman, Matilde. *Sandinista: Carlos Fonseca and the Nicaraguan Revolution.* Durham, NC: Duke Univ. Press, 2000.

Zinni, Anthony, and Tony Kolz. *The Battle for Peace: A Frontline Vision of America's Power and Purpose.* New York: Palgrave Macmillan, 2006.

Zirnite, Peter. "The Militarization of the Drug War in Latin America." *Current History* 97 (Apr. 1998): 166–173.

Index

Small Wars was designed and typeset on a Macintosh OS 10.6 computer system using InDesign CS5 software. The body text is set in 10/13.5 ITC New Baskerville Std and display type is set in ITC New Baskerville Std. This book was designed and typeset by Barbara Karwhite and manufactured by Thomson-Shore, Inc.